A Field of Their Own

A FIELD OF THEIR OWN

Women and American Indian History, 1830–1941

JOHN M. RHEA

University of Oklahoma Press

Norman

This book is published with the generous assistance of the McCasland Foundation, Duncan, Oklahoma.

Library of Congress Cataloging-in-Publication Data
Name: Rhea, John M., 1967– author.
Title: A field of their own : women and American Indian history, 1830–1941 / John M. Rhea.
Description: First Edition. | Norman : University of Oklahoma Press, 2016. | Includes bibliographical references and index.
Identifiers: LCCN 2015035111 | ISBN 978-0-8061-5227-1 (hardback)
ISBN 978-0-8061-6898-2 (paperback)
Subjects: LCSH: Indians of North America—Historiography. | Women historians—United
   States—Biography. | Indian women—United States—Biography. | Historiography—United States—History—19th century. | Historiography—United States—History—20th century. | BISAC: HISTORY / United States / 19th Century. | HISTORY / United States / 20th Century. | HISTORY / Native American.
Classification: LCC E76.8 .R49 2016 | DDC 973.04/9700720252—dc23 LC record available at http://lccn.loc.gov/2015035111

The paper in this book meets the guidelines for permanence and durability of the Committee on Production Guidelines for Book Longevity of the Council on Library Resources, Inc. ∞

Copyright © 2016 the University of Oklahoma Press, Norman, Publishing Division of the University. Paperback published 2021. Manufactured in the U.S.A.

All rights reserved. No part of this publication may be reproduced, stored in a retrieval system, or transmitted, in any form or by any means, electronic, mechanical, photocopying, recording, or otherwise—except as permitted under Section 107 or 108 of the United States Copyright Act—without the prior written permission of the University of Oklahoma Press. To request permission to reproduce selections from this book, write to Permissions, University of Oklahoma Press, 2800 Venture Drive, Norman, OK 73069, or email rights.oupress@ou.edu.

To John and Wauneta Walters, Patricia Rhea, Edna Wilson, Ruth Moeller, Commodore Aldee and Amour Polly Hawkins, Theodore Roosevelt Gee, Jr., Savannah Steele, Harold D. Walters, and especially Bart C. McClenny. It really does take a village.

Contents

List of Illustrations — ix
Preface — xi
Acknowledgments — xv
Acronyms and Abbreviations — xvii

Introduction: "White" Women and the Specialized Field of American Indian Historical Scholarship — 3

Part I:
Women's Early American Indian Scholarship, 1830–1889

1. Women's Rights, American Indians, and Capitol Politics — 15
2. The Washington Vanguard and the Birth of Women's Indian Scholarship — 35
3. American Darwinism, Women, and American Indians — 51
4. Helen Hunt Jackson and the History of American Indian Treaties — 68
5. Alice Fletcher and the Scholarship of American Indian Politics — 80
6. Professionalization and the Twilight of Women's American Indian Scholarship — 105

Part II:
A New Frontier for Women Historians, 1890–1941

7. The Pacific Frontier: Women Historians and a New Kind of Indian History — 123
8. Déjà Vu: Oklahoma Women and the New Ethno-Political Indian History — 163

Conclusion: Women Historians, American Indian History, and Gender Politics — 200

Notes — 207
Bibliography — 241
Index — 281

Illustrations

Helen Hunt Jackson	69
Alice C. Fletcher	81
Alice C. Fletcher with Omaha informant	86
Emma Helen Blair	125
Louise Phelps Kellogg	134
Annie Heloise Abel	140
Rachel Caroline Eaton at Drury College	151
Rachel Caroline Eaton in cap and gown	154
Anna L. Lewis	165
Muriel H. Wright	178
Angie Debo	182

Preface

The seeds for this book were planted in 1976. I remember clearly, distinctly, the first time that I considered the relationship between women and American Indian history. I was nine years old and ensconced, as usual, with my grandmother and great aunts around the old Formica-topped chrome dinner table in my great-grandparent's kitchen. All five of my grandmother's siblings and many of their children and grandchildren were gathered in Snyder, Oklahoma, for the annual family reunion. As tradition dictated, my great-grandmother Armour "Polly" presided over preparation of an old time Oklahoma dinner. For much of the afternoon Armour Polly took the lead in cooking heaps of stuffed, battered, and fried Long John peppers; squash simmered in cream, butter, and sugar; pinto beans, fried catfish, little new potatoes from her garden, green beans and bacon, corn bread, sliced garden tomatoes, and apricot cobbler. After readying five pitchers of iced tea, Armour Polly, then eighty-three years old, retired for a nap while the women pulled their chairs around the table to catch up on family gossip and events of interest.

Being an election year, it was not long before the conversation turned to politics. I can still hear my grandmother asking her twin sister, "Who is Momma going to vote for?" And the deadpan reply, "Carter." Indignantly, my "wealthy" great aunt asked, "Good Lord, why?" Which led to a flawed historical refrain I had heard many times before, "Oh well, that's what Daddy wants and anything to keep the peace. Well you know since Daddy's father fought for the Democrats in the Civil War and the Republicans almost starved him to death at the end, he thinks the Democrats can do no wrong."

But then my grandmother added something new—at least to me—"and of course she's an Indian, so he thinks she doesn't know anything." Perplexed, I exclaimed as only a precocious child can, "Excuse me, but Grandmomma is NOT an Indian." And as only a parent can, my grandmother gave me a look that simultaneously meant, "You be still now" and "you may very well get a spanking later." So, I was still.

Simple as it seemed, my grandmother's statement raised difficult questions. Leaving the issue of possible Indian ancestry aside, I found myself thinking about how women used the "Indian" past to frame personal and political interests. Other concerns would subvert this quandary from my mind over the years, but it resurfaced in college. I read everything I could get my hands on about American Indian history and quickly noticed an intriguing trend, namely that an unusually large number of European American women wrote works of historical scholarship on American Indians in the immediate decades before and after the Civil War. Intrigued, I wondered, "Why Indians?" I examined a range of women's published work on American Indians, along with secondary source biographies and academic treatments of women's Indian scholarship. Some interpretive frameworks proved particularly awkward, foremost the argument that as disenfranchised groups, European American women and Indians were peers bound by a kind of mutual empathy. According to this view, sentimental affiliation—more than anything else—motivated white women's Indian scholarship and concurrent assimilation work.

Considering the glut of women's assimilationist writings that decried Indian "savagery," "barbarism," "brutality," and cultural "perversity," and simultaneously called for coerced Indian assimilation, historical interpretations rooted in the great sisterhood of women and essentialized gender traits were somewhat suspicious. The evidence indicates that European American women's interest in Indian history was driven by personal and cultural agendas—more than mutual empathy or pity. More so, specialized Indian history was intimately linked to the published work of women scholars, rather than to the social and cultural interactions that occurred between European American social reformers (women assimilationists) and American Indians.[1]

The evidence detailing how specialized Indian history emerged does not demonstrate a relationship of rescue, instead it reveals scholarly elitism, academic isolation, and enduring cultural barriers. The validity of women's early American Indian history was measured by its cultural, social, and political distance from actual Indians. Striving for professional "objectivity," European American women's document-driven Indian history was not written at missions, during fieldwork, or in the company of American Indian subjects. Women's early professional work in Indian history also avoided oral interviews, questionnaires, correspondence, and similar kinds of contemporary sources. Anthropological and ethnological observations were particularly taboo. At the time, any of these sources would have marked women's historical scholarship as "biased," or worse, "sentimental." Instead, Indian history written by women was scribed from documentary evidence consulted at libraries, archives, historical societies, and government repositories. For almost a century, cultural, social, political, and economic barriers also delineated the women who could accesses documents and write American Indian history—when, where, and how. This intellectual segregation spanned the preprofessional (1830 to 1889) and early professional (1890 to 1930) periods in American historiography. Indian history was the purview of white women.

By controlling the historical narrative, white women were able to claim an expert status through which they advanced personal interests and goals. Their focus was distinctively pan-Indian, reflecting a national preoccupation with the enduring "Indian Question." In contrast, a smattering of parallel published works by American Indians focused on the historical and political issues facing each author's own tribe. Even in the early professional period Rachel Caroline Eaton, the first Indigenous woman to earn a Ph.D. in American history, continued this intratribal focus with a published history of her own nation—the Cherokees. Not until Choctaw historian Anna Lewis published *Along the Arkansas* in 1932, would an Indigenous woman historian breach the pan-Indian barrier.

Anna Lewis broke through this interpretive divide by redefining the pan-Indian historical narrative in terms of intertribal relations. According to Lewis's formulation, intertribal connections allowed Indian peoples to exercise agency in a kind of "middle ground" that navigated Indigenous and colonial agendas. While Lewis's book remained relatively obscure, her intertribal approach did not. This was poignantly demonstrated by two articles that appeared in Mattie Lloyd Wooten's 1940 anthology, *Women Tell the Story of the Southwest*—a pioneering collection of articles by Western women about Western history.

Wooten's anthology featured the work of both amateur and professional women historians from Texas, New Mexico, Arizona, and Oklahoma. Notably, Wooten's introduction highlighted articles authored by Anna Lewis and Muriel H. Wright, giving special notice to the novelty of work by two Indigenous Oklahoma historians published in the same volume. Lewis contributed a biography of Choctaw political and educational leader Jane McCurtain that emphasized her intertribal influence, while Wright's article detailed the disastrous alliance between the Choctaw and Chickasaw nations and the Confederacy. Lewis's article was written eight years after publication of *Along the*

Arkansas; Wright's article was penned while she conducted research for her comprehensive, *A Guide to the Indian Tribes of Oklahoma.* Both articles challenged the dominant pan-Indian historical narrative by illuminating historical Indigenous political alliances.[2]

For Muriel Wright these intertribal sentiments mirrored her own internal conflict with deeply held assimilationist beliefs. Wright supported assimilation as an abstract goal, but she detested its devastating economic and cultural effects on Indian peoples. In contrast, the turn toward intertribal history was not a contradiction for Anna Lewis, who saw in it a validation of Indian sovereignty. Unlike the trajectory of European American pan-Indian history, in which Indian peoples were forcibly stripped of their cultural and tribal identities and amalgamated into American society as a defeated "race," Lewis's intertribal history focused on the common political interests of distinct, sovereign American Indian tribes and nations. In time European American pan-Indian history would lose its definitive authority within the academy, due in large part to the fact that key Indigenous historians criticized the assimilationist eschatology of pan-Indian history, while advancing their own intertribal and intratribal interpretations.

Early attempts by Indigenous women historians to publish Indian histories through the academic presses were met with negative peer reviews that reflected cultural hegemony, sexism, and conflicts of interest. Nevertheless, they persevered. Indigenous women historians' determination to publish contrarian views of Indian history played a crucial role in steering the academy toward a more critical view of settler colonialism and America's internal imperialism. *A Field of Their Own* offers a century-long look at how key European American and Indigenous women shaped the specialized field of American Indian history.

Acknowledgments

The final leg of the long journey that fit the story of women and American Indian history together for me began at the University of Oklahoma. Albert Hurtado, David Levy, Judith Lewis, Fay Yarbrough, Joshua Piker, Don Pisani, and David Wrobel each played significant roles in helping me sort out answers to the hard questions. Richard Lowitt graciously shared his insights into the complex relationship between Angie Debo and Edward Everett Dale. I am indebted to Paul McKenzie-Jones for discussions that helped me to conceptualize how pan-Indian and intra- and intertribal studies shaped the first century of American Indian history.

Other scholars who were extremely generous with their time, advice, and suggestions include Kate Larson, Susan Gray, Phil Brigandi, Valerie Mathes, Suzanne Crawford, Lynn Musslewhite, Hamilton Cravens, Margaret Sankey, and Peter Bowler. I would like to especially thank David Wrobel and Charles Rankin for their assistance in moving my book toward publication.

Laurie Scrivener and Brian Buckley also provided tireless assistance at the University of Oklahoma Bizzell library. Sunu Kodumthara spent many an evening with me at the Bizzell library reference desk discussing American Darwinism and women Indian scholars. Friend and colleague Anthony Carlson could be counted on for an essential weekly scholar's confab at "The Library," a local ale and pizza joint. JoAnn Palmeri's graciousness at the University of Oklahoma, History of Science Collection made much of my research on American Darwinism possible. I am equally grateful to Anna Cook at the Massachusetts Historical Society Library, and Kate Blalack, Sarah Coates, and David Peters at the Oklahoma State University Libraries Special

Collections. Heartfelt thanks go to Kelly Brown at the University of Science and Arts of Oklahoma, Nash Library, for guiding me through the Anna L. Lewis and Muriel H. Wright collections. Likewise, I owe many thanks to the University of Tulsa McFarlin Library, Department of Special Collections, for their assistance with the John M. Oskison Collection.

I would like to especially thank my manuscript readers, Valerie Sherer Mathes, Rose Stremlau, and Patti Loughlin, for helping make this a much stronger book. Many thanks also go to the University of Oklahoma Press, especially Alessandra Tamulevich, Stephanie Evans, and my superb copyeditor, Jo Ann Reece. Alessandra, Stephanie, and Jo Ann expertly navigated a host of concerns to successfully shepherd my manuscript to publication. The credit for what is deemed good scholarship goes to all those historians who so graciously provided suggestions and shared their expertise, deficiencies and mistakes are entirely my own.

To family, friends, and acquaintances who patiently listened to endless tales of my latest discoveries, newest musings, and the scholarship of long-past women historians, thank you for the priceless dignity offered by simply listening. I know it was not always easy. To those who silently watch from the other side, you are not forgotten. To Bart McClenny, thank you as always for being there listening, caring, encouraging, and making this work possible. You are the best historian I have ever known. To Rachel, Anna, and Muriel, thank you for never giving up—you made history.

Acronyms and Abbreviations

ABCFM	American Board of Commissioners for Foreign Missions
ABHMS	American Baptist Home Mission Society
AAAS	American Association for the Advancement of Science
AAW	Association for the Advancement of Women
AHA	American Historical Association
AHR	*American Historical Review*
AIAA	American Indian Aid Association
AIMA	American Indian Mission Association
AMA	American Missionary Association
BE	Bureau of Ethnology (also American Bureau of Ethnology)
BGCFM	Baptist General Convention for Foreign Missions
BIA	Bureau of Indian Affairs
CIC	Central Indian Committee
IHA	Indian's Hope Association
IMA	Indian Memorial Association
IRA	Indian Rights Association
ITKPA	Indian Treaty-Keeping and Protective Association
KCW	Kentucky College for Women

KSHS	Kansas State Historical Society
KU	University of Kansas
MCJC	Mary Connor Junior College
MM	Mother's Meeting
MVHA	Mississippi Valley Historical Association
MVHR	*Mississippi Valley Historical Review*
NIA	National Indian Association
NIDA	National Indian Defense Association
OAA	Omaha Allotment Act
OIA	Office of Indian Affairs
OCW	Oklahoma College for Women
PF	Progressive Friends
SSTC	Southeastern State Teacher's College, (Durant, Oklahoma)
UC	University of California
UPU	Universal Peace Union
WABHMS	Women's American Baptist Home Mission Society
WBHMS	Women's Baptist Home Mission Society
WICCE	World's Industrial and Cotton Centennial Exposition
WNIA	Women's National Indian Association
WSHS	Wisconsin State Historical Society
WTSTC	West Texas State Teacher's College

A Field of Their Own

Introduction

"White" Women and the Specialized Field of American Indian Scholarship

In 1941 the eminent historian of American Indians, Angie Debo asserted, "Every schoolboy knows . . . Indian warfare was a perpetual accompaniment of American pioneering, but the second stage in dispossessing the Indians is not so generally and romantically known." Debo's perspective in *And Still the Waters Run: The Betrayal of the Five Civilized Tribes* was new, and a dramatic departure from the historical vision of Frederick Jackson Turner. In his 1889 review of Theodore Roosevelt's *The Winning of the West*, Turner had relegated frontier Indian history to "conflicts of the pioneers with the Indians" that "give opportunity for romantic treatment unsurpassed." Four years later, Turner's essay "The Significance of the Frontier in American History" developed the point further, largely relegating American Indian history to the initial stages of European North American colonization.[1]

Unlike Turner, Angie Debo did not confine American Indians to the distant colonial past or to quiet graves on the fringes of the frontier. Debo's Indians were not indistinctly blended with European Americans in the soothing homogeneity of assimilation. Angie Debo's Indians were contemporary, alive, and striving to interact with twentieth century European Americans on their own terms. Yet while her approach signaled a rupture in the Turnerian view of Indians and frontier progress, it also heralded a new topic for professional historical analysis—Indian sovereignty. Bucking a trend among socially and politically conscious women that dated back to the early republic, Debo's scholarship signaled a final phase in European American women's preeminent position as American Indian historians.[2]

Culminating a little over a century of white women's pan-Indian scholarship, Debo's work would lay the foundation for a modern ethnologically and anthropologically informed American Indian history that would critically engage the legacy of assimilation and settler colonialism. This scholarship would quickly entangle European American and Indigenous historians in new kinds of postcolonial arguments over scholarly representations of Indian history. Encompassing a broad range of contentious topics—including European American imperialism, colonization, and cultural hegemony—the new American Indian history challenged the traditional monopoly European American women held in Indian scholarship.

By the time of Debo's death in 1988 a small cohort of largely male American historians had explored aspects of American Indian cultural appropriation, setting the stage for contentious new scholarship. Their analysis focused on the ways that European Americans had appropriated, interpreted, inscribed, and monetized Indian identity and culture through museum and archive collections, western art, popular publications, photography, theater, and film. In helping turn historian's interests from Indian politics to Indian cultural appropriation, Angie Debo's scholarship also contributed to the critical examination of European American imperialism and its legacy.[3]

Yet in looking at European American patrimony in the public consumption of Indian cultures, historians gave little attention to how a select group of preprofessional and professional women scholars became closely identified with Indian history—and claimed it as their own. While a smattering of European American men published Indian scholarship during the century considered in this volume, no professional male historian exclusively published Indian history or claimed it as a specialized field. In contrast, seven of the nine women examined here almost exclusively published work on American Indians during their years of scholarly activity. Helen Hunt Jackson was a noted author and poet before turning her attention to American Indians in 1879, while Emma Helen Blair worked on a number of different historical projects before taking up Indian history around 1909. With the exception of Jackson and Blair whose careers were cut short by early deaths, these women reinforced their status as dedicated Indian scholars for years through their articles in newspapers, magazines, scholarly journals, and published books.

A handful of historians have considered the role that ethnologically minded male and female scholars assumed in creating an American Indian anthropological narrative, but no scholarship has yet examined the closely knit cadre of European American scholars who fashioned the corollary history of American Indians. While both sexes participated in the construction of Indian scholarship, a disproportionate number of women promoted their expertise as Indian scholars and successfully published American Indian history. Some were preprofessional women scholars who functioned on the margins of the women's rights movement, where they used their American Indian scholarship to exert an extraordinary degree of social and political influence. Given the real power eventually wielded by these scholars, it is surprising that historians have not considered how and why women came to play such a preeminent role in shaping specialized American Indian history.[4]

In examining this question, it may be impossible to discuss historical subjects without creating new constructions, and certainly, fifty years of contention regarding who has the right to participate in cultural and historical analysis of American Indian history has solved little, though it did set scholarly parameters. Regarding the *history* of American Indian history these limits have, in fact, served to scatter and obscure the cultural and intellectual threads that bound together a unique contingent of European American women who shaped Indian history for over a century. Reconnecting the historical continuity of these relationships will undoubtedly challenge established boundaries.

Addressing how and why these women constructed American Indian history may raise the specter of a scholarly witch hunt. The purpose of this book is not to indict historians or historical figures, or to devalue compensatory histories about women, but rather to address why a core group of European American women played such a key role in formulating American Indian scholarship. While arguably the chronology can be traced to the first European colonists, the evidence reveals that Indian scholarship began to gain prominence through the work of socially and politically conscious women often linked to the emerging women's rights movement. Regardless of personal or ideological allegiances, they all participated in a concurrent bid for social and political influence.

This volume is specifically built around nine women scholars who published key document-driven histories that definitively shaped the specialized field of American Indian history: Helen Hunt Jackson, Alice Cunningham Fletcher, Emma Helen Blair, Louise Phelps Kellogg, Annie Heloise Abel, Rachel Caroline Eaton, Anna Lazola Lewis, Muriel Hazel Wright, and Angie Debo. Collectively their scholarship marks a distinct trajectory that maps their unmistakable role in constructing Indian history.

Although several of these women are known through biographical treatments, compensatory histories, and issue-specific articles, the history that weaves their lives and legacies together as Indian historians has not been recognized in previous historical scholarship. Eaton, Lewis, and Wright remain comparatively unknown Indigenous Indian historians. Jackson and Fletcher are not considered Indian historians, nor are their pioneering Indian histories generally recognized in the historiography.

In contrast, when considering male history writers there is virtually no academic quibble regarding the status of preprofessional male historians. From Henry Adams to Charles A. Beard traditional scholarship finds no substantial break, each were real historians separated by time, theory, and style, but not historical credibility. In terms of American Indian history the works of Francis Parkman, Josiah Royce, Justin Winsor, George Bancroft, Hubert Howe Bancroft, and Henry Adams, while historiographically contextualized and stylistically distinguished, are nevertheless placed in the historical cannon alongside Western and American Indian historians including Francis Paul Prucha, William Thomas Hagan, and Richard White. But what distinguished these men as real historians? What made them recognized as legitimate experts across all eras of American scholarship, as opposed to mere historical writers or amateur historians?[5]

The answer in part is that they were socially influential men, and other socially influential men said they were legitimate historians. Not only in the professional era, but also in the preprofessional era, a small cadre of well-connected men with complex political and economic relations determined who was an historian and what comprised history. For this reason the overtly imperialistic and often racist Western scholarship of Theodore Roosevelt—work that would be rejected if submitted to a modern university press—has been traditionally deemed legitimate American history, while the much less-biased historical scholarship of Sarah Bolton and Mary Lamb is labeled as amateur—when even acknowledged. In such an environment women seldom held the social or political power to anoint themselves or other women as legitimate historians of the republic. As Peter Novick observed, "It is a sociological truism that nothing contributes more to the status of a vocation than the extent to which it is seen as a male calling."[6]

Yet for preprofessional women who pursued careers in historical scholarship, the path was particularly perilous for reasons other than gender bias alone. Rather than the rigid chauvinism of male historians and their supporters, the permeable, interdisciplinary nature of postbellum scholarship fostered an identity crisis for women interested in American Indian history. Unlike earlier Indian scholarship that tended to rely on uncritical readings of first-hand accounts, hearsay, and questionable secondary sources, mid-nineteenth century scholarship took a decided turn toward scientific accuracy.[7]

Postbellum women scholars who studied American Indian peoples and cultures were required to base their work on actual observations and scrupulously recorded notes if they wished to garner credibility. Curiously, where the use of tarnished tales, secondhand stories, hearsay, and eyewitness accounts had distinguished earlier male scholars as Indian historians, the use of contemporary observation placed women scholars into a kind of historical limbo. In response, women addressed the anthropological and ethnological aspects of their work as "the natural history of Man, especially with reference to America."[8]

By conflating anthropology, ethnology, and history, postbellum scholarship on American Indians blurred the lines between history and studies of social, ethnic, and cultural lifeways. Preprofessional anthropologists, such as Erminnie A. Smith, Zelia Nuttall, Frederic Ward Putnam, John Wesley Powell, and Matilda Coxe Stevenson, called their work a new kind of history or simply referred to their studies as "histories." Their contemporary Helen Hunt Jackson compiled *A Century of Dishonor*, a document-driven Indian history. However, Jackson also penned a fair amount of politically oriented material about American Indians that was considered "sentimental." Straddling the two disciplines, Alice Fletcher considered herself both an anthropologist and historian. Perhaps in this respect she was correct, like Jackson she authored a comprehensive volume of document-driven Indian history, *Indian Education and Civilization*. Though lost to the historiography, Jackson and Fletcher were the first authors of comprehensive American Indian histories that met later professional criteria.[9]

Addressing this scholarly identity crisis, archaeologist Teresa Militello suggests that modern historians and anthropologists should consider the title "avocational prehistorians." Militello argues that this term more accurately describes preprofessional scholars whose work dates from a time period when the terms "anthropology" and "history" were still quite fluid. Somehow, avocational historians seems an imprecise, if not stilted, description.[10]

To reinforce key points in this book, I occasionally use "scholar" when describing preprofessional women who studied and prominently published on American Indian subjects. These women were particularly distinguished by their recognized status as Indian experts. Using American Indian scholar, as opposed to historian, helps avoid the gendered and sexually biased presumptions that separated preprofessional historians into the ranks of amateurs and real historians. The term scholar also acknowledges the widespread multidisciplinary recognition and impact of American Indian scholarship conducted by preprofessional women. It would be impossible to make such connections if the postbellum women who studied American Indians were strictly defined according to the conventions that distinguished midnineteenth century American male historians.[11]

By anointing themselves Indian experts, a small cadre of white women steadily worked toward assuming the influential scholarly positions long claimed by men. For these women the successful construction of true

American Indian scholarship would require that they dominate the intellectual and political discourse about Indians. But an attempt by women to command almost any intellectual discourse in a world controlled by men risked failure. Their success, however limited and fleeting, was remarkable if only because these women had challenged patriarchal authority and prevailed.

Just as remarkable were the achievements of Indigenous women scholars, who eventually acquired a voice within this new narrative and helped reshape the specialized field of American Indian history. The cultural barriers that segregated the construction of American Indian history effectively made it a European American venture for much of its first formative century. Moreover, this early American Indian scholarship and later Indian history was marked by colonial assumptions that tended to amalgamate diverse Indian peoples into pan-Indian histories. Though a few preprofessional Indigenous women writers addressed intratribal and intertribal Indian history, they did not directly challenge the underlying assumptions of pan-Indian historical scholarship.

The reasons for this were complex, revealing both cultural and political differences. American Indian peoples did not have an equivalent collective imperialist mindset and did not hold a racial evolutionist point of view that amalgamated distinct tribes of Indian peoples, cultures, and sovereignties into a single American Indian race. From a practical standpoint, cultures and peoples under constant assault tend to focus on their own immediate problems. For Indigenous authors intratribal and intertribal history was both self-affirming and politically sensible. Formulated by European American scholars, pan-Indian history was an unattractive if not relatively foreign concept to American Indian writers. The pan-Indian approach to history not only distinguished differences in historical conceptualization, it also reflected the social and economic contours that functioned as barriers to Indigenous Indian scholarship. These barriers effectively segregated the publication of American Indian history.

The intimate social and personal relationships that existed between white women who were social reformers and Indian women—studied in detail by Peggy Pascoe, Jane Simonsen, Katherine Ellinghaus, Catherine Cahill, and others—did not inform the American Indian scholarship of professional women historians. Where women social reformers often engaged with living Indian peoples, women historians studied documents and archival sources on American Indians. Indigenous women historians would not breach this professional barrier until 1919, the year Cherokee historian Rachel Caroline Eaton was awarded a Ph.D. in history. The pan-Indian barrier would not be breached by an Indigenous historian until the publication of Anna Lewis's *Along the Arkansas* in 1932.

A NOTE ON TERMINOLOGY

I use the terms "American Indian" and "Indian" interchangeably. Following the convention of the Indigenous historians examined in this book and my personal preference, I do not use the term Native American. The terms "nation" and "tribe" are used interchangeably when context allows, but when addressing issues pertaining to the Five Tribes—Cherokee, Choctaw, Chickasaw, Muscogee (Creek), and Seminole—as organized political bodies, I specifically use the term Five Nations. For clarity and simplicity, I use the term "Indigenous" when noting American Indian women scholars of Indian history. When discussing the political and assimilationist application of ethnological and anthropological studies, I use the term "ethno-political" scholarship.

The term "construction," as used by contemporary American Indian scholars, denotes academic presentations of American Indian cultures, treaties, and politics. The scholarly process of construction encompasses the historical identification, analysis, organization, publication, and regulation of American Indian history. Construction established parameters for the specialized field and promoted its findings. In this context, construction is used as an analytical tool to examine the process by which European American women presented American Indians and their cultures as historical subjects.[12]

On a related note, when emphasizing preprofessional and professional differences this book distinguishes between American Indian scholarship and Indian history. Indian scholarship refers to work rooted in anthropology and ethnology. Much of this publication was driven by linguistics, philology, comparative mythology, and antiquated racial theory. Indian scholarship was not document-driven nor rigidly segregated from contact with American Indians. In fact, its validity was closely tied to intimate interaction with Indian peoples and cultures. In contrast, Indian history refers to "unbiased," "objective," document-driven publication that was strictly segregated from the author's personal observations or intimate contact with Indian subjects. The validity of white women's Indian history hinged on its distance from Indian peoples and their cultures.

The term "pan-Indian history" describes an historical mindset and related scholarship that tended to level diverse Indian peoples into a single cultural, political, and racial unit. The growth of pan-Indian history was corollary to efforts in the late 1800s to develop a solution to the dreaded "Indian problem," as the U.S. government focused its American Indian policy on assimilating all the tribes into European American culture. "Intratribal" history refers to a history of a specific tribe or nation. "Intertribal" refers to histories or interactions involving more than one tribe or nation.

NINE KEY WOMEN WHO SHAPED THE SPECIALIZED
FIELD OF AMERICAN INDIAN HISTORY

A Field of Their Own is not a biographical or compensatory study of women, consequently the narrative does not focus on the chronological lives of these scholars. Excellent comprehensive biographies of Alice Fletcher, Helen Hunt Jackson, Annie Heloise Abel, and Angie Debo already exist. Instead, this volume is an intellectual and cultural history drawing on the biographical information of women who pioneered the specialized field of American Indian history. While this book makes use of diverse life stories, culled from primary and secondary sources related to the central characters, it *focuses* on the historical trajectory outlined by the scholarly activities of nine women whose work definitively shaped the specialized field of American Indian history during its first formative century.

The years examined in this study, 1830 to 1941, encompass the deep cultural processes through which women became intimately associated with American Indian history. Studies of no single decade or era can demonstrate how American Indian scholarship and women were intimately melded together in American culture. Examining the lives and work of Helen Hunt Jackson, Alice C. Fletcher, Emma Helen Blair, Louise Phelps Kellogg, Annie Heloise Abel, Rachel Caroline Eaton, Anna L. Lewis, Muriel H. Wright, and Angie Debo reveals that women's leading role in the construction of American Indian history was a complex venture—one that unfolded over the course of a century.[13]

This book is comprised of two parts containing 8 chapters. In part I, "Women's Early American Indian Scholarship, 1830–1889," chapters 1 and 2 reexamine old presumptions about the origin of the women's rights movement and its relationship to women's scholarly publications on African American slaves and American Indians. Chapter 1 looks at the political ideology, civil rights agenda, and organizational experiences women brought to abolitionism, including public speaking, debate, publication, and leadership roles that women had assumed during their work as American Transcendentalists, evangelists, and political agitators.

Chapter 2 reveals that within this environment of shifting political metaphors, American Indians slowly assumed a place of importance. First recognized by a handful of women evangelicals and abolitionists, Plains Indians were steadily transformed into the cause célèbre of women's emerging maternal patriotism after the Civil War. Sparked by the failure of the postbellum radical civil rights movement, this maternal patriotism sought to validate women's political aspirations through social uplift work. American Indian assimilation soon became the quintessential symbol of this endeavor.

Chapters 3 through 6 examine how American Indian scholarship became a specialized niche for a small cadre of postbellum women scholars. Inspired by the racial evolution theories of American Darwinism, these women sought to unlock the mysteries of the Indian mind, soul, and body. Based on a carefully crafted status as experts on all things Indian, these women scholars deployed their purported ability to turn American Indians into European Americans as a means to cultivate their own political power and personal influence. In these chapters, I give special attention to the often subtle evolutionary thought of Helen Hunt Jackson and Alice Fletcher and how new data, field research, and evolving racial theories reshaped preprofessional women's ethno-political Indian scholarship. Ultimately these developments shifted anthropological authority from Washington, D.C., specifically the Bureau of American Ethnology, to academic institutions. Unable to transition into the academy, preprofessional women scholars were further isolated from professional credibility and publication.

Part II, "A New Frontier for Women Historians, 1890–1941," looks at how Frederick Jackson Turner's Frontier Thesis struck a further blow against racial evolution and helped amplify the history profession's growing distaste for the interdisciplinary application of ethnology and anthropology. Whereas chapter 7 looks at Turner's role in marginalizing nineteenth century women's Indian scholarship, chapter 8 considers his role in promoting the professional careers of early women historians of American Indians. As American anthropology moved from a form of government patronage to the academy and ethnology and anthropology were shunned by professional historians, Alice Fletcher found herself cast into a new scholarly frontier that generally considered her work antiquated, amateur, sentimental, and overly political. Her once highly visible, popular, and government-sanctioned role as an autonomous female authority on American Indians quickly faded.

While most male historians of the time did not, Turner and a few male cohorts promoted promising women graduate students, who were steered toward professional archival and museum work, as well as careers teaching history at women's colleges and in high schools. In these positions women frontier and American West historians came to distinguish themselves as American Indian experts largely because Indian history was one of the few subjects not already claimed by their male colleagues.

Among the small group of women Indian historians who emerged around the turn of the twentieth century, Turner's students Emma Helen Blair and Louise Phelps Kellogg were pioneers of professional Indian history. Blair and Kellogg's Indian scholarship helped increase their visibility as professional historians who worked outside academic institutions. Though not a Turner student, contemporary historian Annie Heloise Abel advanced

Indian history within the academy, further securing it as an important subject for women historians. Rachel Caroline Eaton, a student of William E. Dodd and J. Fred Rippy, broke through the academic barrier when she became the first Indigenous woman to earn a history doctorate. Given their unique status as architects of the new specialized field of Indian history, the work of Blair, Kellogg, Abel, and Eaton is used here to analyze the intellectual trajectory that led to Angie Debo's interest in the anthropologically and ethnologically informed study of American Indian history.

Chapter 8 examines the precarious rise of new women Indian historians and how nineteenth and early twentieth century cultural tensions regarding the legacy of assimilation and American Indian sovereignty came to inform the work of Anna L. Lewis, Muriel H. Wright, and Angie Debo. In particular, I look at how Debo's continuation of Abel's work on the Five Nations was shaped by the Oklahoma Choctaw scholars, Lewis and Wright. Lewis's and Wright's critical influence, along with that of Lewis's brother Grady, pushed Debo beyond the mere study of past Indian politics, established by the Turnerian tradition, toward the study of a more comprehensive American Indian history. While her early work accepted the basic premise of assimilation, from 1935 on Debo's scholarship increasingly foreshadowed later critiques of American internal imperialism.

Finally, the conclusion "Women Historians, American Indian History, and Gender Politics" looks at the scholarly debate between, Lewis, Wright, and Debo and underlines decades of simmering discontent fostered by European American women's hegemonic role in constructing American Indian history. The tension between these three women likewise pinpoints a complicated moment in academic history when European American women's publications on Indians came to be openly challenged by new Indigenous women historians. Lewis and Wright's critiques of Debo's work demonstrate that American Indian women's emerging historical scholarship was not simply an academic exercise, but rather a powerful public assertion of their own Indian identities, tribal interests, and historical insights. Indigenous women historians had finally found their professional voice and American Indian history would never be the same again.

Part I

Women's Early American Indian Scholarship, 1830–1889

CHAPTER 1

WOMEN'S RIGHTS, AMERICAN INDIANS, AND CAPITOL POLITICS

On December 17, 1904, Belva Ann Bennett Lockwood, then in her seventy-fourth year and a noted matriarch of the women's rights movement, an accomplished lawyer, and two-time presidential candidate, stated in testimony before the United States Senate Select Committee on Woman Suffrage, "I come from the District of Columbia, where no man has the privilege of voting, and so long as this state of affairs continues I am just as good and have just as many privileges as any man."[1]

Accompanying Lockwood were Clara Bewick Colby, corresponding secretary of the Federal Women's Equality Association and longtime Indian rights advocate, and Dr. Clara W. McNaughton, vice president of the Federal Women's Equality Association. A triumvirate of accomplished politically active women, they each embodied the reality of Lockwood's subtle observation, namely that postbellum events in the District of Columbia provided Washington women with a unique opportunity to achieve an extraordinary degree of political, economic, and social power. Set in motion by political indiscretion and corruption, the leveling effect of Congress's universal disenfranchisement of the district's males in 1873 proved to be of inestimable value to its women at a precarious moment in the American women's rights movement.[2]

While early women's rights advocates and congressional radical Republicans formed a weak yet enduring political coalition during the Civil War, a coterie of influential women's rights activists—who either lived in or were intimately associated with the capital—coalesced in the late 1860s to form the movement's federal vanguard. In this capacity women such as Victoria

Woodhull, Susan B. Anthony, Elizabeth Cady Stanton, Caroline Dall, Paulina Davis, Sarah Spencer, Isabella Beecher Hooker, Sarah Johnson, and Jocelyn Gage promoted a radical civil rights ideology that profoundly influenced the rhetoric, goals, and popular image of the national women's movement. Suddenly placed on a parallel political and social plane with district men, women gained unprecedented access to Congress and other national seats of power. This amplified influence, coupled with the district's universal disfranchisement, poised Washington women to play a leading role as social activists, reformers, and Indian assimilationists.[3]

Proposed at Gettysburg, Pennsylvania, on November 19, 1863, the "new nation" idealism President Abraham Lincoln promised in his Gettysburg Address offered expanded equality and progressive civil rights. As it had for freed people, new nation idealism would come to have a lasting impact on a broad range of American women. Shaping both the message of the federal vanguard and the everyday aspirations of women across the republic, thought of a new egalitarian nation gave cohesiveness to an otherwise complex network of women's rights agendas that was often demarcated by those who advocated comprehensive as opposed to utilitarian reforms. The new nation era women's rights vanguard united a range of women activists through a new "feminized" professional model that often transcended political division, economic status, and class distinction. Emerging alongside a small far more visible group of women who gained access to the traditionally male professions—law, medicine, business, politics, and academia—the new categories of feminized professional identity were based on self-conferred noninstitutional pedigrees, peer validation, and autonomous disciplinary and procedural criteria. Social commentators and popular media christened these autonomous professionals the "New Woman."[4]

To this end the Washington-based New Woman movement consolidated a preexisting body of ideas about innate competency that advanced women's intrinsic capacity for individuality, self-sufficiency, property rights, political participation, legal equality, intellectual thought, and economic opportunity. Inspired by transcendentalist assertions of each soul's inherent divine perfection, American women in the early women's rights movement embraced competency as their guiding ideology. Side by side, competency and women's professionalization would become the hallmarks of the post–Civil War New Woman movement.[5]

As contemporaries of Belva Lockwood, Clara Colby, and Clara McNaughton, Helen Hunt Jackson and Alice Cunningham Fletcher were also beneficiaries of new nation idealism and women's emerging autonomous professional status in postbellum Washington, D.C. Although Jackson only resided in Washington briefly, like Fletcher her activities in the city included cultivation of political and social connections that later proved beneficial to her Indian activism. By 1904, when Lockwood made her observation about universal district disenfranchisement, Jackson had been dead for almost two decades, while Fletcher still struggled to maintain her autonomous professional status in a late-nineteenth century world that had radically redefined the meaning of professionalization.[6]

Personally spared the heartache of trivialization, Jackson did not live to see professional historians unceremoniously shelve her pioneering Indian history, *A Century of Dishonor* with the work of other Victorian era "scribbling" women. For Fletcher the roller-coaster ride from zenith to nadir of the New Woman movement was trying at best. She made failed attempts to solidify her methods, interpretive systems, and scholarship within academic organizations, ventures that took both a financial and emotional toll. As the century that fomented the Civil War burned out and the next blazed forth, Fletcher watched as her scholarly work and that of other women American Indian scholars was either ignored or, on rare occasion, dismissively noted by later frontier historians. Today, removed by more than a century from the women who fashioned American Indian scholarship, the fragmentation of their history and intellectual legacy need not continue.[7]

Yet venturing into a scholarly frontier and reconnecting the historical and intellectual threads that bound together the new nation and the New Woman is essential to understanding the historical forces that came to identify women with the American Indian cause, and consequently molded Jackson and Fletcher within the preprofessional community of Indian scholars. By framing Jackson as a poet, author, and Indian rights activist and Fletcher as a pioneering anthropologist and Indian social activist, each woman's scholarly contribution has been cleaved from its seminal role in the construction of American Indian history. Jackson and Fletcher's place in historical evaluation has been minimized and their works treated as disconnected compensatory curiosities, obscuring their roles in defining key historical methods and interpretations that shaped academic scholarship on American Indians.

Born in 1830 and 1838 respectively, Helen Hunt Jackson and Alice Fletcher came of age and inclination far too late to participate in the formative years of the women's rights movement, yet their professional lives and intellectual contributions were bound together by its historical development. Where Jackson maintained a curious mixture of progressive idealism and anachronistic social strictures, Fletcher fully supported women's rights. Notably, while Jackson embraced public speaking and women's suffrage, Fletcher did not. Both Jackson and Fletcher nevertheless benefited from women's new and expanding role in public policy. In this manner the women's rights movement proved a liberating experience for many late-nineteenth century women.

However, its inability to cement an expanded range of professional identities within enduring institutions or to foster equal professional partnerships between men and women limited its ability to transform American society. This failure helps to explain why Jackson and Fletcher, unlike George Bancroft, Hubert Howe Bancroft, Francis Parkman, Henry Adams, Justin Winsor, Josiah Royce, and Theodore Roosevelt, are remembered today more as discrete anomalies, than as pioneering American Indian scholars.[8]

The vocational goals of women's rights leaders and women scholars of American Indians often overlapped, but there were significant historical differences. Plotted by the work of Rebecca J. Mead and Sunu Kodumthara, the women's rights trajectory detailing how regional political achievements of western suffragists shaped national success, simply does not apply to the social and political regime developed by women scholars of American Indians. Women's contributions to the construction of American Indian scholarship remained largely a capitol affair. The difference was one of constituencies: Western women could campaign on their own behalf while the majority of American Indians were effectively legal wards of the U.S. Congress, the Interior department, and the Bureau of Indian Affairs.[9]

Unlike the diffused political power of the postbellum women's rights movement, women scholars of American Indians found their political power focused on Washington, because most American Indians remained federally administered non-citizens. Whereas women's suffrage could be decided on the territorial and state level, no territorial or state law could trump federal Indian policy. This fundamental difference reveals why women scholars of Indians cultivated a close political relationship with Congress and the executive branch between 1877 and 1907.

In measuring the actual power exercised by these women scholars, it is important to remember that no suffragist or women's rights leader had the power to walk into the congressional clerk's office, take pen in hand, and amend bills pending before Congress, but Alice Fletcher did. Nor did any suffragist or women's rights leader control the allotment of personal property and land across approximately one-third of North America; Alice Fletcher did. As a special Indian agent, Helen Hunt Jackson wielded similar influence over the lives and property of the Mission Indians of California.

Even among women's rights leaders who were not Indian scholars, American Indian affairs played a prominent role in fostering professional credibility and political stature. Belva Lockwood's pioneering access to the Supreme Court was intimately tied to her position as counsel for the Eastern Cherokees, and both Lockwood and Clara Bewick Colby took in Indian children. As historians Peggy Pasco and Margaret Jacobs note, care for Indian children strengthened women's political credibility as responsible social reformers. The relationship between women's rights and women's American Indian scholarship raises the question, how did a women's rights vanguard emerge in Washington and subsequently give rise to a lateral political movement that fostered Indian scholarship opportunities for women like Jackson and Fletcher?[10]

THE POLITICAL POWER OF IDEAS: TRANSCENDENTALISTS AND WOMEN EVANGELISTS

Traditional historical scholarship on women's rights emphasized the political push for suffrage, tracing the movement's origin to the well-known 1848 Seneca Falls convention. Since the 1980s a growing cohort of historians have challenged this view with new evidence that questions the originality of the Seneca Falls resolutions and the ideological centrality of suffrage. This work has collectively pushed the historical chronology of the American women's rights movement to the era of the Second Great Awakening (1790–1845) and linked the articulation of women's rights to the Transcendentalist movement of the 1830s.[11]

As a cultural product of the Jacksonian age, Transcendentalism has been interpreted as a reaction to orthodox Calvinism, secularization, the growing conservatism of Unitarian reform, and the social chaos created by emerging industrialization. The central egalitarian belief that all "men and women [a]re fundamentally divine" posited Transcendentalism to champion the early republic's burgeoning preoccupation with social assimilation and democratization. Paralleling the cultural impact of Frederick Jackson Turner's Frontier Thesis six decades later, Transcendentalism inspired a growing contingent of women's rights advocates and abolitionists to coalesce amorphous Second Awakening evangelical ideas about equality and intrinsic human rights into an influential social and political ideology.[12]

In organizational decline by the 1860s, Transcendentalism's lasting legacy was its stealthy ability to infiltrate the ideology of affiliated social and reform efforts, where it thrived as an unseen yet powerful intellectual force. As Caroline Healey Dall, a noted Transcendentalist, women's rights activist, and confidant of Jackson and Fletcher related in 1860, "When, in 1844 Margaret Fuller gave 'The Great Lawsuit' . . . she stated with *transcendent* force the argument which formed the basis of the first 'Woman's Rights Convention' in 1848." Dall stated the case more explicitly in her 1895 history of New England Transcendentalism: "The characteristics of the Transcendental movement were shown in the temper of its agitation for the rights of women and the enlargement of her duties."[13]

As with other cultural and social movements, scholarly debate surrounds the origins of American Transcendentalism, yet historical analysis traces its essential social and political reform ideas to a small cadre of New England women fervently dedicated to the emerging politics of human rights. Prominent among them were Elizabeth Palmer Peabody, Margaret Fuller (Ossoli), Pauline Wright Davis, and Caroline Healey Dall. From 1830 to 1850 these women translated Second Great Awakening idealism into a mainstream Transcendentalist rhetoric that helped foment the national abolitionist and women's rights movements. Both abolitionist rhetoric and the politicized imagery of African American enslavement were effectively appropriated by women's rights proponents.[14]

Deftly employed by an emerging group of outspoken liberal women activists, the slave metaphor became political code for the contentious issue of women's rights. The invocation of brutalized, chained, and cowed slaves became a rallying cry during women's abolition lectures, where it was aimed at overturning European American male hegemony. Such public displays not only flouted traditional gender strictures, which forbade female usurpation of male authority, but also came into conflict with the new "separate spheres" gender sensibilities evolving within the emerging American middle class.[15]

The social and intellectual spark that ignited this new outspoken class of liberal antebellum women activists was struck by pioneering challenges to traditional gender and power hierarchies unleashed during the evangelical fury of the Second Great Awakening. Drawing on traditional cooperative gender and labor roles found in American agrarian society, the Second Great Awakening emphasized the personal priesthood and kingship of each believer, inflaming egalitarian sentiment among its male and female converts. Convinced that the end times were at hand, a notable contingent of Second Awakening believers accepted the eschatological assertion that God would "pour out" His "spirit upon all flesh; and your sons and your daughters shall prophesy." Equating prophesy with preaching many evangelicals consequently promoted, or at least tolerated, the public ministry of women preachers. Largely forgotten today, these women ministers forged in the passionate spiritual crucible of the Second Awakening provoked the first national women's rights debate.[16]

Nancy Towle (1796–1876) one of the most illustrious of the Second Awakening preachers asked, "Respecting the preaching of females.... I would reply, 'Where did *Mary, Anna, Deborah, Miriam, Esther* . . . speak,—but in the church?'" Towle added, "May the Lord, raise up a host of *female warriors,*—that shall *provoke* the opposite *party,* from their *indolence.*" Towle's male compatriot Lorenzo Dow, an itinerant Methodist preacher and avid abolitionist, encouraged her religious work and sanctioned women's public ministry. Dow asked, "Why, a *female*, should not be accountable, to God, for her talents, and ministrations,—as the opposite *gender*,—I know not."[17]

Echoing Towle and Dow, Harriet Livermore, one of the most popular women preachers of the late 1820s and 1830s, emphasized the equality of men and women. A skilled sentimental orator, Livermore built on Transcendentalist and Second Awakening egalitarian ideals, eventually linking women's rights with political reform and Indian assimilation. For American women Livermore anticipated a divine transformation, "How long, O Lord . . . ere women shall be clothed with the sun, walk upon the moon, and be crowned with Apostolick [sic] glory?" The political nature of Livermore's religious message prompted one contemporary critic to note, "The objection, after all, is not so much against female preachers, as against the doctrines which some of them may chance to advocate."[18]

In addition to Towle and Livermore, over one hundred evangelical women preachers joined male counterparts in proclaiming the gospel at camp meetings, in private homes, churches, and public meeting houses throughout the northeast. But their zeal did not end there, from 1790 to 1845 a cohort of women preachers took their unique message to every corner of the republic and across the globe, traveling an annual preaching circuit that averaged several thousand grueling miles. Touting the standard theme of evangelical salvation, women preachers also advanced ideas about abolition, free love (consensual marriage), gender role reform, and American Indian assimilation.[19]

A smattering of women preachers served as elders, deacons, and pastors, but most women evangelists ministered to widely dispersed church communities. As passionate abolition and women's rights advocates, women preachers had a profound influence on Northern evangelical church communities. The lasting legacy of this impact was a network of evangelical congregations that shared or at least empathized with abolitionist, women's rights, and Indian assimilation sentiments. These assemblies would serve as safe havens for later liberal women speakers on the emerging abolitionist and women's rights lecture circuit. Ultimately, the evangelical churches cultivated by women ministers were not able to stem the movement's later rejection of women preachers.[20]

The push to end evangelical women's ministry gained momentum by 1830 as new middle-class converts embraced separate spheres ideology. Moving away from their egalitarian roots, new middle-class evangelicals shunned what they considered to be the increasingly disturbing excesses of fringe evangelical sects, such as the Church of Jesus Christ of Latter-day Saints, the Christadelphians, and outspoken women preachers. With the ascension of the new middle class separate spheres ideology and its insistence on the affectation of female domesticity, fiery women preachers who dared to travel unchaperoned and to speak before mixed sex audiences became a religious embarrassment.[21]

By the late 1840s almost all major evangelical denominations banished women from public ministry. Most early Second Awakening women preachers, already aged or retired to married life, accustomed themselves to the change and adopted the new proprieties of middle-class evangelism. Former women preachers transformed themselves into Sunday school teachers, church committee members, and directors of church-related charitable and missionary organizations. A handful of women preachers refused to give up their ministries and related work as published authors, social activists, and public lecturers.[22]

The political legacy of evangelical women preachers had an important and largely overlooked effect on the way later liberal women activists approached public careers. This influence helped bridge the egalitarian and social justice idealism of women evangelical activists and that of liberal women influenced by the Transcendentalist tradition. Women preachers perfected a well-publicized formula expressed in three key areas of economic and social activity—self-promotion, public performance, and remuneration—that foreshadowed women's entry into autonomous professions. This dynamic was crucial to the popular association of women's rights, abolition, and later of American Indian rights with women activists in general. For women preachers the coupling of abolition and Indian advocacy with women's rights helped diminish the charge of self-serving egalitarianism.[23]

Among the ranks of popular women evangelical preachers, Nancy Towle and Harriet Livermore were exemplary as bridges between proponents of evangelical egalitarianism and liberal women social activists. Both shared an interest in expanded roles for women, abolition, and assimilating American Indians. However, Livermore's solitary campaign for the Christianization of western "Jewish" Indians played a crucial role in turning the evangelical zeal of Northern abolitionists toward the American West and Plains Indians. In this context Towle and Livermore nourished significant intellectual and cultural trends among liberal American women.[24]

Given that the scholarly trajectory has steadily moved away from the traditional 1848 Seneca Falls narrative, it is curious that scholarship on Towle and Livermore remains comparatively miniscule, and even more so that their promotion of women's rights and Indian assimilation has been largely overlooked. Recent work argues that in fact Towle and Livermore did not disappear from the American cultural scene and that their ideas continued to exert an influence on American attitudes about women's rights, slavery, and Indians into the 1900s.[25]

NANCY TOWLE, HARRIETT LIVERMORE, AND AMERICAN INDIAN RELIGIOUS HISTORY

Harriet Towle's public ministry began April 20, 1821. During her eleven year mission, Towle traveled over twenty thousand miles preaching in northern and southern states and also took her message across the sea to England and Ireland. In addition to solitary ministry at countless gospel meetings, camp revivals, and evangelical churches, Towle also labored in concert with other women preachers.[26]

Towle's most notable crusade spanned 1830 to 1832 when she traversed the midwestern and southern states. In the South she forcefully denounced slavery warning Southerners, "You are traveling down to hell." Towle also linked Indian and African American advocacy asking, "Will not the tawny Savage race/ And Afric's sable train/ God's word, and righteousness embrace/ Nor wear the slavish chain?" Towle's plea for Indian evangelization was discussed as late as 1893 in a syndicated newspaper article that compared her religious views with those of Harriet Livermore. Noting that Towle was a life-long proponent of women's rights, the article—almost certainly written by Livermore descendent Franklin Benjamin Sanborn—argued that Towle and Livermore were proponents of a radical civil rights agenda.[27]

After retiring from the ministry in 1832, Towle moved to Hampton, New Hampshire, where she wrote a lengthy memoir that included her ideas about equal rights for women. Although recent scholarship claims Towle's influence faded by 1830, her memoir *Vicissitudes* has remained in circulation since 1833. For decades after her death, Towle's publications continued to provide American society with religiously oriented arguments in favor of abolition, women's rights, and expanded Indian missionary work. In this capacity Towle's work spanned the historical eras that bookended the rise of the American middle class. As a recent study noted, "Nancy Towle bridged the ideological gap between the evangelicals and the woman's rights activists."[28]

Harriet Livermore began public preaching following a conversion experience in 1821 and proved such a popular witness that her ministry was eventually propelled into the United States Congress. Livermore delivered widely reported sermons on social, civil, and Indian rights before the assembled U.S. Congress on four different occasions from 1827 to 1839. Scion of a noted political family, Livermore, gained the patronage of John Tyler, Dolly Madison, Andrew Jackson, and the qualified admiration of John Quincy Adams. Like Towle, Livermore's ministry denounced slavery, championed expanded roles for women, and promoted Indian evangelization. But where Towle's interest in Indian souls reflected established sentiment, the scope of Livermore's concern was epic. Around 1831 Livermore asserted that American

Indians were descended from the Ten Lost Tribes of Israel and were destined to recolonize Palestine.

Scholars have speculated that Livermore became acquainted with the Jewish-Indian theory through Joseph Wolff, a popular Jewish convert, charismatic preacher, and evangelical compatriot. Given that Wolff categorically rejected the Jewish-Indian connection during his 1838 American tour, he seems an unlikely prospect. A stronger candidate was Livermore's acquaintance Ga-la-gi-noh, the Cherokee godson and religious disciple of Continental Congress president Elias Boudinot, who was an outspoken proponent of the Jewish-Indian theory. To this end Boudinot published an 1816 theological work that argued American Indians were descended from the Ten Lost Tribes of Israel and destined to play a central role in millennial eschatology.[29]

As Boudinot's religious protégé, Ga-la-gi-noh adopted his godfather's theology, becoming a cautious proponent of the Jewish-Indian theory. Evidence indicates that Ga-la-gi-noh (who assumed his godfather's name in 1819) and Livermore likely discussed the Jewish-Indian theory during an 1830 encounter. They also met and discussed the Jewish-Indian theory again in 1834. Captivated, Livermore was most intrigued with how the two Boudinots situated Jewish Indians within the Christian millennial tradition. According to their interpretation, fulfillment of biblical prophecy required wholesale Indian conversion to Christianity and Indian mass migration to Palestine. Once removed, Christian Indians would capture the temple mound, rebuild the ancient Jewish temple, and initiate Christ's earthly thousand year reign.[30]

From late 1830 Livermore immersed herself in the extant literature on Indian origins, familiarizing herself with both secular and religious arguments favoring the Jewish-Indian connection. By 1832 Livermore's public testimony became a powerful mainstream evangelical counterbalance to the Church of Jesus Christ of Latter Day Saints founder Joseph Smith's unorthodox formulation of American Indian ancestry. Whereas Smith claimed divine revelation for his Jewish-Indian historical assertions, Livermore grounded her argument in the latest philological, anthropological, and ethnological evidence.[31]

With this approach Livermore revealed a pattern that would play itself out over the course of European American women's engagement with American Indian historical scholarship. When Livermore wished to cultivate sentiment and pity for Indian evangelical work, she turned to Indian voices and divine inspiration. However, when she wished to present herself as an expert on Indian history, Livermore quoted from documentary sources and established Indian scholarship. Merging religious and scholarly narratives, Livermore reinforced her claims to divine guidance with contemporary measures of scientific and historical "objectivity."[32]

Inspired by the millennialism of Joseph Wolff, who predicted that Christ would return in 1847, Livermore began a frantic public campaign to Christianize American Indians and pack them off to Palestine. Tapping the American mid-nineteenth century millennial fascination, in 1832 Livermore delivered a passionate sermon before the U.S. Congress begging for its support of wholesale Indian conversion and migration to Palestine. In attendance, President Andrew Jackson saw in Livermore's scheme a corollary to his own Indian removal efforts and agreed to help bankroll Livermore's western evangelistic venture. Additionally, Jackson directed General William Clark, the famous western explorer and superintendent of Indian Affairs to extend his help.[33]

Livermore's western venture eventually placed her among the Osage Indians encamped outside Fort Leavenworth Indian Territory (in present-day Kansas). As a missionary Livermore was known among the Indians as "Wahconda's wakko" (purportedly meaning God's woman), but as a zealous millennialist who advanced an improbable Indian colonization scheme she was known to the U.S. Indian agents as a meddling devil. Relations between Livermore and the agents became so strained that they pilfered her meager belongings in a spiteful attempt to drive her away.[34]

Accepting the doom of her western mission, Livermore returned to the East Coast for a whirlwind speaking tour touting the need for Indian evangelization. With funds solicited from devoted supporters, Livermore immigrated to Jerusalem in 1833 intent on establishing a religious colony for American Indian converts. Palestinian officials proved hostile to her plan. By 1837 a penniless Livermore abandoned her dilapidated, uninhabited American Indian colony in Palestine and returned to North America. Livermore's childhood friend Quaker poet John Greenleaf Whittier arranged lectures in Pennsylvania and Washington, D.C., to help her meet debts and fund future evangelical work.[35]

Between 1837 and 1849 Livermore returned to Palestine two more times. During her travels Livermore lectured on both sides of the Atlantic, touting American Indian conversion and their colonization of the Holy Land. Following Livermore's return to the United States in 1849, she published *Addresses to the Dispersed of Judah*, in which she continued to promote Indian-Jewish Zionism. A work that intellectually straddled the American Missionary Association's 1846 formation, *Addresses* sheds light on Second Awakening millennialism and the important role Jewish-Indian theory played in casting evangelical efforts westward.[36]

Equally important, Livermore's work reflected an ideological shift among American antiquarians and anthropologists who, from the late 1840s, had distanced themselves from American Indian ocean migration theories.

Giving ground and demonstrating political savvy, Livermore's 1849 publication equivocated on the matter, casting the Jewish-Indian theory as likely true rather than as established fact. This caveat aside, *Addresses to the Dispersed of Judah* did not equivocate on the issue of Indian-Jewish Zionism. In cultural terms Livermore's national engagement with the subject helped bond the dual agenda of saving and civilizing western Indians to the evangelical and Northern liberal ethos. Over the next four decades this agenda evolved into a broad national effort aimed at "civilizing" and assimilating American Indians. Though frustrated by numerous pitfalls, Indian assimilation advocates never lost Livermore's driving sense of millennial urgency.[37]

In the late 1860s Livermore retired from preaching, lecturing, and publication. Her sixteenth and final book, *Thoughts on Important Subjects*, was published in 1864. Four years later Livermore died in a Philadelphia alms house. During her almost five decades of public activity, Livermore's work fanned the flames of the era's millennialist interest in American Indians and helped keep the cause of their Christianization alive well into the twentieth century.[38]

In addition to Towle and Livermore a host of liberal women outside the active evangelical fold sparked parallel venues for women's public activism beginning in the 1830s. As Towle and Livermore's generation of women preachers faded, a growing contingent of liberal women public speakers continued to press for the old evangelical and Transcendentalist goal of an egalitarian society. Stripped of stifling religious language and translated into the comparatively soothing rhetoric of Transcendentalist ethics, the rustic egalitarianism of earlier women preachers was transfigured into the new political language of liberal women activists. Reminiscent of Livermore, these women set themselves on a path to Washington, D.C., where they sought to hinge their own brand of abolition, women's rights, and American Indian acculturation to political power and national action.

DISTINCTIONS BETWEEN WOMEN'S ANTI-REMOVAL AND ANTISLAVERY CAMPAIGNS

Although the particular work of each differed, liberal women activists advocated a liberation ideology that often reflected Transcendentalist sentiments, most notably the right to individuality, self-competency, and universal civil rights. Notable liberal women activists and public speakers included Julia Ward Howe, Ernestine Potowski Rose, Angelina Grimké, Sarah Grimké, Clarina Howard Nichols, Paulina Kellogg Wright Davis, Lucretia Coffin Mott, and Lydia Maria Child. Against this rising tide of outspoken women activists, a reserved but influential group of conservative benevolence workers coalesced to challenge liberal women's social agendas and promiscuous presence in the public realm. Cheered on by powerful allies who also championed separate spheres ideology, conservative women such as Catherine Beecher and Lydia Sigourney fostered a national debate that pitted their demure social sensibilities and modest political initiatives against foes they characterized as "strong-minded" women dedicated to social upheaval.[39]

Shunning public venues, Catherine Beecher used the printed word to rebuke outspoken liberal women and rally those sympathetic to her cause. Beecher noted, "A woman may seek the aid of co-operation and combination among her own sex, to assist her in her appropriate offices of piety, charity, maternal and domestic duty," but she cautioned against action that "throws a woman into the attitude of a combatant." Beecher particularly warned women against public speaking, "because it draws them forth from their appropriate retirement, to expose themselves to the ungoverned violence of mobs, and the sneers and ridicule of public places . . . [to] carry forward the measures of strife."[40]

The outspoken abolitionist Angelina Grimké passionately replied to Beecher's reproach with a provocative monition of her own: "While I live, and slavery lives, I must testify against it." Grimké added, "If I should hold my peace, 'the stone would cry out of the wall, and the beam out of the timber would answer it.'" Both conservative and liberal women agreed on various aspects of American social reform, but the possibility for cooperation ended with their respective public agendas. Regardless of their overlapping moral convictions, the social divide separating antebellum conservative and liberal women largely corralled their work into irreconcilable camps.[41]

Catherine Beecher's conservative cohort of women benevolence workers were distinguished from liberal women's rights and abolition advocates by their strict adherence to a silencing public decorum dictated by separate spheres ideology. In theory middle-class women were relegated to the quiet role of domestic consumer, comforting wife, and altruistic mother—the so-called "house nun." In reality the coy public silence claimed by conservative women served more as a middle- and upper-class pedigree than as an actual mark of refined womanhood. Yet, the constraints of this silent social affectation shackled the public voices of leading conservative women benevolence workers and relegated their political activism to publication and statements by male proxies. The defining public silence of Beecher and her coterie is born out in a study by Alisse Portnoy, which suggests that antebellum conservative women were ultimately distinguished by their refusal, or at least grave reluctance, to speak in public—especially before mixed sex audiences.[42]

For each group the stakes were high, indeed their disagreement over women's proper social and political roles drove an ideological war that came to define the causes to which liberal and conservative women were most closely aligned. The breech that developed between these women sheds light on two long-term developments within the liberal women's camp: why liberal women activists originally turned their Indian assimilation interests toward the American West, and how their early concern for Christianizing and civilizing western Indians eventually blossomed into a definitive postbellum political movement.

Two key factors drove American Indian assimilation to the background of liberal women's national agenda—until after the Civil War. The first was the ongoing cultural dispute concerning women's proper political and social role in the republic, while the second concerned the image of the "downtrodden Indian" as an unattractive metaphor for liberal women and their reform goals. Nowhere were these distinctions more clear than in the 1829 to 1838 anti-removal and antislavery campaigns.[43]

The conservative women's Indian anti-removal campaign was effectively an extension of the 1818 anti-removal campaign. A reaction to President James Monroe's interest in relocating Southern Indians west of the Mississippi, the 1818 campaign joined Quakers and the American Board of Commissioners for Foreign Missions (ABCFM) in a counterploy. The anti-removal campaign essentially promoted a nationalized assimilation program intended to help southern Indians retain their traditional homelands. Anti-removal efforts ultimately culminated in the 1819 Indian Civilization Fund Act, which empowered the president to "employ capable people," mostly Quaker and ABCFM missionaries, to implement Indian acculturation. The act also provided for an annual ten thousand dollar stipend rarely appropriated by Congress. As a centralized approach, the Civilization Fund was the first attempt to organize an Indian assimilation program at the federal level.[44]

Making use of the opportunity, Quakers and the ABCFM raised funds for Indian missions and propelled a throng of proselytizers southward to assimilate the "savage" Indians. Quakers raised well over thirty thousand dollars for the effort, while the ABCFM came in second with twenty thousand dollars in contributions. Lagging in funds and fearing Quaker hegemony, the ABCFM shrewdly authorized women missionaries for the first time in its history. The ABCFM's action in this matter further encouraged the public to identify women with Indian politics and social intervention.[45]

A well-documented course of events reveals that by the late 1820s early assimilation efforts came into irreconcilable conflict with the land interests of Southern states. This tension played itself out in the bitter congressional Indian removal debates of 1826 to 1830. Anticipating the legislative success of removal forces, ABCFM corresponding secretary Jeremiah Evarts launched a national campaign to again thwart Indian removal. But unlike national sympathies during the 1818–19 effort, this time political conditions were quite different. While religious organizations expended tens of thousands of dollars on new Indian missions and assimilation work, with an eye toward preserving Indian land claims, the Southern states (particularly Georgia), with enthusiastic presidential support from Andrew Jackson, were determined to proceed with removal.[46]

Reflecting ABCFM fears of impending failure, especially the loss of capital raised by women laity, Evarts enlisted the help of Catherine Beecher. In concert with her close friend and ally Lydia Sigourney, Beecher fashioned a national women's anti-removal petition campaign. From the beginning, Beecher and Sigourney's effort would be socially and politically reserved.[47]

When Beecher and Sigourney inaugurated their anti-removal campaign they were so afraid of male criticism that they worked anonymously. Popularly deemed *The Ladies' Circular*, the petition solicited, "benevolent women of the United States" and urged them to use "prayers and exertions to avert the calamity of removal." Promoted through Christian journals and women's benevolent societies, Beecher and Sigourney's work was eventually assumed by the Ladies' Association for Supplicating Justice and Mercy Toward the Indians. In calling women to benevolent political action, *The Ladies' Circular* warned supporters to exercise caution in their public activities and limit exertions to "that influence in society that falls within her lawful province."[48]

Garnering fifteen hundred signatures by 1831, the petition's rhetoric reflected standard ABCFM policy denouncing forced removal as counterproductive. Petitioners specifically feared that Indian removal west of the Mississippi would spawn renewed "savagery." Moreover, women supporters resented nullification of their personal and financial efforts to Christianize southern Indians. Attracting the attention of emerging abolitionist leaders who drew parallels between government Indian policy and slavery, the anti-removal campaign suffered a fatal blow when Jeremiah Evarts died suddenly in 1831. Not only did Beecher and Sigourney lose their patron, they also lost their public voice.[49]

In contrast, the women's antislavery petition campaign encompassed a broad range of liberal women and lasted well into the Civil War. The intensity of women's abolition zeal propelled them far beyond the influences that conservative women deemed within their "lawful province." The work of supporters in several states, the women's abolition campaign framed its fight against slavery in apocalyptic imagery that rejected gendered attempts to impose silence or restraint. As one woman contributor to the abolitionist journal *Liberator* noted, "I am not bound to conciliate the affections of any man." Sarah Grimké more directly counseled, "The idea is inconceivable to me that Christian women can be engaged in doing God's work . . . yet must ask his blessing . . . through the lips of a man."⁵⁰

Key women's abolition organizations were established in Rhode Island (1832), Massachusetts (1833), Pennsylvania (1833), and New York (1835). Of these the Philadelphia Women's Anti-Slavery Society exercised considerable influence, hosting both the second and final national women's antislavery conventions in 1838 and 1839. Philadelphia women would prove crucial to the success of the women's antislavery movement, forging ties that united the interests of evangelical and liberal women. A similar merging of religious and secular interests would be repeated in the mid-1800s by Pennsylvania women activists for Indian rights.⁵¹

Early on, women in the American abolitionist movement realized the impact of imagery, specifically the "speechless agony of the fettered slave." Borrowed from British abolitionists, the chained slave image became a powerful emblem for American women activists. Angelina Grimké noted, "Until the pictures of the slave's sufferings were drawn and held up to public gaze, no northerner had any idea of the cruelty of the system." At the first women's antislavery convention in 1837 a resolution noted, "We regard anti-slavery prints as powerful auxiliaries." Women's rights and Indian rights advocate Lydia Maria Child made the connection more explicit in 1838, "Remember them that are in bonds as bound with them." The chained slave image proved to be such a powerful metaphor that proponents of women's rights would continue to employ it for almost a decade after the Civil War. Like Nancy Towle and Harriett Livermore, liberal women were associated with a political agenda that encompassed the civil rights of both African Americans and European American women.⁵²

Yet, attractive as the slave metaphor proved for liberal women, the image of the vanishing Indian was equally unattractive. Though Child and a handful of liberal women publicly supported the anti-removal campaign, antebellum women's rights advocates did not adopt American Indian imagery for their movement. Widely seen at the time as a free, but backward people unable to meet their own needs or make useful contributions to the nation, American Indians were generally considered an impotent, dwindling race. Though pitied, the image of the "cowed Indian" dependent on the magnanimity of European American males proved to be a repulsive political image for liberal women.⁵³

Abolitionist's conventions, meetings, and lectures drew intense, often heated public criticism, but their main focus was the antislavery petition drive, and liberal women played a leading role in this effort. Regardless of their locale, women's antislavery groups and related organizations shared a common goal until 1848—securing federal legislation to abolish slavery in the District of Columbia. Heralded by Congressman John Quincy Adams, the antislavery petition campaign was crafted according to contemporary understanding of constitutional powers. In antebellum America, most politicians believed congressional authority to abolish slavery was limited to the federal district—if at all.[54]

Both abolitionist and proslavery forces came to believe that success in the District of Columbia campaign would have national ramifications, providing a blueprint for universal African American abolition and a path toward African American suffrage. For abolitionists the prospect encouraged heroic determination, while for proslavery forces the spectator of freed federal district slaves provoked fanatical obstructionism. As the leading abolitionist in Congress, John Adams proposed a politically savvy compromise in 1838. Billed as "compensated emancipation," Adam's legislation offered a financial incentive for freeing federal district slaves, but the bill sparked intense proslavery opposition and Adams quickly retreated on the matter. A decade later Adams's bill was reintroduced to withering criticism and was quickly withdrawn by Representative Abraham Lincoln. The antislavery campaign was effectively disconnected from the District of Columbia cause following the death of John Adams in 1848.[55]

To the consternation of conservative women, by 1831 the Indian anti-removal petition, abolition, and women's rights were equally identified with women activists. Specifically, the anti-removal campaign and abolition petitioning were widely seen as the work of meddling Northern women and their "Sunday school" cohorts. Public and political anxieties were expressed by future president John Tyler, who complained, "Woman is to be made the instrument of destroying our political paradise, the Union of these states; she is to be made the presiding genius over the councils of insurrection and discord." Tyler pointedly warned, "She is to be converted into a fiend, to rejoice over the conflagration of our dwellings and the murder of our people." Political fear regarding the momentum of abolition activities became so great that in 1836 legislative opponents imposed a gag on further congressional antislavery debate. By 1837 women's antislavery petitioning was so politically provocative that conservative women renounced political activity at the national level and cast a wary eye toward further action on behalf of American Indians.[56]

These ideological and gendered anxieties also played out in the slavery debates that rocked the early interdenominational tendencies of the American Board of Commissioners for Foreign Missions. Within the ABCFM, abolitionist oriented Congregationalists, Presbyterians, and Methodists joined with evangelicals to denounce the organization's toleration of slave labor used by southern Indians and southern mission stations. Unrelenting, ABCFM leadership argued that slave labor was indispensable to southern missions and essential to Indian agriculture. In the face of ABCFM recalcitrance, abolitionists soon came to interpret the organization's southern Indian assimilation work as proslavery.[57]

This heated internal debate eventually led to formation of the rival American Missionary Association (AMA) in 1846. Dedicated to abolition, the AMA refused to accommodate slave labor and, to this end, rejected missionary and assimilation work among southern Indians. Turning some of its interests toward the non-slaveholding western tribes, the AMA for a time channeled flimsy Northern (and women's) concern for American Indian assimilation westward. However, around 1861 the AMA began to emphasize African American civil rights, and by 1865 the organization had exclusively turned its attention to that goal. Reflecting a shift in public interest, by 1869 the AMA attracted meager donations. In irreparable decline by 1874, the AMA never recovered its former influence. Coinciding with the AMA's slump, from 1869 on American Indian assimilation was largely subsumed by President Ulysses S. Grant's Indian Peace Policy. Under Peace Policy provisions, the quasi-official Board of Indian Commissioners assumed a senior role in efforts to Christianize and assimilate western Indians.[58]

In turn, early Baptist interest in Indian evangelization was fractured by the machinations of an aggressive Kentucky missionary and political operative named Isaac McCoy. An early advocate of Indian removal, McCoy pressed northern Baptist missionary societies to offer their support. Under intense pressure from McCoy, several northern Baptist state associations sent memorials to Congress in favor of removal, but northern Baptists remained deeply divided on the subject. The same was true of the northern Baptist General Convention for Foreign Missions (BGCFM). Though strongly encouraged to embrace removal as a potential boon for northern Baptist missions, the BGCFM board nevertheless retained grave moral doubts. Northern opinion remained so divided that Francis Wayland, a leading Baptist educator and economist corresponded with McCoy and the Baptist anti-removal camp in an effort to resolve the issue.[59]

In the early 1840s McCoy established ties with southern proslavery, pro-removal Baptists who worked in concert with him to form the pro-removal American Indian Mission Association (AIMA) in 1842. AIMA immediately provoked the wrath of northern abolitionists, while its subsequent political activities aroused enmity among northern Baptists who feared being associated with AIMA's Indian removal agenda. Consequently, northern anti-removal Baptists threw their support behind the AMA mission to the Plains Indians. The westward gaze of northern Baptists would eventually help foster the Philadelphia-based women's Indian Treaty-Keeping and Protective Association (ITKPA).[60]

The ITKPA and the national women's Indian assimilation movement were foreshadowed by the 1859 American Indian Aid Association (AIAA). Born of an impassioned campaign by Quaker activist and veteran of the Oregon Indian wars John Beeson, the AIAA—with Philadelphia, New York, and Washington, D.C., branches—was the first truly national American Indian assimilation organization. Ideologically allied with the Progressive Friend's (reform Quakers) and embracing the abolitionist prohibition against assimilation work among the southern tribes, the AIAA structure was egalitarian, interdenominational, and nonsectarian.[61]

Espousing a set of ideas later enshrined in President Grant's 1869 Peace Policy, the AIAA called for American Indian removal to protected reservations. To administer these reserves, the AIAA envisioned autonomous reservation governments that would oversee the dispersal of farm allotments and govern daily life. Additionally, the reservation governments would be charged with promoting agriculture, animal husbandry, and European American style education. To monitor the new reservations and their governments, the AIAA proposed a specially trained corps of European American male *and* female missionaries, arguing that men were best suited for administration, while women were better equipped to impart the finer points of civilization.[62]

Although the AIAA repeatedly called for a national Indian policy summit, its direct efforts proved ineffectual at the national level. The AIAA did, however, make a lasting impression on Quaker and evangelical women assimilationists and their allied organizations. Foremost among these, the Pennsylvania Universal Peace Union, with which Lucretia Mott, Susan B. Anthony, Julia Ward Howe, Amelia Quinton, and Mary Bonney were associated, shared AIAA goals and idealism. While the AMA and the AIAA existed on the periphery of women's antebellum civil rights activity, their Indian assimilation work and egalitarian idealism exerted a persistent ideological influence on the social reform interests of women's rights advocates and the institutional structures they would create after 1865.[63]

THE ROAD TO WASHINGTON AND INDIAN SCHOLARSHIP

Cultivated by early evangelical zeal and later by rejection of slave labor, liberal women's interest in Plains Indian assimilation proved paltry at best. Trailing women's rights momentum to the nation's capital, Indian "reform" would eventually emerge as a lateral interest pursued by activists on the movement's margins. Embraced by postbellum "maternal patriots," women's mid-nineteenth century Indian reform efforts linked both "sentimental" social activism and Indian scholarship. Women Indian scholars listened, watched, and reported what they observed while out among their living subjects—their protocol was not objectivity, independent verification, and peer review. Professional historians would later criticize this work as biased, irredeemably polluted by personal and political sentiment.

Cracks first appeared in this approach to Indian scholarship when Helen Hunt Jackson and Alice Fletcher published their "objective" American Indian histories. Jackson's 1881 volume, *A Century of Dishonor*, and Fletcher's 1888 *Indian Education and Civilization* report were the first comprehensive, archive researched, document-driven Indian histories. Addressed to a white male political audience, both publications shunned hearsay, anecdotal evidence, and personal observation in favor of primary source documents detailing legal and political interactions between the United States and various Indian peoples. Though Jackson and Fletcher's scholarly careers straddled both the sentimentalist Indian reform movement and document-driven Indian scholarship, their 1881 and 1888 publications blazed an objective trail for later professional women historians. The path to this new objective Indian history would pass directly through Washington, D.C.[64]

CHAPTER 2

THE WASHINGTON VANGUARD AND THE BIRTH OF WOMEN'S INDIAN SCHOLARSHIP

Between the founding of the American Indian Aid Association (AIAA) in 1859 and the creation of the Indian Treaty-Keeping and Protective Association (ITKPA) in 1879, no national Indian political association attracted significant attention from women's rights proponents. From 1859 to 1879 women's rights supporters were overwhelmingly concerned with abolition and promoting their own civil rights. Even the Washington women's rights vanguard that coalesced between 1868 and 1872 with its narrow women's rights focus, still clung to the tried and true political imagery of abolition.

Although the Washington women's rights vanguard would play an important role in achieving African American civil rights and black male suffrage, political misfortune would quickly sever women's historic ties to abolition imagery. An examination of the rise and fall of the Washington vanguard illuminates why women's rights proponents moved so quickly from the political rhetoric of abolition to the politics of American Indian assimilation. It also reveals how, following the vanguard's demise, the rise of maternal patriotism and the lateral diffusion of women's activism created new opportunities for women's American Indian scholarship.

THE RISE AND FALL OF THE WASHINGTON WOMEN'S RIGHTS VANGUARD

The postbellum renaissance of American West expansion promised new opportunities for women's rights and the suffrage cause. Susan B. Anthony and Elizabeth Cady Stanton promoted the 1867 Kansas suffrage campaign and the American Woman Suffrage Association indicated interest in expanding the cause westward; however, an influential cohort of women continued to focus their attention on the nation's capital.[1]

Stemming from the antislavery campaign, liberal women's interest in Washington took concrete form by the late 1860s—through the campaign to enfranchise District of Columbia African American males. Buoyed by the radical Republican–abolitionist political alliance that helped pass the 1867 Kelley Suffrage Act, which conferred the right to vote on African American males in Washington. D.C., a women's rights vanguard began to coalesce in Washington around 1868. A community of like-minded liberal women, the vanguard was dedicated to revolutionary social and political change. To this end its members, such as Victoria C. Woodhull, Isabella Beecher Hooker, Mary Walker, Susan B. Anthony, Elizabeth Cady Stanton, and Sarah Spencer among others, worked to steer African American civil rights momentum to their own political advantage.[2]

The federal district territorial campaign gained momentum after 1869 when property owners, politicians, Washington power brokers, and their congressional allies, frustrated by decades of federal mismanagement, proposed refashioning the district as a territory. Spurred to action by the capital city's embarrassingly antiquated, war-ravaged infrastructure, high property taxes, and anachronistic municipal politics, reformers drafted a bill to authorize territorial status for the entire district. The legislation passed Congress and was signed into law by President Ulysses S. Grant. On January 27, 1871, the Territory of Columbia succeeded the District of Columbia. Almost from the beginning the establishment of Columbia Territory portended doom for African American male suffrage—yet the Washington women's rights vanguard continued to agitate as if universal suffrage was just around the corner.[3]

In reality the new territorial government accelerated the demise of universal male suffrage. Rather than reforming the federal district, territorial rule continued to promote the notorious political machine that melded freedmen's poverty and desperation into a voting block easily manipulated by white politicians. The reconstructed district government, intended to streamline and economize badly needed municipal improvements, instead opened Columbia to a wider assortment of shady contractors, uninhibited graft, and the outright incompetence of Ulysses S. Grant's political appointments. Increasingly higher property taxes and massive ill-planned, mismanaged improvement projects prompted two congressional inquiries in 1872. Although territorial officials were largely acquitted by Republican comrades, the inquests raised lingering doubts about the desirability of Columbia's universal male franchise. African American male voters, whose very livelihood depended on ballot box support for notorious construction projects, were damned if they did and impoverished if they did not.[4]

In 1873 African American male voters, and virtually the entire territorial administration, were the subject of a third and fatal round of congressional review. Already exceeding a statutory debt limit of ten million dollars—by approximately ten million dollars—territorial property taxes had increased by approximately 100 percent. Additionally, city officials had printed dubious territorial bonds in a desperate bid to cover the enormous debt of a corrupt public works program. Having driven hundreds of Washingtonians to sell their holdings, the territorial government became an almost universally despised symbol of graft, corruption, and failed African American male suffrage. The financial meltdown of Columbia Territory, national recession, and the embarrassing media circus surrounding its political circle pushed jubilant Congressional segregationists and humiliated champions of African American civil rights into a rash political solution that did away with the nation's first postbellum universal male suffrage experiment.[5]

On June 30, 1874, in a rare show of political unity, southern conservatives joined radical Republicans in stripping Columbia of territorial status and the franchise. In its place Congress vested district authority in a joint committee, which would implement the will of Congress through its three congressionally appointed commissioners. Practically speaking, the congressional district joint committee became Washington's new municipal government. For most European American males the end of territorial rule, high property taxes, and the federal assumption of Columbia debt seemed a fair trade for losing the vote. But for African American men the end of universal male suffrage signaled a stunning reversal of their political rights—a loss that would play out again and again across the nation. To women in the District of Columbia, who never had the right to vote, this sudden male disenfranchisement would prove a fortuitous political boon. For the time being the Washington vanguard and women's rights proponents found themselves disconnected from the revolutionary emancipation they had anticipated and the slave–freed people metaphor that had so powerfully served their struggle for over four decades.[6]

THE BIRTH OF WOMEN'S INDIAN SCHOLARSHIP

In the wake of the new government act for the territory of Columbia the Washington women's right vanguard was strangely quiet. With the exception of a few petitions continuing to ask for women's suffrage in the District of Columbia, a very unlikely proposition given the disenfranchised status of the district's male voters, and a brief sixteenth amendment push for women's suffrage, the vanguard and women's rights leaders made no public comment on the new situation in the district. At the helm of the vanguard, Victoria Woodhull, already diminished by her own actions, had largely faded into the political background following her failed 1872 presidential bid.[7]

During this uncertain time for liberal women's political fortunes, liberal and conservative distinctions became more flexible, if not fluid. Straddling an anachronistic gender role of female domesticity and a sea change in public attitudes about women speaking in public, young conservative women increasingly defined their middle- and upper-class status in terms of community social benevolence and local organizational work. Consequently, new conservative women, who felt women should act for the benefit of their own homes and communities, moderate women, who limited their support for women's rights to local applications, and liberal women, who argued that women should engage in a wide range of public pursuits and should have the right to vote, often found common interests that transcended individual politics. This new dialog fostered the formation of politically diverse women's networks.[8]

Reflecting this change, the Washington vanguard also began to transform from a radical cadre of liberal women into an allied community of women dedicated to women's suffrage and women's social and economic empowerment. Revolutionary ideology soon gave way to more attainable ideas and goals. Embracing mainstream political sensibilities, the Washington vanguard evolved into an informal confederation of social reform–minded women.[9]

Following their 1874–77 political disappointments, Washington women's rights proponents reconsidered their role in American society. Hitting on a new strategy, many women's rights advocates began to refashion themselves as "maternal patriots," emphasizing their own purity, morality, and womanly benevolence. These women contended that as virtuous white American mothers, raising virtuous white American children in virtuous white American homes they were best suited to address the dire social problems arising from immigration, rural to urban migration, industrialization, and the so-called "Indian problem." Maternal patriotism repositioned women activists to create new political constituencies, brandish new forms of political influence, and prompt Congress to act on a variety of social legislation. By placing radical social and economic change on the back burner, women social reformers would find Congress amenable to some forms of change deemed in the national interest. As a political strategy maternal patriotism proved extremely successful, both for leading activists and those on the margins of the women's rights movement. But among maternal patriots no other group of women would acquire the extraordinary degree of political power that was exercised by late-nineteenth- and early twentieth-century women scholars of American Indians.[10]

PENNSYLVANIA, WASHINGTON, AND WOMEN'S INDIAN SCHOLARSHIP

Between 1874 and 1877 the women's rights movement turned its eyes toward the Trans-Mississippi West and began a new phase in American politics. Universally branded suffragists, Northern and Midwestern women's rights proponents deepened their connections to Western women, creating political networks that linked women from Washington and across the nation with women in the West. By the end of Southern Reconstruction the American West came to play an important role in Washington women's social and political outlook, as they increasingly evoked maternal patriotism to justify their newfound interests in Indian assimilation and the westward march of European American Christian civilization.

Almost five decades in the making, the national women's Indian assimilation cause first took form in Pennsylvania among the old battle-hardened evangelical and Quaker abolitionists. As Amelia Stone Quinton, one of the founding members of the Indian Treaty-Keeping and Protective Association noted, "The small philanthropic public ... though zealous for the colored race, [was] barely beginning to waken to a sense of Indian wrongs."[11] More than simply a retooled metaphor, American Indian assimilation displaced the push for African American civil rights and became one of the leading interests of women social activists.[12]

The first women's Indian assimilation organization with truly national aspirations to emerge in the postbellum era, the ITKPA was headquartered in Philadelphia and grew out of Philadelphia educator and Baptist social activist Mary L. Bonney's interest in the welfare and evangelization of "Oklahoma Indians." Bonney's initiation into Indian activism can be traced to a dramatic May 1, 1877, church program presented by American Baptist Home Mission Society (ABHMS) General Missionary to the Indians and former head of the Indian Territory Union Agency, George Washington Ingalls.[13]

Titled, "Missionary Work Among Indians," and augmented with images from a "stereopticon," Ingalls's "familiar lecture" at the Philadelphia First Baptist church gave a selective account of his time as an Indian agent and Baptist missionary in Nevada and Indian Territory (present-day Oklahoma). Ingalls's show was part of a national ABHMS campaign that encouraged Baptist women to form local branches of the Chicago-based Women's Baptist Home Mission Society (WBHMS). The financially crippled ABHMS saw the WBHMS as a source of much needed revenue and initially encouraged its expansion. Founded in 1877 as a largely autonomous organization by a cadre of missionary minded Baptist women, the WBHMS was devoted to charitable and missionary work among southern freedwomen and Indigenous peoples in Indian Territory, with a special emphasis on elevating the status of "degraded" Indian women. Almost two weeks after Ingalls's visit, Bonney and fellow women parishioners established a WBHMS branch at Philadelphia First Baptist Church on May 17–18, 1877. Bonney was elected one of two vice presidents at the inaugural branch meeting.[14]

For two years Bonney and her WBHMS colleagues labored to collect money and goods for Indian charity and the related efforts of two Indian Territory Baptist missionaries. Between 1878 and 1879 Bonney's WBHMS branch raised $922.90 (the equivalent of $22,200 in 2015 dollars) to this end. Funding success aside, the Philadelphia WBHMS efforts were threatened by two events that occurred between 1879 and 1880.[15]

In the spring of 1879 a rival women's Baptist missionary group in Boston, the Women's American Baptist Home Mission Society (WABHMS) conspired with the cash-strapped all-male American Baptist Home Mission Society (ABHMS) to dissolve the WBHMS board and place it and its treasury under a new body administered by the ABHMS. Bonney and her WBHMS colleague Amelia Stone Quinton likely feared that an ABHMS takeover would erase their hefty financial investment in Indian Territory mission work and stymie their future efforts on behalf of Indian women. In response, Bonney and Quinton took initial steps to protect their Indian efforts by forming a "special committee" within the Philadelphia WBHMS branch. While the WBHMS ultimately won their battle against the ABHMS, the victory did not come until mid-1880, and by that time another crisis had prompted Bonney and Quinton to definitively separate their Indian efforts from the WBHMS.[16]

Following an 1879 visit to Indian Territory, Ingalls alerted the public to an unprecedented European American intrusion onto Indian lands. Ingalls warned that "desperadoes" were gaining a foothold and threatened to erase almost a half-century of Baptist missionary work in Indian Territory. Alarmed by concurrent newspaper reports of Missouri senator George Graham Vest's proposal to organize an "Oklahoma Territory" and open it to white settlement, Bonney and Quinton took further steps to form a separate Indian political action committee within their local WBHMS branch. This committee, later named the "Indian Treaty-Keeping and Protective Association" (which would eventually become the Women's National Indian Association) would not formally separate from the WBHMS and become an independent organization until June 3, 1881.[17]

The ITKPA shared a political and intellectual geography with neighboring activists, including Philadelphia Protestant Tractarians, ecumenical evangelicals, members of the peace movement, and the intellectual constellation that revolved around John Beeson, Lucretia Mott, Henry B. Whipple, and William and Mary Ross Welsh. Moreover, the ITKPA's spiritual home, the First Baptist Church, was adjacent to a leading hotbed of Indian missionary and political activism—the Protestant Episcopal Church. Reflecting its intellectual environment, the early ITKPA espoused a sentimental "Indian Reform" rhetoric, with goals common to the American Indian Aid Association, the Pennsylvania-based Indian's Hope Association (IHA) and other nineteenth-century evangelical social reform movements.[18]

This common legacy was also shaped by two earlier organizations: The Progressive Friends (PF) founded in 1854 and the Universal Peace Union (UPU) founded in 1866. Apart from PF and UPU egalitarianism, Bonney and Quinton's ITKPA also embraced the postbellum ecumenism gestating among northern evangelicals. Far from a nondenominational movement, this new interdenominational cooperation stressed unity of evangelical Christian belief, Christian pacifism, and the political strength of coordinated evangelical social work. Retaining strong denominational affiliations, interdenominational evangelicals crossed sectarian lines to work in a variety of emerging Christian social outreach programs.[19]

The Philadelphia-based Indian's Hope Association, located a few blocks from ITKPA operations, seems to have particularly influenced Bonney and Quinton. Founded in 1868 by wealthy philanthropist William Welsh and his wife Mary Ross Welsh, the IHA grew out of an earlier Episcopal women's missionary organization quaintly known as the Mother's Meeting (MM). Operated from the Welsh's palatial mansion, the IHA drew a constant stream of curious visitors, missionaries, women social workers, and Indian "reformers." The IHA was not modest in its influence, sounding a clarion call to other Christian women on Philadelphia's historic Chestnut Street.[20]

Based on their pervasive northeastern reach, the IHA remained a strong regional women's Indian assimilation organization until William Welsh's death in 1878. Thereafter, Welsh family interest in Indian assimilation was increasingly co-opted as a cause célèbre by William Welsh's artist-socialite nephew, Herbert. The IHA blazed a trail for women as Indian assimilationists, but its primary function as an Episcopalian mission limited its national appeal. Although the IHA continued to limp along after 1878, from that year forward Bonney and Quinton would effectively claim the Philadelphia Indian reform spotlight.[21]

Bonney, an Episcopal convert and avid women's rights proponent, and Quinton, a zealous educator, social activist, and reserved women's rights advocate who had worked in New York "almshouses, infirmaries, prisons and in the women's reformatory," both hitched their political futures to an Indian reform movement that would become noted for its three national petition drives. The initial Indian reform petition presented by Bonney, a political novice, was a factually flawed document, quickly withdrawn from public view. In contrast the next petition (recognized by historians as the first), jointly penned by Bonney and Quinton, was a carefully worded memorial that reflected the long held treaty-keeping and assimilationist views of the AIAA, IHA, and others. Perhaps drawing a lesson from Bonney's first embarrassing attempt, the two women based their new petition on well-researched Indian treaties and applicable U.S. statutes. Though framed in "sentimentalist" rhetoric, Bonney and Quinton's entreaty paid close attention to Indian political history as recorded in government records and archival documents.[22]

As educators who stressed the importance of math, science, and logic in their pedagogy, Bonney and Quinton were familiar with the rigorous methods and evidential practices of academic work. Bonney "taught her students to think . . . [and] equipped them with her methods, to go out into the world as independent thinkers and actors." Quinton, as the wife of a history professor and astronomer was exposed to the (then) accepted standards of historical and scientific research. Amelia's husband, Professor R. L. Quinton, augmented the family income with lectures at Haverford College and other locales, addressing the history of early Christianity, astronomy, and geology. Archival research and documentation of historical detail would come to distinguish ITKPA memorials and literature. While the kind of petitioning engaged in by ITKPA members comprised one of the few political options available to women before they gained the right to vote, ITKPA petition work provided a handful of members with the opportunity to hone their research skills and perfect their understanding of Indian political history.[23]

Quinton's research into the history of Indian treaties for the first petition helped cultivate ITKPA women's political credibility. Unlike contemporary assimilationists, who generally relied on antiquated moral and sentimental rhetoric to advance their goals, Quinton and Bonney bolstered their arguments with historical documentation. Reflecting this tact, Bonney presented a paper at the 1881 Women's Baptist Home Mission Society annual meeting titled, "The Indian Question." Likely drawing on Helen Hunt Jackson's recently published, *A Century of Dishonor*, Bonney "gave many facts of the history of this people, of their treatment by whites since 1849."[24]

Bonney and Quinton's first public petition, circulated nationally with the help of WBHMS women, garnered thirteen thousand signatures and was presented to President Rutherford B. Hayes and Congress in February 1880. In May 1880 Bonney and Quinton took additional steps to distinguish their efforts from the WBHMS, forming (with two other branch members) an interdenominational "ways and means committee." Bonney and Quinton called this group the "Central Indian Committee" (CIC). Funded by Bonney, the CIC continued their petition work and expanded the effort into other states. On December 1, 1880, Bonney and Quinton received permission from their First Baptist branch WBHMS and the national WBHMS to operate as an independent organization.[25]

Inspired by a series of popular 1880 newspaper articles published by Helen Hunt Jackson outlining historical instances of U.S. Indian treaty abrogation and wrongs, Bonney and Quinton's second petition, in addition to repeating the first's plea for treaty fidelity, also raised the issue of voluntary United States citizenship for American Indians. The day before the petition's presentation in Congress—on January 28, 1881—Helen Hunt Jackson placed a copy of her recently published book, *A Century of Dishonor*, "on the desk of every member of Congress." Quinton and Jackson were in the congressional galleries when the petition was presented and returned for floor discussion. Quinton noted Jackson's "anxious interest . . . [in] quotations made from her book in the Senate speeches." Though boasting fifty thousand signatures, the second petition did not attract lasting attention in Congress.[26]

In June 1881 the CIC formally separated from the WBHMS, becoming a distinct organization with national reach. Christened the Indian Treaty-Keeping and Protective Association, its membership ratified a constitution and Quinton soon expanded the organization's reach to five states. Quinton and Bonney also formulated a new committee structure that fashioned the ITKPA into a national multidenominational organization.[27]

Reflecting the women's rights sentiments of the AIAA and the women-only membership of the IHA, the ITKPA remained a women's organization. However, while Quinton and Bonney supported women's rights, Quinton insisted that the ITKPA steer clear of fractious women's rights politics in order to focus on the assimilation cause. Taking this course, the ITKPA fostered an accommodating political environment for conservative, moderate, and liberal women. In turn, the ITKPA's neutral women's rights politics facilitated the contributions of such politically diverse women as the liberal suffragist, ethnologist, and scholar, Alice Fletcher, and the conservative poet, author, and social activist, Helen Hunt Jackson. Rather than mixing their lot with suffrage, ITKPA women turned their full political attention to promoting treaty fidelity, American Indian citizenship, and the allotment cause.[28]

Paralleling their fellow assimilationists' concern that Grant's Peace Plan was insufficient, Bonney and Quinton concluded by late 1881 that American Indians were in danger of perishing in the exterminating havoc of settler colonialism. Their solution was to subject Indians to the same "rights" and property laws European Americans lived under. This new position became the basis for Quinton and Bonney's third petition to Congress. Allotment and related assimilation ideas were not new, however the ITKPA's third petition was the first formulation of a comprehensive national Indian policy based on universal allotment. The ITKPA's new policy effectively launched the organization as a powerful player in the national arena of Indian assimilation politics.[29]

As a political organization, the ITKPA proved quite effective not for its stunning legislative successes, but rather for its keen strategic instincts and shrewd tactical moves. Cumulatively, ITKPA political power stemmed from its ability to present well-argued positions supported by "extracts from Government records revealing its numberless broken compacts with Indians." Key to this approach was Quinton's realization that sentimentalist appeals of the past were no longer effective at the nation's capitol. Negative congressional reaction to the third petition and the rapidly changing goals of national Indian reform activists doomed the long tradition of mawkish Indian "reform" rhetoric.[30]

Introduced February 21, 1882, by senate sponsor, Senator Henry L. Dawes of Massachusetts, the third petition asked for fidelity to Indian treaties, universal education for Indian youth, social welfare for Indian women, allotted Indian land, and U.S. citizenship for Indians. Responses from senators Preston B. Plumb of Kansas and Henry M. Teller of Colorado—both accomplished lawyers—were strategic attacks on the ITKPA's new agenda. Plumb linked sentiment for Indians to inexperience and contended that recent western conflicts actually stemmed from "strict observance" of U.S.-Indian treaties. Dismissing ITKPA concern for Indian women, Plumb confidently asserted, "You cannot get an Indian any more than a Mormon woman to advocate change of the relations that exist now between the Indian woman and the male members of the tribes."[31]

Senator Teller snidely remarked that Senator Dawes was "full of pathos and full of enthusiasm, but utterly lacking in common sense." Pointedly speaking up to Quinton and Bonney seated in the Senate gallery, Teller echoed Plumb's assertions regarding the petitioners' naiveté and gullibility. Agreeing with Plumb, Teller insisted that a "little time spent on the frontier would convince them . . . it is not so easy to educate an Indian." Reiterating Plumb's arguments on treaty fidelity, Teller concluded that Indian misfortune did not "come entirely from a failure . . . of the government to maintain its treaties. . . . [or] an improper treatment by the people of that section."[32]

Although Quinton later noted Plumb and Teller's "objection hotly stated," she exercised keen political savvy. Resisting a direct and potentially futile political confrontation with the senators, Quinton redoubled her efforts to ground ITKPA politics in "public and official records." Taking an approach that would eventually press a select group of Washington, D.C., women into action, Quinton emphasized the need "for publishing the facts regarding both Indian capacities and the long oppressions." Quinton was determined to overcome Congressional critics with well researched and documented evidence.[33]

Reacting to legislative hostility, the Peace Policy's lackluster achievements, and a new political landscape that valued facts over sentiment, the ITKPA refashioned its organizational image and goals. Regarding this transformation Quinton stated, "The initial impulse of this movement had been an impassioned outcry for justice, and the faithful carrying out of stipulations supposed to be for the welfare of the Indian." Motivated in part by Plumb and Teller's "objection hotly stated," Quinton redoubled her efforts and "read in public libraries and gained information in many ways." She concluded that "the treaties were often frauds, and the reservation system itself was the greatest of all hindrances to Indian civilization." Quinton's new "conviction... was embodied in press articles... and was soon the opinion throughout the Association." To further advance this new agenda Quinton embraced a host of women allies—most notably Helen Hunt Jackson and Alice Fletcher. Having associated themselves with the ITKPA (Jackson in 1879 and Fletcher sometime between 1881 and 1882), Jackson and Fletcher proved invaluable, using their Indian scholarship to further the organization's national goals.[34]

The ITKPA was renamed the National Indian Association (NIA) in 1881, and in 1883 rebranded itself the Women's National Indian Association (WNIA). Ultimately, the WNIA shaped women's postbellum American Indian scholarship in three ways: It brought together a wide range of conservative, moderate, and liberal women; it prioritized comprehensive Indian treaty and historical document research; and it galvanized the careers of autonomous professional women who studied American Indian peoples and their pasts. As a contributing force, the WNIA played a crucial role in the development of women's American Indian scholarship. In this respect, Fletcher and Jackson's association with the WNIA proved a shrewd choice that mutually benefitted all parties.[35]

HELEN HUNT JACKSON AND THE GHOST OF EDWARD B. HUNT'S BRAIN

Helen Maria Fiske Hunt Jackson was born October 15, 1830, to Deborah Vinal Fiske and Nathan Welby Fiske. Nathan Fiske was a Congregationalist minister and professor of languages and rhetoric at Amherst College. Deborah Fiske was a self-educated connoisseur of literature and a feeble consumptive. Under doctor's orders to maintain "perfect quietness and entire rest from talking, walking, working, and everything," Deborah often sent her younger children to stay with relatives. Helen Fiske was sent to boarding school. The cumulative effect on Helen would be indelible: she became convinced life was unusually precarious and the maladies that threatened it were unleashed by overexertion.[36]

Despite an unsettled childhood, Helen was raised a strict Calvinist. Schooled in the gendered middle-class affectations of the age, Helen's intellectual and academic curiosities were nevertheless encouraged by both parents, but this nurturing environment soon came to an end. When Helen was only fourteen Deborah Fiske died. Following her father's death three years later, Helen resided temporarily with her aged maternal grandfather. Unable to care for a teenaged girl, Helen's grandfather soon placed her in the care of a Boston lawyer, who continued her education in the most prestigious private schools of the day. By young adulthood Helen Fisk was well grounded in a classical liberal education.[37]

During an 1851 New York visit, Helen met Edward Bissell Hunt, brother of New York governor Washington Hunt. Edward, then "a lieutenant in the Army Corps of Engineers," was also a well-respected scientist, civil engineer, and fellow of the American Association for the Advancement of Science. When the two met, Edward was in New York to present a paper at the AAAS on the nature of gaseous pressure. Smitten, Helen and Edward were married six months later and set up housekeeping. In addition to domestic paraphernalia, Helen Hunt had access to her husband's vast library. It is not known if she made use of it, but given that Edward encouraged Helen's interest in literature—introducing her to several well-known literary figures—it is reasonable to assume she perused his book collection.[38]

Helen Hunt's intellectual pursuits were curtailed with the birth of her first child, Murray, in 1852. Murray died of a brain tumor in 1854. After a period of mourning and with great anticipation Helen and Edward's second child, Warren, was born in 1855 and for almost a decade all seemed well.[39]

In spring 1863 Edward Hunt published a treatise titled, *Union Foundations: A Study of American Nationality as a Fact of Science*. Addressing the raging battle at hand, Edward's book championed unionism by identifying it with inherently "American" biological and geographical features. In his section discussing American federalism, Edward linked the growth of western-style governments to advanced brain evolution. Hunt discussed at length the parts of brain function and their similarity to town, county, state, and national governments. Linking political and physical quality to quantity, Hunt drew the following parallel: "Structural rank can be almost measured by brain-preponderance."[40]

On October 2, 1863, Edward Hunt died in the Brooklyn Naval Hospital. The tragic events leading to his death occurred following the test of a prototype torpedo for the U.S. Navy. Against his assistant's advice, Edward climbed down a rickety ladder into the unlit underwater launching chamber following a flawed launch. Improperly vented, the chamber had filled with poisonous fumes, which prompted Edward to make a hasty retreat. Ten feet into his assent Edward was overcome by the toxic gases and fell to the floor violently hitting his head. Rescued several minutes later and rushed to hospital, Edward was found to have suffered a "concussion of the brain." Shortly afterward, Edward became comatose and died two days later.[41]

Within a year, Helen Hunt suffered another debilitating blow. Her remaining child, Warren, contracted diphtheria in 1865. As he lay slowly suffocating, his face progressively turning blue, Helen extracted a promise that once on the other side he would send her a sign. Following Warren's death Helen remained barricaded in her room for several months awaiting word that never came. In a cathartic moment Helen finally accepted her child's passing and emerged from her chamber convinced that human personality could not survive death. The experience sharpened Helen's conviction that rapid change discombobulated the brain, resulting in insanity, death, or both.[42]

Warren's passing, together with that of Edward and Murray, left Helen with the unshakable conviction that matters effecting the brain must be approached judiciously. For Helen believed that sudden change could literally kill. Following the death of her family, Hunt's literary production increasingly noted physical, specifically brain, health. Ultimately this concern shaped Hunt's support for the ITKPA's "gradual" approach to Indian assimilation. Helen Hunt feared that rapid change would drive American Indians to insanity and death. Drawing on these themes in 1879, Helen noted, "I shall be found with 'Indians' engraved on my brain when I am dead."[43]

In 1873 the widowed Helen Hunt, suffering from bronchitis, traveled to Colorado Springs, Colorado, seeking a cure. While there Helen met William Sharpless Jackson, a local banker, railroad investor, and Quaker. The two married in 1875 and made their home in Colorado Springs. Four years later Helen Jackson returned to the East Coast to participate in the 1879 birthday festivities for her old friend, Oliver Wendell Holmes. During her stay Jackson attended a public lecture by Standing Bear and Susette and Francis La Flesche, who were in Boston protesting Ponca Indian removal from Nebraska. Inspired by a cause that fit into her middle-class maternal sentiments, Jackson embraced the crusade for Indian treaty fidelity. Before returning to Colorado Springs, Jackson affirmed her new social consciousness with a visit to the Indian Treaty-Keeping and Protective Association (ITKPA) offices in Philadelphia.[44]

Taking up her famous pen, Helen Hunt Jackson authored numerous letters to newspaper editors attacking treaty infidelity and Ponca removal. Several of Jackson's letters specifically condemned Interior secretary Carl Schurz's handling of the matter. Garnering public attention, her squabble with Schurz further awakened public sentiment to the Ponca cause. Mirroring the ITKPA call for comprehensive scholarship on Indian legal and treaty histories, Jackson began archival research that would culminate in publication of the most important Indian scholarship of her career, *A Century of Dishonor*.[45]

ALICE C. FLETCHER: EARLY ANTHROPOLOGIST, ETHNOLOGIST, AND INDIAN SCHOLAR

Alice Cunningham Fletcher was born March 15, 1838, in Havana, Cuba, to Thomas G. Fletcher and his wife, Lucia Adeline Fletcher. A Dartmouth graduate, Thomas Fletcher was a lawyer by profession, while Lucia was described as a well-educated woman deeply concerned with the intellectual growth of her children. Wracked with tuberculosis and hoping for recovery, Thomas relocated his family to Cuba in 1837.[46]

Unimproved after several months, Thomas and his family returned to New York in late 1838. A year later, Thomas died. Following her husband's death, Lucia moved the family to Brooklyn, New York. Records indicate that Lucia enrolled Alice in the prestigious Brooklyn Female Academy sometime between 1846 and 1847. There Alice likely studied agriculture, music, geography, history, natural history, natural philosophy, chemistry, and astronomy.[47]

Little is known about Alice Fletcher's life between 1850 and 1872, except that she studied history and literature, toured Europe, and eventually taught in private schools. By 1872 Fletcher developed an interest in women's rights and worked as governess for the wealthy Conant family in Connecticut. Fletcher's employer, Claudius B. Conant, magnanimously continued to pay her "a large salary" for several years after her work as a governess ended. Conant's death in 1877 ended Fletcher's stipend, and the financial crisis of 1878 wiped out her savings. Fletcher initially turned to the public lecture circuit for self-support, later finding more secure work through noted anthropologist Frederic Ward Putnam.[48]

Drawing on her natural science and history background, Fletcher crafted a wildly popular lecture series titled "Ancient Americans." Delivered in fall

1879, the presentations soon attracted sponsorship by the Minnesota Academy of Sciences. Focusing on ancient American Indians and the mound builders, Fletcher's lectures reflected both a growing postbellum interest in Indian history and the emerging role of autonomous professional women in American society.[49]

During this difficult period, Fletcher also cultivated important social and political relationships, most notably in the Sorosis club of New York, out of which grew the Association for the Advancement of Women (AAW). Modeled on the American Association for the Advancement of Science (AAAS), the AAW—which Fletcher helped found in 1873—proved a valuable vocational and scholarly resource. Through the AAW Fletcher befriended fellow member Mary Putnam, cousin to Frederic Ward Putnam, and Maria Mitchell, who was known for promoting women in the sciences. Friendship with Mary Putnam also provided Fletcher the opportunity to cultivate vocational prospects through Frederic, Mary's cousin. Frederic, director of the Peabody Museum of American Ethnology and Anthropology, was a noted advocate of women scholars.[50]

With Mitchell's help Fletcher secured the rank of AAW secretary, becoming one of Mitchell's favored candidates for scientific promotion. Mitchell's contention that "science needs women" no doubt reinforced Fletcher's growing interest in anthropology and ethnology. Fletcher's attraction to the human sciences would lead to tutelage under noted preprofessional anthropologist Frederic Ward Putnam. As permanent secretary of the American Association for the Advancement of Science (AAAS) and an associate of the Harvard University School for the Collegiate Instruction of Women, Putnam was well situated for the promotion of women anthropologists. Putnam first secured a position for Fletcher on an 1878 shell mound excavation sponsored by the Peabody Museum and, thereafter, secured her membership in both the Archaeological Institute of America and the AAAS. In 1879 Fletcher was not the first female member of the AAAS; she was preceded by Erminnie Smith, who joined the AAAS in 1876, and was followed by Zelia Nuttall in 1886 and Matilda Coxe Stevenson in 1892.[51]

As an AAAS member Fletcher joined section H (anthropology) and presented papers on anthropological and ethnological subjects. By 1879 Fletcher also began anthropological training at the Peabody Museum under Putnam's direction. Fletcher's study with Putnam continued for approximately two years. In October 1881 Fletcher journeyed west for ethnological study among the Lakota, Dakota, and Omaha Indians. By the time Fletcher began Indian fieldwork she was familiar with the latest ethnological and anthropological scholarship.[52]

A NEW SCHOLARSHIP FOR A NEW ERA

By 1881, Helen Hunt Jackson and Alice Fletcher were firmly established on autonomous career paths as American Indian scholars. Jackson pioneered Indian treaty and legal history in her 1881 *A Century of Dishonor*—a scholarly trajectory that continued with Fletcher's 1888 *Indian Education and Civilization* report. Where Jackson presented a document-driven Indian history wedged between an introduction and conclusion dripping with passionate appeals for justice to American Indians, Fletcher's volume of document-driven Indian history was distinct both in style and content from her ethno-political Indian scholarship.

Jackson's *A Century of Dishonor* would be dismissed after her death as a naïve work best suited to the tastes of "maudlin fanatics," while Fletcher's *Indian Education and Civilization* would be indiscriminately conflated with the general corpus of her anthropological and ethnological scholarship when considered by professional historians. Arguably, both Jackson and Fletcher promoted their own intellectual and political competency by grounding their two historical works in "public and official records" several years before the American academy embraced document-driven history as a profession. Jackson and Fletcher's Indian histories not only affirmed the archival scholarship eventually privileged by male academicians such as John Franklin Jameson and Frederick Jackson Turner, but also foreshadowed the work of professional women historians who established the specialized field of American Indian history. Ironically, Jackson and Fletcher were not remembered for their pioneering Indian histories, but rather for their Indian reform activism. Much of Jackson's Indian reform publications and Fletcher's anthropological and ethnological scholarship would be dismissed as biased or "sentimental" by professional historians. But for a time, Jackson and Fletcher achieved distinction within the permeable preprofessional realm of American Darwinism and women's Indian scholarship.

CHAPTER 3

AMERICAN DARWINISM, WOMEN, AND AMERICAN INDIANS

The historical trajectory that attracted women's rights proponents and socially conscious women to American Indian assimilation included a distinctively political flare, reflecting new tactics that emerged following the dissolution of the image of the slave as a metaphor for women's rights and subsequent disintegration of the radical equal rights campaign. Historian Louise Newman refers to this change as a process in which, "White women increasingly developed their own institutions . . . charitable societies . . . and organizations focused on 'municipal housekeeping,'" These new pre-professional structures allowed women to "influence men's political forums and play a direct part on the formulation of social policy."[1]

Most notably, this transformation resulted in an unexpected and normalizing conflation of women's social reform causes. Socially and politically active women, regardless of ideological bent, were popularly identified as the "New Woman." Effectively "flattening out" into a wide range of lateral interests, these new women "became increasingly visible and active as political agents," who effectively melded the use of "demonstrations, petitions, boycotts, lobbying, and pamphlets to express . . . [their] political views and consolidate . . . power." Among their causes no other as readily facilitated patriotic maternalism as did the campaign for American Indian assimilation.[2]

At the intellectual core of this emerging movement were a hand-full of women scholars who variously published prototypical scientific and academic works on American Indian anthropology, ethnology, and history. Ultimately, the political winds that swept these interests westward would come to tarnish the intellectual legacies of women scholars of American

Indians. Julie Des Jardins notes that it was precisely the sticky political veneer of such "progressive" women's scholarship that helped to compartmentalize and obscure the pioneering work of women within the preprofessional American history community. Produced during the heyday of American Darwinism, publications on American Indians by Helen Hunt Jackson and Alice Fletcher were notable victims of this backlash. Although Jackson was not an anthropologist or ethnologist, her single volume of Indian history, like Fletcher's, was nevertheless tainted by its link to American Darwinism and assimilation politics.[3]

Not that preprofessional American history written by male scholars was apolitical. The iconic scribes—Henry Adams, George Bancroft, Josiah Royce, Francis Parkman, Hubert Howe Bancroft, Justin Winsor, and Theodore Roosevelt—all embraced versions of a popular political agenda that interpreted westward expansion as both inevitable and beneficent. While individual formulations varied, the early male history community generally favored westward expansion, and male historians were notably indifferent to the fate of Indian cultures uprooted by European American settlement. Adams, Parkman, Bancroft, Winsor, and Royce did incorporate elements of American Indian anthropology and ethnology in their works, but as a whole the scope of male historical scholarship was far more concerned with chronicling Indian "pacification" than with discussing the finer points of Indian assimilation.[4]

In contrast Helen Hunt Jackson and Alice Fletcher were deeply concerned with methodologies for assimilating Indians into the mainstream of American life. To this end each woman played a key role in standardizing a distinct set of analytical tools for the study of American Indian cultures and histories. Jackson standardized the use of archival research and document analysis as a hallmark of Indian political history. Fletcher advanced philology, linguistics, ethnology, phrenology, mythological, ethnology, and preprofessional anthropology as useful tools for the study of American Indian life and the development of assimilation policy. Ultimately, both Jackson and Fletcher would deploy document-driven Indian history at key junctures in their Indian activism.[5]

AMERICAN DARWINISM, WOMEN SCHOLARS, AND AMERICAN INDIAN EVOLUTION

Helen Hunt Jackson and Alice Fletcher are often depicted as Indian rights proponents, however their venture into the complicated world of assimilation scholarship ran counter to the modern understanding of Indian rights, such as sovereignty and cultural integrity. Jackson and Fletcher were not devoid of concern for Indian peoples nor did they lack admiration for aspects of

Indian life. As European American women, their cultural and scientific assumptions were shaped by over three centuries of fascination with the trans-Allegheny territory and its peoples. This attraction paradoxically envisioned the American West as simultaneously a mystical place of rare and haunting beauty and a virtually unlimited source of land and raw materials. Parallel but far more troubling, the European American view of Indians followed a narrative that blended depictions of an enchantingly exotic, noble people with horrifying tales of their indelible depravity, unredeemed savagery, and unpredictable brutality.[6]

Such conflicting thoughts were embedded in both Jackson's and Fletcher's views of American Indians. Helen Hunt Jackson often recorded her perceptions of American Indian cultures as a composite of exotica, tragedy, and martyrdom. While on her spring 1880 European tour—recuperating from the travails of writing *A Century of Dishonor*—Jackson visited the Copenhagen, Denmark, Museum of Ethnology. Afterward she noted that it featured:

> portraits of all the most distinguished of our Indian chiefs; a whole corridor filled with glass cases full of their robes, implements, weapons, decorations; several life-size figures in full war-dress . . . they were far more wonderful, being wrought by an uncivilized race, living in wilderness, with only rude paints, porcupine quills, and glass beads to work with. My eyes filled with tears, I confess, to find at last in little Denmark one spot in the world where there will be kept a complete pictorial record of the race of men that we have done our best to wipe out from the face of the earth[7]

During an 1881 western excursion to the Sioux Reservation, Dakota Territory, Alice Fletcher noted her perceptions of both Indian exotica and Indian "barbarism":

> *September 18, 1881*, Passed Indian on the way—was told he was an old man. He was gay. A small red and black shawl, plaid, wound like a turban around his head. A wood colored checked shirt, buckskin leggings, a shawl wound in some curious way so as to form breeches

> *September 21, 1881*, The Sioux drove them out and great battles took place in the valleys . . . James and John Springer remember one of these great battles. Their father, mother and family were all killed. The little boys hid under a raw buffalo skin . . .

> *September 30, 1881*, Wajapa was delighted to use the Opera-glass, he said, "This will be good when we get far away from houses and then when any one is coming we can see who they are, whether friend or enemy!" A delicious bit of barbarous remains.[8]

Championing the assimilation of American Indian peoples, Jackson and Fletcher nevertheless lamented their roles in dismantling Indian societies and cultures. Unfortunately, each woman's guiding political goals were grounded in their desire to save "extinguishing" Indians. Driven by a misguided moral certainty, genuine cultural appreciation for Indian peoples languished. American Darwinism, with its blessed assurance of Northern European supremacy would inform both Fletcher's unrelenting devotion to coercive Indian assimilation and Jackson's advocacy of gradual acculturation.[9]

Epistemologically dating to Thomas Jefferson's administration, this "evolutionary" view of Indians and the American West was grounded in the historical legacy of American developmentalist ideology. Developmentalists apportioned ethnic, social, and cultural characteristics along a complex trajectory of racial development that mingled environmental, biological, and cultural qualities. Eventually, heated antebellum debates over African slavery helped to further solidify American cultural attitudes about racial distinctions. By 1860 leading American intellectual and scientific thinkers had absorbed these ideas and subsequently injected them into the American understanding of evolutionary theory. The conflation of environmental factors, biology, and culture as a single quality called "race" emerged as a defining characteristic of American Darwinism. The persistence of this synthesis—and its assumptions—well into the first decade of the nineteenth century reveals the facile nature of later attempts to distinguish a separate Gilded Age "social" Darwinism.[10]

For early American Darwinists the devil was in the details, and there they sharply departed from later Darwinian orthodoxy. The absence of a provable mechanism for biological inheritance blurred the lines between behavior and instinct and between environmental conditioning and biological mutation. In an age ignorant of genetic processes, American Darwinists consistently identified an individual's biological and cultural characteristics with his or her race. Individual qualities were regarded as reflections of group characteristics, consequently individuals were ultimately deemed pliable only on the group level. With both moral and ethical conviction American Darwinists asserted that while a person might rise above individual limitations, they could not individually rise above their racial characteristics.[11]

Nowhere was the blending of racial and evolutionary theory more evident than in the American Darwinist scholarship of John Wesley Powell. As head of the Bureau of Ethnology (BE) and Alice Fletcher's employer, Powell emphasized American Darwinism within the institution. In 1885 Powell matter-of-factly told a *Washington Post* reporter, "It is true that the scientific men in the bureau under my charge are evolutionists—that is they accept some form of evolution." A year later Powell made an address to the Anthropology Society of Washington titled, "From Barbarism to Civilization," in which he asserted, "Races grow . . . yet all of us do not grasp so great a thought."[12]

Powell's insistence that races grow had a profound influence on Alice Fletcher's own ideas about racial evolution. In an 1891 speech to the Washington Woman's Council titled, "Our Duty toward Dependent Races," Fletcher noted the regenerative "possibilities of latent powers which new conditions and fostering care may develop with those races." Pointing to method, Fletcher added, "Through thousands of years men have been struggling on this little world . . . his only effective weapon . . . has come from his power of brain work." Other racial evolution proponents such as Nathaniel Southgate Shaler and Frederic Ward Putnam also played important roles in shaping how Alice Fletcher formulated her scholarship, but they were primarily involved in the autonomous professional aspects of her life.[13]

Jackson and Fletcher each gleaned a different focus from contemporary thought on racial evolution. Jackson sought to move public opinion toward the gradual assimilation goals she shared with the Indian Treaty-Keeping and Protective Association. In contrast, Fletcher embraced the push for rapid dissolution of Indian tribal identity and communal land use. But irrespective of these methodological differences, Jackson and Fletcher's devotion to racial evolution ultimately cast them into the red hot crucible of Washington Indian politics.[14]

Reflecting the era's evolutionary optimism, Jackson insisted, "Bigger if not better creatures have come and gone ahead of us, and bigger and better may be yet to come, who will study our inexplicable skeletons with as scientific and quenchless an interest as we study fossils today." More specifically, in 1883 Jackson drew on contemporary racial evolution sentiments to construct a biting critique of Spanish secularization and its effects on California Indians. Jackson argued that secularization was a radical break from what she considered the comparatively measured acculturation practices of the California Spanish missions. Noting that secularization reflected "a singular lack of realization of the time needed to make citizens of savages," Jackson complained, "The Indian communities attached to the missions were . . . formed into pueblos . . . the missions secularized." Jackson lamented, "It is strange how . . . civilized peoples forget that it has always taken centuries to graft on or evolve out of savagery anything like civilization."[15]

Alluding to evolutionary anthropologist Henry Lewis Morgan's well-publicized stages of racial progression, Alice Fletcher emphasized the continuous arch of Indian "evolution." Fletcher contended, "Scholars are recognizing that . . . aboriginal conditions on this continent throw light on the . . . development of human society and its institutions." Further identifying American

Indian history with evolutionary processes, Fletcher predicted, "The time seems not distant when students of man's culture will turn hither for evidence needed to fill gaps." Confidently, Fletcher asserted, "America is the 'fossil bed' where are preserved stages of progress unrecorded in written history."[16]

Taken as a whole, Fletcher and Jackson's evolutionary views were in accord with the era's American Darwinist trend, which united both the anthropological methodologies and the assimilationist politics of American West and American Indian scholars. At the helm of this new movement, a select group of men and women distanced themselves from the existing morass of antiquated antebellum pseudo-scientific speculation. In place of inherited assumptions about the natural world and unproven, often fanciful, ethnological theories, this coterie launched an ambitious methodological reform based on systematic observation, documented investigative practices, and published scholarship. Alerted to underutilized and under-evaluated American West geological, mineral, fossil, botanical, biological, and ethnological sources, these American Darwinists cast their scholarly ambitions westward. Mobilized by a plethora of western political, economic, and infrastructure innovations, a motley crew of American Darwinists carried their cultural agendas and analytical equipment westward in unprecedented numbers. As their interests turned west, so did the general thrust of American anthropology and ethnology.[17]

Among the horde of new western scientific explorers, the work and worries of Edward Drinker Cope and Othniel Charles Marsh would loom large and set the stage for an evolutionary oeuvre rooted in the trans-Mississippi West. Famous, or perhaps infamous for their "bone wars," Cope and Marsh's work revealed an ancient American West filled with dinosaurs. Cope and Marsh's fossil discoveries literally transformed American Darwinism by giving it tangible form through ancient skeletal reconstructions dug from western clay and displayed in Northern museums. For American Darwinists, Cope and Marsh's work validated both the truth of evolution and the reality of its operation in the American West.[18]

Yet of all the bizarre fossils found in the American West, the most startling proved to be Cope's *Anaptomorphus Cope*, excavated at the valley of the Big Horn River, Wyoming Territory, in 1881. Cope immediately sent word of his find to the national media noting, "This skull is remarkably similar . . . to the human skull." But Cope's description went further, actually proclaiming *Anaptomorphus Cope* to be the illusive "missing link." Cope reported, "The characteristics of the formation of the human skull are clearly defined—so clearly as to be remarkable." Cope insisted, "I consider this skull as the earliest indication of the existence of man." Cope's legitimate, if not overblown, analysis of the fossil specimen encouraged the racial evolution sentiments of budding ethnologists like Alice Fletcher. Based on the work of Cope and others, Fletcher would come to believe that European American culture could literally transform Indian brains.[19]

The postbellum American West scientific mania and its concordant mission to discover and document human evolution spawned two rival scientific methodologies, paleontology and anthropology. Although beyond the scope of this book, the hotly contested battle for public funds and recognition would be won by anthropologists, who argued that understanding the human past trumped the general study of ancient life. The ascendency of anthropology as a federally sanctioned field of study would prove crucial to the status of early American Indian scholars like John Wesley Powell and his protégé Alice Fletcher. It was in this climate that Powell and his closest associates codified a definitive set of ethnological practices intended to elevate Bureau of Ethnology (BE) credibility, build the scientific and scholarly reputations of BE anthropologists, and exercise hegemony over American Indian scholarship.[20]

Fashioning a unified national anthropological and ethnological code proved difficult for Powell and the bureau. Powell had to overcome a long-established nineteenth-century conflation of anthropology and ethnology that effectively blurred the operational distinctions between ethnological work focused on a single human group and the more general anthropological analysis of human beings. Further confounding Powell's task, the Smithsonian, the BE's parent institution, identified both anthropology and ethnology as the study of "the natural history of man" and "the past history of man." Fortuitously, Powell's efforts were bolstered by Henry Adams, a distinguished dean of American history. Adams encouraged famed anthropologist Lewis Henry Morgan to support Powell in his efforts to advance a non-Paleolithic history of North American Indians. Ultimately Powell succeeded through a forceful enumeration of his plan.[21]

In a frank 1879 letter to the secretary of the Smithsonian, Powell asserted the Bureau of Ethnology's primacy in the study of North American anthropology stating, "It is the purpose of the Bureau of Ethnology, to organize anthropologic research in America." Citing special congressional authority to set BE policy, Powell defined anthropology as the general study of human beings (races) and ethnology as its various branches.[22]

The divisions in Powell's schema broadly encompassed "Somatology, Philology, Mythology and Sociology." Attention was also given to regional studies: "Habits and Customs, Technology, Archeology . . . especially in California, Arizona, New Mexico, Colorado, Utah, and part of Wyoming." Curiously Powell expressed interest in mapping the "History of Indian Affairs including treaties, cession of lands by Indians; removals; progress in industrial arts; distributions of lands among them; schooling."[23]

Powell's ethnological scope paralleled the interests of the Indian Treaty-Keeping and Protective Association. However, as an honorary ITKPA member, Alice Fletcher proved to be the only BE employee to pen a comprehensive Indian history that addressed treaties, cession of lands, removals, progress in industrial arts, land distribution, allotment, and education. While Powell ostensibly valued the study of Indian political histories, over the next two decades his personal efforts and institutional interests would focus on demonstrating linguistic and cultural parallels between American Indians and other "barbaric" peoples. Across the entirety of Fletcher's career she would share this cultural-linguistic focus with Powell. In a 1905–1906 study of the Omaha tribe written with Francis La Flesche, Fletcher expressed hope that comparative philology might help "solve some of the problems presented by this extensive linguistic stock."[24]

The root of Powell and Fletcher's philological interests dated to the early days of racial evolution. A range of European and American proponents argued that language and brain evolution were linked definitively, marking racial status in the evolutionary hierarchy. "Higher" and more refined language indicated advanced races, with Europeans—English and Germans—predictably placed at the pinnacle. Based on this vainglory, influential American Darwinists came to believe that simply teaching "lower" races to speak English would prompt an evolutionary response measurable in new brain growth.[25]

Hoping for this end, Powell and Fletcher supported boarding school efforts to root out American Indian languages in favor of English. The extent to which American Darwinists embraced this flawed linguistic pedagogy was revealed at the 1890 Lake Mohonk Conference. Speaking to assembled guests, Princeton University president James McCosh embraced the English language as an important medium for Indian assimilation and as a miraculous vehicle for physical evolution. McCosh insisted, "English language ... should be required of every pupil." McCosh continued, "Their own tongues tend to narrow the intellect, and are not fitted to impart and express the ideas which expand the mind and excite higher aspirations." According to McCosh, learning the English language would contribute to "a process of evolution ... continued for several ages." The end of this process, he asserted, "will lead to the enlargement of the [Indian] brain as an organ of the mind." McCosh related that in the "British West Indies ... a hatter could tell you at what time a company of negroes had been brought to a plantation by the size of their brain." Emphasizing this point McCosh noted, "those who had been longest in the country and in contact with civilized men having larger heads than those who had been introduced more recently."[26]

Unable to attend the conference, Fletcher sent a letter that mirrored McCosh's position. Fletcher noted that American Indian "progress has been slow because of isolation of language and the habits formed by old reservation lines and precedents, which not only affect his habits, but his modes of thought." Agreeing with McCosh's sentiments, Fletcher affirmed her faith in assimilation noting, "It has been proven over and over again that man can be educated and civilized." Fletcher's BE boss, Powell also shared her faith in the transformational power of language and its necessary role in American Indian assimilation.[27]

Powell's linguistic, philological, and mythological focus reflected the American Darwinist template for racial evolution, however, as scholarship his work was densely written and often abstract—not the kind of material that riveted public attention or fired political wills. As head of a government-funded agency Powell could not afford to alienate the public or Congress. To maintain Bureau of Ethnology hegemony over American Indian scholarship Powell had to continually cultivate popular and government interest. To this end Powell and his associates launched a concerted effort to enlist a "large number of persons including missionaries and teachers among the Indians, Indian agents, Army Officers, scholars connected with colleges of the United States and others."[28]

Powell's recruitment of social workers, Indian Office bureaucrats, military personnel, and academics created a fertile environment for the political agendas and scholarly aspirations of emerging anthropologists and ethnologists. Among these Powell's promotion of a small cadre of preprofessional women anthropologists unwittingly placed an official BE stamp on "sentimentalist" American Indian politics and scholarship. Where Powell constrained himself to dense (often dry) anthropological treatises, Alice Fletcher augmented her repertoire with exciting ethnological tales recounting life among the Omahas, among the Nez Perces, and during *The Hako: A Pawnee Ceremony*. Though their literary styles differed, Powell and Fletcher remained intellectually bound by their commitment to American Indian scholarship and assimilation.[29]

INDIGENOUS WOMEN'S SCHOLARSHIP VERSUS THE AMERICAN DARWINIST ASSIMILATION NARRATIVE

John Wesley Powell, Alice Fletcher, and Helen Hunt Jackson knew American Indians, but they did not seek indigenous critiques of their assimilation views or scholarship. Powell's western explorations—particularly the 1869

"Geographic Expedition," Fletcher's sojourn among the Omahas and later the Nez Perce tribe, and Jackson's encounter with Standing Bear and Francis and Susette La Flesche did not foster scholarly peer relationships with American Indians. Though Fletcher would later "adopt" Chief Joseph La Flesche's son Francis, as Joan Mark notes, "He lived as a son in the household, and Alice exercised over him a mother's authority." More precisely, though Francis would eventually become a respected anthropologist in his own right, for years he remained under Alice Fletcher's close supervision. Francis did not achieve complete legal autonomy until the Omahas were granted citizenship in 1887—the year he turned thirty.[30]

Although American Indians were not invited to critique the ethno-political narrative, three indigenous writers published book-length responses between 1883 and 1898 that were intended for European American audiences. In order of publication, these were: Sarah Winnemucca, *Life Among the Piutes: Their Wrongs and Claims* (1883); Sophia Alice Callahan, *Wynema: A Child of the Forest* (1891); and Susette La Flesche (with Fannie Reed Giffen), *Oo-Ma-Ha Ta-Wa-Tha: Omaha City* (1898). Susette La Flesche also penned short assimilation critiques in an introduction to her husband's book, *The Ponca Chiefs* (1880) and in an introduction to William Justice Harsha's, *Ploughed Under* (1881). Susette La Flesche also published a series of articles for the *American Nonconformist* (Washington, D.C.) and the *Lincoln Independent* (Nebraska). A brief survey of the lives and publications of Winnemucca, Callahan, and La Flesche reveals both their parallels to and distinctions from Helen Hunt Jackson and Alice Fletcher's Indian histories.[31]

Perhaps the best known of the three, Sarah Winnemucca Hopkins's life has been examined in great detail by recent biographies. The salient points of her story reveal an often harsh life that offered few comforts. Against great odds Winnemucca learned to speak, read, and write English at an early age. As a "culture broker," Winnemucca used her mediation skills to advance the interests of her people—the Northern Paiutes.

Sarah Winnemucca (Thocmentony) was born 1844, in a Northern Paiute camp situated on the banks of Humboldt River. Her father was a Shoshone named Poito and her mother Tuboitonie, was a Northern Paiute. Sarah's grandfather, Tru-ki-zo, also known as Chief Truckee, initiated first contact with European Americans and eventually served as John C. Fremont's guide on the Great Basin Expedition. Approximately 1857 Tru-ki-zo moved his daughter, Tuboitonie and her children to San José, California, where they worked in town and at local ranches. While in San José, Winnemucca briefly attended a Catholic mission school with her sister. Racial prejudice brought a swift end to their formal education, but Winnemucca continued studies on her own, teaching herself to "speak on paper." Given her mastery of the

English language, Winnemucca was singled out for employment as a United States military interpreter and tribal liaison.[32]

Early in her work for the army, Winnemucca utilized her ability to speak on paper in a desperate bid to help her people. On April 4, 1870, Winnemucca sent a letter to Major Henry Douglas that frankly asked, "What is the object of the government in regard to Indians?" Denouncing Indian Agency fraud, she offered a solution, "Guarantee that [Paiutes] can secure a permanent home on their own native soil, and that white neighbors can be kept from encroaching on our rights." The letter made a deep impression on Douglas and was subsequently reprinted in *Harper's* magazine and national newspapers. Winnemucca would continue to draw on her position as a culture broker, writing and eventually lecturing on behalf of the Northern Paiutes and other Indian peoples.[33]

In 1872, after a series of devastating conflicts with European American colonial settlers and the U.S. Army, the Northern Paiute and Bannock tribes were forcibly removed to the Malheur Indian Reservation. Winnemucca was removed as well, though her work afforded her free passage off the reservation. By 1878 new conflicts with settler colonists erupted into the "Bannock War" and both the Bannocks and Northern Paiutes were forcibly removed to the Yakima Reservation in Washington Territory.[34]

More an internment camp, Yakima initiated a decade of starvation, privation, and death for the Northern Paiutes. Responding to the pitiful situation, in 1879 Winnemucca drafted an affidavit to Interior secretary Carl Schurz explaining the situation and asking that he return the Northern Paiutes to the Malheur reservation. Building on her previous public speaking experience, Winnemucca also traveled to southern California and the Pacific states to give a series of lectures intended to draw national attention to the Yakima atrocities. During her time at Yakima, Winnemucca met and courted an Indian Service subagent, Lewis H. Hopkins. The two were married December 5, 1881, and within days Winnemucca planned a new speaking tour in the eastern states. A variety of difficulties postponed the engagements until 1883.[35]

Winnemucca's lectures varied at each locale, but she always touched on common themes, notably Indian Service corruption, agent maleficence, cruel missionaries, and a general indigenous right to land ownership and personal liberty. During the eastern tour Winnemucca augmented her case with documentary sources. When discussing agent corruption at Malheur she noted a "printed report in the United States statutes," found by her husband Lewis Hopkins in the "Boston Athenæum." According to Winnemucca the report revealed a twenty-five thousand dollar misappropriation by the Indian agent. Like Helen Hunt Jackson and Alice Fletcher, Sarah Winnemucca appealed to the "objectivity" of public documents to bolster her credibility.[36]

Sometime after 1881 Winnemucca befriended the Boston Brahmins Elizabeth Palmer Peabody and her sister Mary Tyler Peabody Mann. Purportedly at Elizabeth Peabody's prompting, Winnemucca penned an autobiography that Mary edited for publication. Presented to the public in 1883, *Life Among the Piutes: Their Wrongs and Claims* was a damning indictment of United States dealings with the Northern Paiute and Bannock Indians. Textual evidence indicates an awareness of Helen Hunt Jackson's 1881 book, *A Century of Dishonor*, but Winnemucca does not mention it in her narrative. Cutting against Fletcher and Jackson's assimilationist views, Winnemucca staunchly supported Northern Paiute tribal sovereignty. Rejecting the standard American Darwinist racial hierarchy, Winnemucca advanced her tribe's social and cultural structure as parallel, if not democratically superior to the United States noting, "We have a republic as well as you . . . the council-tent is our Congress, and anybody can speak . . . women and all." Winnemucca's staunch support for Northern Paiute sovereignty and intertribal cooperation, stood in stark contrast to the pan-Indian assumptions and assimilationist goals advanced by Jackson and Fletcher.[37]

Making full use of the political opportunities afforded by publication, Winnemucca included a petition in the back of her book. Unlike the Indian Treaty-Keeping and Protective Association's contemporary third petition, which opened the door to "modified or abrogated" treaties and allotted land held in trust, Winnemucca called for restoration of the Malheur reservation, full and free land in severalty, and return of the Paiute prisoners interned at Yakima. These pleas were partially met by 1886.[38]

In 1884 with the help of the Peabody sisters and Northern philanthropists, Winnemucca opened a bilingual Paiute school in Lovelock, Nevada. In a circular to local trustees, Winnemucca appealed to tribal ties, "Brothers and sisters . . . many of you are my aunts and cousins . . . we are one race . . . your blood is my blood." Pleading for students she frankly observed, "A few years ago you owned this great country, today the white man owns it all." She noted that this was because of "education." Cutting against the American Darwinist tide, Winnemucca admonished her audience, "You have brains same as whites, your children have brains, and it will be your fault if they grow up as you have." The school proved a great success, but changes in United States Indian policy after 1887 forced the school to close. The students were shipped off to government boarding schools. Four years later Winnemucca died at her sister's home in Montana.[39]

Sophia Alice Callahan was born on January 1, 1868, in Sulphur Springs, Texas. Her father, Samuel Benton Callahan, was listed on the 1898 Dawes roll as one-eighth Muscogee (Creek) "by blood." Alice's European American mother, Sarah Elizabeth Thornberg Callahan, was the daughter of a local

Sulphur Springs Methodist minister. According to the antiquated blood quantum calculation used by the Dawes Commission Alice Callahan should have been listed as one-sixteenth Muscogee, but the final rolls show her as one-eighth. In the Muscogee nation Samuel Callahan operated a vast ranching and farming enterprise, owned slaves, and during the War of the Rebellion he held a Confederate military position. After 1862 Samuel served as the Muscogee and Seminole delegate to the Confederate Congress.[40]

After the Civil War, Samuel Callahan variously served as House of Kings clerk (Muscogee Senate), in the Muscogee National Council, Muscogee Supreme Court clerk, and eventually as chief justice of the Muscogee Supreme Court. Samuel also served as editor of the *Muskogee Indian Journal* and as superintendent of the Wealaka Boarding School. Alice Callahan benefited from her father's wealth and political power, both of which afforded her an education and teaching positions in the Muscogee nation.[41]

Though much of Alice Callahan's early life remains obscured, it is known that in 1886 she taught school in Okmulgee, Muscogee nation, and in 1887 she joined the Mary Watson chapter of the Harrell International Institute's juvenile missionary society. In the first week of September 1887 Alice and a friend, Lettie Edwards, departed for a years' study at the Wesleyan Female Institute in Staunton, Virginia. Both returned to the Muscogee nation in June 1888. Callahan spent that summer in Sulphur, Texas, presumably with relatives. In the fall of 1889 Callahan won first place for her essay, "Lawyers," at the Muskogee Indian International Fair—international in this instance meaning intertribal.[42]

Likely galvanized by the success of her essay, Callahan completed *Wynema: A Child of the Forest* sometime between 1889 and 1890. Published by subscription though H. J. Smith and Company in 1891, orders for *Wynema* were taken at Cyrus Beatie Gilmore's "Post Office Bookstore" in the city of Muskogee and peddled door to door by H. J. Smith book agents for twenty-five cents a copy. The audience for *Wynema* was likely small and local. H. J. Smith and Company filed for bankruptcy in 1893 and was succeeded by E. A. Weeks and Company. E. A. Weeks seems to have dropped *Wynema* from its catalog by the end of 1893. Alice Callahan died from inflammation of the lungs (likely pneumonia) on January 7, 1894, at the age of twenty-six.[43]

A work of historical fiction, *Wynema* loosely paralleled Callahan's life, following the exploits of Wynema, a young Muscogee girl who dreamed of opening her own school. Crucial to understanding the complicated message of Callahan's *Wynema* is familiarity with its literary twin, Alfred Benjamin Meacham's 1876 volume, *Wi-ne-ma: The Woman Chief*. A former superintendent of Indian Affairs and chairman of the Modoc Peace Commission, Meacham was able to draw on official documents from his time as a government employee. Meacham's account gave a romanticized, if not skewed account of the "Modoc War," with special attention to his own rescue by a Modoc woman he named Winema.[44]

The real life Winema went by the name Toby Riddle and was married to a white man named Frank Riddle. Meacham's *Wi-ne-ma* recounts the crucial role that mixed marriage and "mixed race" Modocs played in confronting settler colonialism and navigating U.S. Indian policy. In contrast, Callahan's attempt to coalesce *Wynema* around generic "mixed race" and mixed marriage Indian characters never solidified into more than an awkward literary device. Callahan's inability to resolve the racial and cultural tensions between the European American, "mixed race," and mixed-culture characters in her novel likely reflected her own conflicted background as one-eighth (possibly one-sixteenth) Muscogee. It is not clear to what extent Callahan interacted with Muscogee citizens or engaged with Muscogee culture.[45]

Struggling to find a unifying theme, Callahan addressed issues of social justice, land allotment, and the massacre at Wounded Knee. In terms of political critique, *Wynema* discussed allotment, but did not question racial evolution. Although Callahan personally seems to have been against redistribution of land, in the *Wynema* narrative she also presented anti-allotment as an educated European American sentiment to be embraced by American Indian protégés. Throughout her novel, Callahan consistently framed political power as a European American prerogative.[46]

Callahan further complicated the allotment critique by pitting "civilized" Five Nations citizens against the "western tribes." This subject is introduced in an exchange between Wynema and her European American teacher Genevieve. Initially favoring allotment as an important step in compelling "lazy Indians" to "cultivate" land, young Wynema is prompted to change her mind. Calling Wynema to task, Genevieve proclaims, "If your land were divided it would become a state . . . do you think your western tribes sufficiently tutored in . . . civilization to become citizens of the United States?" Wynema chastened, replied, "What a superficial thinker I am not to have understood this!" Distinguishing the "civilized" Five Nations from Plains tribes, Callahan muddled the allotment debate. While Callahan's motives are not clear, this complex, seemingly contradictory treatment likely reflected contemporary debate within the Five Nations. Exempted from allotment by the 1887 Dawes Act, Five Nations citizens argued its virtues and vices until finally forced to accept allotment under terms of the 1898 Curtis Act. In this context, *Wynema* is a unique window into the political thought of Five Nations citizens during the "inter-allotment" years.[47]

Like Sarah Winnemucca's *Life Among the Paiutes*, Alice Callahan's *Wynema* addressed contemporary tribal politics, particularly property and cultural rights, but was not rooted in government documents and archival sources. Where Winnemucca cited a lone document procured by her husband, Callahan referenced a few uncited newspaper articles. As a short, subscription paperback book published by a "dime novel" firm, *Wynema* was not written for a politically engaged readership. Where Winnemucca's autobiography reached an audience numbering in the thousands, *Wynema* probably reached only a few hundred.[48]

Unlike Winnemucca's pre-allotment (and Callahan's pre–Curtis Act) publications, Susette La Flesche's 1898 *Oo-Mah-Ha-Ta-Wa-Tha: Omaha City* was published fourteen years after the largest Omaha reservation land allotments. Susette La Flesche (Inshata Theumba) was born in 1854 to Joseph La Flesche (E-sta-mah-za) and Mary Gale La Flesche, at Bellevue, Nebraska (Omaha reservation). Joseph's father was a French fur trader and his mother a member of the Ponca tribe. Mary's father was an English surgeon and her mother of Iowa descent. Joseph La Flesche, the adopted son of an Omaha chief, Big Elk, inherited the position following Big Elk's death. Chief Joseph was one of the 1854 signatories to the treaty that ceded traditional lands and created the Omaha Reservation. Susette spent the first fifteen years of her life on the reservation, where she attended the Presbyterian boarding school.[49]

In 1869 Susette La Flesche was enrolled in the Elizabeth Institute in New Jersey, where she studied English, elocution, Latin, French, German, drawing, and music. Upon graduation in 1875 Susette returned to the Omaha Reservation and taught at the government boarding school. In May 1879, following the forced removal of the Poncas, Susette accompanied her father to the Ponca reservation in Indian Territory and found disease, malnutrition, starvation, and death. Upon her return, Joseph and Susette worked with *Omaha Daily Herald* (Nebraska) editor Thomas H. Tibbles to litigate the famous Standing Bear case. Joseph La Flesche formulated the simple, but brilliant legal argument that Standing Bear was a human being entitled to full civil rights.[50]

In fall 1879 Henry Tibbles arranged for Susette La Flesche, Standing Bear, and Francis La Flesche to go on an eastern tour to popularize the Poncas' plight. Serving as Standing Bear's interpreter, Susette La Flesche also gave addresses on her own. On the first leg of the tour Susette asked a capacity audience at a local Omaha church, "I love my people . . . I have told them that they must learn the arts of the whites and adopt their customs, but how can they when the government sends the soldiers to drive them about over the face of the earth?" Throughout the allotment and assimilation period, Susette La Flesche would champion accommodation, tempered with the autonomy of unencumbered citizenship, unrestricted property rights, and full civil rights as a model for U.S. Indian policy. This approach would bring Susette into conflict with contemporary Indian rights leaders like Alice Flectcher who argued that American Indians required coerced assimilation and tutelage. Susette married Thomas Tibbles in 1881.⁵¹

Susette continued her writing career into the late 1890s, giving particular attention to political critique. Sometime between 1897 and 1898 she was approached by Fannie Reed Giffen about coauthoring a souvenir book for the upcoming Omaha, Nebraska, Trans-Mississippi International Exposition. Slated for June to November of 1898, the Omaha "world's fair" promised grand architecture, electric lights, and an exotic "Congress of Indians." This convocation, racialized and commercialized by promoters, boasted the "last opportunity of seeing the American Indian as a savage." Trumpeting assimilation, promoters noted, "The government work now in progress will lift the savage Indian into American civilization . . . [and] will wipe off the maps of the United States the Indian reservation . . . [and] the reservation Indian."⁵²

Whatever sponsors had intended, Susette La Flesche did not follow suit. *Oo-Mah-Ha-Ta-Tha: Omaha City*, situated the Omaha tribe squarely within Omaha city's past and present. Reminding their audience that Omaha began with an injustice to the Omaha people, the authors presented a copy of the 1854 treaty that ushered the city and reservation into existence. Following the treaty, the authors presented a biographical sketch of each Omaha signatory. Directly challenging the assimilation and allotment narrative, the authors featured, "Wa-ja-pa's letter." This 1879 epistle, addressed to Eastern activists, asked for full civil rights (citizenship), an end to government oversight, demilitarization of the reservation, and unencumbered land titles. Wa-ja-pa insisted, "We wish to keep what is ours."⁵³

Although Sarah Winnemucca, Sophia Alice Callahan, and Susette La Flesche addressed allotment and assimilation, *Life Among the Paiutes*, *Wynema*, and *Oo-Mah-Ha-Ta-Tha* were not intended to be comprehensive Indian histories. These publications touched on intertribal sentiment, but each was driven by an agenda narrowly focused on the distinct intratribal political interests of each author's family and tribe. In part this reflected the economic, political, and social distance—as well as institutional discrimination—that isolated American Indians from documents related to tribal politics and history. But it also revealed stark cultural and political realities that were significantly different from those facing preprofessional and professional white women who published document-driven Indian history. Indigenous works would have a distinctly personal, intimate, intratribal focus, while historical volumes by European Americans had a more impersonal, general pan-Indian gaze.⁵⁴

The political and institutional wall that segregated the survival interests of individual tribes and their members from the pan-Indian assimilation agenda of European American activists and scholars also delineated who would write preprofessional American Indian history. Individual tribes, nations, and tribal members would challenge the goals of European American assimilationists—sometimes in print—but no American Indian would write a published document-driven Indian history before the first decade of the twentieth century. Helen Hunt Jackson and Alice Fletcher not only pioneered this kind of Indian history, they foreshadowed white women's hegemony over the field in the coming decades. But first, Jackson and Fletcher's path to publication on American Indian history would take each woman into the smoldering political crucible of settler colonialism and United States Indian policy.

CHAPTER 4

HELEN HUNT JACKSON AND THE HISTORY OF AMERICAN INDIAN TREATIES

Helen Hunt Jackson was a widely read popular poet and author, whose first published work dated to 1865. A childhood friend of Emily Dickenson and later Ralph Waldo Emerson, Jackson enjoyed a successful publishing career. Unencumbered by antiquated notions that equated female decorum with public silence, Jackson nevertheless avoided public speaking and found the women's rights movement, particularly suffrage, distasteful. Shunning the women's rights mantle, Jackson existed at best on the movement's far periphery. Jackson's political activism, like that of Catherine Beecher four decades earlier, was largely confined to print.[1]

The historical record does not reveal precisely when Jackson became interested in Indian activism, but most sources date her political awakening to the Ponca removal controversy in 1879. That fall Jackson penned a series of protest letters to newspapers outlining her sentiments on the forced Ponca removal. Following an early December 1879 book review of Thomas Tibbles's *The Ponca Chiefs*, Jackson initiated library research intended to back her sentiments with documentation. Given that her criticism was primarily directed at Interior secretary Carl Schurz, who majored in history and philosophy at Bonn University (Germany), Jackson's new tack proved prudent.[2]

Quoting Indian office reports, U.S. statutes, and Indian treaties archived at New York's Astor library, Jackson wrote a December 15, 1879, letter to the *New York Tribune* decrying the nebulous legal status of American Indians. On December 19, 1879, Secretary of the Interior Schurz made a detailed reply to Jackson's letter that brought into question her historical understanding of U.S. government treaties with Indians. Jackson replied with further

Helen Hunt Jackson, ca. 1880. Popularly known as an Indian rights activist, Jackson published the first near comprehensive "document-driven" Indian history in 1881. Courtesy of the Ramona Bowl Museum, Hemet, California.

documentation, carrying on a protracted newspaper dispute with Schurz. The last of December, Jackson noted in a personal letter, "I do not want to leave a loophole of attack on a single assertion." Jackson's "Indian Rights" newspaper letters in late 1879 and early 1880 demonstrated a growing mastery of Indian treaties and Indian office documentation. On January 21, 1880, Jackson informed William Hayes Ward, editor of the *New York Independent*, "I am hard at work . . . writing . . . the history in short of the gov[ernmen]ts['] dealings with the Indians for the last 100 years."[3]

THE FIRST DOCUMENT-DRIVEN PAN-INDIAN HISTORY

Four years before Helen Hunt Jackson's death from cancer in 1885, Thomas Henry Tibbles, principle editor of the *Omaha Herald* christened her, "Helen Hunt, the Colorado historian of the good Indians." He described her as "fair, fat and forty." As Alice Fletcher would discover, Tibbles's wit was irreverent, however, his presentation of Jackson as an historian of American Indians was not frivolous. After meeting Jackson during his Boston tour with Standing Bear and learning of Jackson's Indian activism, Tibbles "turned over to her [his] whole mass of [Indian] records," which "she spent months classifying." His records included documentation compiled during the Ponca removal controversy, including court transcripts from Standing Bear's successful 1879 habeas corpus petition. Jackson's in-depth analysis of Tibbles's records helped develop her archival and research abilities, skills that played a key role in lending credibility to Jackson's 1881 publication, *A Century of Dishonor*.[4]

For a time Jackson would hold the distinction of being the solitary American historian of Indian treaties, legal activities, and politics. Both Tibbles and the Women's National Indian Association (WNIA) widely praised her historical scholarship and touted Jackson's achievement in chronicling treaty history. For her part, Jackson framed *A Century of Dishonor* in moral terms, as "a shameful record of broken treaties and unfulfilled promises." She added, "The history of the border white man's connection with the Indians is a sickening record of murder, outrage, [and] robbery." Tibbles noted that his own records were published in Jackson's "book . . . where they formed the Ponca chapter and part of the Appendix." Regarding Jackson's efforts during the Ponca controversy Tibbles added, "I strongly doubt we could have won without her." Amelia S. Quinton of the WNIA praised *A Century of Dishonor* for revealing "Truthful and thrilling records." Quinton further noted, "The facts there given from undisputed sources must intensely interest the reader . . . while also correcting many errors." A review of the book, cited by Quinton, proclaimed, "To citizens who feel that their own honor is involved in that of the government, the title of this book is gravely significant." As an honorary member, political activist, and scholar, Jackson maintained a relationship with the WNIA until her death in 1885.[5]

Yet, for over a century the scholarly connection between Jackson's *A Century of Dishonor* and the Women's National Indian Association has been obscured by the critique of a male historian whose own scholarship is noted for its strident advocacy of American imperialism. In Theodore Roosevelt's *The Winning of the West*—a largely undocumented historical narrative—the future president savaged Jackson's *A Century of Dishonor*, defining it as a sentimental rather than intellectual work. Though Jackson's book was scrupulously documented, Roosevelt sniffed, "As a history it would be beneath criticism, were it not that the high character of the author ... ha[s] given it a fictitious value ... quoted by the large mass of amiable but maudlin fanatics."[6]

Roosevelt halfheartedly noted that Jackson had "the most praiseworthy purpose—to prevent our continuing any more injustice to the Indian," however, this did not mitigate the fact that his critique was a harsh public dismissal of her scholarship on U.S.-Indian treaties. More so, while Roosevelt's comments were certainly unfair, in a much more damning way they struck at the heart of Jackson and the WNIA's mutual interest in Indian treaty and legal history. By pegging *A Century of Dishonor* as a singularly sentimental work, Roosevelt effectively obscured Jackson's intellectual contribution to the evolving structure of WNIA Indian scholarship.[7]

The historical record does not reveal complex conversations or deep philosophical exchanges between Jackson and WNIA leaders Mary L. Bonney and Amelia S. Quinton, but all three initially shared similar views on assimilation—ranging from voluntary allotment and elective citizenship to a measured process of acculturation. However, of the three, Jackson advocated a particularly light touch, usually framing her assimilation suggestions as "voluntary." At first Bonney and Quinton preferred to call their Indian proposals "gradual," but they changed their position and began to promote legally mandated assimilation by 1882. Jackson's assimilation views, best described as "gradualist," remained consistent until her death in 1885. Their early common sentiment was reflected in Jackson and Quinton's contemporary statements. The 1881 WNIA petition, coauthored by Quinton, called for keeping all treaties "with the Indians until they are changed by the mutual and free consent of both parties." The accompanying letter, penned by Quinton, stated that the nation should "make it to the interest of the Indian tribes among us *voluntarily* to become citizens of the United States, and not by the coercion of Acts of our Congress." Jackson articulated a similar view, arguing that "to administer complete citizenship of a sudden ... to all Indians ...

would be as grotesque a blunder as to dose them all . . . with one medicine." She concluded, "It would kill more than it would cure."[8]

Reflecting Jackson's gradualist views, *A Century of Dishonor* outlines legal and treaty histories of the Delaware, Cheyenne, Nez Perce, Lakota and Dakota, Ponca, Winnebago, and Cherokee tribes. Jackson argued that near-ubiquitous treaty abrogation, removal and resettlement, and European American settler colonialism disrupted American Indian efforts to "civilize" at their own pace. Embracing the proposals of Minnesota Episcopal bishop Henry Benjamin Whipple and Dutch Reformed Church cleric Julius Hawley Seelye, Jackson argued, "All judicious plans and means for their safety and salvation must embody provisions for their becoming citizens as fast as they are fit, and must protect them till then in every right and particular." A brief examination of the first and second chapters of *A Century of Dishonor*—concerning land rights and the Delawares—illustrates Jackson's point.[9]

Jackson's introductory chapter presents a sophisticated analysis of American Indian land rights, shrewdly distinguishing between right of ownership, as asserted by the United States, and right of occupation, an Indian treaty right. Jackson's position on Indian land rights was remarkably insightful, foreshadowing the analysis of twentieth century post-colonial historians. Building on the right of occupation, Jackson's Delaware chapter traces their legal and treaty interaction with Europeans from Hendrik Hudson's first contact in 1609 through events culminating in 1880. Recounting Colonial Era and U.S. treaties, the chapter's pivotal point centered on the 1795 Treaty of Greenville which encompassed eleven tribes, including the Delawares, also known as the Western Confederacy. The treaty established a boundary line ostensibly demarcating the limits of settler colonialism and outlined paltry annuities to be paid in exchange for large cessions of Western Confederacy land.[10]

The treaty stipulation that most concerned Jackson was article five, guaranteeing "the Indian tribes who have a right to those lands are quietly to enjoy them—hunting, planting, and dwelling thereupon so long as they please without any molestation from the United States." Jackson noted that by 1818 the Delawares were pressured into surrendering treaty land and removed west of the Mississippi to new land, guaranteed by an 1829 supplementary treaty provision. In 1854 the Delawares were again compelled to relinquish land to the United States. Additionally, their remaining lands in present-day Kansas were to be surveyed for allotment.[11]

Jackson dryly commented that, after sending one hundred and seventy men to fight for the Union in 1862, the Delawares were compelled a half-decade later to give up their 1854 reservation rights and move to Indian Territory. Although the Delawares proved themselves excellent ranchers and farmers—producing five thousand head of cattle, seventy-two thousand bushels of grain, and thirteen thousand bushels of potatoes annually—harassment, cattle theft, and violent attacks by colonial settlers forced the tribe to leave Kansas around 1867. Noting the repeated disruption of Delaware society Jackson concluded, "Such uprooting, such perplexity, such loss, such confusion and uncertainty, inflicted once on any community of white people anywhere in our land, would be considered quite enough to . . . blight its prospects for years."[12]

Careful documentation and analysis aside, Jackson's gradualist sentiments were soon obscured by the passion of her politics. Following *A Century of Dishonor*'s publication, Jackson placed specially commissioned, red leather editions embossed with, "Look upon your hands! They are stained with the blood of your relations," at the desks of every member of the forty-seventh Congress—three hundred and seventy-seven in all. Jackson also sent an autographed copy to President Chester A. Arthur. The tactic galvanized supporters and incensed opponents. Jackson's book, though polarizing, did not capture the nation's attention, however it did contribute to congressional investigations of the Ponca removal controversy and the creation of a presidential commission led by General George Crook. In the spring of 1881 Jackson accepted a proposal by *Century Illustrated Magazine* to write four travel articles about southern California. Ultimately, Jackson's experiences during her West Coast sojourn, particularly at the Indian villages, would compel her to become an advocate for the Mission Indians of southern California.[13]

Jackson finalized her travel and writing plans with *Century* magazine's editor, Richard Watson Gilder in fall 1881. After a brief visit to New York, Jackson traveled by train to Los Angeles, arriving in December 1881. Over the next few months she visited numerous West Coast locales, including the Bancroft Library where she researched material for her upcoming articles, ancient Franciscan missions, and several Indian villages, including Luiseño, Cahuilla, Cupeño, Ipai, and Soboba settlements. Jackson's sojourn in southern California proved decisive in shaping her views about the dire need for an involved, but cautious federal assimilation (through education), land management (with protected reservations and private property), and a selective allotment program for California Indians.[14]

Jackson's visit to Soboba village proved quite disturbing, because in observing the dislocation and suffering there, she drew a parallel to the effects of removal on the Poncas and other Plains Indians. Following additional investigation, Jackson uncovered a complicated history of Spanish-Mexican land grants and subsequent faulty, if not fraudulent surveys that swindled Soboba village's Indians, mostly Serranos, out of their historic claims. Jackson's research on Soboba village prompted her further inquiries into the general status of California Mission Indians and an enduring interest in their plight.[15]

While Jackson would address the concerns of California Indians in terms of guaranteed reservations, selective allotment, and federal oversight, many California Indians hoped to secure U.S. citizenship as well as land titles that honored traditional grants acquired during Spanish and Mexican rule. Unfortunately, California Mission Indians found that their grants were not honored by European Americans. As with Plains Indians the issues confronting California Mission Indians involved European American encroachment, outstanding land claims, and their status as residents of the United States. Given the problems facing Indians at Soboba village and other Mission Indians, Jackson concluded that Interior department policies had failed to protect Indian land interests. The 1881 tour convinced Jackson that Mission Indians would likely perish without a substantial overhaul of federal Indian policy in southern California.[16]

In a June 1882 letter to Secretary of the Interior Henry Teller, Jackson outlined the situation and insisted that without government intervention Indians at Soboba village would "be driven off their lands." Jackson contended that Soboba village Indians "want a title given to them individually. . . . They do not want a land title in common with their tribe." Boldly Jackson added, "I suppose it would be entirely out of the question . . . for the Interior department to send a woman along with a commission of investigation, and let the woman write the report!" Given her celebrity and penchant for letters to the editor, it seems reasonable to conclude that Teller understood Jackson's question as both a request and a threat likely to appear in print.[17]

Reflecting the political influence of a powerful coalition that respected her work, including senators, Indian office commissioner Hiram Price, and President Chester A. Arthur, Jackson received notice in summer 1882 of her appointment as "Special Agent to report on the Mission Indians." According to her commission, Jackson was charged with identifying public domain sites for permanent (reservation) settlements, providing detailed descriptions of Mission Indian land holdings, and reporting recommendations. Jackson was also given permission to work with respected California conservationist Abbot Kinney and hire a translator. In mid-February 1883 Jackson arrived in Los Angeles, and over the next several months she visited each Mission Indian settlement with Kinney. Jackson and Kinney were appalled by the grinding poverty they encountered and the outrageous manner in which non-Indian settlers had swindled or appropriated Indian land.[18]

At tour's end Jackson returned to Colorado Springs, Colorado, where she began work on the official report. Completed in early July 1883, the fifty-six page *Report on the Condition and Needs of the Mission Indians of California* made eleven recommendations. Among these the report called for "resurveying and marking existing reservations; removal of all white settlers from reservations; removal of the Indians or the upholding and defending of their claims." In an effort to secure reservation land, Jackson and Kinney specifically asked for "patenting with a twenty-five year trust period ... both old and new reservations to Indian residents." Addressing education and health, the report called for boarding schools, comestible provisions, and medical care. To ensure that government supplies were properly distributed Jackson and Kinney requested "two inspections a year for each village and settlement." Regarding legal rights, the report recommended hiring "special attorneys for cases relating to mission Indians." To protect vulnerable populations, Jackson and Kinney advocated "purchasing two tracts of land [on] ... the Pauma Ranch ... and the Santa Ysabel ranch" and incorporation "of the San Carlos and other Indian groups north of the mission agency boundary under jurisdiction of the mission agency."[19]

In their report Jackson and Kinney advocated a gradual movement toward Alice Fletcher's land in severalty scheme as codified in the 1882 Omaha Allotment Act. Unlike Fletcher, Jackson and Kinney did not support immediate coercive allotment. However, they did recommend "that all these Indian's reservations ... be patented to the several bands occupying them [and] the United States to hold the patent in trust for the period of twenty-five years ... as has been done for the Omaha Indians." Reflecting Jackson's gradualist views on allotment the report concluded, "Some of them are fit for it now, and earnestly desire it, but the majority are not ready for it. The communal system ... satisfies them."[20]

After submitting the report to Commissioner Price, Jackson launched a concerted effort to help marshal a bill enshrining the study's main findings through Congress. In a November 6, 1883, letter to Price, Jackson inquired about publishing the report in pamphlet form and thanked him for offering free copies. Jackson noted that she could place two hundred, "so that every copy will tell," and "that at least fifty will receive especial notice in the press." Jackson's efforts were not immediately successful; the Mission Indian bill failed to pass. But Jackson continued to campaign for the bill until her death in 1885. The Mission Indian bill finally became law in 1891.[21]

FROM THE POLITICS OF INDIAN HISTORY TO THE POLITICS OF HISTORICAL FICTION

The personal calamities surrounding Helen Hunt Jackson during her first three decades provoked her life-long fear of physical overexertion, especially of the brain. A number of Jackson's publications noted dire consequences resulting from physical and mental exhaustion. Addressing various topics, including the domestic realm and travel, five of Jackson's major works written between 1876 and 1885 referenced mental deterioration caused by fatigue and sudden environmental change. *Mercy Philbrick's Choice, Hetty's Strange History, Bits of Travel at Home, Bits of Talk about Home Matters,* and *Zeph* each linked physical overexertion to mental decay—especially in women and children.[22]

Jackson's fears about fatigue and brain degeneration informed her views on assimilation, as attested by her *Century* magazine articles, "Father Junipero and His Work," and "The Present Condition of the Mission Indians in Southern California." After Jackson's death, both articles were reprinted together as a brief book titled, *Father Junipero Serra and the Mission Indians of California.* The *Century* articles reveal that Jackson admired the gradual but determined assimilation program of early Spanish Catholic missions, which she pegged as the mechanism of Spanish imperial expansion fifteen years before historian Herbert Eugene Bolton's treatise, "The Spanish Mission as a Frontier Institution." Idealizing what she considered to be early Spanish efforts to gradually ease West Coast American Indians into a European-style agricultural economy, the *Century* articles painted a romantic image of Spanish and American Indian collectivism.[23]

Jackson's quixotic vision of Spanish colonialism depicted the Catholic Church as a moral organ of civilization pursuing a centuries-long benevolent venture in Indian assimilation. However, she felt this effort was ruined when political authorities eventually "set ten years" as sufficient time to assimilate the Indians and secularize the missions. Sending an admonishment to American coercive assimilationists, Jackson warned that greed destroyed Spanish California and Mexican California, and delivered the region and its Indians to the United States. American greed, she warned, might yet deliver California to new owners.[24]

Together, these sources shed light on the formation of Jackson's assimilationist ideology and her fear that Indians were being forced to embrace European American culture too quickly. Following the disappointing failure of the California Mission Indians legislation, Jackson began work on what would be her final publication. Wanting to "write a story that would do for the Indian . . . what *Uncle Tom's Cabin* did for the Negro," Jackson found inspiration in the story of a homicide she heard about while among the Cahuilla Indians of southern California. The murder case involved two Cahuilla Indians—Ramona Lubo and her husband Juan Diego—and a European American man, Sam Temple, the teamster who killed Juan. Built around a fictionalized account of the case, Jackson's novel *Ramona* compared Spanish and Mexican assimilation methods to European American assimilation efforts.[25]

Ramona is set in the aftermath of the Mexican-American War, during early California statehood. The novel's main character, Ramona, is a "mixed-blood" Mission Indian (European American–Indian). After the death of Ramona's foster mother, Senora Ortegna, Ramona is raised by Ortegna's sister, wealthy Spanish-Mexican sheep rancher Senora Moreno. Moreno raises Ramona as her daughter and as a sister to her own son, Felipe. Although Moreno equally despised Indians and the new American overlords, she raised Ramona as a valued member of her family. During the annual sheepshearing conducted by a band of local hired Indians, Ramona fell in love with Alessandro, the band leader's son.

Against Moreno's wishes Ramona and Alessandro eloped. Thus began their long journey across southern California in search of a permanent home. Driven from a series of homesteads by American colonial settlers, the couple moved with their young daughter to a cabin in the San Bernardino Mountains. Discombobulated by the constant turmoil of harried relocation and the grinding prejudice of European American settlers, Alessandro began a slow descent into insanity. Blaming himself for believing a "full-blood" Indian could successfully assimilate into European American society, Alessandro was dealt a final blow when his daughter, "Eyes of the Sky," suddenly died because the local European American doctor could not be compelled to treat her.[26]

Ramona soon bore another daughter, but Alessandro was already in the grip of madness. Overwhelmed by sorrow and delirium, Alessandro walked to a nearby community where he rustled Jim Farrar's horse and rode it home. Farrar, an American colonial settler tracked Alessandro to his mountain cabin where he angrily shot him in front of Ramona. Following a rigged trial that set Farrar free, Ramona returned to live with Moreno and Felipe. In a bid to escape the prejudice of European American settlers, the three moved to Mexico. Once south of the border Felipe revealed his love for Ramona and the two soon married. Felipe and Ramona had many children of their own, but Jackson noted, "The most beautiful of them all, and it was said the most beloved . . . was the eldest: The one who bore the mother's name . . . Ramona, daughter of Alessandro the Indian."[27]

In *Ramona* Jackson dramatically portrayed her fear of rapid assimilation and its dire effect on American Indians. Ramona, a "mixed-blood" Indian, was raised from childhood in a Spanish-Mexican family and readily assimilated. In contrast Alessandro, a "full-blood" adult Indian, was excluded from United States citizenship, subjected to constant discrimination by European

American settlers, and was ultimately unable to assimilate into American society. Alessandro's fate paralleled the numerous stories of injustice recorded in *A Century of Dishonor*—he was effectively barred from political, social, and economic participation in American life. The final chapter of *Ramona* presented a clear indictment of U.S. Indian policy in California. Only by moving to Mexico's more congenial and accepting Catholic culture did Senor Moreno, Felipe Moreno, Ramona Moreno, and their children find peace.[28]

Although *Ramona* did not ignite an American passion for Indian rights, as Jackson had hoped, it did inspired a unique travel culture in southern California. Ramona Lubo, one of many Cahuilla Indians purported to have been the basis for Jackson's *Ramona*, gained a notable following among European American collectors of Indian baskets, crafters who wove Indian-style baskets, and women assimilationists. Lubo's Ramona's Star basket pattern—depicting the heavenly abode of her departed husband, Juan Diego—came to symbolize the brutality of American westward expansion. Jackson would live only one more year following publication of *Ramona* in 1884. On August 12, 1885, in a morphine-induced delirium, Helen Hunt Jackson succumbed to cancer of the stomach.[29]

Jackson's 1881 presentation of Indian history was a pathbreaking venture. No previous scholar had published a comprehensive study of Indian treaties based on documentary sources. Though dealt a devastating blow by Theodore Roosevelt's facile critique, *A Century of Dishonor* did not completely disappear from academic discourse. In addition to sporadic scholarly citation since 1881, *A Century of Dishonor* was reprinted by Harper and Row in 1965 with a preface by noted American West historian Andrew Rolle. The University of Oklahoma Press issued a critically acclaimed reprint in 1995, prefaced with a lengthy introduction by Jackson scholar Valerie Sherer Mathes. Scholarly analysis of *A Century of Dishonor* continues to the present.[30]

Jackson died before seeing the full effect of her Indian activism or the popular success of her historical fiction *Ramona*, but during her lifetime, *A Century of Dishonor* bestowed a measured degree of political influence. While belittled by Jackson's critics, the publication galvanized her allies and cultivated an aura of expertise around her that culminated in an official appointment. Though Helen Hunt Jackson and Alice Fletcher came to write document-driven Indian treaty histories by different avenues, both took up the format in a bid to elevate their positions among the American public, Indian activists, and political allies. Where moral sentiment alone failed to advance Jackson's Indian activism, Fletcher's personal ethnological observations eventually proved insufficient as well.

At crucial junctures in their Indian activism, both Jackson and Fletcher enhanced their roles as Indian experts by appealing to the objective authority of public documents. As legal instruments, government reports, official records, and archived documents were deemed legitimate chronicles of political history. As documentation of male political acts, archived documents were also considered trustworthy. By citing archived documents, Jackson and Fletcher anointed their treaty histories with intellectual authenticity. Ultimately the success of Indian reform legislation made this kind of preprofessional history obsolete, but for a season it proved an effective political tool. Foreshadowing both the demise of women's preprofessional ethnopolitical scholarship and the rise of women's professional Indian history, Fletcher's document-driven monograph had the distinction of signaling both the twilight of one era and the dawning of another.

CHAPTER 5

ALICE FLETCHER AND THE SCHOLARSHIP OF AMERICAN INDIAN POLITICS

On a cold, blustery September evening in 1881, Alice Fletcher and her traveling companions took refuge in a country boarding house just outside Florence, Nebraska. Chilled, shivering from a long wagon ride in the freezing rain, Fletcher and company gathered around a heating stove and began to make small talk with their host, Mrs. Smith. Curious, Smith asked Fletcher, "What do you do?" Fletcher's brief reply prompted Smith to quiz, "What is Ethnology?" Fletcher tried to explain, but found she "couldn't do it."[1]

As a budding preprofessional ethnologist and anthropologist, Fletcher was on the first leg of her 1881–82 field expedition to the Omaha Reservation and still quite green. During a hard winter and dreary spring, Fletcher took copious notes and conducted hundreds of interviews that helped her develop a succinct ethnological philosophy. Shunning the sweeping racial studies of Morgan, Powell, and Brinton, Fletcher focused on American Indian social life and political history. Over the next two decades Fletcher would perfect the political application of her Indian scholarship. A curious irony of Fletcher's ethno-political career was that it led her to write a trailblazing, document-driven pan-Indian history.

DISCOVERING "HER MAJESTY'S" ETHNOLOGICAL EMPIRE

The story of how Alice Fletcher created an ethnological empire and commodified American Indians is not easily told. It is a troubling tale marked by moral contradictions and heartbreaking ethical failures. By all accounts Fletcher was a pleasant, mild mannered, jovial woman noted for debilitating

Alice Fletcher at her writing desk. Alice Fletcher, a noted preprofessional anthropologist and ethnologist, helped identify American Indian scholarship with women activists and scholars in the popular mind. Courtesy of the National Anthropological Archives, Smithsonian Institution (4510).

bouts with arthritis and a striking resemblance to Queen Victoria. As a friend and colleague Fletcher was widely known to be kind, thoughtful, and loyal. As a scholar she coauthored several important works on Indian culture and a comprehensive study of the Omaha tribe that remains a respected standard among anthropologists. As an assimilationist she was widely heralded by European Americans and a small, devoted cadre of American Indians as a benevolent and well-intentioned advocate. Yet paradoxically, she also holds the infamous distinction of having done more to destroy American Indian cultures than any single figure in North American history.[2]

In large part, Fletcher's political and scholarly interests determined this course. Reflecting three closely related policies advanced by the Indian Treaty-Keeping and Protective Association and the Bureau of Ethnology, Fletcher's work would embrace social and cultural assimilation, land allotment in severalty, and compulsory Indian education. Unfortunately for both Fletcher and her victims, this radically uncompromising route to ethnological notoriety was built on the pain and suffering of fellow human beings. Fletcher would not comprehend the degree of misery she caused until almost a full decade after her first allotment venture in 1883. A close analysis of Fletcher's emerging scholarship while camping among the Oglala Lakotas and Omahas in 1881–82 reveals the political trajectory that would indelibly shape her career.[3]

Alice Fletcher's first tentative steps toward establishing her credentials as an Indian scholar, assimilationist leader, and federally sanctioned ethnologist were taken during her 1881 Nebraska and South Dakota tour. Inspired by an 1879 encounter with Standing Bear, Susette La Flesche, and Francis La Flesche—Ponca and Omaha Indians who were on a speaking tour in the East protesting Ponca removal and federal land policies effecting the Omahas—Fletcher decided to augment her budding ethnological credentials with an informal scientific expedition among the Oglala Lakota and Omaha Indians. To date no evidence has been found that indicates women Indian activists had prior knowledge of Fletcher's trip. However, while still on the expedition both Alice Fletcher and Susette La Flesche forwarded papers addressing Indian social customs to the annual meeting of the Association for the Advancement of Women (AAW) in Buffalo, New York. Since Fletcher and La Flesche were not present, their papers were read by two women in attendance. Afterward, Amelia S. Quinton gave a short presentation detailing activities of the Indian Treaty-Keeping and Protective Association.[4]

As a member of the AAW board of directors and chair of its topics and papers committee in 1880 and 1881 respectively, Fletcher had interacted with Amelia Quinton prior to her 1881 AAW presentation, though to what degree and in what manner is not known. Though tenuous, Fletcher did have a connection with Quinton, and presumably with other women Indian activists, around the time she left for her Omaha fieldwork. These interactions, though preliminary, suggest that Fletcher did not blindly venture west and happen upon American Indians who she could represent as political commodities, rather she journeyed there to find them.[5]

By the second week of September 1881 Fletcher was already in Nebraska. Between mid-September and early October she was introduced to various Oglala Lakota, Omaha, and Ponca tribal members by Thomas Henry Tibbles, a mercurial journalist who had taken up the Ponca and Omaha cause; Susette La Flesche Tibbles, daughter of former Omaha chief Joseph La Flesche; and Ezra Freemont, an Omaha associate of Joseph La Flesche. Meticulously chronicling her observations in a diary and field notebook, Fletcher followed a carefully laid plan to insure that her western scientific effort would not be dismissed as mere travel writing or sentimental musings. Two months before her trip, Fletcher had implored John Wesley Powell of the Bureau of Ethnology to "send [her] a copy of the instructions issued by the Smithsonian Inst. for the study of Indian Peoples." Having met Powell the previous year (1880) in Boston, Fletcher wrote, "You will hardly recollect me . . . I told you that I hoped to undertake this work and you generously offered to aid me."[6]

Pitching her project as a unique study of Indian women and their habits, Fletcher noted, "I trust that being a woman I may be able to observe & record facts & conditions that are unknown or obscure owing to the separation of the male & female life." Although the calculated rhetoric was one that Fletcher would later deploy when seeking funds or support from the Bureau of Ethnology and her East Coast network of women's rights proponents, her Indian scholarship did not focus on Indian women. To demonstrate the depth of her ethnological interests Fletcher also enclosed for Powell a pamphlet, outlining her 1879 lecture series on ancient American peoples. Fletcher concluded with a deliberate missive, "I shall be at the Scientific Ass. on Monday and Tuesday & hope to [meet] you personally."[7]

Almost three months into the trip Fletcher had not received a reply from Powell, who was no doubt concerned that her request for ethnological aid might eventually include a request for funds—a suspicion that would prove correct. Clearly disappointed, Fletcher chided Powell, "Sir: It was quite a disappointment not to receive the promised letter indicating points you would think it well for me to particularly observe in Indian home life." Expecting Powell to follow Putnam's correspondence approach to ethnological instruction, Fletcher found his inattention exasperating, if not dismissive. Casually noting letters of recommendation from Colonel Garrick Mallery and Frederic Ward Putnam, Fletcher felt confident in explicitly pressing her earlier financial hint, "Will you please give me any assistance that you can in this work?" Again Powell did not reply, so Fletcher was forced to proceed hoping that her careful overtures to Powell would bear fruit. Left to her own devices, Fletcher freely melded her political interests with her developing ethnological methodology.[8]

Between September 17 and October 30, 1881, the Tibbles-Fletcher party visited the Omaha Reservation, Winnebago Reservation, Santee Sioux Mission complex, and Rosebud Agency—traversing several hundred miles in cold, rainy weather. Frayed camping equipment and well-worn wagons added further discomfort.[9] But the equipment and transportation were not the only things falling apart. Relations were deteriorating between Fletcher and the self-appointed Indian expert Thomas Tibbles.[10] By the time they reached the Winnebago Reservation and the Santee Sioux Agency, Tibbles, a peevish and occasionally vulgar man, provoked unpleasant exchanges with Fletcher. Emblematic of Tibbles's growing animosity was his decision to belittle Fletcher with the nickname, "Highflyer." Tibbles's slur was a tacky translation of "Ma-she-ha-the" (Sweep-of-an-eagle's-wing), an Omaha name bestowed on Fletcher by Wajapa, also known as Ezra Freemont, who served as her guide. As relations worsened between Fletcher and Tibbles, he abruptly ended Susette La Flesche's unofficial role as Fletcher's translator. Driven by petty jealousy, Tibbles's action effectively derailed Fletcher's ethnological inquiry among the Oglala Lakotas. In response, Fletcher considered parting company. Fletcher decided she would return to the Omaha Reservation with Ezra Freemont as her guide—not that their relationship was ideal.[11]

A member of the Omaha Citizen's Party village (Win-dja'-ge), Freemont began to accommodate European American culture in the early 1870s by working as an agency policeman and carpenter. In 1881 the forty-year-old Freemont, rechristened Wajapa by Fletcher, claimed one hundred and sixty acres, of which approximately fifty were in production, including hay. Fletcher's records show that in the spring of that year Wajapa planted twenty-five acres in wheat, fifteen in corn, and a nine-acre garden boasting potatoes, onions, cabbage, tomatoes, beans, squash, beets, cucumbers, and muskmelon. In addition, Wajapa and his wife owned three cows, two pigs, twenty-two chickens, four turkeys, and two ducks, in which they took great pride. Although an advocate of accommodation, Wajapa also cherished the fact that his Ponca father had served as a band leader and his grandfather as a chief.[12]

In 1881, forty-three year old Alice Fletcher was of modest means, unemployed, unmarried, childless, essentially property-less, and homeless. In Wajapa's eyes Fletcher seemed a person of low status both by European American and Omaha standards. Fletcher's tenuous position, reinforced by Tibbles's jealous sarcasm and her own assertive personality, eventually proved too much for Wajapa to accommodate. By mid-September Fletcher began to note Wajapa's increasing "moodiness."[13]

A cathartic climax came one stormy night when the arthritic (and occasionally crippled) Fletcher insisted that Wajapa place a waterproof canvas beneath the poles of the Plains Indian teepee the party planned to sleep in. Through long experience Plains Indians had discovered a simple way to prevent rain from traveling down teepee poles (which extended through the smoke vent) to the floor, where the drips made a sodden mess. This was accomplished by using thin sticks that extended from the outer edges of the fire pit up to the point where the teepee poles joined at the center of the smoke vent. These sticks effectively channeled rainwater into the fire where it evaporated. Wajapa, well aware that Fletcher's plan would guide streams of water to the floor considered her venture foolish and voiced his opposition. Fletcher in a fit of anger snapped, "You speak to us as if we were children."[14]

Having reached his breaking point, Wajapa spent the next two hours standing outside sulking in the pouring rain while a chastened Fletcher prepared for a miserable slumber on the muddied teepee floor. Later that night Wajapa slipped into the teepee, wrapped himself in a buffalo robe and fell asleep. The next day Fletcher, in danger of losing her prospective guide, engaged Wajapa in "games, cracking jokes and having a thoroughgoing jolly time."[15]

Fences mended with Wajapa, Fletcher laid plans with the Indian agent at Fort Randle to part company with Tibbles. Before leaving the garrison, Fletcher took time to relax, read, and cultivate important social and political connections. During her respite Fletcher studied Lieutenant Thomas M. Woodruff's essay, "Our Indian Question." Addressing many of Fletcher's concerns since embarking on the journey, Woodruff's proposals struck a chord and helped Fletcher coalesce a host of amorphous ideas into a political agenda that would guide her American Indian scholarship for the next three decades.[16]

Overwhelmed and occasionally frightened by close contact with the "heathen" and "different race" she encountered during the sojourn, Fletcher found Woodruff's essay particularly illuminating. An ardent assimilationist, Woodruff proposed separating U.S. Indian policy into three categories. The first involved "wild" nomadic Indians who were to be placed under military oversight and forced into cattle ranching. Next, the "idle and dependent agency Indians" would be forced into farming. Finally, "civilized Indians" under government tutelage, were to be given U.S. citizenship, land in severalty, and placed under local and state law. For Fletcher, Woodruff made attractive distinctions that clearly moved her political and scholarly path away from "wild Indians" and steered her toward "civilized Indians," such as Susette and Wajapa.[17]

Paralleling the Indian Treaty-Keeping and Protective Association's emerging political agenda, Woodruff's essay also emphasized flexibility in Indian treaty compliance, an accelerated push toward allotment, and compulsory Indian education. As one of three award-winning essays in a national competition considering "Our Indian Question," Woodruff's article promised broad appeal. Given Fletcher's high praise for Woodruff's work, it is not surprising that a blueprint for Indian ethno-political scholarship was already forming in her mind.[18]

At the end of October Fletcher, finally freed of Thomas Tibbles's spiteful interference, and Wajapa made their way back to the Omaha Reservation. There Fletcher found the Omahas well into the third decade of reservation life and divided into an uneasy confederation of three villages. Bi-ku-de, the agency village, was dominated by traditionalist ranchers who resisted assimilation. Jan-(th)ca'-te was considered a moderate village whose members harvested nearby trees for lumber and kindling. Win-dja'ge, the progressive Presbyterian mission village, embraced land allotment and agriculture.[19]

At Win-dja'-ge, Fletcher found perfect ethno-political subjects—Joseph La Flesche, Wajapa, and the resident Citizen's Party members. With many of the villagers already living in wood frame or log homes situated on farms allotted in 1871, the Win-dja'-ge Omahas seemed ideal candidates for Fletcher to

An Omaha Indian informant with Alice C. Fletcher in Macy, Nebraska. While much of Fletcher's work merged her assimilationist politics with anthropological fieldwork, her massive 1888 *Indian Education and Civilization* report was meticulously researched and documented. Courtesy of the National Anthropological Archives, Smithsonian Institution (4500).

study and push toward final assimilation. Derisively called the "Make-Believe-White-Men village" by other Omahas, Win-dja'-ge became the focus of Fletcher's interests for the remainder of 1881.[20]

In her pioneering biography of Alice Fletcher, Joan Mark addressed Fletcher's ethnological and political interaction with the Omahas by consulting Fletcher's well-known 1881 "Camping with the Sioux" manuscript, her personal correspondence, and Fletcher and Francis La Flesche's 1911 publication, *The Omaha Tribe*. Other scholars, such as Omaha historian Mark J. Awakuni-Swetland, followed suit using related material for informative analysis of Omaha political, social, and cultural agency. No scholarship exists linking the intellectual, scholarly, and political nexus shared by Fletcher, Helen Hunt Jackson, and other American assimilationists associated with the ITKPA. It was precisely this union of politics and scholarship that made Fletcher and Jackson's work so provocative and consequently of public interest. Other detailed Indian ethnological scholarship, such as that by Bureau of Ethnology linguist James Owen Dorsey, did not garner a comparable degree of public attention. Analysis of Fletcher's long-ignored 1881 "Omaha

Allotment Field Notebook" (OAFN) helps fill these historical gaps by illuminating a previously hidden scholarly blueprint that reflected Jackson and Fletcher's concerns and those of their associates.[21]

Composed during the last two months of her western tour, the November to December 1881 OAFN chronicles information about Win-dja'-ge village and its people, including maternal and paternal lines of descent, tribal affiliation (Omaha and Ponca), social and cultural data, 1871 allotments, and Omaha pleas for valid land titles. Comprising three hundred and ninety-one unnumbered faded pages, the notebook records a unique moment in Plains Indian allotment history. More so, the OAFN reveals the evolution of Fletcher's political determination to press Congress for a general Omaha allotment act and, subsequently, the authority to sever Omaha cultural and family ties.

The Omaha Reservation in present-day Nebraska was created by treaty between the Omaha tribe and the United States government in 1854. Among various provisions, including land cessions, the treaty also called for allotment in severalty. Article six of the treaty stated, "The President may, from time to time, at his discretion, cause the whole or such portion of the land hereby reserved . . . to be surveyed into lots." Aside from the fenced farms associated with Win-dja'-ge village and limited plot cultivation at the remaining villages, no reservation land was allotted by the federal government in the decade following the 1854 treaty.[22]

As part of negotiations for the cession of Omaha land to the Winnebago tribe in 1865, a delegation, dominated by Win-dja-ge leaders and progressive chiefs called for a general survey and allotment of Omaha lands. Following concerted efforts by Win-dja'-ge leaders and Omaha agent Edward Painter, survey work was finally completed in 1867. At that time Painter tried to compel all the Omahas to take land in severalty by restricting their government provisions, but that tactic failed. The initial allotment process ended in 1872, with approximately two-hundred Omahas, a minority, taking land in severalty. Alice Fletcher's reapportionment of the earlier 1871–72 allotments and the final compulsory allotment would cause enduring enmity. Many of the Omahas were dissatisfied with the soil quality and location of their new allotments.[23]

The blast of Washington's fury against American Indians between 1870 and 1871 proved a watershed moment in federal Indian relations—especially for the Omahas. The 1870 Cherokee Tobacco case established Congress's right to administer Indian lands and alter or essentially abrogate treaties with Indian peoples. Subsequent legislation spurred by the High Court's decision officially ended the treaty-making process with American Indians. While Congress pledged to observe treaty provisions made before 1870, its actions effectively ended any pretense by the federal government to recognize Indian sovereignty. By 1871 the Omahas—and all American Indians—were almost solely at the mercy of Congress and those who could bend its ear.[24]

Adding misery to insult, federally sanctioned buffalo kills were decimating traditional Plains Indian economies. With the declining bison herd intertribal competition for the remaining buffaloes increased, often forcing Omaha hunting parties into armed conflict with other tribes. Unable to freely pursue buffalo hunting, all segments of Omaha society were pushed toward allotment and European American style agriculture. Yet for all the effort spent on destroying buffalo herds, funds to capitalize Indian farming ventures were not forthcoming. Congressional penny-pinching would stymie Omaha agricultural prospects for decades.[25]

A bittersweet sidebar emerged in 1874 when the Omaha's former beneficiaries, the Winnebagos, successfully lobbied Congress for an additional twelve-thousand acre land grant from the Omaha Reservation. In return Congress doled out eighty-two thousand dollars to the Omahas through the reservation agent. A small amount was spent on agency infrastructure, such as a new infirmary, but most of the money was never seen by the Omaha people. Meager payments aside, the 1874 "sale" brought to light a far more disturbing fact—the allotment documents given to Omahas between 1867 and 1871 where virtually worthless department of the Interior land certificates. No Omaha actually held legally binding title to their land allotment.[26]

The reservation was in turmoil. In the eyes of the law, Omahas from the ceded land were homeless, and ultimately forced to rely on the agent and tribal generosity. Moreover, the concurrent forced removal of the Omaha's sister tribe, the Poncas, to Indian Territory caused further anxiety. As if matters could not get worse, 1878–79 Missouri River flooding destroyed Win-dja'-ge village crops and prompted the removal of their saw and grist mills to agency headquarters.[27]

A definitive blow came in 1879, when the Omaha and Winnebago agencies were combined and the new agent moved his operations to the Winnebago Reservation. With no capital for agricultural work, valueless land certificates, limited access to the government agent, and fearing forced removal to Indian Territory, by 1881 many Omahas felt the dissolution of their reservation was imminent. This tragic spate of events weighed heavily on Wajapa during Fletcher's 1881 expedition. Depicted in her diary as sulky and plodding, Wajapa was not the simple minded "savage" described by Fletcher. Wajapa's moodiness no doubt reflected both the grave situation back home and his own efforts to sort out those who would be loyal and effective European American advocates for the Omaha tribe.[28]

An 1882 newspaper story titled, "A Boston Girl Joins an Indian Tribe to Learn Their Traditions," bears further witness to how this desperate situation affected Fletcher and Wajapa between November 1881 and February 1882. The article noted that Indian agent George W. Wilkinson, "on taking charge" of the Omaha and Winnebago reservation, had found "Miss A. C. Fletcher . . . with them and nearly starved." Fletcher did not reveal this information to her East Coast friends, nor did her communications with them appeal for much-needed humanitarian relief. During her sojourn among the Omahas, Fletcher's solicitations were limited to assimilation policy, such as her November 12, 1881, missive to the War Department requesting help in securing education for "the children of Sitting Bull's band in Bishop Ware's Mission schools." Fletcher's concern rarely stepped beyond the magic circle of allotment and compulsory education.[29]

Alice Fletcher had witnessed assimilation pedagogy at the Santee Manual Training School—arithmetic, multiplication, subtraction, poetry recitation, English—and it made a lasting impression. A cause dear to racial evolutionists, European American education was believed to transform the brain, stimulating lucid "civilized" thought. Fletcher would advance compulsory Indian education and its civilizing properties for almost three decades.[30]

No daily record exists of Fletcher's November to February stay at the Omaha Reservation, but her 1881 "Omaha Allotment Field Notebook" gives a good impression of the ethnological and political issues that occupied her mind. A ragged note pasted inside the front cover listed seven questions that shaped her work: "Who were the originators of the Citizen's Party? How organized? What started it? When did they ask for titles? Who did they ask? Do they ever meet? What do they plan?" The remainder of the note gave a rough list of Omaha Citizen's Party members who considered themselves the most progressive. Win-dja'-ge residents were already establishing a pecking order for their interactions with Fletcher. From the beginning, Fletcher's Indian commodification would be bifurcated, a venture in which her vision would be tested against that of the Win-dja'-ge community.[31]

The first thirty pages of Fletcher's OAFN record a series of Omaha stories demonstrating close kinship bonds, extraordinary loyalty to white men and a fierce devotion to European American culture. Two of the records are particularly striking, revealing the politics behind what the speakers wished to convey and what Fletcher wished to hear. In a vignette titled "Dora's father" Fletcher hastily noted:

> Dora . . . worked at mission. Dora's father was taking a woman [and] her children home a blizzard came up—children & woman suffering . . . dug a hole

took off his clothes made them comfortable . . . went away for help. After severe struggles located a lodge—his feet [and] hands frozen solid. The women and children escaped [death][32]

In the second story the Omaha speaker related:

An Omaha Indian was fighting during the war [,] was with an officer. Officer wounded—Indian caught the officer laid him beside a dead horse flayed the skin laid it over the officer and then defended the officer single handed—after wards carried him miles to a fort to safety. Much afterward Indian came to the fort—officer saw him & thanked him[33]

Each story indicted the speaker was aware that his or her words would be repeated to a broader audience. Given that Fletcher was associated with Thomas Tibbles and that BE ethnologist Thomas Dorsey had worked among the Omahas for two years before her arrival, it would be hard to imagine the Omahas thought otherwise. Fearing that a failure to secure land titles might lead to land loss and removal to Indian Territory, the Omahas told stories that were clearly composed for East Coast, if not congressional ears. To this end Omaha representatives took great pains to emphasize their loyalty to the United States and their desire for valid land titles.

The narrative of Fletcher's OAFN revealed both the Win-dja'-ge village political structure and the immediate concerns of the Omaha Citizen's Party. Susette and Francis La Flesche's father, former Omaha chief Joseph La Flesche, was the most prominent Win-dja'-ge leader. The "civilized" qualities of Joseph La Flesche's French father and the loyalty of his Ponca-Omaha mother were noted in Chief Joseph's OAFN narrative: "Susette's grandmother [Chief Joseph's mother] took her husband on her back & carried him several miles to where he could have white surgeon care & get well. Husband wounded by a Sioux."[34]

Notations that followed indicated a close relationship between the Omaha and Ponca tribes. Other short ethnographic stories in this section related Omaha marriage traditions and sexual mores. On page thirty-four of the OAFN Fletcher suddenly turned from cultural inquiry and began a demographic and property tabulation that would fill the remaining three hundred and fifty-seven sheets. Tersely she noted, "Louis Saunsoci no. 254 N.E. 1/4 of Section 25 of township 25 north of 9—160 acres Interpreter 1843 to 1878—sight lost since interpreter." Saunsoci would prove to be one of four mixed-blood Omahas to provide Fletcher with information. Out of the remaining fifty-three Omahas Fletcher interviewed, ten were original members of the Win-dja'-ge village noted in an 1855 census, ten were relatives of original Win-dja'-ge villagers, and seven comprised the tribal police force. In all forty-six of the men recorded in OAFN were full-blood Omaha-Ponca, four were half French, one was a fourth French, one white, and one undisclosed. The small number of subjects recorded in OAFN reflected temporary migrations caused by 1881–82 crop failures. Several hundred Omaha families left the reservation that winter to hunt small game, while a small contingent was left to guard homes and equipment.[35]

Motives for providing Fletcher with information varied between mixed-blood English speakers and full-blood Omaha speakers. Mixed-blood Omahas were much less concerned about U.S. citizenship and acculturation, succinctly focusing on land titles. Full-blood Omahas spoke at length about their love for democracy, law, United States citizenship—and of course land titles. Louis Saunsoci, listed as half French simply stated, "I want a title to my farm." William Provost, also half French tersely stated, "I want to get a title to my lands." In contrast, To-oh-ka-hah (Arthur Ramsey), a full-blood Omaha made an elaborate statement noting, "I belong to the citizen's party . . . I was one of its originators." Ramsey continued, "We want to become citizens. . . . We wish to have laws like the white men, to have courts to appeal to, and to have good titles to our lands." Referencing hard times, Ramsey added a plea for help, "This year we have made nothing, our crops were so poor."[36]

Wajapa, Fletcher's full-blood Omaha guide demeaned his life before accommodation, "Before I began to farm I was just a wild Indian, doing as I pleased, going round the country looking for death." Yet all was not well, Wajapa noted, "We have no government on the reserve. . . . We have trouble all the time, which we would not have if we had government and law. . . . We want these." Notably, Wajapa worried about the legal security of Omaha lands, "There are persons living on the reserve who have certificates of allotment; they believe that the land is theirs, and that they can always keep it . . . I know differently." Referring to the 1871–72 Interior department allotment paperwork, Wajapa emphatically stated, "I know that the certificates are not good . . . I want a title to my land, then the land will be mine." Issuing a warning to Fletcher and her superiors, Wajapa added, "We are going to ask for our titles. . . . As long as the government does not give them, we will ask until the government gets tired." Wajapa reiterated, "We won't stop asking till we get our titles."[37]

Another full-blood Omaha, Joseph Merrick, mirrored Wajapa's concerns lamenting, "I went on my farm with my certificate . . . [and] soon lost faith in it for the people told me it was good for nothing." Appealing to a power higher than Fletcher, Merrick pleaded, "I hope God will help us get [real] titles." Merrick concluded, "I belong to the party that wishes to become like white people . . . and to be citizens."[38]

Full-blood Omaha-Ponca participants consistently addressed two concerns. First, they did not want to be forced off their reservation to Indian Territory—this made the issue of legal land titles paramount. Second, they argued that if they did not have unencumbered rights as citizens, then the fruits of their labor would be appropriated by settler colonists. For Fletcher's subjects clear land titles were not the problem, but rather the solution. Little did they know allotment would come on Fletcher's terms.

What is most striking about Fletcher's OAFN is its union of the personal and the political, the historical and the legal. Fletcher's elaboration of Indian culture and her machinations for assimilation were not diffused into the sweeping arcs of universal race patterns, but rather remained grounded in meticulously recorded demographic and property data. In carefully detailed notes Fletcher monotonously chronicled maternal and paternal lines of descent, blood quantum, tribal affiliation, reservation residence, treaty terms, land use, allotments, agricultural production, and domestic and farm inventories for the households of fifty-three Omaha men.[39]

Fletcher's detailed Indian ethno-political work was unique for the period, revealing Omaha anxieties about the security of their 1871 allotments. More so, the OAFN revealed Fletcher's intention to reshape the very heart and soul of Omaha tribal life by restructuring land use and the manner in which Omaha families lived, loved, and learned. Little did the Omahas realize in the winter of 1881 that "the woman who came from the east," would compel them to take English names, assign unalterable tribal affiliation, re-survey and forcibly allot reservation land, and whisk their children and young married couples hundreds of miles away to boarding schools. But then, there is no record of Fletcher ever sharing the OAFN with her Omaha subjects.[40]

While the progressive and moderate Omahas hoped Fletcher would prove a loyal champion and that their narratives would foster peace and security, they were unaware that she was already setting plans in motion that would change their lives forever. In fact, on Fletcher's first day at the Omaha Reservation she had penned a dramatic and revealing appeal to an eastern ally. Addressed to "My dear Mrs. Clapp," a Washington socialite, staunch New York abolitionist, and wife of former Government Printing Office chief Almon M. Clapp, the letter demonstrated Fletcher's connection to a broad range of socially and politically active Washington women interested in the Indian assimilation cause.[41]

Fletcher's missive couched her interests in the rhetoric of maternal patriotism, "Here I am far away in miles and farther still in circumstances. . . . My study of the life, conditions and mode of thought of Indian women is full of interest and instruction." Reiterating the difficulties of her venture she noted, "It was needful that I should do this in order to accomplish my scientific work." A plea for monetary support was accompanied by a request that Mrs. Clapp have the letter "read in the churches—or read & published in a paper." Fletcher sanctimoniously added, "Only let it do the work if so God wills." Like her Omaha subjects, Fletcher was composing stories to be retold back East. In closing, Fletcher asked Mrs. Clapp to "Give my love to Mr. Clapp and all our friends."[42]

By the end of December, Fletcher demonstrated the full range of her political repertoire with a pleading epistle to an unlikely ally. Dated December 31, 1881, Fletcher's letter to the staunch segregationist and state's rights proponent, Alabama senator John Tyler Morgan was void of the cloying narrative typical of her letters to women friends and acquaintances. Matter of fact, Fletcher informed Senator Morgan, "Today I mail a package registered to your address. . . . It is the petition of 53 Omaha Indians asking that titles be given them to the land on which they have worked and practically homesteaded." Justifying her political agenda she offered, "Scientific study connected with the home life of the Indians brought me here . . . the living cry of those with whom I found myself so claimed my ear and heart—that I feel I must do something to help.[43]

Excusing her informality by claiming she "never drew up or designed a petition" and was "not versed in official language," Fletcher asked Senator Morgan to take pity and present the petition to Congress. Fletcher continued, "Justice passes beyond the fateful line which isolates this reserve from the blessings of civilization and with the early morn of the new year winds its way across the continent to the Senate chamber." There, Fletcher hoped, "the Father of all mankind be with you as you voice this cry."[44]

On January 11, 1882, Senator Morgan—second ranking member of the Senate Indian Affairs committee—presented the *Memorial of the Members of the Omaha Tribe of Indians for a Grant of Land in Severalty*. Over the next month the petition languished in Congress, meanwhile Fletcher continued to cultivate political allies. A February 4, 1882, letter to Senator Henry L. Dawes—chairman of the Senate Indian Affairs committee—and a February 8, 1882, letter to Interior secretary Samuel J. Kirkwood included core ideas, phrases, and terms from Fletcher's letter to Morgan indicating a broad strategy. The end of February saw Fletcher's departure for Washington, where she engaged in a whirlwind campaign to secure legislation for Omaha allotment.[45]

Fletcher's activities following her arrival in Washington bear witness to both the lateral influence of the Washington women's rights movement and Fletcher's keen ability to bend the machinery of government to her own desires. Passage of the Omaha Allotment Act (OAA) in early August 1882 proved a coup for Fletcher and demonstrated the newfound political muscle of maternal patriotism. Herbert Welsh's Indian Rights Association was not constituted until December 1882, a fact that underscores the political power of women assimilationists.[46]

Fletcher would claim years later, "I heard nothing of that little petition in which the Omahas asked to have their houses secured to them," and likewise that she received no help in furthering the 1882 Omaha Allotment Act—neither was true. On February 4, 1882, Fletcher received a reply to her December 31, 1881, letter to Morgan. The senator noted he was sending her a copy of the petition as published in the Congressional Record with marginal "remarks of Mr. [Senator] Dawes . . . which are appreciative, and very favorable." Morgan added, "He [Dawes] is the chairman of the committee on Indian Affairs in the Senate." Concluding with sentiment, Morgan sanctioned Fletcher's quest, "I know no higher public duty of men and women than to aid these people to see the 'light that shineth in the darkness.' . . . Yours to command, Jno. T. Morgan." Fletcher had pierced the inner sanctum of United States Indian policy.[47]

After receiving Senator Morgan's letter, Fletcher penned replies to Morgan and Dawes pleading for Omaha allotment. Fletcher justified her actions, contending that the Omahas wanted legally binding titles and had no other advocate. Fletcher's general thrust indicated that sale of Omaha land without provision of valid titles for existing Omaha allotments would lead to the reservation's wholesale liquidation and transform the Omaha Indians into a band of homeless paupers. Upon arrival in Washington, Fletcher immediately began assembling a political coalition composed of congressional wives, leading members of the Association for the Advancement of Women (AAW), and the Women's National Indian Association (WNIA)—formerly ITKPA. Letters from the wives of key senate Indian Affairs committee members demonstrate that Fletcher was not only discussing Omaha allotment privately, but was also using her Omaha Allotment Field Notebook to craft public lectures for organizational meetings. Sarah Ann Davis Crapo, wife of Senator William Wallace Crapo, and Laura Sunderland, a popular Washington social activist, arranged for Fletcher to speak before leading AAW and WNIA women on the Omaha allotment bill.[48]

By mid-spring 1882 a cohort of Washington women had mobilized behind Fletcher's cause. They were led by Senator Henry Dawes's wife, Electra Sanderson Dawes. On April 24, 1882, Electra Dawes invited Fletcher on a joint mission to solicit support from Hiram Price, commissioner of Indian Affairs, and Interior secretary Henry M. Teller. Within a month Fletcher received another invitation via the prestigious Mount Vernon Seminary for Women in

Washington, D.C., to meet with "Mr. and Mrs T——r" (most likely the Tellers) and discuss "Indian affairs." On May 16, 1882, Anna Laurens Dawes, Senator Dawes's daughter, forwarded a letter from Dr. Emily Talbot of Boston inviting Fletcher to speak before the American Social Science Association on the matter of Indian "schools, land, homes, anything which will tend to advance their *civilization*." Anna Dawes noted in her cover letter, "She [Emily Talbot] recently wrote asking father if it would be desirable to have a paper read before the coming meeting of the Social Sciences Ass -, on Indian education." Anna added, "You will be pleased to hear that Mrs. Teller thinks you are charming & have most sensible ideas. Let us hope she thinks all Indians are like you!"[49]

March brought unforeseen blessings for Fletcher and her ethno-political goals—at the temporary expense of Amelia Quinton and the Women's National Indian Association. In March 1882, *Cherokee Advocate* editor, Daniel H. Ross, launched a biting critique of Amelia Quinton, the WNIA, and their drive for Indian assimilation and allotment. Ross accused the WNIA of launching a political "movement" that had acquired such a profound hold "upon the public mind" that "it will never 'down' . . . until it has encompassed the Indians with all necessary safe guards, or smothered them to death in the exuberance of its misdirected friendship." Arguing that the WNIA lacked personal knowledge of Indian cultures, Ross warned that in their "zeal to be 'up and doing' there is some danger, indeed great danger of our friends doing some of us harm instead of good." Ross explained, "It is a mistaken idea to suppose that United States citizenship and the holding of land in severalty is the only panacea for all the ills to which we [Indians] are exposed." Reiterating his position Ross stated, "Making lands a chattel has never been popular among the Indians. . . . To these dear friends we would simply say handle us gently." Ross cautioned WNIA activists, "When disorganized and homeless, as some of the tribes are in some of the Territories, give them . . . permanent homes as far removed as possible from the cupidity of your own people."[50]

Quinton made a comprehensive reply, but the blow had already been delivered. Arguing there were no more unencumbered western lands to guarantee Indian "remoteness," Quinton insisted that "voluntary" allotment was necessary. Her contention, however, rang hollow given Quinton also proclaimed that compulsory land in severalty was inevitable.[51]

Ultimately Quinton was not able to answer Ross's key criticism—that East Coast women who did not live among Indians lacked sufficient understanding to craft policies for wholesale Indian social and cultural change. Quinton and the WNIA's diminished luster thrust Fletcher—one of the few European American women scholars who could claim direct experience with Indian tribes—to the forefront of assimilation politics. In 1882 Fletcher truly became the queen of American assimilation.

Reflecting her elevated status among Washington assimilationists, the month of May brought Fletcher a flood of contributions and lecture engagements. Two such events were sponsored by Senator Joseph R. Hawley, a longtime American Indian assimilationist, and his wife, Harriet Foote Hawley, chairman of the Washington (WNIA) Indian Committee. The flurry of interest also included publication offers for the narrative of Fletcher's Omaha expedition. However, Fletcher's crowning moment of political approbation came when she delivered an address on Omaha allotment before the United States Senate Committee on Indian Affairs.[52]

Fletcher's political activities in Washington were shaped by a vast information network encompassing the Omaha-Winnebago reservation, allies in Indian education, missionaries in Nebraska, and supporters at the Indian boarding schools. Among these, George W. Wilkinson, Alfred L. Riggs, Richard Henry Pratt, C. L. Hall, Alice M. Robertson, and M. C. Wade kept Fletcher apprised of Omaha and European American sentiments in the field. This information proved invaluable to Fletcher given that the pending Omaha allotment legislation technically required tribal consent.[53]

Ultimately, Fletcher placed her distinctive mark on the Omaha Allotment Act of 1882. Other scholarship has argued that Fletcher rigged the legislation through a stealthily inserted amendment that required all the Omahas to be allotted *before* any reservation land could be sold. The evidence does not support this interpretation given the 1882 act does not contain that provision. In fact, what bothered Fletcher was the absence of allotment language in the original bill. Fletcher's concern was intensified by Interior secretary Teller's blunt assertion, "If the Indians have received patents . . . they are the owners in severalty of their respective allotments and it is immaterial whether it be called a fee title or by some other name."[54]

Secretary Teller's and Senator Dawes's preference for retaining the reservation system and allowing the Omaha tribe to lease, rent, or sell unassigned reservation land further stymied Fletcher's plans. Such "gradual" sentiments did not interest Fletcher whose goal was to immediately slate "civilized" Omahas for allotment, cajole the remaining Omahas into accepting allotment, and finally to extend Nebraska state law over the Omaha Reservation. Although favoring allotment and eventual sale of surplus land to raise capital, Fletcher was against legislation that only provided for the hasty sale of fifty thousand reservation acres.[55]

Largely reflecting the input of western politicians who hoped to open the Omaha Reservation to European American settlement and white Omaha farmers, the gestating bill would have effectively opened the Omaha

Reservation to non-Indian settlement. Fletcher's response was to "Get hold of the bill" in the congressional clerk's office and insert language calling for immediate allotment. Under her own authority Fletcher refashioned a land-sale bill into the nation's first act for mandated allotment in severalty. The groundwork Fletcher laid—carefully cultivating the support of powerful Washington politicians and politically influential women's organizations—enabled her amendments to proceed through Congress.[56]

Finally, after nine months of aggressive lobbying, *An Act for the Sale of Part of the Reservation of the Omaha Tribe of Indians in the State of Nebraska and for Other Purposes* was signed into law by President Chester Arthur on August 7, 1882. Senator Dawes immediately sent Fletcher a note stating, "The bill in regard to the Omaha Indians ha[s] become law...I congratulate you." Seven months later on March 16, 1883—the same month that fellow honorary WNIA member Helen Hunt Jackson was tapped as an Interior department special agent to investigate conditions among the California Mission Indians—President Arthur appointed Alice Fletcher a U.S. special allotment agent to the Omahas. Fletcher had successfully used Indian scholarship to transform herself into a political operative and federal agent.[57]

The Omaha Allotment began in March 1883 and ended in June 1884. In the course of her work Fletcher allotted 75,931 acres to 1,194 Omahas. Fifty thousand reservation acres were sold to European Americans and 55,450 were held in reserve for future Omaha generations. Fletcher also participated in a WNIA program that lent money for home construction and farm improvements to allotted Omahas. Stressing assimilation, married Omaha couples were given preferential consideration. Although the Omahas faced an uphill battle, their wealthy East Coast creditors carefully tracked repayments.[58]

Without Indian Office permission, Fletcher also launched a cattle ranching venture with Ed Farley on eighteen thousand acres of reserved Omaha land. Ed Farley was married to Rosalie La Flesche, Joseph La Flesche's daughter and Susette and Francis La Flesche's sister. The operation came into question when U.S. Attorney General Benjamin H. Brewster concluded that under the 1882 Omaha Allotment Act, allotted Omahas could not lease their land for grazing. Brought to a head by her old nemesis Thomas Tibbles, Fletcher's involvement in the Farley cattle venture proved a political mistake that temporarily tarnished her influence among Washington benefactors.[59]

With the completion of her Omaha allotment work in 1884, Fletcher again scrambled for cash. Through Frederic Ward Putnam, Fletcher's financial needs were eventually met by an endowed Peabody Museum associateship. The award reflected Putnam's growing confidence in Fletcher's ethnological abilities and his gratitude for the rare and beautiful Omaha cultural items she donated to the institution, among which were two ceremonial pipes, a sacred tent, and a number of eagle thighbone whistles.[60]

Fletcher's Peabody endowment added to her scholarly heft, which in turn prompted new publications. Among these were works on Omaha culture, Indian education, Winnebago culture, Lakota culture, Omaha traditions, allotment, Indian physiognomy, and an 1885 tribute to the late Helen Hunt Jackson. In all Fletcher published nineteen monographs and articles between 1882 and 1885.[61]

Most of Fletcher's ethno-political scholarship was anchored to Francis La Flesche, an Omaha man without whom much of her ethnological work would have been difficult, if not impossible. The son of Joseph La Flesche, Francis met Fletcher during her 1881 sojourn, and the two quickly developed a rapport. In fall 1881 Francis was sent to Washington to serve as an interpreter for the Senate Indian Affairs committee. Later, Francis served in the Indian office and eventually published work as a respected anthropologist in his own right. For many years Francis La Flesche acted as the Washington eyes and ears of Win-dja'-ge village.[62]

Although a twenty-four-year-old adult, Francis La Flesche was still considered a ward of the United States, unable to stay in Washington without a guardian. In 1882, Fletcher became Francis's official overseer in return for access to his cultural knowledge. Until 1887, when a provision in the Dawes Act conferred U.S. citizenship on the Omahas, Francis allowed Fletcher to place him in her charge hoping that through his influence the Omaha and other American Indian cultures would be more accurately recorded for posterity. Until her death in 1923, Francis would prove an invaluable contributor to Fletcher's scholarly works—except for one.[63]

A SEASON TO REMEMBER: ALICE FLETCHER
AND THE POLITICS OF INDIAN HISTORY

The years 1885 to 1887 were anomalies in Alice Fletcher's career. For the previous six years Fletcher had labored to establish herself as one of the nation's preeminent experts on American Indian peoples and cultures. However, in fall 1884 Fletcher's work began to shift from ethnological study toward document-driven American Indian history—a reorientation that would last for approximately two years. Fletcher's brief change in scholarly approach was sparked by a grand convergence of political and social forces that threatened to derail, or at least delay the coercive allotment movement.[64]

Appointed in 1882, Secretary of the Interior Henry M. Teller, though an assimilationist, did not favor allotment and remained suspicious of allotment schemes throughout his three-year tenure. General John Eaton and John

Dewitt Clinton Atkins, respective heads of the Education and Indian offices—the Interior divisions specifically charged with Indian affairs—were devoted assimilationists who favored coercive allotment. In addition to interdepartmental tensions, the Education and Indian offices were still reeling from former Interior secretary Carl Schurz's public dispute with Helen Hunt Jackson over Ponca removal and related charges of gross corruption, mismanagement, and treaty violations. Subsequent congressional investigations by the House and Senate and damning charges by Indian rights activists brought threats of legislative intervention and budget cuts to the agencies.[65]

In addition to congressional scrutiny, the Women's National Indian Association, the Indian Rights Association (IRA), and the National Indian Defense Association (NIDA) also kept allegations of Interior department and Indian office fraud and mismanagement before public view. In a particularly pointed 1884 attack NIDA's official organ, the *Council Fire and Arbitrator*, pegged Alice Fletcher's Indian office allotment work as a case "where land in severalty has been given to Indians before they were prepared for so radical a change." In the face of such withering criticism, the Education and Interior offices needed a loyal ally to champion their cause. But more than a savvy spokesperson, they needed a respected scholar who could marshal facts, organize an effective argument, and successfully prosecute their case before Congress and the American people.[66]

Commissioner John Eaton spied a promising candidate at the September 4–7, 1884, American Association for the Advancement of Science (AAAS) annual meeting. As vice president of AAAS section I—Economic Science and Statistics—Eaton presided over a session in which Alice Fletcher read a paper that presented Omaha allotment as a rousing success. Titled, "Lands in Severalty to Indians; Illustrated by Experiences with the Omaha Tribe," the paper contended that coercive allotment was not only prudent, but also the only viable solution to the "Indian problem." As a founding member of the American Historical Association (AHA) and an early advocate of document preservation and archival research, Eaton likely found Fletcher's document-driven, statistic laden presentation of particular interest.[67]

Sixteen days later, September 23, 1884, Fletcher participated in the Lake Mohonk Conference of Friends of the Indian. Held at a resort in Ulster County, New York, the annual Lake Mohonk Conference attracted both politicians and social reform activists interested in "solving" the Indian problem. During the regular sessions, Fletcher presented a paper on Indian citizenship, arguing that recent experience with the Omahas revealed that reservation lands could be rapidly allotted with no social or cultural ill-effect.[68]

A key feature of the 1884 Lake Mohonk agenda was Senator Henry L. Dawes's explication of the "Coke bill." According to Dawes, the bill awarded immediate tribal (communal) title to reservation lands with the option to allot when agreed to by two-thirds of male members. Allotted land titles were to be held in trust by the federal government for twenty-five years. Fletcher vigorously objected to tribal title, frankly stating, "The principle is wrong." Calling for immediate and coerced allotment in severalty, she suggested holding titles in trust for no more than ten years. Fletcher concluded, "The only way out for the Indian is right out into our civilization."[69]

In October 1884 Commissioner Eaton made his selection for Education and Indian office advocate by inviting Fletcher to fashion an exhibit demonstrating Omaha progress for the 1885 New Orleans World's Industrial and Cotton Centennial Exposition (WICCE). Advertised as the reconciliation of Northern and Southern economic and political might, the New Orleans exposition promised a national audience for innovators in industry, social reform, and politics. For their part, the Education and Indian offices planned a massive display intended to showcase educational and social reform. To match expectations, Fletcher contemplated an elaborate plaster model display, but financial constraints limited her to a series of photographs depicting Omaha life before and after mandatory allotment and a map of the allotted Omaha Reservation. Accompanying the pictorial exhibit, Fletcher prepared a thirty-three page pamphlet comprised of twelve engravings depicting Omaha life dispersed through an extensive annotated text based on her Omaha allotment presentation at the 1884 American Association for the Advancement of Science. Titled, *Historical Sketch of the Omaha Tribe of Indians in Nebraska*, the booklet was reserved for distribution to WICCE attendees "who expressed an interest in Indian advancement."[70]

It is not clear when the series of twenty-three exhibit photographs were taken, however, they received their first public viewing January 8, 1885, at the Fourteenth Annual Conference of the Board of Indian Commissioners. Offered with "a map of the Omaha reservation," Fletcher informed her audience that the pictures illustrated the unalterable fact that "the Omahas have crossed the line; they now have land in severalty." Explaining that the photographs illuminated the "past and present condition of the Omahas," Fletcher contended, "The salvation of the Indian is to get them out among Whites."[71]

As confirmed by written instructions, Fletcher's 1885 WICCE commission was to last for three months. Fletcher departed Washington on February 23 and arrived in New Orleans on February 26; her exhibit was shipped separately and did not arrive until several days later. On February 27 Fletcher presented a paper before the International Education Association titled, "An

Historical Sketch of the Omaha Tribe of Indians in Nebraska." Based on her 1884 AAAS address, the paper demonstrated Fletcher's keen awareness that her position as an Indian policy expert depended on her mastery and skillful presentation of historical documentation. Over the next few days Fletcher gave several ethnological talks and served as a popular docent at the Carlisle Indian boarding school exhibit.[72]

When Fletcher's exhibit material finally arrived, Lyndon A. Smith of the Education office mounted the photographs for display on two screens. Having attracted large crowds, Fletcher reported to Indian commissioner John Atkins that her efforts made a deep impression on visitors. Fletcher particularly noted that "a large number of the pamphlets" were distributed, and additional copies were mailed to religious organizations and Indian policy activists. The glowing report was reinforced with a special exposition award acknowledging her "illustrations for Indian progress."[73]

Sometime before Fletcher's arrival in New Orleans, the Senate Indian Affairs committee headed by Henry Dawes directed U.S. Commissioner of Education John Eaton to provide a report on the status of Indian education and civilization. The committee, then in the process of debating allotment legislation, wanted an accurate gage of Indian assimilation efforts. In particular, the committee wanted a legal assessment of reservation lands—both allotted and unalloted—and statistics on Indian education. In response, Eaton provided a hastily compiled report based on Selden Noyes Clark's 1876 census of the American Indian population titled, *Are the Indians Dying Out? Preliminary Observations Relating to Indian Civilization and Education.* Unfortunately for Eaton, Clark's forty-three page review of U.S. Indian populations, Indian schools, and Indian missions was eight years out of date and woefully inadequate for the committee's needs. The brief "Indian Education and Civilization" report was returned to the Education office on February 25, 1885, with instructions for substantive "revision and amendment." Commissioner Eaton needed a scholar and an accomplished editor. Based on her previous publication and proven mastery of American Indian education and assimilation statistics, Eaton handed the project to Alice Fletcher.[74]

"Assisted by a portion of the clerical force of the Department of Statistics [Education office]" Fletcher began work on the report in early May 1885. Fletcher labored at the Education office archives and the Library of Congress until September when she attended the American Association for the Advancement of Science annual meeting with Francis La Flesche. Afterward, in early October, Fletcher attended the concurrent 1885 Board of Indian Commissioners meeting and the Lake Mohonk conference, an event where her new document-driven research made a lasting impact on United States Indian policy.[75]

The keynote address of the Lake Mohonk conference was delivered by Senator Dawes, explicating recent Senate work on the Coke-Dawes bill. Expressing agreement with his colleague from the House, Congressman Robert Coke of Texas, Dawes continued to champion tribal title to lands with the option for voluntary allotment. Objections were raised, but Dawes was finally convinced by Alice Fletcher's presentation of statistics, legal statutes, and documentary evidence purporting to prove the beneficial effect of coercive allotment. Armed with a map, photographs, laws, and a comprehensive list of Indian treaties, reservation allotments, and unalloted reservations, Fletcher pushed for both compulsory Indian education and mandatory allotment in severalty. Reflecting the majority view, Fletcher joined in passing a set of resolutions to that effect. Dawes assented, and along with Amelia S. Quinton of the Women's National Indian Association and other activists, Fletcher was appointed to a platform committee charged with lobbying recently elected President Grover Cleveland and his secretary of the Interior, Lucius Lamar. Fletcher concluded her remarks at the conference with a tribute to the recently departed Helen Hunt Jackson noting, "Let us be faithful, and complete what she has left us to do."[76]

Fletcher devoted the next ten months to drafting the *Indian Education and Civilization* report. Originally planned as a massive "history of each existing tribe," financial constraints limited Fletcher to a minutely detailed cultural, educational, treaty, legal, and land history of the tribes slated for allotment in the Dawes-Coke bill (later known as the Dawes General Allotment Act). In final form, Fletcher's *Indian Education and Civilization* report comprised six hundred and ninety-three pages divided into twenty-two chapters.[77]

The first three chapters, devoted to the sixteenth, seventeenth, and eighteenth centuries respectively, charted European imperialism in its Spanish, French, and English forms. Finding each despotic, Fletcher concluded the third chapter with a generally positive overview of American assimilation efforts since the Revolution. Chapters four through six gave short histories of the Indian service, the creation of reservations, and Indian education. Chapters eight through twenty-one gave detailed histories of twenty-two reservations and associated tribes. The final chapter was an overview of nineteenth-century Indian missionary work and ended without a conclusion—likely reflecting the abrupt end of her appropriation two months earlier.[78]

Completed in 1887 and published in 1888, Fletcher's solitary volume of document-driven Indian history emerged just as she was thrown into one of the worst trials of her career. Reviled by Thomas and Susette Tibbles, who loudly complained to the Indian office and the Senate Indian Affairs committee about Fletcher's administration of Omaha allotment and her involvement in the Omaha cattle ranching venture, the Interior department opened an investigation. While far from silencing Fletcher's support for pending allotment legislation, the investigation did limit her public influence among the organized assimilationists. At Thomas Tibbles's behest, the Indian Rights Association also began its own inquiry into Fletcher's allotment work, Omaha leasing practices, and the Omaha cattle venture. The lengths to which the IRA's James E. Rhoads and Charles C. Painter went to foster Omaha dissent decidedly turned Fletcher against the organization and its leadership. Although denied by Fletcher, her correspondence with Joseph La Flesche suggests that she had a stake in Ed Farley's cattle enterprise.[79]

The immediate result of the Interior's inquiry and IRA accusations was that Fletcher diverted her limited time and resources to self-defense. Consequently, though Fletcher significantly shaped the final version of the 1887 Dawes Act, the WNIA and IRA played a far more visible and self-congratulatory role. Notably, while most Win-dja'-ge villagers proclaimed loyalty to Fletcher, during the Interior's investigation a few hedged their bets with donations to the WNIA. Records show that in 1887, Wajapa, Sin-da-ha-ha, Tae-on-ka-ha, Noah La Flesche, and Ma-wa-da-ne contributed a total of seventy-two dollars to the WNIA Indian Home Building and Emergency Fund. By the end of 1887 Fletcher successfully quashed all charges and quickly regained her political and scholarly stature.[80]

Following passage of the Dawes Act, Fletcher was again appointed an allotment agent. Between 1887 and 1892 Fletcher allotted land, sometimes diplomatically, often through coercion, and occasionally by force to the Winnebagos and Nez Perces. During her work—and that of other Indian office agents—Fletcher's *Indian Education and Civilization* report proved a valuable tool for deciphering legal questions raised by the Dawes Act. For the next two decades the report would be cited by legal and educational sources as a definitive text on Indian treaties and legal history. Though a trailblazing historical work, Fletcher's *Indian Education and Civilization* report was not admitted to the historiographical cannon, nor did it erase the troubling legacy of her ethno-political scholarship.[81]

Galvanized by historical information gleaned from the report, Alice Fletcher's Indian activism cost the Winnebago and Nez Perce tribes dearly, both in terms of cultural loss and several hundred thousand acres of private property. As a direct result of Fletcher's successful push for mandatory allotment in severalty, American Indian peoples lost about ninety million acres of the approximately one hundred and fifty million acres the tribes held in 1887. Ninety thousand landless Indians were effectively made into vagrants, while thousands more were torn from their homes and shipped off to government boarding schools. Ultimately, Fletcher's maverick history text proved the handmaiden of her ethno-political scholarship.[82]

As pioneers of document-driven pan-Indian history, Helen Hunt Jackson and Alice Fletcher were the first American scholars to pen comprehensive histories of American Indians based on archival, public, and government documents. Yet, *A Century of Dishonor* and the *Indian Education and Civilization* report were still products of their time. The institutional and political forces that Jackson and Fletcher accessed through their Indian histories would dramatically change by the late 1890s. Moreover, passage and implementation of mandatory assimilation and allotment legislation quelled political and scholarly interest in historical works detailing Indian treaty, property, and legal history.

By the 1890s new institutions would overshadow the ability of the Bureau of Ethnology, the Office of Indian Affairs, and private Indian activists to define American history—particularly the history of the American West. American Indian history would be absorbed into academic Frontier and American West historical scholarship where it would languish on the periphery as nostalgic memories of peoples and cultures erased by the swift tide of European American progress. Eventually, new political realities within the academy would again compel European American women to produce document-driven American Indian histories.

CHAPTER 6

Professionalization and the Twilight of Women's American Indian Scholarship

At the dawn of the academic professionalization boom in 1889, Alice Fletcher was interviewed by a Washington, D.C., *Evening Star* correspondent for an article featuring the city's "Women Who Serve Science." Regarding Fletcher's scholarly achievements, the reporter noted, "What she has accomplished does not seem to be so very much, because she sees so much still to be done in the future." Fletcher continued her work well into the next decade, but her distinguished career as a leading preprofessional anthropologist was already in decline. As the human sciences moved away from government sponsorship and began to professionalize in the academy, professional status was increasingly restricted to those with degrees in their specific fields. Likewise, scholarly publication, long the standard for establishing personal expertise and intellectual credibility, was increasingly limited to a new generation of emerging academic specialists. Alice Fletcher's last peer-reviewed publication on work pertinent to her field appeared in the 1912 *American Anthropologist* journal.[1]

While the preprofessional era facilitated women's American Indian scholarship and allowed a handful of women to exercise a significant amount of political power through those studies, the academic professionalization of history and anthropology marked the erosion of their scholarly and political status. More damning, professional anthropologists, historians, and scientists called into question the racial theories that underpinned women's Indian scholarship. In destabilizing theories of racial evolution, anthropologists, historians, and scientists also helped alter the historical narrative of the American West.

This reconfiguration of history would recast the western conquest as a singular tale of inevitable European American progress. The earlier work of women Indian scholars would not find a niche within this new history. Western frontier expansion would become the specialty of professional male historians.

In an opportunistic move that increased their own professional stature, women historians took up American Indian political history because it was the only subject not claimed by their male colleagues. Retooled as an "objective" nonpartisan study of treaties and legal relations with the United States, the new Indian political history was almost exclusively identified with women historians. In this early phase, much of this new Indian history would be written by women historians employed outside the academy. Until the mid-twentieth century American Indian history was largely associated with women's colleges, state historical societies, museums, and historical archives, where the majority of professional women historians were employed. Even as women made significant strides in American society, higher education, and professional vocations, gender continued to demarcate the American historical narrative.[2]

ANTHROPOLOGY AND WOMEN

The professionalization of anthropology played a key role in the decline of American Darwinism and women's American Indian scholarship. Woven into the intellectual, political, and legal structure of John Wesley Powell's Bureau of Ethnology, American Darwinism and the ethnological scholarship it spawned shaped the BE mission, American Indian law, and federal Indian administration. Yet for all its influence, American Darwinist scholarship had an Achilles heel—it was predicated on the precarious notion of racial evolution.

The first spark of several firestorms that would eventually consume American Darwinist scholarship was not cast by the emerging cohort of late-nineteenth century genetic theorists, nor the American eugenics movement. Based on mounting evidence that racial identity did not reflect a single unity of environmental, biological, and cultural factors, John Wesley Powell moved to separate BE ethnological scholarship from American Darwinism. Powell gave the outline of this new approach in his 1889 American Association for the Advancement of Science (AAAS) presidential address.[3]

For her part, Alice Fletcher was basking in the sunlight of success in 1889. Fletcher rejoiced with passage of the Dawes Act in 1887. She relished critical acclaim for her comprehensive Indian treaty and legal history published in 1888 and was elated by the news of her induction into the prestigious

Literary Society of Washington. Rubbing shoulders with "members drawn from different sections of society," including John Wesley Powell, Matilda Coxe Stevenson, and Senator Joseph R. Hawley, Fletcher was well placed to secure a prominent positon in the emerging anthropology profession. Unfortunately, this transition was aborted in May 1889 when she received orders from the Indian office to allot the Nez Perces in Idaho. Fletcher's triumph in promoting the Dawes Act proved a bittersweet victory; it unexpectedly tied her to grueling, isolated, old-fashioned ethno-political work just as the world of anthropology was transforming. While preprofessional women anthropologists would not be able to transition into permanent professional positions in academic anthropology departments, a small cadre would reestablish themselves as noted anthropological fieldworkers. Although Fletcher received a lifetime fellowship from the Peabody Museum in 1890 that freed her from financial worry, it was not an academic position and it did not confer professional status. Ultimately, ill-health, unfortunate circumstances, and a lack of academic credentials would prevent Fletcher from becoming a professional anthropologist.[4]

In 1890, a year after Fletcher began her new allotment assignment, Powell explicitly made his case for the study of human cultures as opposed to the old racial groups. Culling racial categories and characteristics, Powell announced, "There are no ethnic groups of mankind which can be satisfactorily demarcated . . . the world has been covered with a network of streams of blood which science cannot unravel." Redefining human phylogenesis as a cultural phenomenon, Powell cleaved the effects of culture and society from the study of biological characteristics. Powell proclaimed, "The process of human evolution being not biotic, but cultural, the study of mankind gives rise to a new realm of science, which is denominated 'anthropology.'" Most radical of all, Powell suggested that anthropology itself "might . . . be called the science of culture, and perhaps still better the science of the humanities."[5]

Freed from the conflating effect of American Darwinism, each human culture was now set to become an individual area of study. The scholarship of American Indian cultures, already specialized by Alice Fletcher, Matilda Coxe Stevenson, Zelia Nuttall, and others, nevertheless remained contentious, because federal Indian policy continued to shape Bureau of Ethnology Indian research. More so, BE affiliated scholars like Fletcher, intellectually shackled by their own roles in promoting Indian assimilation, proved recalcitrant.[6]

Anthropology at academic institutions and museums largely embraced cultural relativism. The Interior department, Indian office, and Bureau of Ethnology, long steeped in Indian assimilation policy and the concurrent interests of entrenched assimilationist bureaucrats, found it extremely difficult to change course. As late as 1900 Fletcher used assimilationist rhetoric to describe American Indians as "a race in a state of culture antecedent to that in which our earliest literature and music flourished." Similar sentiment was expressed in 1907 by Commissioner of Indian Affairs Francis E. Leupp who proclaimed, "Results attained at present indicate ... that pursued through a few generations acquired habits will become fixed and [will] be transmitted by heredity, thus establishing characteristics which distinguish the sturdy white citizen." As a new generation of academic anthropologists scrutinized the Indian ethno-political scholarship produced by government institutions, few realized the extent to which the Department of the Interior, Office of Indian Affairs, and Bureau of Ethnology were ossified by federal statutes, congressional oversight, judicial precedent, and institutional habits. It was there, between the government ethnologists and the new academic anthropologists that significant fractures first appeared in the old postbellum community of American Indian scholars.[7]

John Wesley Powell's push to redefine anthropology came at the dawn of profound methodological and institutional changes within the American social sciences (humanities). But just as Powell began his bid to reinvent the Bureau of Ethnology's preeminent role in American anthropology, the social sciences began fragmenting into discrete professional disciplines. Ultimately, professionalization would situate anthropologists within academia where they would be pitted against historians in institutional battles for relevancy and funding. The move toward professionalized anthropology served to erode the status of preprofessional scholars of American Indians and undermine the BE's preeminent role in American anthropology.

The well-documented rise of professional anthropology reveals that in 1886 Frederic Ward Putnam, director of the Harvard University affiliated Peabody Museum of Natural History and a mentor of Alice Fletcher, petitioned Harvard University to establish a graduate program in anthropology. After four years of rigorous campaigning, Harvard finally established its Department of American Archaeology and Ethnology, which offered the nation's first advanced degree in anthropology. As chair of the new department, Putnam developed a three-year program that required work in "the laboratory, museum, lectures, field-work ... exploration and in the third year some special research."[8]

A graduate anthropology program followed at Columbia University and was soon joined by graduate anthropology programs at Chicago and Pennsylvania. By 1912 the Harvard, Columbia, Berkeley, Chicago, and Pennsylvania programs had awarded a total of twenty anthropology doctorates to male students and by 1928 had awarded the Ph.D. to fifty-three men and nine women. Though impressive, this growth fell short of the doctorates awarded by university history programs. As an academic profession, anthropology did not produce the number of specialists it had under BE leadership.[9]

A significant shift in sex ratios among anthropologists also occurred as the discipline moved from the control of government agencies, quasi-private museums, and autonomous organizations to academic institutions. Since the mid-twentieth century American historians have focused on women's postbellum entry into higher education as indicative of a general rise in women's academic status, but a survey of women anthropologists before and after the professional era brings this assumption into question. Between 1890 and 1935 there was a precipitous decline in new women anthropologists.[10]

The 1870 to 1890 growth in preprofessional women anthropologists was the result of Frederic Ward Putnam's personal efforts as permanent secretary of the American Association for the Advancement of Science and director of the Peabody Museum of Natural History. As AAAS secretary Putnam encouraged women to join section H, the anthropological division. In his capacity as director of the Peabody Museum, Putnam also mentored a number of promising female anthropology students. By 1890 Putnam's protégés included Frances E. Babbit, Fanny D. Bergen, Virginia K. Bowers, Alice C. Fletcher, Fanny Hitchcock, Anita Newcomb McGee, Jeannette Robinson Murphy, Zelia Nuttall, Erminnie Smith, Jennie Smith, Sara Y. Stevenson, Cordelia A. Studley, and Laura O. Talbot.[11]

From 1884 to 1890 Putnam cultivated more women anthropologists than were produced by Harvard, Columbia, Berkeley, Chicago, and Pennsylvania universities combined during the decades from 1891 to 1930. When considered in terms of doctorates awarded, the decline in women anthropologist's professional status after 1890 becomes clear. Between 1891 and 1930 graduate anthropology programs accepted one hundred and twenty-four doctoral students, of these only eighteen were women. A doctorate in anthropology was not awarded to a woman until 1913—twenty-two years after the first doctorate in anthropology was conferred on a male student. Harvard did not produce a woman doctor of anthropology until 1944—fifty years after it first awarded the degree to a male student. Of the eighteen women doctoral students accepted into programs between 1891 and 1930 eleven received their doctorates.[12]

As the study of anthropology transferred to the university setting, the status of preprofessional women's Indian scholarship declined. Navigating a more flexible interdisciplinary scholarship before 1890 allowed women to cultivate their expertise in both anthropology and history. By the end of the nineteenth century, women scholars of American Indians were increasingly isolated from both disciplines. Professional anthropologists were often distant, but they did not reject preprofessional women scholars' ethnological work out of hand. However, professional historians proved unwilling to accept the work of noncredentialed women scholars as legitimate.[13]

Dominated by male Americanist historians who embraced Manifest Destiny and American Indian irrelevancy, history's early interdisciplinary tolerance had been in question since the American Historical Association was founded in 1884. Racial evolution was not yet taboo among the historical set, but as a matter of professional objectivity historians were unwilling to accept the ethno-political baggage of women's American Indian scholarship. By 1893 most historians were backing away from American Darwinism. In its place leading specialists in American history and culture elaborated a triumphalist view of European American westward expansion. Out of step with the new Anglo-Saxon narrative of western conquest, women's earlier Indian scholarship was largely ignored by the emerging profession.[14]

HISTORY AND WOMEN

The origin of professional American history is well documented, but a brief survey reveals that it can be traced to the generation of privileged American male students who pursued higher education at German universities between 1880 and 1890. By 1889, "more than one hundred and fifty American students [we]re pursuing their post-graduate studies in German universities." It was in Prussia that a generation of young American history students, such as Justin Winsor, Herbert Levi Osgood, Frederic A. Bancroft, Edward A. Ross, Albert Bushnell Hart, James Harvey Robinson, William E. Dodd, and Herbert Baxter Adams learned the German approach to academic history. Alice Fletcher visited Europe in 1894, but the records show that she did not study the German historical method.[15]

The German model that would be employed by Hart at Harvard, Robinson at Columbia, and Adams at Johns Hopkins focused on creating what James Franklin Jameson called, "a community of investigators," who were "concerned with pursuing their own research while training the next generation; elevat[ing] the professional historian to expert status; control[ing] a complex set of investigative methods and . . . root[ing] out all superfluous speculation and political agendas." This approach allowed male historians like Adams and his colleagues to promote academic history as the final court of review for historical truth. Unlike "literary" predecessors and women scholars of American Indians, Adams and his colleagues considered their work to be objective history free of opinion, emotion, political agendas, and ideological bent.[16]

Professional objectivity relied on documentary sources, and the early American history profession was committed to archival research and documentary verification. Influenced by such German notables as Leopold von Ranke, professional American historians were not given to the prosaic flourishes and undocumented hearsay characteristic of preprofessional histories. In this sense the new profession of history aspired to be an objective science.[17]

To this end professional American historians shunned the oral traditions and secondhand accounts found in the works of preprofessional historians like Frances Parkman, Hubert Howe Bancroft, and Josiah Royce. Reflecting changing political and cultural interests, Americanist historians came to focus almost exclusively on European American history. From the mid-1890s on, these professional historians generally proved hostile to histories that ranged far beyond American Anglo-Saxon social and cultural development. Ironically, though they were objective document-driven histories, both Helen Hunt Jackson's *A Century of Dishonor* and Alice Fletcher's *Indian Education and Civilization* report fell through the historiographical cracks.[18]

The archival focus of the history profession was intimately linked to the newly formed American Historical Association. Founded in 1884 and chartered by Congress in 1889, the AHA provided a national platform for professional historians and served as an important intellectual forum for historical theory. Equally important, the 1889 congressional charter required the Smithsonian to publish free of charge a yearly report on AHA activities. The resulting *Papers* and *Annual Report* diffused AHA scholarship across the nation.[19]

Among the AHA's professional contributions, founding member James Franklin Jameson lauded the creation of state and local historical societies and archives, which "were unknown" before 1884, and the promotion of university history departments. Jameson specifically noted the AHA's role in championing full-time history professors—of which there were only fifteen in 1884. Though not exclusively composed of professionals, the AHA was indispensable in making American history a profession.[20]

A NICHE FOR WOMEN HISTORIANS

Over the last three decades scholarship on the American historical profession has advanced two plausible, but flawed theories regarding the early experiences of professional women historians. These arguments hold that either male founders of the profession refused to admit women, or conversely they refused or failed to promote women historians. Consequentially, most women historians were largely shut out of the profession in universities and forced to take jobs in government and public archives, historical societies, women's colleges, and high schools. Neither argument explains why a small group of professional male historians cultivated several hundred women graduate students and promoted their employment as professional historians—outside the realm of comprehensive universities.[21]

The answer is found in the practical (and opportunistic) needs of early academic historians. Albert L. Hurtado notes in his biography of American borderlands historian Herbert E. Bolton that male historians' willingness to accept female students reflected several concerns, headed by admission targets and departmental funding. Frontier historian Frederick Jackson Turner's motive was more immediate—to fulfill his own research and academic needs. Turner and later his male protégés—Herbert E. Bolton and Edward Everett Dale—mentored many of the degreed women produced by the early history profession. While a comparatively large number of women were eventually awarded the history M.A. and Ph.D., only a few found faculty employment at universities. So, why were the majority of women historians employed outside the academy until well into the first half of the twentieth century?[22]

A reexamination of the evidence, specifically data compiled by Jacqueline Goggin, reveals that women graduate students were trained by professional male historians, who did not believe women should hold faculty positions at coed universities. In this matter, male historians reflected contemporary views about women's employment in the "public" sphere. With few exceptions, male historians directed their female graduates toward archival work at new national, state, and local historical societies, and government record repositories. The new profession quickly produced a glut of women historians, who filled available archival positions. As public history jobs tightened, women historians were directed toward employment at women's colleges, high schools, and secondary schools. Turner, in particular believed that women historians' most valuable contribution was at the K-12 level, where they would promote American identity and American culture.[23]

Ultimately, what gave credence to the idea that women were barred from the history profession was the testimony of women graduate students who made unsuccessful bids for postgraduate employment in coed university history departments—only a handful would acquire tenured faculty positions before the 1960s. The fact that many of the first women historians linked professional status to coed academic positions served to obscure the large number of women graduates produced by history departments and their work as professional historians outside the academy. This clarification should not obviate the fact that promoting women historians outside academia largely served utilitarian purposes, chiefly the cultivation of competent archivists and document curators.[24]

Acceptance of women graduate students coincided with a dramatic increase in female applicants. Considering that the 1884 American Historical

Association constitution did not specifically bar women members and the American Association for the Advancement of Science anthropology section H accepted women, historians have deduced that history and anthropology were equally attractive to female students. Related is the assumption that women's admission to historical studies (human sciences and history) was proportionate to the general influx of postbellum female graduate students. A survey of graduate anthropology and history data proves this assumption is incorrect and reveals a unique sexual division of labor in the history profession.[25]

When anthropology began to professionalize in 1890 there were approximately fifty preprofessional women anthropologists and ethnologists. From the beginning of professionalization of the discipline around 1890 until 1935, academic anthropology produced eighteen women doctorates. When history began to professionalize around 1884 there were only two recognized women historians—Martha Lamb and Sara Bolton. Between 1890, when the first formal academic history programs were established, and 1935 the history profession awarded three hundred and thirty-four Ph.D.s to women.[26]

Given their general acceptance in higher education, it is improbable that women flocked to history graduate programs indiscriminately. Part of what made history more attractive to women were the employment opportunities in archival work, public history, public schools, and women's colleges. While anthropology placed field research and related archival and museum work under departmental control, archival, repository, and museum work remained largely autonomous. Moreover, public schools and women's colleges rarely offered anthropology courses, whereas history was usually a required subject. The evidence strongly suggests that few women were attracted to anthropology graduate programs because postdoctorate employment as an anthropologist was limited to academic appointments decidedly favorable to men. In contrast a history M.A. or Ph.D. offered women alternative employment if work in academia proved out of reach.[27]

An examination of the American Historical Association's role in professionalizing American history reveals that the AHA's founders envisioned a profession roughly divided between academic and public vocations—a demarcation that lent itself to a sexual division of labor. In the annals of American humanities, the history profession stands alone in developing a gendered vocational division. This dual trajectory of labor reflected the gender biases and expectations of the day, however there were a few exceptions. A small cohort of professional male historians worked in public history and taught at women's colleges and high schools. Likewise, a handful of professional women historians—such as Margaret J. Mitchell (University of Oklahoma,

1917–22) and Annie Heloise Abel (Johns Hopkins, 1910–15)—held faculty positions at comprehensive universities.[28]

THE AMERICAN HISTORICAL ASSOCIATION, PUBLIC HISTORY, AND WOMEN HISTORIANS

The AHA grew out of an 1883 paper titled "New Methods of Study in History," read by Herbert Baxter Adams before the American Association for the Advancement of Science. Adams's paper outlined his vision for a national "organization of research" to be called the "American Historical Association." The AHA coalesced in the fall of 1884 with the adoption of a constitution defining the organization's guiding principle as "the promotion of historical studies." Although the AHA expressed concern for manuscript collection and the establishment of archives, this did not become a formal policy until its fourth annual meeting under President Justin Winsor. Winsor's presidential address, "Manuscript Sources of American History: The Conspicuous Collection Extant," codified the long-standing interest in collecting and preserving manuscripts as an AHA policy.[29]

Spurred to further action by Cornell history professor, Moses Coit Tyler's 1889 paper, "The Neglect and Destruction of Historical Materials in this Country," the AHA absorbed the task of archival promotion into its organizational structure. Responding with shock to the widespread loss of American primary sources, the AHA appointed a special committee to consider assistance to "the National Government in collecting, preserving and calendaring American historical manuscripts." As a direct result of this committee's work, the AHA received a congressional charter that specifically charged it with the "promotion of historical studies . . . [and] the collection and preservation of historical manuscripts."[30]

The AHA charter also prompted a concerted effort to establish state and local archives and modern historical societies staffed by trained historians. Special attention was called "to the superior opportunities which college libraries and historical societies afforded for . . . [manuscript] preservation by permanent institutions and in fire-proof repositories." AHA members were urged to persuade owners of historical manuscripts "to provide for their security and usefulness through such means." The AHA was so successful in promoting state and local historical societies that by 1894 there were three hundred and fifty-eight, spanning every state in the union.[31]

Regional historical societies maintained close working relationships with university history departments, specifically professors who made use of their collections, advised future collection work, and recommended promising graduate students for employment. However, historical societies remained largely separate in their funding, administration, and hiring decisions. Directorships and administrative positions usually went to men, particularly at the larger more affluent societies. Curatorial, archival, library, and secretarial positions went to professionally trained women historians. A notable example was Frederick Jackson Turner's student Dr. Louise Phelps Kellogg, who began her career as Reuben Gold Thwaites's chief assistant at the Wisconsin State Historical Society immediately following her graduation.[32]

A detailed analysis of the three hundred and thirty-four women who received advanced history degrees between 1890 and 1935 is beyond the scope of this volume, however a survey of the evidence indicates that most women Ph.D. and M.A. graduates were guided to employment in history archives, museums, public education, and women's colleges. This pattern is revealed through a brief review of women graduate students taught by two of Frederick Jackson Turner's male students, Herbert Eugene Bolton, at the University of Texas and University of California, and Edward Everett Dale, at the University of Oklahoma. Between 1900 and 1935 Bolton chaired the M.A. committees of one hundred and eighty-eight women and the doctoral committees of five women. In terms of gender ratio, Bolton mentored one hundred male M.A.s and sixty-six male Ph.D.s. Women who received their degrees under Bolton went on to work in historical societies, public education, and women's and religious colleges. A similar pattern occurred with Edward Everett Dale's students. Dale was the doctoral committee chair for both Anna L. Lewis in 1930 and Angie Debo in 1933. Dr. Lewis eventually served as history department chair at the Oklahoma College for Women until her retirement in 1956. Dr. Debo briefly held positions at the West Texas State Teachers College and the Panhandle-Plains Historical Museum. Later, after years of unemployment Debo held several comparatively brief positions at Oklahoma A&M College, including a teaching stint after it became Oklahoma State University of Agricultural and Applied Sciences in 1957.[33]

AND ALONG CAME TURNER: AMERICAN EXCEPTIONALISM AND WOMEN'S INDIAN HISTORY

Often cast as a theoretical historian, Frederick Jackson Turner was also a practical, if not opportunistic, scholar. Trained in an age of burgeoning American nationalism and westward expansion, Turner sensed public interest in a new national narrative. As a young scholar Turner concluded, "American history needs a connected and unified account of the progress of civilization across the continent." His eventual thesis that "The existence of an area of free land, its continuous recession, and the advance of American settlement westward, explain American development," would captivate U.S. historians for much of the twentieth century. Branding western "free land" as an unencumbered frontier quietly awaiting settlement by a "fit people," rather than the confiscated property of dispossessed Indian peoples, Turner helped fashion an historical lie. With theoretical finesse, Turner neatly disposed of American Indian history and with it the troubling legacy of racial evolution and ethno-political scholarship. Turner's West was seen as a virgin landscape uncomplicated by the facts of its own multicultural history. This version of the American West would not be shackled with "romantic treatments" of the "conflicts of the pioneers with the Indians," rather it would replace the complicated history of western ethnic diversity with the fantasy of benign Anglo-Saxon settler colonialism.[34]

In its velvet treatment of conquest, Turner's theory gave European American expansion a new decorum. Yet his proposal was not so novel as to be unrecognizable within the history profession or American culture. Turner's "Frontier Thesis" was roundly praised by such notable authorities as Francis A. Walker, Brooks Adams, and John Fiske. Most gratifying for Turner, Theodore Roosevelt complimented his research noting, "You have struck some first class ideas, and have put into definite shape a good deal of thought which has been floating around rather loosely."[35]

The Frontier Thesis approach to American Indians signaled a sea change in how American history would be presented to the nation. Turner described "the frontier [a]s the outer edge of the wave—the meeting point between savagery and civilization," where "primitive Indian life" compelled the federal government to "the determination of peace and war with the Indians, the regulation of Indian trade, the purchase of Indian lands, and the creation of new settlements as a security against the Indians." Within a couple of paragraphs Turner neatly reduced the whole of North American Indian history to a few definitive political interactions with European Americans.[36]

By redefining the position of Indians in American history and dismissing the underlying presumption of assimilation, Turner advanced a new approach to American racial politics. Reflecting the essay's theme of national Anglo-Saxon ethnic and cultural unity, Turner stated, "If one would understand why we are today one nation, rather than a collection of isolated states, he must study this economic and social consolidation of the country." Making clear that it was not the proper subject for an historian, Turner added, "In this progress from savage conditions lie topics for the evolutionist." Turner's vision of progress circumscribed a narrative of parallel decline and marginalization for American Indians—the passing of a former peoples whose relation to American history was delineated by trade agreements and land treaties, and settled by removal. Here, a new line of scholarship was to emerge for women marginalized in the nascent history profession.

Indian political history, largely ignored by male historians, became an interest of Turner's women students, who quickly made it their own scholarly domain.[37]

Having set in motion the historical inscription of American Indians as pacified treaty makers and the invisible minions of an expanding imperial power, Turner's Frontier Thesis gained increased relevance immediately following the Spanish-American War. Posited by historians Brooks Adams and John Fiske, and politicians Theodore Roosevelt, Woodrow Wilson, William McKinley, and Elihu Root as a model for enlightened democratic imperialism, this new approach to Indian history would also garner attention from male expansionists at the U.S. Office of Insular Affairs and in the U.S. territorial government of the Philippines.[38]

By the mid-1890s, impatient with the pace of Indian assimilation, male expansionists began to argue that American Indians were sufficiently acculturated and the West was definitively settled in order to justify calls for termination of federal guardianship of the tribes. Ironically, the social and cultural havoc wrought by assimilation would now be cited as proof that Indians were ready to fend for themselves. By the end of the 1898 Spanish-American War, male expansionists would declare Indian assimilation complete and propose a similar venture for new U.S. possessions in the Pacific. To this end, male expansionists would look to Indian treaties and legal history for guidance. The efforts of these expansionists to reshape the historical narrative into a propaganda tool would also have a devastating effect on the status of preprofessional women scholars of American Indians.[39]

ALICE FLETCHER'S MELANCHOLY END

The decade following the Spanish-American War was rife with social and political conflicts, but few were as colorful as the battle between male expansionists and maternal patriots. Competing for attention from the same constituencies, each group posited themselves as saviors of the nation and protectors of American culture. Expansionists pressed their interests through foreign policy, while maternal patriots advanced their cause through social reform activism, most notably Indian assimilation politics.[40]

Maternal patriots staked out a distinct role in the arena of Indian assimilation. Although predominantly male Indian rights groups existed, with the exception of Herbert Welsh's Indian Rights Association (IRA) no other group had the national organization or influence to claim equal status with the Women's National Indian Association (WNIA). When Herbert Welsh's claims are put to the test, evidence shows a marginal if not negligible IRA role in marshaling allotment legislation. William T. Hagan's definitive work on the

IRA suggests that Welsh's political claims were largely the hyperbole of a narcissistic man. Welsh's pretensions to the contrary, the WNIA remained the premier Indian assimilation movement well into the 1890s.[41]

Tensions came to a head when the era's most prominent expansionist, Theodore Roosevelt—then a member of the U.S. Civil Service Commission—gave a talk before the 1892 Lake Mohonk Conference. Just back from a tour of the Nebraska reservations, Roosevelt called federal Indian guardianship into question. Concluding with a biting critique of alcoholism, social disorder, and limited agricultural success on the Omaha Reservation, Roosevelt yielded the floor to Alice Fletcher, who was on leave from her allotment duties in Idaho.[42]

Fletcher believed she had seen the genesis of a new Omaha social and economic order when she visited the reservation in 1890, and she was taken aback by Roosevelt's assessment. Politically savvy, Fletcher directed her response only to dissolution of the reservation system and Indian citizenship. Roosevelt refrained from further criticism of the Omahas and picked up Fletcher's new lead. Calling for a radical change in federal-Indian relations, Roosevelt proposed, "We have got to make them citizens.... We have got to make them understand that they have to sink or swim on their own merits." Fletcher's concurrence proved a watershed moment for women's Indian activism and women's American Indian scholarship.[43]

The events surrounding Fletcher's 1892 trek to Lake Mohonk and her subsequent appearance at the 1893 Chicago World's Columbian Exposition illuminate the extent to which women's preprofessional Indian scholarship was being displaced across the professional spectrum. For Fletcher, 1892 proved a dismal year. That spring she learned that her old mentor Frederic Ward Putnam had chosen an academic anthropologist, Franz Boas, as his chief assistant at the Chicago Exposition. Feeling that she was infinitely more qualified for the position, Fletcher was heartbroken by Putnam's decision.[44]

Additionally, as the Winnebago agent struggling through a difficult assignment with a tribe not disposed toward allotment, Fletcher found her work far less glamorous than it had been a decade before. After Roosevelt's biting critique at Lake Mohonk and the disappointing news from Putnam, Fletcher returned to Idaho and oversaw the sale of five hundred thousand surplus acres in the Nez Perce reservation. Fletcher then returned to Washington and climbed into her sickbed where she remained in a deep depression for several weeks.[45]

Fletcher recovered by turning her attention to three papers she intended to present at the Chicago World's Columbian Exposition. Adopting a new sensitivity to professionalism, Fletcher dropped assimilation rhetoric to focus on Omaha religious and social music. Two months before Turner presented his famous essay on the American frontier in Chicago, Fletcher presented her work before the Chicago exposition's anthropology conference. To Fletcher's dismay, a derivative paper presented by a former colleague, Professor John Fillmore, eclipsed her own. On a subject in which Fletcher hoped to gain professional credibility, she was outmaneuvered by a lazy thinker and a professionalized system rigged against her. Again, Fletcher returned to Washington and took to her sickbed.[46]

Mirroring Fletcher's experience, preprofessional anthropologist Matilda Coxe Stevenson read a paper addressing Zuni ceremonial life at the Congress of Women at the Chicago Exposition. There is no evidence to indicate that Stevenson's male Bureau of Ethnology colleagues attended, though her presentation was later published by the BE. Unlike papers read by professional male anthropologists, neither Fletcher's nor Stevenson's papers garnered academic attention, nor were they published in professional academic journals. Although Fletcher and Stevenson had high hopes for their Chicago scholarship, they were not able to overcome the new professional chasm that divided preprofessional women's Indian scholarship from that of professional historians and anthropologists.[47]

After 1892 Fletcher curtailed her relationship with the Lake Mohonk conference. Eschewing assimilation, Fletcher took up the Indian citizenship cause and turned her scholarly attention to the study and preservation of American Indian music and cultures. Fletcher's interest in Indian citizenship signaled a change in the old assimilation politics—reflecting her own disappointment with the course of Indian assimilation.[48]

With her unpleasant 1892 Lake Mohonk experience in mind, Fletcher returned to the Omaha Reservation in 1899 and found the tribe in turmoil. This time she no longer saw the Omahas through the eyes of a young idealistic assimilationist, but with the wizened gaze of a sixty-one-year-old woman. Fletcher found the Omaha social and cultural disorder heartbreaking. Though she would never publicly admit her lifework had been fundamentally flawed, she did note, "No people can be helped if they are absolutely uprooted." Based on what she saw at the Omaha Reservation, Fletcher determined to preserve what she deemed best in Indian cultures. Fletcher's new agenda was eventually taken up by the General Federation of Women's Clubs and promoted well into the 1920s as a reformed assimilation goal.[49]

Fletcher's modified assimilation campaign would not prove the most popular twentieth-century approach to U.S. Indian policy. Where Fletcher's new agenda reflected a sense of remorse, impatient advocates of expansionism embraced a hasty and ill-informed campaign to wrap up Indian assimilation and apply its methods to subjects in the newly acquired U.S. dominions. For expansionists, the American frontier had progressed beyond the nation's borders and well into the Pacific realm.[50]

Reflecting Roosevelt's impatience with federal guardianship, a new generation of expansionists pushed to bring the long saga of Indian assimilation to a close. Looking toward the new U.S. Pacific possessions, they saw Indian assimilation as a template for American colonization in the Philippines. As Theodore Roosevelt argued in an 1899 speech not long after he was elected governor of New York, "Every argument that can be made for the Philippines could be made for the Apaches, every word that can be said of Aguinaldo could be said for Sitting Bull." Roosevelt asserted, "As peace and order and prosperity followed our expansion over the lands of the Indians, so they will follow us in the Philippines." The stage was set for a new kind of American Indian history constructed by the first generation of professional women historians.[51]

Part II

A New Frontier for Women Historians, 1890–1941

CHAPTER 7

The Pacific Frontier

Women Historians and a New Kind of Indian History

As it had for Helen Hunt Jackson and Alice Fletcher, American westward expansion called a new generation of women to author document-driven Indian histories. For nineteenth-century women scholars, American imperialism began on the western bank of the Mississippi River and looked toward the setting sun. In contrast, for the first generation of professional women historians, twentieth-century American imperialism began on California's shoreline and ended where the sunset melted into the Pacific Ocean. At the conclusion of the Spanish-American War, this imperial gaze quickly fell upon the Philippines.

In 1980 Walter L. Williams argued that American Indian policy shaped United States policy in the Philippines. Williams's scholarship linked Theodore Roosevelt, Brooks Adams, William McKinley, and other expansionists to the belief that American Philippines policy should mirror trans-Mississippi western settlement and Indian assimilation. Williams suggested that the conflation of Pacific expansion with Manifest Destiny played a key role in lending credence to Frederick Jackson Turner's articulation of American exceptionalism. Ultimately, the American Philippines colonial venture withered. In 1902 President Theodore Roosevelt began drawing the Philippine occupation to a close, in part because the much touted assimilation project was not working.[1]

Although American expansionists imagined close similarities between Philippine colonial history and American Indian assimilation history, in reality they were little more than parallel. Nevertheless, a handful of expansionist scholars—championed by political allies—purported to address a dire foreign policy issue. Presenting an "objective" account of treaties, laws, and judicial precedents linking Filipino and American Indian colonial history, these scholars advanced their work as informative for U.S. policy in the Pacific Islands. Filipino and Indian political history seemed promising areas of study.[2]

Magnified by congressional debate over Pacific colonization, this emerging historical narrative provided one woman from outside the academy with a rare opportunity to publish historical scholarship. As coauthor of new nationally important work on the Philippines, Emma Helen Blair earned the respect of academic peers without challenging the history profession's sexual division of labor. An examination of Blair's scholarly genesis demonstrates why the link between expansionists and early professional women historians was both tenuous and short-lived. More so, Blair's troubled encounter with expansionist scholarship illuminates her turn toward American Indian political history.

EMMA HELEN BLAIR AND ASSIMILATION POLITICS IN THE PACIFIC REALM

Emma Helen Blair's brief work as an expansionist scholar, and later as an Indian historian, was made possible in part by Frederick Jackson Turner's promotion of women graduate students. In fact, Turner awarded the first history doctorate earned by a woman to Kate Asaphine Everest in 1893, and of the seven history doctorates bestowed on women between 1893 and 1900, at least two were earned under Turner's direction. While Turner believed the work women historians with M.A. and Ph.D. degrees did at the secondary and high school levels was essential to promoting American identity, he thwarted their bids for faculty appointments at universities. For women graduates seeking employment at professional archives, museums, libraries, women's colleges, and high schools, Turner penned glowing letters of recommendation. A notable example was Emma Helen Blair—one of Turner's least-known, but most historically significant pupils.[3]

Unlike Turner's better-known student Louise Phelps Kellogg, biographical information is sparse for Emma Helen Blair, a little-known figure in Wisconsin and American historiography. The details of Blair's early life are sketchy and barely illuminate her graduate work with Turner. Her obituaries and college catalogues show that in 1874 Blair graduated from Ripon Women's College, Madison, Wisconsin, where she earned a B.A., and afterward she worked in public education, as an editor, and as registrar of the Milwaukee Associated Charities. With the intention of burnishing her social science credentials, at the age of forty-one Blair enrolled in the University of Wisconsin.

Emma Helen Blair, ca. 1911, photograph by Reuben Gold Thwaites. Blair, an early student of Frederick Jackson Turner, was one of the first professional historians to focus on American Indian history as a specialized field of study. Courtesy of the Wisconsin Historical Society (WHS-23529).

Between 1892 and 1894 Blair studied sociology, economics, and history and earned a Bachelor of Science degree. She began history graduate work under Turner, but that was terminated for unknown reasons before she earned an advanced degree. At an unknown date Blair enrolled in the Ripon College Spanish program. Records indicate that by 1906 Blair had earned a M.A. in Spanish. In 1909 the University of Wisconsin awarded Blair an honorary history M.A. in recognition of her professional work as a translator and historian.[4]

From 1894 until her death from cancer in 1911, Blair worked under the direction of Turner's associate Reuben Gold Thwaites at the Wisconsin State Historical Society (WSHS). The circumstances of her employment are unknown, but it seems reasonable to assume that Turner helped Blair secure the WSHS position, given his close friendship with Thwaites and his later claim to have shaped Blair's scholarship. At the WSHS Blair first worked as a librarian and curator cataloging state newspapers. From 1896 to 1901 Blair's early scholarship involved translation and copyediting for Thwaites's monumental seventy-three volume work, *The Jesuit Relations and Allied Documents*. As Thwaites's assistant editor Blair gained insight into how historical manuscripts were selected, translated, and readied for publication.[5]

Blair likely acquired much of her appreciation for American Indian cultures and history from Thwaites during her time at WSHS. Thwaites was known for his interest in American Indian peoples, and much of his publication focused on the complex social, political, and economic interactions that existed between American Indians and European Americans in the old Northwest. Reflecting this interest, Thwaites's and Blair's *Jesuit Relations* focused on yearly reports sent by French Jesuit missionaries to their North American and French superiors as well as supplementary documents spanning 1610–1791. According to Thwaites, the volumes were intended to illuminate the lives and historical acts of both French colonists and American Indians.[6]

Whatever Thwaites's influence, Blair took an active interest in American Indian history. A letter she sent to the *American Anthropologist* journal in fall 1900 commenting on an article authored by Alice C. Fletcher in the previous issue, testified to Blair's budding interest in American Indian history. Blair noted, "I have read with much interest Miss [Alice] Fletcher's account of the visit to France in 1827 of a party of Osage Indians." After providing additional information on the incident, Blair concluded with research suggestions for Fletcher including material from *Jesuit Relations*. There is no evidence that Blair ever met Fletcher in person or shared correspondence, but Blair's *American Anthropologist* letter and citations in her final publication demonstrate her detailed knowledge of Fletcher's scholarship and a familiarity with Indian Rights Association (IRA) publications. Cumulatively, this evidence suggests a tenuous link between the ethno-political scholarship of preprofessional women scholars of American Indians and professional women historians' emerging interest in Indian history. The association would prove short-lived.[7]

Blair's translation and copyedit work on *Jesuit Relations* so impressed Thwaites that he asked her to work on two additional manuscripts: *A New Discovery of a Large Country in America by Father Lewis Hennepin* and *Original Journals of the Lewis and Clark Expedition, 1804–1806*. As with her work on the previous volumes, Blair's new translation work further exposed her to the complex story of American Indian cultures and history. *A New Discovery of a*

Large Country was based on translated colonial French fur trade documents detailing French and Indian social and economic relations, while *Original Journals of the Lewis and Clark Expedition* glorified Anglo-Saxon individualism and westward expansion into American Indian homelands. In deference to the great evangelist of American imperialism and his popular history of Western conquest, the *Lewis and Clark Expedition* preface read, "To Theodore Roosevelt . . . this first publication of the Original Records of their 'Winning of the West' is most respectfully dedicated."[8]

While working on *The Jesuit Relations*, Blair began a curious professional relationship with Western history publisher Arthur Henry Clark and editor, bibliographer, and archivist James Alexander Robertson. Publications by this scholarly triumvirate would weave together American Pacific colonization, Indian assimilation, and the academic work of respected American historians—notably Frederick Jackson Turner, Henry B. Lathrop, Edward Gaylord Bourne, and Herbert Eugene Bolton. Inspired by the raging national interest in America's Pacific dominions, Blair noted in a 1902 letter to Edward E. Ayer, "I have just made arrangements with a publisher for the issue of a series (covering more than fifty volumes) to comprise documents relating to the early history of those islands." Ayer, a wealthy Chicago businessman, influential Newberry Library patron, and collector of books and manuscripts on Indians and the American West, would prove an important ally in Blair's eventual bid to publish with the Arthur H. Clark Company.[9]

Blair's letter to Ayer sheds light on her emerging relationship with the newly established Arthur H. Clark publishing house and the manner in which Philippine colonial history became linked to Indian and American West scholarship. Clark, a British citizen, began his American publishing career following a chance meeting with General Alexander C. McClurg. Impressed by his enthusiasm for the vocation, McClurg offered Clark a job with his Chicago-based publishing house in 1889. Clark remained there until 1892.

After an unsuccessful bookstore venture that ended in 1893, Clark found employment with rival bookseller, the Burrows Brothers Company in Cleveland, Ohio. At Burrows Brothers Clark became close friends with one of the firm's principle customers and Blair's future employer, Reuben Gold Thwaites. Both men would play a pivotal role in Blair's eventual turn to Indian scholarship.[10]

Through Thwaites, Clark developed an interest in Mississippi Valley history, particularly seventeenth- and eighteenth-century Jesuit influence in the region. Seizing the chance to further his own publication interests, Thwaites proposed a multivolume translation of French, Latin, and Italian sources on Jesuit activities in the Mississippi Valley. Following an intense lobbying campaign by Thwaites and Clark, Burrows Brothers agreed to fund translation and publication. Work began in 1896. Over the next four years Clark and fellow Burrows Brothers employee James Alexander Robertson worked on the project with Thwaites and Blair. Blair served as a translator for the series—her first published scholarship.

While working on the Jesuit volumes, Blair and Robertson developed a close friendship that would continue for several years. This association deepened between 1900 and 1901 when Robertson, still a Burrows Brothers employee joined Blair at the WSHS full time to work on a comprehensive index for the project. Completed in 1901, the seventy-three volume *The Jesuit Relations and Allied Documents* received critical acclaim.[11]

Although *The Jesuit Relations* proved a financial success for Burrows Brothers, Clark left the firm in 1901 over a contractual dispute. With his recent publication success in mind, Clark founded his own Cleveland, Ohio, publishing firm devoted to frontier and American West topics. The Arthur H. Clark Company publishing house opened in 1902.[12]

Between 1902 and 1903 Blair's friendship with Thwaites, Clark, Ayer, and Robertson proved invaluable to her publication career. Noting the acclaim of Thwaites's Burrows Brothers publication and hoping to cash in on a burgeoning national interest in the Philippines, Blair and Robertson approached Clark with a proposition. Knowing that Ayer had called for the collection of Spanish colonial documents following the Spanish-American War, and remembering Thwaites's own interest in Spanish American colonial documents, the duo proposed a multivolume translation of Spanish North American and Spanish Pacific colonial documents. Blair and Robertson suggested eminent historian Edward Gaylord Bourne direct the project, further tempting Clark.[13]

Titled *The Philippine Islands, 1493–1803*, Bourne's introduction set the tone for the first year's work. Declaring the American Indian assimilation project completed, he proclaimed the "negro" and the "Malay" (Filipinos) as the nation's two remaining "race problems." Foremost, Bourne contextualized the study as demonstrating the role Spain played in North American Anglo-Saxon colonization. Tracing Spanish influence from 1493 to the 1803 Louisiana Purchase, Bourne structured the first five volumes around Turner's Frontier Thesis. Frederick Jackson Turner's input was noted in the editorial acknowledgments, where Blair and Robertson thanked him for his personal assistance.[14]

Completed in early 1903, the first five volumes depicted Spain as a beneficial and civilizing influence in the Americas. While generally well received by academics and the American public, U.S. Governor of the Philippines William Howard Taft (1901–1903) vehemently disagreed with the assessment of Spanish colonialism in *The Philippine Islands*. For Taft and his chief adviser James Alfred LeRoy, the Protestant Anglo-Saxon lads who landed at Jamestown and whose descendants later marched into Manila, Havana, and San Juan did not succeed a civilized Spanish empire, rather they drove out a barbaric Old World Catholic regime steeped in medieval ignorance and tyranny. LeRoy publically voiced this view in biting critiques published as reviews in the *Nation* (1903) and the *American Historical Review* (1904). Specifically, LeRoy accused Bourne of advancing a pro-Spanish viewpoint through a narrow selection of translated documents.[15]

Blair responded to LeRoy's blunt appraisal with a pointed refutation, noting that Bourne was a respected scholar of the North American Spanish colonial era. Blair stressed that *The Philippine Islands'* editorial board did not have an agenda regarding the Spanish colonial venture. Moreover, regarding what LeRoy characterized as the need for "a broadening of scope," Blair noted that Robertson was then currently in Seville, Spain, conducting research at the Archivo General de Indias and planned to survey Spanish colonial era documents in Madrid, Simancas, Rome, Paris, London, Manila, and Mexico. In refuting LeRoy's critique of Bourne and Robertson, Blair had also advanced a rigorous defense of her own work.[16]

In August 1903, likely responding to government pressure, Clark abruptly named James LeRoy new director of the *Philippine Islands* series. The appointment was curious given that Leroy had no previous experience in historical scholarship or serious publication. Nevertheless, Taft and LeRoy finally wielded sufficient power to shape Philippine scholarship. Utilizing the authority of his new position, LeRoy quickly pushed Bourne to the periphery and proceeded to fashion the remaining *Philippine* volumes into a running critique of the Spanish colonial regime.[17]

In LeRoy's hands the immediate publications depicted Spanish depravity while lauding precolonial "Malay" (Filipino) culture. Executing a comprehensive revision of the project, LeRoy soon turned the focus of the series to the whole of Spanish Pacific colonization. LeRoy's ultimate goal was to demonize Spanish colonialism, while portraying American expansion as both a liberating and civilizing force.[18]

For his part Bourne was unimpressed with Leroy's scholarship. Resenting his displacement by a politically connected amateur boor and historical simpleton, Bourne turned away from the Clark project. Bourne worked instead on his *Spain in America, 1450–1580*, which would eventually appear as volume three of Albert Bushnell Hart's massive series, *The American Nation: A History*. In the introduction Bourne refuted LeRoy's scholarship by embracing an inclusive view of Spanish history in America "from the birth of Christopher

Columbus to the beginning of the continuous activity in colonization by the English."[19]

For his part, though Turner had advised Blair and Robertson on the Philippines project, he did not comment on the turn of events with LeRoy nor did he make further suggestions for the volume. Like Bourne, much of Turner's time after 1903 was devoted to his own pending contribution to the Hart series titled, *The Rise of the New West*. Marshaling material from his numerous magazine and journal articles, Turner's contribution reiterated the east to west trajectory of his Frontier Thesis.[20]

Unlike Bourne and Turner who were able to professionally distance themselves from *The Philippine Islands* project, Blair and Robertson were obligated to complete their work. For his part, Robertson apparently accepted the plunge into government propaganda with few questions. Blair adapted, but never forgave LeRoy for commandeering the project. Forced upon her as contrived scholarship, LeRoy's editorial control distressed Blair. While it is not entirely clear what Turner and Thwaites thought of LeRoy (if they gave him much thought at all), they strongly encouraged Blair to take up American Indian history when *The Philippine Islands* project ended in 1909. James Alfred LeRoy's influence over American historical scholarship also ended in 1909—with his death from tuberculosis.[21]

Taking Turner and Thwaites's advice, in 1909 Blair immediately turned her attention to research on American Indian history. Blair's resulting scholarship comprised a two-volume publication titled, *The Indian Tribes of the Upper Mississippi Valley and Region of the Great Lakes*. Although Clark deemed *The Philippine Islands* a failure—he lost twenty thousand dollars on the venture—apparently under Turner's and Thwaites's influence he agreed to publish Blair's work.[22]

Clark's decision to publish Blair's book was all the more daring considering that *The Indian Tribes* merged translated historical documents and Indian political history with ethno-political scholarship and Indian rights sentiment. Conceivably, this marriage of the accepted and the near taboo in professional history was the result of Blair's inexperience—she was primarily a translator of historical documents and did not have a Ph.D. in history. However, this argument is complicated by the fact that Blair was a nationally acclaimed peer-reviewed historian whose work involved skilled interpretation, analysis, and meticulously researched annotations. Additionally, Turner critiqued much of Blair's scholarship, including *The Indian Tribes*, before publication. At first glance, *The Indian Tribes* seems to be a disturbing contradiction—a professional-era Indian history sprinkled with preprofessional ethno-political scholarship—all with Frederick Jackson Turner's stamp of approval. But a closer look suggests that Blair, who was battling cancer at the time, transformed a painful personal tragedy into a unique opportunity to navigate the otherwise irreconcilable politics of contemporary professional objectivity and her own Indian rights sentiment. Blair, the old social worker and charities administrator, wanted to use her professional skills as an Indian historian to publish one final book that she hoped would tangibly benefit American Indians.[23]

Dedicated to "Frederick Jackson Turner, who has long led the van of research in the history of the great Middle West, and has done most to make known its importance in the development of the American nation," Blair's *The Indian Tribes* was a curious blend of documentary translations, Indian political history, ethnological material, and blatant assimilationist politics. Blair's semiprofessional status (as the recipient of two M.A.s) gave her entrée to Turner's professional guidance on Indian political history and Thwaites's expertise on document sourcing, translation, and indexing. Additionally, Blair drew upon a complex network of ethnologists and Indian rights activists to inform the sections of her book that detailed ethnological data and assimilation politics. Although not definitive evidence, the chronology of material in *The Indian Tribes* strongly suggests that the professional historians consulted for it, most notably Turner, did not know about the later ethnological and assimilation additions—at least until after Blair's death.[24]

The structure that Blair selected for *The Indian Tribes* is curiously similar to that used by Helen Hunt Jackson for *A Century of Dishonor* thirty years earlier. Blair's main text, like Jackson's, is a fairly objective document-based history. Likewise, both Blair and Jackson's introductions and appendices resemble the other's, with the introductions making a sentimental appeal for "justice" (assimilation) and the appendices presenting American Indian letters and articles from leading ethnological and Indian rights sources. While it is possible that Turner and Thwaites indulged Blair as she weakened and grew progressive ill between 1910 and 1911, the importance each man attached to professional credibility makes this highly unlikely. Blair clarified the matter in a short preface to volume two's "Addenda," noting that because of her "serious illness and to avoid delay in publication," the eminent American Bureau of Ethnology social scientist Paul Radin had "kindly revised proofs for the second half of volume II and prepared the following additional information." Moreover, Blair noted, Gertrude M. Robinson prepared the index.[25]

The first volume contained Blair's translations of two treatises on early Midwestern American Indian cultures by the French fur trader and colonial official Nicolas Perrot and the French colonial official Claude-Charles Le Roy. The first half of volume two continued with the Le Roy translation, followed by the memoirs of American Major Morrill Marston and American Thomas Forsyth, an Indian agent. These four documents were well known to Turner and Thwaites, and it is entirely reasonable to assume they reviewed the first half of the manuscript, since Blair thanked each for their critiques and suggestions. However, as Blair clarified, neither Turner nor Thwaites reviewed the remainder of the text.[26]

Volume two concluded with a lengthy appendices in three parts (A, B, and C) intended to "bring the work down to the present day and render it a connected and homogeneous whole." Beginning with early French contact, appendix A is a condensed biography of Nicolas Perrot prepared by Blair. Appendix B is comprised of material written by Alice C. Fletcher, Henry W. Henshaw, Franz Boas, and James Mooney that Blair culled from the Bureau of Ethnology's *Handbook of American Indians*. Blair intended the ethnological material from appendix B to illuminate "the present condition of the Sioux, Potawatomie, and Winnebago tribes." Appendix C presents a selection of ethno-political letters, written by various Christian clergy, pleading for missionary support and Indian "rights."[27]

While it seems improbable that Turner or Thwaites would have accepted the ethnological and Indian rights politics in the appendices as objective, much less professional, Blair's blatant sentimental advocacy of Indian rights in the introduction to the work would have likely provoked friction with her old mentors. Reaching into the misty past of Indian activism, Blair recycled almost every sentimentalist trope used by assimilationists over the preceding century. Proclaiming her desire to banish the degraded image of American Indians depicted in the popular press, Blair hoped her final publication would reveal that "the Indian is very much the same kind of being that his white brother would have been if put in the red man's place."[28]

Yet for all its ethno-political baggage, the heart of Blair's *The Indian Tribes* was a solid Turnerian text, and it did affirm the early stages of Americanization proposed by Turner. Moreover, book reviews by the popular press unanimously praised *The Indian Tribes*, as an important and readable American Indian history, while professional historians were more sedate. The *American Historical Review* (*AHR*) rather banally reported, "Miss Blair spared neither labor nor space in illuminating the original narratives with generous notes and annotation," but more frankly concluded her project had "been realized with indifferent success," largely "because of the character of the materials welded together." Yet, most critics agreed with the *AHR* reviewer's final assessment: "There is certainly no doubt as to the great service which has been rendered to students of American history by the publication . . . in . . . English translation of these source materials."[29]

Choosing to dismiss Blair's parting plea for Indian rights, fellow professional historians emphasized her service as an archivist and translator. But

Blair's work had already transcended that distinction, she was not ultimately remembered as a translator but rather as an important historian of the Midwest and American Indians. Ironically, in a 1905 *Dial* article titled "The Problems of Translation," Blair had already rejected the notion that her work was mere rendition, contending instead that skilled translation is a valid historical scholarship that serves as the basis for "forming its own conclusions as to events, affairs, and men." By blurring the often gendered boundaries between historical translation and historical scholarship, Blair helped elevate the status of other professional women historians who published significant historical translations. This precedent would have a lasting effect on both the Arthur H. Clark Company and on Blair's WSHS colleague, Louise Phelps Kellogg.[30]

By selecting documents that examined the "Indian character and the policy of the whites toward the dispossessed Indian tribes" for her final publication, Blair unwittingly helped Arthur H. Clark refocus his publishing interests on history of the American West. Moreover, after their brief scholarly foray into transpacific American imperialism, Blair's work also signaled a renewed emphasis on North American and Mississippi Valley scholarship among Turner's closest allies. More directly, *The Indian Tribes* marked the continuing influence of women historians at one of the nation's premier frontier archives—the Wisconsin State Historical Society. Yet, in spite of Blair's measured success, professional interest in American Indian history still lagged. The development of American Indian history as a specialized field of study would be continued by Blair's friend and WSHS colleague, Louise Phelps Kellogg.

LOUISE PHELPS KELLOGG: A FIELD ALL HER OWN

Louise Phelps Kellogg was Frederick Jackson Turner's second female doctoral student. Kellogg, a Wisconsin native, entered the Madison graduate history program in 1895. If not for her sex, Kellogg might have been a Turner protégé. In fact Kellogg was among a small cadre of students who enrolled in Turner's original History of the West class—the first of its kind taught at an American university. Just six months her senior, Turner initially found Kellogg an ill-prepared student, but he came to respect her diligence, analytical skills, and originality. Under Turner's direction Kellogg studied early American frontier history, an interest reflected in her 1897 B.L. (Bachelor of Literature) thesis, "The Formation of the State of West Virginia."[31]

In 1898, with Turner's blessing, Kellogg applied for and was awarded a Boston Education Association fellowship that paid for a years' study in Europe. Overseas, Kellogg completed classes at the London School of History and

Louise Phelps Kellogg at her desk. Encouraged by her doctoral committee chair, Frederick Jackson Turner, much of Kellogg's Midwestern scholarship focused on American Indian history. Courtesy of the Wisconsin Historical Society (WHS-15343).

Economics and later at the Sorbonne. Before her studies in England ended, Kellogg also conducted research at the Public Record Office in London. While finishing her classwork at the Sorbonne, Kellogg published her first professional history article in the September 1899 issue of *Le Revolution Françoise*—in French. Returning to the University of Wisconsin, Kellogg was awarded an assistantship and taught ancient and medieval history courses for Charles Homer Haskins, who was away on sabbatical. Utilizing research from her time at the London archive, in 1901 Kellogg successfully defended her dissertation, "The American Colonial Charter: A Study of English Administration in Relation Thereto, Chiefly after 1688." Kellogg's dissertation won the American Historical Association's Justin Winsor prize for the best dissertation on American history and was later published in the 1903 AHA annual report. With doctorate in hand Kellogg expected to find a full-time faculty position with a university history department, but the position never materialized. As a woman noticeably hard of hearing, Kellogg was not an ideal candidate for academic employment in Turner's eyes, yet her skill as a researcher, scholar, and teacher earned high praise. Indeed, after Kellogg returned from her year of study in Europe, Turner helped her secure the one-year assistantship in ancient and medieval history and a university fellowship for the following semester. Accolades aside, Kellogg was slated, like most women historians, for a position outside the academy.[32]

While it was not generally known to women historians, in recommendation letters and private correspondence male mentors and colleagues often characterized them in whole or in part as either disturbingly willful, physically impaired, grotesquely unattractive, distastefully unusual, or lacking in personality. Symptomatic of this prejudice, women historians were scrutinized for real, imaginary, or nonsensical defects that purportedly made them unfit for academic careers. Reflecting pervasive sexism, this stealthy institutional chauvinism helped justify the disproportionate consignment of women historians to careers at historical archives, museums, women's colleges, and high schools. Women historians like Kellogg and Blair, who used publication to reach beyond the professional anonymity of sexually segregated vocations, came to occupy a kind of scholarly limbo—recognized but without standing in the academy.[33]

Even if their work justified academic accolades, if not faculty employment, women historians' purported defects helped absolve the culpability of those who relegated them to nonacademic careers. Kellogg's hearing impairment allowed Turner to easily mark her as a promising but flawed prospect. Upon graduation Kellogg was directed toward a one-year research position at the highly esteemed Wisconsin State Historical Society—Turner having worked behind the scenes to this end. As a research assistant Kellogg worked under the direction of longtime Turner friend and colleague, WSHS Secretary Reuben Gold Thwaites.[34]

While an accomplished archivist and scholar, Kellogg was not a maverick. In fact Thwaites, like Turner, initially considered her suggestible and easily manipulated. On a superficial level, Kellogg's pliable nature seemed an advantage to Thwaites. Where Blair had proven an independent thinker and willful historian, Kellogg presented herself as a loyal scholar and employee. However, under her own authority and at WSHS expense, Kellogg published several acclaimed volumes on American Midwest history, numerous pamphlets, and journal articles—in addition to the work assigned by Thwaites and his successor. Arguably, Kellogg's lifelong devotion to publication revealed both her strategic accommodation and personal agency within a vocation dominated by men.[35]

As they had with Emma Helen Blair, Turner and Thwaites also influenced Kellogg's interest in American Indian history. Turner was mainly preoccupied with archival documents detailing colonial and early republic

American Indian history. But Thwaites demonstrated what Turner called, "a catholicity of views" that lead Thwaites "as early as 1876 . . . [to] publish a [biographical] sketch of the Indian chief Oshkosh." Moreover, Turner noted that as WSHS secretary, Thwaites "visited remaining Indian tribes in their old homes, interviewed their chiefs . . . and incidentally was obliged to be host . . . to delegation after delegation of these Indians." Turner added, "At [Thwaites's] summer home in Turvillwood the Winnebago . . . still made annual hunting trips." As Kellogg would discover, Thwaites's view of Wisconsin and Midwestern history was permeated by American Indian peoples and their histories.[36]

Although frontier and Midwestern histories were popular at the time, Thwaites and Kellogg collaborated on a number of published volumes that were heavily weighted toward Indian political history. In turn, Thwaites also encouraged Kellogg to expand her own research on Indian history in the Midwest. This scholarly persuasion was reflected in Kellogg's first WSHS journal article, "The Fox Indians during the French Regime," published in 1908. A meticulously researched piece, "The Fox Indians," followed the contours of traditional political history.[37]

Notably, the Fox article is illustrative of Kellogg's later Indian political histories. Kellogg followed a clear chronology, first discussing Fox migrations and how the tribe came to inhabit "Wisconsin territory." Later, French colonialists made first contact with the Fox tribe through the ministrations of a fur trader and minor official named Nicolas Perrot. Following a familiar pattern outlined by Turner in his Frontier Thesis, the French quickly moved to establish commercial relations with the Fox tribe. However, the relationship soured when the Fox determined French traders were "deceitful, arrogant, and brutal." Tensions soon lead to warfare. After approximately sixty years of intermittent conflict with "New France," the Fox ultimately made a strategic decision to side with their old colonial enemies during the "French and Indian" war. Following French defeat, the Fox Indians "were inclined to the English interest." Reflecting Turner's assessment of colonial French and Spanish collusion with American Indians, Kellogg argued that the French tendency to "congregate tribes around a French post, induced friction that produced war." Kellogg concluded, "The Fox were the entering wedge of ruin for the French dominion in America," and the tribe's "obstinate resistance . . . set in motion forces that gave . . . the Great West to the English speaking race."[38]

As the only fulltime American professional historian with a special focus on Indian history, Kellogg played a key role in developing the WSHS's national reputation for frontier scholarship. Having studied under Turner and mastered his proficiency in Midwestern history, Kellogg proved to be an invaluable editorial assistant for Thwaites, and in return he proved an invaluable guide to archival research and historical publication. Years later Kellogg would note, "He taught me my trade."[39]

While in Thwaites's employment Kellogg found little time for her own work, publishing only a few short monographs and papers under her name. Though an amiable and generous scholar, Thwaites was a relentless taskmaster. During her first year at WSHS Thwaites assigned Kellogg to work with Blair and Robertson—under his direction—translating and editing his seventy-three volume series *Jesuit Relations*. This project was immediately followed by Thwaites's eight-volume series of Lewis and Clark journals, which Kellogg edited. Over the next decade Kellogg worked directly with Thwaites, helping to translate and edit his three-volume series *Revolution on the Upper Ohio, 1775–1777*, and his thirty-two volume *Early Western Travels*. Ultimately, Kellogg's grueling work with Thwaites significantly broadened her knowledge of colonial French, Spanish, English, and American Indian history.[40]

Reuben Gold Thwaites's death in 1913 proved a turning point in Kellogg's publication. Although Kellogg completed their joint projects already in progress, notably *French Advance on the Upper Ohio* (1916) and *French Retreat on the Upper Ohio* (1917), she also took a series of steps that established American Indian history as a defining feature of her work. This was accomplished through the publication of a series of popular newspaper articles on local Indian lore, and a short but significant peer-reviewed article titled, "Indian Diplomacy during the Revolution in the West." She also published an acclaimed two-volume set exploring colonial and American Indian relations, *Frontier Advance on the Upper Ohio, 1778–1779* (1916) and *Frontier Retreat on the Upper Ohio, 1779–1781* (1917), and *Early Narratives of the Northwest, 1634–1699*, which examined French and Indian relations in the Great Lakes and the northeastern Mississippi Valley regions.[41]

Over the next two decades Kellogg published two more esteemed volumes on French, English, and American Indian relations in the old Midwest: *The French Regime in Wisconsin and the Northwest* (1925) and *The British Regime in the Northwest* (1935). In recognition of her extensive publication and scholarly distinction, the University of Wisconsin awarded Kellogg an honorary Doctor of Letters degree in 1926. Four years later, Kellogg was elected the first woman president of the Mississippi Valley Historical Association—forerunner of the Organization of American Historians. In 1937 Kellogg and esteemed Spanish borderlands historian Herbert Eugene Bolton were jointly awarded honorary doctorates by Marquette University for their contributions to the history of southwestern Catholic missions. Kellogg's tenure at WSHS, during which time she had either "written, edited, indexed or proofread" each of the society's several hundred publications, lasted until her death in 1942.[42]

A search of Kellogg's published works will not produce many titles that directly reference American Indians. Kellogg's Indian histories, though extensive, are called "frontier, "old Midwestern," or "Midwestern" history, following the precedent established by her mentor, Reuben Gold Thwaites. Like Thwaites, though the bulk of her publications focused on American Indian history, Kellogg's professional credibility was based on her reputation as a frontier historian. Unlike Emma Helen Blair's work, which was published through the Arthur H. Clark Company, the WSHS board funded or underwrote Kellogg's publications. As the nation's premier frontier historical society, WSHS promoted frontier history and frontier historians. Nevertheless, through prodigious scholarly output both Blair and Kellogg made a permanent contribution to American Indian historical scholarship. Crucially, Kellogg's long career as a public historian and published author demonstrated that professional women historians could take up American Indian history without evoking the discredited excesses of women's preprofessional ethno-political scholarship.

A few male frontier historians, such as James Alton James the author of *Indian Diplomacy and the Opening of the Revolution in the West*, dabbled in American Indian history, but their interests were faint and their publications sparse. Kellogg on the other hand epitomized scholarly productivity—in a very real sense her voluminous work exploring European American and American Indian relations became her history. By championing objective Indian history, Kellogg reaffirmed the traditional connection between European American women and American Indian scholarship, and in the absence of significant male scholarly interest she also pioneered the writing of professional Indian history. In this regard Kellogg blazed a trail for other women historians who helped make American Indian history a specialized field within the history profession.[43]

Yet the part of Kellogg's scholarship that focused on American Indians did not prompt widespread interest among American historians. Indian history was still considered a fringe subject that did not warrant specialized study in the male dominated academy. While Kellogg found a comfortable niche for American Indian history and women historians in frontier scholarship, she did not demonstrate the singular importance of American Indian history. The question remained, were Indians more than tangential to American history? The unequivocal answer would come from a woman historian who successfully bridged the regional chasm that divided male American historians of her day.[44]

ANNIE HELOISE ABEL AND THE SPECIALIZATION OF INDIAN POLITICAL HISTORY

While Louise Phelps Kellogg laid the groundwork for defining American Indian history as a specialized interest, the scholarship of Annie Heloise Abel would bring it to fruition. Born in 1873, Annie Abel was a native of Sussex, England, who immigrated at age twelve to the United States, where she joined her father, mother, and siblings on a farm outside Salina, Kansas. Annie's parents, George and Amelia, had immigrated to Kansas with four of their children in 1884, but Annie remained behind with a relative in England. The year of Annie Abel's arrival, 1885, found Kansas booming. The new state's progress was conspicuous in its profusion of well-funded public schools.[45]

Abel attended Salina high school, graduating in 1893, and for the next two years she taught in the Kansas public school system. In 1895 Abel was accepted at the University of Kansas (KU). As a state resident, Abel's undergraduate classes were free of charge. An ambitious student, Abel received a B.A. with honors in 1898. Following KU graduation, Abel taught for a year at the Thomas County high school, and afterward she took a job at KU as a manuscript reader for the English department. The job required Abel and a cohort to grade student essays for each of the university disciplines. Within a year Abel tired of marking "about 45,000 pages of manuscript," and resigned her position. Soon after, Abel was accepted by the KU graduate history program where she studied "Anglo-Saxon, Middle English and American History."[46]

Abel's M.A. chair was the eminent historian Frank Haywood Hodder, who devoted his scholarly attention to state formation on the American frontier. Hodder, a tedious but respected historian of Kansas, was embroiled in a statewide controversy involving his interpretation of the Kansas slavery debate by the time he became Abel's thesis chair. Amateur historian John Speer of the Kansas State Historical Society (KSHS) accused Hodder of slandering antislavery partisans and contended that Hodder's work downplayed the moral and ethical arguments of Kansas abolitionists. Under attack by Speer, who was politically connected, Hodder soon found his KU position in jeopardy. The bloody battles of bleeding Kansas were not yet ready for the objective scrutiny of professional historians.[47]

Clearly shaken, Hodder consulted his KU colleagues. Their unanimous recommendation was that he should drop the matter and focus on the broad sweep of American history. Agreeing, Hodder publicly retreated from Kansas history and the slavery issue. Reflecting this reversal, Hodder also maneuvered his graduate students away from subjects touching on the Kansas slavery debate—though not specifically away from Kansas history. This unfortunate chain of events would definitively shape Abel's work.[48]

Annie Heloise Abel, ca. 1901–1904. As the first woman historian to focus on Indian history within the academy, Annie Heloise Abel successfully pushed American Indian scholarship westward. Courtesy of the University Archives, Kenneth Spencer Research Library, University of Kansas.

Abel's interest in American Indian history began in England. As a British citizen who became a naturalized American, Abel interpreted American Manifest Destiny as a natural extension of British colonialism. Abel's tendency to equate an idealized British imperial benevolence with an idealized view of American Manifest Destiny reflected a popular late-nineteenth century British mindset that shaped her early intellectual development. As a graduate student at KU, Abel interpreted abolition and American Indian assimilation policy as legacies of British imperial benevolence, and she was keen on examining this connection through the lens of Kansas history.[49]

The aspiring historian quickly found that present history proved to be past politics. Given Hodder's own recent difficulties, Abel's interest in exploring a correlation between British colonialism and American westward expansion alarmed him. Realizing the subject could not be addressed without delving into slavery, abolition, and the Civil War, Hodder encouraged Abel to focus instead on Indian politics at the state level. Hodder believed that his protagonists would find Indian politics, a subject largely deemed outside "white" history, of little concern. After some deliberation Abel decided to write her thesis on "Indian Reservations in Kansas and the Extinguishment of their Title."[50]

Abel's thesis effectively circumvented the concerns Speer and his KSHS compatriots raised about Hodder's Kansas slavery study. As important, in the opening paragraph Abel fashioned an argument that she would use to navigate the perils of Northern and Southern regional sentiment throughout her career as an Indian historian. Taking up Turner's focus on the national significance of westward expansion, Abel shrewdly dismissed slavery arguing, "Those of us who are accustomed to regard the tariff, the national bank and negro slavery as the all-important issues . . . forget how intimately the aborigines were concerned in that estrangement of the North and South." Replacing slavery as the pivotal dispute in American history with Indian removal-assimilation, Abel asserted, "The 'Great American Desert' . . . was destined to be the testing-ground . . . of the two principle theories connected with the sectional conflict—squatter sovereignty and Indian colonization."[51]

Abel's argument effectively killed two birds with one stone. First it established a politically safe narrative for addressing those areas in which she felt U.S. national ethics were damaged by abrogation of the British colonial humanitarian legacy. Second, it allowed her to draw Southern history into the westward sweep of Turner's Frontier Thesis without including a damning indictment of Southern slave mongering. With this two-pronged attack Abel revealed that the North and South were equally complicit in Indian removal and the appropriation of Indian lands. By disavowing the centrality of the issue of slavery, Abel fabricated an historical contrivance that diplomatically reunited the North and South in a grand westward sweep. Abel would spend the remainder of her career as an Indian scholar burying the true cause of the Civil War under Indian treaties, Indian removal, Indian wars, and Indian reservations.[52]

After defending her master's thesis June 6, 1900, Abel was successfully encouraged by Hodder to pursue a doctorate at Cornell University in Ithaca, New York. There Abel studied American history with Moses Coit Tyler, a venerable founding father of the AHA. Unfortunately, Tyler died within months of Abel's arrival. Unimpressed with the remaining faculty and plagued by financial difficulties, Abel returned to Lawrence, Kansas, in 1901. To make ends meet and pay for graduate tuition at Kansas University, Abel taught history and politics at a local high school from 1901 to 1903. Her luck changed in early 1903 when she and KU colleague Frank J. Klingberg were awarded Bulkley (Yale University) scholarships in American history.[53]

With their awards in hand, Abel and Klingberg were admitted to the Yale history doctoral program in 1903, where Abel studied under Edward Gaylord Bourne. Having just distanced himself from the Arthur H. Clark *Philippine Islands* project, Bourne encouraged Abel to expand her M.A. thesis into a broad dissertation topic that looked at Indian removal as a national event. Abel settled on "The History of Events Resulting in Indian Consolidation West of the Mississippi." Abel's scholarship helped further redirect Bourne's own interests toward the Mississippi Valley, while for Abel it circumvented the long-simmering North-South dispute among American historians. Nowhere was this tension more palpable among academics than within the membership of the American Historical Association.[54]

Abel joined the AHA in 1903, but she proved too shy to engage the politics of regional history within the organization. Perhaps this was best for an aspiring western historian, because the AHA's internal power struggles would cause enduring fissures in the history profession. While the 1915 revolt against founding members Herbert Baxter Adams, John Franklin Jameson, and Frederick Jackson Turner is well-known, few are aware of the earlier role dissatisfied Southern historians played in helping Western historians split from the AHA.[55]

Regional academic tensions dated to the early 1890s, and by the early 1900s the ambitions of Western historians wedded the frustrations of Southern historians. Western historians felt the AHA, particularly its journal the *American Historical Review* did not give sufficient attention to pre- and trans-Mississippi history of the American West. Southern scholars were particularly annoyed with the AHA's tendency to link Southern history with the specter of slavery. By 1908 this Western and Southern discontent culminated in a separate historical association devoted to Mississippi Valley history and named the Mississippi Valley Historical Association (MVHA). While an apt solution to the concerns raised by disaffected Western and Southern historians, the MVHA did not soothe Southern sensitivity to historical treatments of the "peculiar institution." As an aspiring Western historian Annie Heloise Abel's career prospects rested on her ability to navigate the regional sensitivities of MVHA members, particularly those allied with the Redeemer view of Southern history.[56]

While Abel would become a celebrated member of the AHA, the editorial board of the *AHR* notoriously discriminated against women scholars whose interests fell outside the Northeast. More damning, *AHR* editor John Franklin Jameson disliked Abel's writing and was particularly unimpressed with her scholarship. In contrast the MVHA's *Mississippi Valley Historical Review* (*MVHR*), under Clarence W. Alvord's editorship, was known for publishing the work of women historians. While Abel's dissertation won the AHA Justin Winsor award and was published in the 1906 *Annual Report of the American Historical Association* (against Jameson's wishes), the bulk of her published articles would appear in the *MVHR*. Publication in the *MVHR* demonstrated Abel's ability to navigate the organization's Southern and Western sentiments.[57]

GONE WITH THE WIND: ETHNOLOGY, SLAVES, AND COLONIAL HUMANITARIANISM

The intellectual environment that shaped Abel during her Yale doctoral work reflected a professional trend toward comity—particularly decorous peer review and academic solidarity in public. This sentiment also characterized the profession's approach to North-South regionalism. While a less flattering but largely diplomatic Southern history was promulgated in the pages of the *AHR* by Herbert Baxter Adams and John Franklin Jameson, AHA member William Archibald Dunning of Columbia University successfully published misleading scholarship on imaginary Reconstruction outrages and so-called Negro rule. Dunning avoided insulting his Northern peers outright by making African Americans responsible for both the Civil War and its aftermath. Adams, Jameson, and Dunning aside, most AHA members were unwilling to openly fuel professional dissension. The practical effect was that American history remained captive to a North-South narrative defined by unwritten but well-known parameters. Colleagues expected fellow American historians to avoid inflammatory rhetoric or polemical scholarship that might foster animosity. Ultimately, keeping regional interests bound within a professional code of conduct gave form to what historian Peter Novick called the professional regime of *"credat emptor"*—or very nicely disputed history.[58]

As Hodder discovered in his own experience with the slavery debate, inflaming regional discontent could harm one's career. When Abel proposed her dissertation subject to Edward Gaylord Bourne and George Burton Adams in 1903 the professional stakes could not have been higher, and for their part neither would follow a graduate student down a rabbit hole. Having already linked British colonialism and United States Indian policy, Abel found that her deepening interest in American slavery pointed her on a dangerous professional path. Fortunately, Abel's studies with Bourne and Adams helped her develop a winning dissertation strategy that avoided regional pitfalls.[59]

Abel's class notes from this period shed light on how Bourne and Adams helped shape her early ideas about the North American British colonial project into a refined critique of American humanitarian failures. As scholars, Bourne and Adams had developed national reputations for their respective Americanist and European scholarship. With Adams, Abel focused on the American application of English constitutional history and law, while Bourne pointed her attention to British colonial policy in the early republic.[60]

Abel's outline for Adams's "British Constitution" seminar reveals the extent to which he sharpened her admiration for British colonialism. Abel underscored Adams's contention that "Constitutional governments are derived from England wherever they are found. . . . English institutions have made a conquest of the whole world." Abel also enrolled in Adams's "Magna Carta and English History to the Tudors" seminar. In her Magna Carta class notes Abel exclaimed, "This is an outline of what we most need in History. . . . It introduces the elements of our own race and institutions.[61]

With Bourne, Abel studied South American constitutions and colonial American charters. Abel also took Bourne's "American History from Madison to Lincoln" seminar, which focused on the constitutional crisis surrounding the Louisiana Purchase. The seminar discussion was built around Max Farrand's 1904 *AHR* article, "Compromises of the Constitution." Farrand argued that scholars incorrectly privileged the Constitutional Convention slavery debate, when in fact the admission of western states proved a far greater concern.[62]

Citing a private discussion with Frederick Jackson Turner, Farrand argued that the old East Coast states (North and South) feared the prospect of new western states more than the extension of slavery. Consequently, the new Constitution gave Congress virtually unrestricted jurisdiction over new U.S. acquisitions and territories. For Abel the implication was profound: Farrand clarified a matter suggested by Abel's M.A. thesis—the federal government had constitutional authority to administer the Louisiana Purchase, including the power to create Indian reservations, an Indian territory, and an all-Indian state. Abel gave this idea mature form in her dissertation. Enlarging her M.A. thesis, she argued that Indian removal and plans for an Indian state west of the Mississippi originated with Thomas Jefferson. It seems likely that Abel's dissertation was also shaped by Nathaniel T. Bacon's 1901 *Yale Review* article, "Some Insular Questions," which touched on Jefferson's support for an Indian colonization plan out West.[63]

Drafted between 1903 and 1905, Abel's "The History of Events Resulting in Indian Consolidation West of the Mississippi," was based on the assertion that "Removal ... was ... absolutely original with Jefferson." Her dissertation traced Jefferson's early removal rhetoric through to the Indian diaspora initiated by John Quincy Adams. Abel's argument built on the premise that American Indian policy from Jefferson to Jackson followed the humanitarian principles of British colonialism—namely moving subject peoples toward either assimilation or sovereign status.[64]

Abel based her contention on Jefferson's proposed 1803 constitutional amendment, which would have provided a legal framework for acquiring the Louisiana Territory and setting part of it aside for Indian colonization. Though a brilliant work of historical analysis, her dissertation's tactical triumph was in its regional reconciliation. Ascribing Northern and Southern removal to distinct chapters, Abel described the process as a truly national effort consistent with Jefferson's intentions. At the head of the federal removal effort Abel discovered two Southerners, President James Monroe and Vice President John C. Calhoun. Abel lauded both men for their humanitarian efforts. In Abel's hands, the Southern role in Indian removal became one of balancing the demands of an expanding and ambitious European American population with the moral obligation to protect, civilize, and Christianize the Indians.[65]

Examining Georgia's role, Abel argued that prior to Indian removal the state had not benefited from significant Indian cessions, consequently Georgia's large non-Indian farming and mining populace had no hope of acquiring additional land. Reversing the traditional critique of Georgian land greed, Abel held that much of Georgia's removal mania resulted from "unfavorable" Indian treaties, and she argued that Jefferson acquired the Louisiana territory with the intention of alleviating civil strife in Georgia.

However, Abel ultimately deemed Indian removal an institutional and moral failure, because "The Indian state, which Calhoun had hinted at and [Virginia governor James] Barbour had planned, was never created." Abel noted, "The best criticism that can be passed upon Indian removal is that it was a plan too hastily and too partially carried into execution for its real and underlying merits ever to be realized." She concluded the result of this swift and incomplete venture was that "before the primary removals had all taken place, the secondary had begun, and the land that was to belong to the Indian in perpetuity was in the white man's market."[66]

By linking western settlement to Indian removal rather than the contentious issue of slavery, Abel found a safe way to promote her argument regarding the abrogation of America's humanitarian heritage—and the westward movement of American history—without provoking sectional controversy. Abel broke through the regional history ceiling in large part by outwitting all-to-delicate Southern historical sensibilities. It was a short triumph.[67]

Where Abel's dissertation might otherwise have taken its place on a dusty shelve alongside the scholarship of her contemporaries, the novelty of her argument and the influence of her committee members (and their AHA leadership positions) guaranteed that her work would reach a wider audience. In a gesture meant to honor the dying Bourne and the aged Adams, as well as Abel, in 1905 the AHA Justin Winsor Prize committee selected her dissertation and published it in the AHA annual records—but not without dissension. An unfavorable "anonymous" critique (by Jameson) appended the publication. Mirroring private remarks made to Andrew C. McLaughlin, Jameson's review sniffed that Abel's dissertation had been written with "not much literary skill nor with great insight into the political affairs of men." More specifically, Jameson contended that Indian removal schemes predated Jefferson and Indian sovereignty effectively ended with Grant's Peace Policy.[68]

The record does not reveal Abel's response to Jameson's remarks, but with the admission of Oklahoma as a state she found occasion to revise her dissertation thesis. In a paper read before the 1907 AHA annual meeting she asserted, "The recent admission to statehood of Oklahoma, with its mixture of red, black, and white inhabitants, marks the definitive abandonment of an idea that had previously been advocated at intervals for more than a hundred years." Notably, Abel backed away from her contention that Jefferson originated Indian removal. Abel concluded, "After 1878 there was practically no thought whatsoever of allowing the aborigines a separate existence as an integral part of the Union, and the spasmodic efforts of a hundred years . . . failed." Abel had, in fact, responded to Jameson.[69]

As noted in her dissertation, the logical progression of Abel's scholarship should have been a history of the removed tribes since 1866. Abel's 1907 AHA paper had already prepped the intellectual ground and marshalled preliminary research. This scholarly course would have required extensive use of sociological, anthropological, and ethnological material. However, in the interval between the presentation of Abel's 1907 AHA paper and its publication in 1909 two events would undercut this trajectory.

In February 1908 Abel's mentor and professional guide, Edward Gaylord Bourne, died. This void was filled by Bourne's close colleague George Burton Adams, Abel's well-liked graduate European studies professor and doctoral committee member. Already an advocate, Adams became her new professional mentor.[70]

Adams's election to the AHA presidency in December 1908 seemed a professional boon for Abel, but his inaugural address cast a shadow over the immediate development of her Indian scholarship. Titled, "History and the Philosophy of History," Adams's address solidified a set of amorphous historical guidelines favored by Frederick Jackson Turner and Western historians. Regarding the late-nineteenth century assent of social sciences within the academy Adams proclaimed, "There arose a variety of new interests, new groups of scholars formed themselves . . . all concerned with the same facts of the past which it is our business to study." Adams complained that the "new sciences" were so "severely critical" of professional historians that "our right to the field is now called in question, our methods, our results and our ideas are assailed."[71]

Adams proceeded to delineate the offenders: political science, "geographers" (evolution theorists), economic theorists, sociologists, and folk-psychologists. These five, all within the purview of anthropology and ethnology, were denounced as a fifth column chipping away at the validity of historical scholarship. Adams warned, "In my opinion this allied attack upon our field of history by the five divisions . . . is not an affair of the moment." Against this assault Adams called on professional historians to remember, "All science which is true science must rest upon the proved and correlated fact. . . . It can have no other foundation than this." Dismissing the work of those who would displace professional historians, Adams added, "Generalization from hasty observation, from half-understood facts, is useless [as history] and often worse than useless."[72]

Eschewing contemporary interdisciplinary practices, Adams resolutely affirmed the study of documents noting, "The field of the historian is, and must long remain, the discovery and recording of what actually happened." While other historians were free to disregard Adams's sentiments and indeed the matter was far more contentious within the profession, Abel's career prospects were closely tied to her mentor's good graces. As such Abel's hope to "continue the present work along the line of the effect of the actual removals," effectively came to a close. The trek down that path would have to wait for another historian.[73]

Over the next two decades Abel's American Indian scholarship unfortunately parroted the racial sentiments of the time. Based in part on research she conducted while a historian for the U.S. Office of Indian Affairs, where she was hired part-time in 1913, in 1915 Abel published *The American Indian as Slaveholder and Secessionist*. A response to Woodrow Wilson's resegregated Washington, Abel's work brazenly mollified the Southern segregationist sentiments of the new administration. The deftness with which Abel warped American Indian history in order to placate the new Southern regime offers a disturbing insight into the political plasticity of Indian scholarship.[74]

The American Indian as Slaveholder and Secessionist was aimed at a segregationist audience with the intent of leveling Northern condemnation of Southern states and their racial policies. Abel noted, "The Confederacy was offering ... [the Five Tribes] political integrity and political equality and was establishing over ... [their] country, not simply an empty wardship, but a bonafide protectorate." Abel continued, "They were slave holding tribes ... supposed ... to have no interest whatsoever in a sectional conflict that involved the very existence of the 'peculiar institution.'" In ascribing blame for Confederate sympathies within the Five Tribes, Abel asserted, "The federal government left them to themselves at the critical moment ... and then was indignant that they betrayed a sectional affiliation."[75]

Reflecting the political environment of the day and Abel's awareness of the Wilson era's federal racial policy, she included an unusual and largely disingenuous disclaimer: "The author deems it of no slight advantage ... that her educational training so largely American as it is, has been gained without regard to a particular locality." Abel further noted that she "belongs to no section of the Union, has lived, for longer or shorter periods in all sections, and has developed no local bias." Abel emphasized that it was her "sincere wish that no charge of prejudice can, in ever so small a degree, be sustained by the evidence, presented here or elsewhere." A longtime resident of the Sunflower State, Abel acquired her B.A. and M.A. at the University of Kansas where she carefully navigated the contentious legacy of "bleeding Kansas." Abel's assertion that she retained no regional bias was at best puzzling. Given that she was desperate to keep her part-time job at the Office of Indian Affairs (OIA), her declaration did not have to be true, only politically effective.[76]

In 1915 Abel also published documents that she discovered in the OIA archive as *The Official Correspondence of James S. Calhoun while Indian Agent at Santa Fé and Superintendent of Indian Affairs in New Mexico*. This publication was informative, not so much for what it revealed about Calhoun, but rather for Abel's lengthy introduction outlining OIA politics and funding. While she was politically cautious, a read between the lines reveals that Abel's sudden burst of publication between 1913 and 1915 constituted a bid to retain funding for her OIA position and was clearly aimed at Southern Democrats who served on the congressional Indian Affairs committees. An historian who began her career studying Indians in the context of British colonial policy, Abel no longer saw Indian history as a regional bridge, but rather as a lifeline for a precarious position in public history.[77]

Between 1915 and 1916 Abel took a more secure position as an assistant professor at Smith College, a women's college in Northampton, Massachusetts, and by 1916 she became a full professor. Much like Kellogg's work at the WSHS, at Smith Abel began to publish annotated volumes of original documents she discovered during her tenure at the OIA. Additionally, in 1919 Abel published a companion volume to *The American Indian as Slaveholder* that addressed the contentious issue of Indian military service in World War I. Thus *The American Indian* began a series.[78]

Titled *The American Indian as Participant in the Civil War*, volume two reflected the assimilation ideology of Abel's former OIA boss, Cato Sells. A Wilson appointee, Sells empathized with the notorious Indian "Americanization" program of Rodman Wannmaker and Joseph Dixon. Like Dixon, Sells fervently believed that Indian service in World War I would lead to full assimilation. Concurrence with Sells proved a professional boon for Abel.[79]

The American Indian as Participant in the Civil War placed Indians into the most quintessentially nostalgic role of the Wilson era—as Civil War combatants. Adding historical weight to Sells's view, Abel's scholarship helped quash antiquated arguments that characterized Indian men as lazy, ignorant, shiftless, disloyal, and treacherous savages. In Abel's second volume, Confederate Indians were depicted as honorable, loyal, principled Americans who imperiled their fortunes and their lives for freedom. Indeed, Abel's depiction of Cherokee Confederate General Stand Watie was strikingly similar to contemporary valorizations of Robert E. Lee. Abel's conclusion cast Confederate Indian soldiers as victims of the Lost Cause noting, "The Indian had made an alliance with the southern Confederacy in vain."[80]

Abel's Indian removal series was completed in 1925 with publication of *The American Indian under Reconstruction*—the third and final volume, which traced the trans-Mississippi removal saga to 1866. Abel argued that American Indians who participated in the Civil War—as Unionists or Secessionists—were victims of failed Confederate aspirations and Union incompetence. Abel concluded that the renegotiated treaties of 1866 were far more severe than Union demands placed on Rebel states seeking readmission to the Union. Echoing the dominant thesis in Reconstruction scholarship, Abel transformed the Five Tribes into quintessential Reconstruction victims. Abel's scholarship left the removed Indians as little more than broken wards of a fickle federal overlord, an image that would not be corrected for almost two decades.[81]

A scholarly career that began with an inquest into the relationship between American Indian removal and British colonial policy, ended with Abel's portrayal of Indians as the ultimate Civil War casualties. The scholarly ease with which Abel moved the slaveholders of the Five Tribes to the role of valiant secessionists and American military heroes, and finally to pitiful victims of Reconstruction, reflected both the rapidity with which the national Civil War narrative changed and the degree to which Abel's own professional viability was bound with it.

The remainder of Abel's professional career steered from Indian scholarship toward document publication. Following the trail blazed by Thwaites,

Blair, and Kellogg, Abel concluded her academic enterprise with the publication of colonial era documents including, *Chardon's Journal at Fort Clark, 1834–1839*, and *Tabeau's Narrative of Loisel's Expedition to the Upper Missouri*. However, even this scholarship would prove a link to the next generation of women scholars of American Indians.

For a season Abel's interest in publishing colonial era documents detailing European American and American Indian relations would be paralleled in the work of three indigenous professional women historians of American Indians—Rachel Caroline Eaton, Anna L. Lewis, and Muriel H. Wright. Each would publish their own document-driven Indian histories. Although Eaton, Lewis, and Wright's publications signaled a new phase in American Indian history, they did not bring Abel's plan for a postbellum Five Tribes pan-Indian history to fruition. The culmination of Abel's work would have to wait for another Oklahoma woman historian.

Almost three decades after Abel's *The History of Events Resulting in Indian Consolidation West of the Mississippi* was published, Angie Debo took up Abel's proposal for a post-1866 study of removed Indians. Critical interaction with fellow Oklahomans Lewis and Wright would prove crucial to Debo's venture, but before this scholarly triumvirate could lock intellectual horns the old cultural barriers that separated American Indians from writing academic history had to be breeched.[82]

RACHEL CAROLINE EATON: THE FIRST PROFESSIONAL INDIGENOUS WOMAN HISTORIAN

Rachel Caroline Eaton is believed to be the first Oklahoma American Indian woman to earn a doctorate and most likely the first American Indian awarded the Ph.D. for history. Eaton's master's thesis, published through the George Banta Publishing Company in 1914, is believed to be the first document-driven Indian history published by a professional woman historian of American Indian descent. Like the preprofessional Indigenous writers Sarah Winnemucca, Alice Sophia Callahan, and Susette La Flesche Tibbles, Eaton's professional scholarship focused on the intratribal history of her own people, rather than the pan-Indian history long dominated by European American women.

As a published professional historian Eaton broke through enduring cultural barriers that barred American Indians from writing document-driven Indian history. Notably, she did it as an academic within the academy. What is known of Eaton's life and American Indian scholarship is tantalizing—her work represented the first Indigenous historian's voice raised in protest against European American women's long domination of Indian history.[83]

Rachel Caroline Eaton at Drury College, ca. 1895–96. Eaton completed her undergraduate work at Drury College in Springfield, Missouri. Between 1873 and 1893 Drury College attracted a steady stream of students from the Five Nations. Courtesy of the Eaton family.

Rachel Caroline Eaton was born July 7, 1869, on the Arkansas–Cherokee Nation line outside Maysville, Arkansas. Later, the Eaton family moved to the Claremore Mound area. Rachel's father, George Washington Eaton, was a Confederate veteran, farmer, rancher, and oilman. Rachel's mother, Nancy Elizabeth Ward Williams Eaton, was a descendent of famed Cherokee "Beloved Woman" Nancy Ward. Nancy Eaton died on September 21, 1896, roughly two months after Rachel's twenty-eighth birthday. Rachel attributed her interest in history to her mother, noting that Nancy Eaton was "one of the last of the fireside historians of her race, whose vital interest in her people constrained her to repeat their story . . . until it was rooted and grounded in my memory from earliest childhood." Years later Anna L. Lewis would express similar sentiments about her Choctaw mother.[84]

Rachel's father was a European American from Texas where he fought for the Confederacy in "Company B, Morgan's Battalion, Texas Cavalry, under [Captain Milton M. Boggess] and Lieutenant Charles [Leroy] Morgan." At the conclusion of the war George Eaton traveled to Arkansas where he met Nancy Elizabeth Ward Williams. Following a brief courtship George and Nancy were married on May 17, 1868, and shortly thereafter they bought a small farm outside Maysville, Arkansas. Rachel and a brother, Calvin, were born on the family farm.[85]

In 1874 the Eaton family moved to the Cherokee Nation where they settled in the Claremore Mound area. There George Eaton engaged in farming and cattle ranching, later branching off into the mercantile trade, real estate, and oil. Engaging in his oil pursuits, George Eaton discovered what he erroneously named "radium water" while drilling a test hole just outside Claremore. Actually nonradioactive and sulfur-rich, Eaton's radium water would give rise to the twentieth-century Claremore Mound "bath" craze. A savvy businessman, George built the Mendenhall Bathhouse not far from the radium water well site and promoted the entire venture as "Radium Town." George Eaton put Claremore Mound on the map.[86]

The mound itself had historical significance for Rachel Eaton. Site of the infamous Strawberry Moon battle "fought between the Osages and the Cherokees in the spring of 1818 . . . the culmination of a long-standing feud between the two tribes," the towering limestone dome that formed "Claremore mound" provided imaginative and intellectual fodder for Rachel's mind. Written into the geography and culture of the area, the battleground and its lore was described by the young historian as a "story composed of many sources . . . based on the written records and the hill which stands as the immutable background of this tragic encounter." The antiquity of the event was given contemporary relevance by the "arrowheads, battered tomahawks, and bits of colored beads" that Rachel Eaton found scattered across the hill.[87]

In 1874 the Claremore Mound community gave birth to the town of Claremont, later renamed Claremore in 1882. While the exact date is unknown, sometime between 1882 and 1888 Rachel Eaton entered the Cherokee National Female Seminary located just outside Park Hill, a Cherokee Nation town approximately sixty-two miles northeast of Claremore. The female seminary was within walking distance of Park Hill, onetime home of legendary Cherokee chief John Ross and *Cherokee Phoenix* newspaper editor, Elias Boudinot. Dubbed the "center of Cherokee culture," Park Hill also boasted the Park Hill Publishing House. Rachel's time at Park Hill likely intensified her interest in John Ross and proved invaluable for her later research.[88]

Accounts conflict regarding the year of Rachel Eaton's graduation from the female seminary. The building burned on April 10, 1887, and was not rebuilt until 1889. Emmet Starr, M.D., a noted "genealogist and historian of the Cherokee people," gave the date of Eaton's commencement as June 28, 1888. Following graduation Eaton enrolled in Drury College, a small liberal arts institution in Springfield, Missouri, that was popular with Cherokee Nation students. In 1895 Eaton graduated from Drury with a bachelor's degree cum laude. Eaton promptly returned to the Cherokee Nation where she acquired a faculty position at the Cherokee National Female Seminary and taught in the Claremore public school system.[89]

On December 25, 1901, Rachel Eaton married James Alexander Burns, a fellow 1888 graduate of the Cherokee national seminary. The Cherokee Male Seminary was located three miles northwest of Park Hill, and it is reasonable to assume Rachel and James became acquainted as students. Regardless, not long after graduation from the Cherokee Male Seminary James taught in the Claremore school system, and in 1896 he became superintendent of schools in Heber, Arkansas. Two years later James was hired as superintendent of the Claremore public school system. The same year, 1898, James was a founding member of the Indian Territory Teachers Association. In 1900 James organized the Nowata, Cherokee Nation, public school system and became its first superintendent. James also owned a farm in Sageeyah, Cherokee Nation, served as district court clerk, and later entered the real estate market, owning a share in the Citizen's Hotel of Nowata.[90]

In 1905 James and Rachel Burns attended summer classes at the University of Chicago. Ten years earlier James had worked for a Chicago collection firm, so presumably he was familiar with the city. The following year Rachel enrolled at the University of Chicago and began her master's degree work in history and anthropology. In 1911 she was awarded the A.M., the University of Chicago's equivalent of M.A. degree, for her fifty-two page thesis titled, "John Ross." Following graduation Rachel accepted a job as an assistant in the history department at the Industrial Institute and College for the Education of White Girls in Columbus, Mississippi. Eaton remained in the magnolia state for the duration of the 1911–12 term. Between 1911 and 1913 Eaton also conducted research that enabled the expansion of her brief master's thesis into a two hundred and twelve page manuscript. In 1914 Eaton's manuscript was published by the George Banta Publishing Company of Menasha, Wisconsin, as *John Ross and the Cherokee Indians*. Though various sources identify the 1914 Banta publication as either her master's thesis or her later dissertation, it was neither. Eaton expanded her short thesis and published it as a book *before* it was crafted into an edited dissertation.[91]

In 1913 Eaton accepted a positon at the Lake Erie Female Seminary in Painesville, Ohio, and the following year she accepted a position as dean of women and history department chair at Trinity College in Waxahachie,

Rachel Caroline Eaton in cap and gown, ca. 1919. Eaton was the first Indigenous woman to earn the Ph.D. in American history and the first Indigenous author of a document-driven professional American Indian history. Courtesy of the Eaton family.

Texas. During summer and fall breaks Eaton returned to Oklahoma to visit family and friends in Claremore and Tulsa. In summer 1917 Eaton accepted an additional position as secretary of the wartime Oklahoma Defense Council. Around 1918 Eaton resigned her position at Trinity University and moved to Alamogordo, New Mexico, with her brother Joel Merritt Eaton. Joel suffered from tuberculosis, and it was thought that the dry climate might help his condition.[92]

By 1919 Eaton was back in Claremore teaching at the Claremore high school. Between 1918 and 1919 Eaton reduced her 1914 Banta publication to a one hundred and fifty-three page manuscript, which she submitted as her University of Chicago doctoral dissertation. Two years later Eaton privately published the dissertation through Star Printery in Muskogee, Oklahoma, however it was distributed by the University of Chicago library. The dissertation and later 1921 publication, both titled *John Ross and the Cherokee Indians*, added a third chapter titled, "The Coming of the Missionaries," eliminated William E. Dodd's preface, and reduced the text by fifty-nine pages.[93]

Cherokee chronicler Emmet Starr noted that Rachel and James divorced but did not reveal the reason or date. From 1914 James does not appear to have accompanied Rachel to Mississippi, Ohio, or Texas. Notably, the couple was childless. While in Mississippi, Rachel began to refer to herself as Caroline B. Eaton, a practice she continued through her employment in Texas. Upon return to Claremore in 1919, Rachel referred to herself as either Mrs. R. C. Eaton or Rachel Caroline Eaton. Following a one-year teaching stint in Claremore, Eaton ran for Rogers County superintendent of schools on the 1920 Democratic ticket (Claremore is in Rogers County). Eaton would purportedly retain the position for two consecutive terms. Eaton was party to a suit brought against the Rogers County superintendent of public education in 1924, so she likely served at least a term of four years. The record does not indicate history research or publication during Eaton's tenure as Rogers County public school supervisor.[94]

After retiring from her elected position, Eaton began work on an expanded version of *John Ross and the Cherokee Indians*. As a prerequisite, she spent a year conducting further research in Chicago. Afterward Eaton kept two residences—one in Oklahoma City and one in Tulsa—to facilitate research and writing at the respective metropolitan archives. In 1935, Eaton's health began to fail and she returned to her old home in Claremore. The same year she submitted her revised and expanded manuscript to the University of Oklahoma Press. Titled "A History of the Cherokee Nation," the manuscript was rejected by the press in December 1935. The following year Eaton was elected to the Oklahoma Hall of Fame "as one of Oklahoma's outstanding women." Two years later, on September 20, 1938, Rachel Caroline Eaton died of breast cancer at her home in Claremore.[95]

Given that current scholarship mistakenly conflates Eaton's 1911 master's thesis with her 1914 book, her 1919 dissertation, and her 1921 dissertation reprint, a brief examination of each will help contextualize similarities and differences. Eaton's unpublished manuscript is not currently available for scholarly review and remains unpublished. In the preface to Eaton's master's thesis and 1914 book, she credited Professor Edward Morris Sheppard of Drury College, Missouri, with encouraging her to publish on Cherokee history. Sheppard, who filled various faculty positions, including president of Drury College, was a well-known Missouri geologist and amateur historian of some accomplishment. Noted for his collections of flora and fauna, Sheppard was tapped to organize the Missouri state exhibit at the 1904 Louisiana Purchase Exhibition in St. Louis. His 1934 eulogy noted, "For years . . . [Sheppard] has been interested in the early history of the aboriginal tribes and early explorers of Missouri and the Southwest, and has made many valuable investigations."[96]

The organization of Eaton's fifty-two page thesis, "John Ross" established the basic chapter divisions, subjects, and content for each of its permutations up to 1921. The first chapter related Ross's early life along the Coosa River in Alabama, and this was followed by a chapter that briefly described the boundaries and social geography of the old Cherokee Nation. Eaton's strong sense of Cherokee nationalism was voiced in her references to pre- and post-removal Cherokee "possessions" and her pride in Cherokee civilization. Chapter three looked at Ross's role in early military confrontations, treaties, his election as Cherokee chief, the suit against Georgia, and his heroic efforts to avoid Cherokee removal. The fourth and fifth chapters discussed removal, establishment of the trans-Mississippi Cherokee Nation, Civil War destruction, and Ross's final role in the 1866 Reconstruction treaty. Until the revised 1935 manuscript, each of Eaton's publications followed this outline. The historical record does not reveal why Eaton chose to expand and publish her master's thesis as a book prior to reworking the material for her doctoral dissertation, however, sources strongly suggest she took this course to head off an ambitious competitor.[97]

In 1908, the second year of Eaton's M.A. work at the University of Chicago, she established the Rogers County Sequoyah Historical Society. Meeting with seventeen amateur historians—including Emmet Starr—at George Washington Eaton's home in Claremore, the group pledged itself to "preservation . . . of Indian relics in the Cherokee capital at Tahlequah." Eaton was elected president at the first meeting. In the coming months the society focused on collecting material pertaining to the lives of Sequoyah and John

Ross. In addition to its community role, Eaton saw the society as an important document repository for her graduate work. In her 1914 publication Eaton noted that "abundant use has been made of the manuscripts placed at my disposal by the Sequoyah Historical Society." Like many of her male academic counterparts, Eaton cultivated her own archival source.[98]

Eaton's efforts came to fruition in 1911 with the publication of her master's thesis, "John Ross." The accomplishment was soon overshadowed by a statewide announcement trumpeting Colonel Augustus E. ("Gus" or "Gustavus") Ivey's plan to publish a definitive "Cherokee History." In addition to advertising his intention in nine Oklahoma newspapers, Ivey also touted it in the October 1911 edition of *The Indian's Friend*—the official organ of the Women's National Indian Association. A polarizing Cherokee lawyer, journalist, and political figure associated with Elias C. Boudinot and the Boomer cause, Ivey emphasized, "The book will include the career of Chief John Ross" and added that the publication would be "completed in two years."[99]

Whether Ivey's plan to publish by 1913 compelled Eaton to act or not, in 1912 the Sequoyah Historical Society began to focus on the life of John Ross. A year later on October 3, 1913, it was announced that "Miss Eaton will . . . finish her history of John Ross, which she expects to have ready for the printers by the first of the year." In fact, *John Ross and the Cherokee Indians* was released by George Banta press approximately thirteen months later. Eaton's hometown newspaper noted, "It is historical throughout, and gives the history of the Cherokee people as drawn from numerous authentic records." Eluding to its unique status as the first document-driven Indian history written by a professional Indigenous historian, the editor concluded, "We believe this book the first one covering in a thorough manner the period mentioned from strictly authentic sources."[100]

Like her thesis, the 1914 publication was dedicated to Eaton's mother, Nancy. Written with an eye toward her dissertation, the book was completed under the direction of her dissertation committee chair, noted historian of the South William E. Dodd. Expanding on the biographical treatment in her master's thesis, Eaton's book included new material on Indian removal, Cherokee reestablishment, re-destruction (the Civil War), and the final effort to reconstitute the Cherokee Nation.[101]

John Ross, the hero of Eaton's book, was presented as a messianic figure determined to save Cherokee culture and sovereignty from termination. Eaton gave special attention to Ross's role in forging post-removal Cherokee nationalism out of seemingly irreconcilable tribal divisions. In this, Eaton's book mirrored her Chicago mentor William E. Dodd's 1914 revision of Southern history and American post–Civil War nationalism, *Expansion and*

Conflict. The concluding page of Eaton's book echoed the pro-nationalist sentiments of the final paragraph of *Expansion and Conflict*, noting Ross "was first, last and always a Cherokee Indian, a citizen of the Cherokee Nation which was to him a sovereign, independent nation."[102]

Between Eaton's tenure at the Lake Erie Female Seminary in Painesville, Ohio, and her time at Trinity University in Waxahachie, Texas, she reworked her 1914 book into a dissertation. In substance the text remained the same, structurally, however, it changed. Removing fifty-nine pages, Eaton also separated her treatment of missionaries from chapter two, "Early History of the Cherokees," shortening and refashioning it as a new third chapter, "The Coming of the Missionaries." Successfully defending her dissertation in 1919, Eaton had it privately published through Star Printery, Muskogee, Oklahoma, in 1921. The dissertation reprint was distributed through the University of Chicago library, but does not seem to have been commercially marketed. The 1919 dissertation and 1921 reprint included exactly the same text. The master's thesis and 1914 book are similar in subject and structure to the 1919 dissertation and 1921 reprint, but differ from the latter in length and chapter order.[103]

Following Eaton's retirement from politics in the late 1920s, she spent a year in Arkansas conducting research later augmented with material from Oklahoma City, Tulsa, and other archives. By 1935 Eaton fashioned the new material into a manuscript titled "A History of the Cherokee Nation." Though this work is not available for scholarly analysis, sources have verified that the manuscript is a reworked expansion of Eaton's 1921 published dissertation. Roughly the first half of the manuscript is an edited version of the 1921 publication, and the remainder covers Cherokee Nation history to the 1930s. Sources indicate that the manuscript advocates both women's suffrage and treaty and citizenship rights for the Cherokee freed people. In this, Eaton's sense of justice proved remarkably consistent. Breaking through the academic ceiling to become the first Indigenous professional woman historian of American Indians, Eaton's scholarship still did not breech the pan-Indian barrier. Like Sarah Winnemucca's *Life Among the Piutes* fifty-two years earlier, Eaton's "A History of the Cherokee Nation" focused on the history of her own people.[104]

When Eaton submitted her completed manuscript to the University of Oklahoma Press for consideration on June 7, 1935, she expected a prompt reply. In late June Eaton compelled a close friend, Mrs. C. M. Mackey, wife of a noted Oklahoma City civil engineer to check on the review process. Unfortunately Eaton's main contact, Editor-in-Chief Joseph A. Brandt, was hospitalized shortly before her manuscript arrived at the press. In Brandt's absence acting editor Savoie Lottinville notified Eaton on June 26, "We are putting it through the customary procedures of reader's reports . . . and we expect . . .

to have some decision for you within the next three weeks." Lottinville added, "The manuscript looks as if it were an interesting possibility for our Civilization of the American Indian Series."[105]

Revealing a degree of desperation, Eaton replied to Lottinville on June 28 asking if the press had "progressed far enough with the critical reading of my manuscript to give me any assurance that it will qualify for a place in your Civilization of the American Indian Series." Fearing rejection Eaton queried, "If there is some doubt . . . I feel I should be seeking elsewhere for a publisher if I am to see my book in the hands of the public before some other author." Eaton prodded, "I understand that there are at least two working on a subject similar to mine." Expressing doubt in Lottinville's interest, Eaton frankly noted, "I regret that Mr. Brandt, himself, is unable to pass upon it . . . though I am sure the manuscript is in safe and expert hands."[106]

A few days later, Lottinville replied to Eaton noting trouble finding reviewers for the manuscript, but assuring her, "We are only too anxious to have your work under consideration for inclusion in our Civilization of the American Indian series." Lottinville added, "I hope that you will find it possible to allow us the necessary time for handling the manuscript." Eaton gave the press a month before her next inquiry.[107]

On August 9 Eaton wrote Lottinville asking, "At your earliest convenience will you please inform me what decision you have reached concerning my manuscript?" Pressing the matter Eaton noted, "It is necessary for me to have the information as soon as possible in order to reply to various inquiries that are coming in almost daily." More graciously Eaton concluded, "Thanking you for past favors and considerations, and hoping that Mr. Brandt has recovered his health."[108]

Joseph Brandt's heath had recovered. An August 10, 1935, letter to Eaton revealed that Lottinville had actually taken no action on her manuscript. Brandt reported, "I will have to obtain the reports of two readers before I can come to a decision." Three months after Lottinville suggested the review would be completed in three weeks, Brandt added, "I expect it will require at least a month to obtain reader's reports." Eaton did not reply[109]

A month and a half later, Eaton sent a brief note asking, "My dear Mr. Brandt, have you been able to reach any decision regarding my History of the Cherokee Nation?" Now pleading Eaton asked, "May I hear from you at your earliest convenience. Please." Four days later Brandt informed her, "I have just received the first reader's report on your, 'History of the Cherokee Nation.'" Brandt apologized, noting the first reader "held the manuscript for more than a month."[110]

Almost thirty days later Brandt made a startling revelation to Eaton, "At last I have my reports on the two histories of the Cherokee Nation." Unknown to Eaton, the press was not simply reviewing her manuscript, they were pitting it against a competing submission. Brandt continued, "I asked the readers to consider both manuscripts from our point of view and to recommend the manuscript they thought best suited for our purposes." Seven months after her initial inquiry, Brandt informed Eaton, "Both readers recommended the publication of the other manuscript." Brandt continued, "Both readers feel that your manuscript would be more popular but each feel that your manuscript was not as definitive as the other." In conclusion Brandt offered, "One reader felt . . . that you occasionally revealed a bias. . . . The second . . . that you were [s]ubjected to . . . a too-partisan, pro-Cherokee point of view."[111]

Joseph Brandt's reply revealed that ethnological, particularly "ethnic" scholarship, remained taboo in the academy. More so, old, repackaged ideas about Indians and race weighed heavily on his decision. Within a year Angie Debo submitted her manuscript "As Long As the Waters Run" (original title) to the OU Press. It too was ultimately rejected as culturally and politically biased.[112]

University of Oklahoma Press records indicate that the second manuscript, *A Political History of the Cherokee Nation*, written by University of Oklahoma history professor Morris L. Wardell received preferential treatment. Gaston L. Litton, a noted archivist, author, and reader for the University of Oklahoma Press reported that Wardell's book "recorded the confused and conflicting parts without bias and with care." Reflecting this view Brandt noted to Eaton, "I think it extremely unfortunate that the two happened to coincide in their writing but under the circumstances, all I could do was to select the best from our particular standpoint."[113]

Wardell's preferential treatment went beyond mere institutional favoritism. While penning his own manuscript, Wardell was asked to review a competitor's submission in 1933. Noted Cherokee author and Angie Debo's future Oklahoma Federal Writer's project coeditor John Milton Oskison submitted a manuscript, titled "Unconquerable, the Story of John Ross, Chief of the Cherokees, 1828–1866," that was also rejected by the OU Press. Reviewers Morris L. Wardell, Grant Foreman (a respected Five Tribes scholar), and James J. Hill (University of Oklahoma assistant librarian) variously branded Oskison's manuscript unscholarly, partisan, and poorly written.[114]

Although Wardell regretted the decision because of his "personal acquaintance with Mr. Oskison," he found the manuscript "unscientific" and "biased." Specifically, Wardell objected to Oskison's work because it was written from a Cherokee point of view. In terms of professional ethics, Wardell should not have been allowed to review a competitor's manuscript.[115]

In spite of finding Oskison's text "sketchy," "biased," "argumentative," and not at all "scientific," Wardell offered that it could be "rewritten in a few weeks and made ready for publication by the university press." Oskison flatly refused. Given that Wardell's report also noted, "It would require a good deal of revamping which I think his views would not allow him to do," his revision suggestion appears more calculated than genuine. Comparatively, Eaton's submission was far superior to Oskison's, but she was not offered a revision option.[116]

The names of Eaton's two manuscript readers and their reviews have not been discovered. It would be disturbing if, in fact, Wardell reviewed her submission. Regardless of Wardell's role in the review process, the readers deemed Eaton's manuscript "too-partisan," with a "pro-Cherokee point of view." Because the two reviews are likely lost to history, the record is not clear regarding institutional politics, however sexual, racial, and cultural biases were clearly recorded in black and white.[117]

In the end Eaton may have had the last laugh. Considering the intellectual and academic legacy of Eaton's scholarship, it is reasonable to assume that *John Ross and the Cherokee Indians* shaped William E. Dodd and J. Fred Rippy's student Angie Debo during her M.A. work at the University of Chicago. A 1915 *AHR* book review by Annie Heloise Abel found that while Eaton's 1914 publication was burdened with numerous typographical errors and an inadequate index, the text "is practically the first truly historical Indian biography that has been produced." In an unsigned 1915 *MVHR* book review, William E. Dodd replicated in entirety his preface for Eaton's 1914 book which stated, "It is a well written chapter in our own national history which no student can afford to overlook."[118]

Perhaps Debo did not overlook Eaton's scholarship. Following her master's work at the University of Chicago, Debo was accepted as a doctoral candidate by the University of Oklahoma history department in 1929. Debo penned several seminar papers at the University of Oklahoma on Indian history and in 1932 published an article titled, "Southern Refugees of the Cherokee Nation." Notably, Debo's article addressed two of Dodd's historical interests— the South and Cherokee Indians. Reflecting a pro-sovereignty view, Debo published *And Still the Waters Run: The Betrayal of the Five Civilized Tribes* eight years later. Abel and Eaton's scholarship very likely shaped Debo's development as a professional Indian historian.[119]

Yet, before Debo's epic indictment of human greed and maleficence could congeal, she would first have to tussle with two pioneering Indigenous American Indian scholars, Anna L. Lewis and Muriel H. Wright. Together these three women would break through significant barriers in American Indian history. Anna Lewis would have the distinction of being the first Indigenous scholar to challenge the traditional European American pan-Indian historical narrative through publication. Muriel Wright, longtime editor of the *Chronicles of Oklahoma* and expert guide to the Oklahoma Historical Society archives, would widen the breach in 1951 with her critically acclaimed treatment of the Indian tribes of Oklahoma.

Almost four decades prior, male historians branded interdisciplinary work anathema in the profession—with a particularly pronounced disgust for ethnology and anthropology. Though Lewis and Wright were not personally close with Debo, the fierce intellectual friction that existed between them created a scholarly bond, which definitively established Indigenous women's place within the history profession and infused the specialized field of American Indian history with a new ethnological, anthropological, and intertribal sensitivity. From Rachel Caroline Eaton the torch first passed to Anna Lewis.

CHAPTER 8

DÉJÀ VU

Oklahoma Women and the New Ethno-Political Indian History

The scholarly journey that culminated in Anna L. Lewis's pioneering 1932 "middle ground" study, *Along the Arkansas*, also succeeded in breaching the long dominant European American pan-Indian historical narrative. Bridging the preprofessional and professional eras, political realities affecting each American Indian tribe largely directed Indigenous narratives and comparatively rare publications toward intratribal concerns. Even in the early professional period, the social, political, and economic realities confronting Indian peoples, who had navigated centuries of invasive imperialism, coercive assimilation, and continuing property theft, prompted Rachel Caroline Eaton to focus on the history of her own people.

Shortly after Eaton completed her 1914 publication *John Ross and the Cherokee Indians*, the last vestiges of the Cherokee national government were shuttered by order of the U.S. Department of the Interior. Unfortunately, just as intertribal historical narratives began to emerge as a powerful foil to traditional European American pan-Indian histories, Eaton's health gave way. Though contemporaries, Eaton would not join the emerging scholarly triumvirate of Anna Lewis, Muriel Wright, and Angie Debo. While sources suggest that Eaton's final unpublished manuscript moved toward an intertribal sensitivity, it was Anna Lewis who finally broke through the pan-Indian barrier. Lewis's *Along the Arkansas* addressed regional Arkansas Valley intertribal relations, while it critiqued European imperialism. Reflecting her own sentiments, Lewis's scholarship helped reinforce Indian support for Indigenous sovereignty.

In contrast Muriel Wright, though nostalgic in her treatment of Indian history, championed assimilation and termination. For Wright, Indian treaties established tutelage reserves, not independent republics or sovereign tribes. Wright's 1951 publication, *A Guide to the Indian Tribes of Oklahoma*, offered a survey of tribal histories that noted their respective assimilation and termination efforts and ironically verified that American Indian peoples and cultures yet survived. Together, Lewis and Wright subjected Debo's early scholarship to rigorous intellectual scrutiny, each illuminating different, often opposing aspects of the sovereignty debate. Each Indigenous historian would play a key role in shaping *And Still the Waters Run*, Debo's penultimate indictment of European American imperialism.[1]

DOWN IN THE OLD NATION

Anna Lezola Lewis was born October 25, 1885, near the town of Cameron in the Choctaw Nation. Her parents were Elizabeth Ann Moore Lewis, a Choctaw citizen, and William Ainsworth Lewis, an enterprising European American rancher. A landless Southern refugee from postbellum Georgia, William Lewis migrated to the Choctaw Nation in 1872 where he settled in the vicinity of Kully Chaha. Choctaw law stipulated that as a European American William Lewis could not remain in the nation or claim land without acquiring Choctaw citizenship—either by tribal adoption or through marriage to a Choctaw citizen. In 1877 William Lewis solved this dilemma when he married Elizabeth Ann Moore, purported great-granddaughter of traditionalist Choctaw chief, Nita-oshe. Between 1877 and her death in 1899 Elizabeth Lewis gave birth to ten children—seven survived infancy. Through marriage to Elizabeth, William gained citizenship in the Choctaw Nation and use of the tribe's collectively held land. With access to Choctaw grazing pastures, William Lewis quickly built a highly profitable range cattle business, and he eventually ventured into banking. By 1883 William and Elizabeth were of sufficient means to hire European American missionaries as governesses for their younger children.[2]

During childhood Anna Lewis was kept close to Choctaw culture and history. Through the influence of her mother and maternal relatives, Anna was given instruction in Choctaw tradition. From a young age she was trained as a Choctaw "wise person" and entrusted with tribal lore. Early instruction in Choctaw culture, language, and history would deeply influence Anna Lewis as an educator and professional historian.

Years later, as chair of the Oklahoma College for Women's history department, Lewis established a small campus museum with an impressive array of pan-Indian artifacts, including a spinning wheel from the home of John

Anna L. Lewis, ca. 1950s. A student of Herbert Eugene Bolton and Edward Everett Dale, Lewis was awarded the University of Oklahoma's first history doctorate in 1930. Courtesy of the University of Science and Arts of Oklahoma, Anna Lewis Collection, Nash Library, Chickasha, Oklahoma.

Ross, a Comanche feathered warbonnet, a Comanche "beaded feather-tipped ceremonial wand that belonged to Tauwr," a pipe from the prehistoric mounds near Newkirk, Oklahoma, and a Comanche belt and beaded neck pouch containing a "mescal bean." Lewis also published articles on Choctaw history and culture that emphasized tribal independence. In public lectures Lewis explored various Indian origin stories and the history of Five Tribes removal. A pervasive theme in Lewis's scholarship was Indian sovereignty and minority rights. She argued, "Peoples all over the world cannot be free, free to carry out their ideas of civilization, free to do the things they enjoy unless they are *economically independent.*"[3]

Educated in early Choctaw subscription schools where the assimilationist pedagogy of Northern missionaries included cruel racial taunts, Lewis developed a lifelong aversion for institutional and racial bigotry. As a young student caught in the midst of tribal debates concerning practical versus classical curricula, Lewis weighed the issues and developed a favorable opinion of classical studies. Both experiences led the future educator to conclude that all children deserve a compassionate, unbiased, and competent liberal education.[4]

Lewis's sentiments, reinforced by the Choctaw Nation's moral and financial support for higher education, galvanized her intention to attend college and pursue an academic career. When she turned fifteen, Lewis was enrolled in the Tuskahoma Female Academy (TFA), a local Presbyterian boarding school for college-bound Choctaw women. Following her graduation in spring 1903, Lewis enrolled in the Mary Connor Junior College (MCJC) in Paris, Texas. Both geographically and culturally desirable, the facility appeared to satisfy Lewis's educational and professional requirements. For reasons unknown, Lewis stayed at the MCJC less than a year.[5]

Following her return to the Choctaw Nation in 1904, Lewis enrolled in a summer Normal School near Hartshorne, Choctaw Nation. That fall, at the age of nineteen, Lewis received her teaching certificate. Residing in her father's home near Cameron, Lewis applied for jobs at local public schools, picking up positions in Bokchito and Durant, Choctaw Nation. With her sister Winnidell away at boarding school and her aging father unable to care for the house, Lewis assumed the domestic responsibilities and care of her younger siblings. Lewis became deeply attached to her maternal role, but the arrangement proved short lived.[6]

In early 1905, Lewis's father married "sight unseen . . . an old maid from Georgia," named Eula Stroup. The Lewis children considered their stepmother "a hard woman to like." Eula displayed neither motherly sentiment nor cultural affinity. Moreover, the new Mrs. William A. Lewis challenged Anna's relationship with her siblings, her domestic procedures, and ultimately her right to live in her mother's Choctaw Nation home. Faced with the prospect of being ejected from the family residence by an enterprising European American woman, Lewis took two important steps that would dramatically improve her future.[7]

As a citizen of the Choctaw republic Anna Lewis was entitled to a land allotment under the terms of recently signed United States legislation. The

1898 Curtis Act, which amended the 1887 Dawes General Allotment Act, mandated individually allotted homesteads for citizens of the Five Nations. On November 22, 1905, at 9:00 A.M. "Annie Lewis," then twenty years old received deed to two hundred and forty acres in northwest Bryan County (Choctaw Nation). Lewis's allotment was over one hundred and fifty miles from her family's ranch near Cameron.[8]

Aimed at the dissolution of traditional cultural ties, allotments were awarded without regard to current residence or traditional family plots. Consequently, like many Choctaw allottees Lewis did not have an attachment to her land and did not intend to engage in agricultural production. Instead, Lewis thought of her land as a real estate investment that could be sold as needed. Toward the end of 1906, when events in her father's house did finally force Lewis to monetize her allotment, against her father's wishes, she found it a fortuitous boon.[9]

According to U.S. statute, Choctaw allottees were required to stake a one hundred and sixty acre homestead on their allotments. The homestead was taxable and inalienable for twenty-one years. The first year one fourth of the remaining eighty acres could be sold, another fourth after three years and the remainder after five years. For the rest of her life, land transactions would help finance Lewis's higher education, the purchase of two homes, and occasional trips—including a summer European tour in 1924.[10]

Lewis's financial resources also allowed her to consider undergraduate studies. Setting her sights on an associate's degree, she made arrangements in 1906 to attend a Kentucky junior college closely associated with the Choctaw Nation. Surviving accounts do not reveal the institution's name, but evidence suggests it was the Kentucky College for Women (KCW), also known as Caldwell College. Like the Mary Connor facility, KCW was a Protestant Christian institution. However, unlike the Connor junior college, which was informally allied with Southern Baptists, KCW was administered by a local Kentucky Presbyterian group.[11]

Socially and politically KCW exhibited a progressive Southern racial policy inherited from the college's Northern abolitionist founders. KCW's political bent was put into practice by mandatory college and community social uplift projects coordinated with the Young Women's Christian Association. Officially far from radical in outlook, KCW did provide Lewis with opportunities for greater personal freedom and a comparatively moderate intellectual and political environment.[12]

In 1908 Lewis returned to Oklahoma after two terms of study at KCW. Years later a biographical sketch reported that Lewis came back, because "she was homesick." At the very least, Lewis finished her junior college work and did not wish to remain in Kentucky. Moreover, events in the newly formed state of Oklahoma likely made her feel culturally isolated and politically impotent in Kentucky.[13]

When Lewis returned to Oklahoma she found that the Twin Territories she left behind—one an actual territory opened to European American settlement and the other Indian Territory, comprised of five sovereign Indian nations—had been merged into a single state. In this new order the sovereign interests of the Five Nations and Plains tribes did not have representation, nor were women given the vote. Surveying this terrible injustice, the future historian noted with irony that Oklahoma entered the national federation as a liberal beacon, boasting one of the most progressive state constitutions in the Union. The contradiction between the state's progressive stand on labor and social welfare could not be easily reconciled with its treatment of American Indians and women. To address the situation Lewis turned to a readily available public forum—the classroom.[14]

Returning to the Bokchito school system, Lewis taught Choctaw children who were entranced by a fellow tribal member recently returned from studies in Kentucky. Given that Lewis spoke the Choctaw language and incorporated Choctaw culture into her pedagogy, it is not surprising that she was as beloved by her high school pupils as she would be by her future college students. At the end of the 1913 term Lewis accepted a teaching position in Durant, Oklahoma, some fourteen miles west of Bokchito. Again she found herself teaching a predominantly Choctaw student body. While working in Durant, Lewis met a young woman who would change the course of her academic journey.[15]

The name of Lewis's friend in Durant has been lost to posterity. Winnidell Gravitt Wilson, Lewis's niece noted the unnamed woman and recorded the momentous event: "A friend wanted to go to the University of California at Berkeley . . . she asked Anna [Lewis] to go with her." Lewis, "knowing the reputation of that school and thinking this was an opportunity she might not attempt alone," decided to accept the offer. No other record of her preparations or journey to California are known to exist. Sometime in 1913 Lewis made final arrangements and departed for California.[16]

In 1913 Lewis began coursework to complete her undergraduate requirements at the University of California (UC). As an undergraduate Lewis developed a strong interest in the history of the American West, particularly settler colonialism. Her course work completed in 1915, Lewis was awarded the *Artium Baccalaureatus* (A.B.) degree.[17]

Lewis's sister Winnidell joined her at UC in 1915. Like Lewis, Winnidell monetized her allotment to fund undergraduate study. At Berkeley, the two sisters shared living expenses and helped each other with course work. Toward the end of 1915, Lewis started preliminary research for her master's degree under the direction of Herbert Eugene Bolton. At the time, Bolton was working on the manuscript for *Spanish Exploration in the Southwest, 1542–1706,* while putting together a compendium of papers from the Panama-Pacific International Exposition, as well as juggling classroom responsibilities and his work with graduate students.[18]

Given that Bolton steered four graduate students to master's degrees and one to a doctorate in 1915, his scholarly output was astounding. Even with this workload, as an adviser, mentor, and committee chair Bolton remained constant, clear, concise, practical, and competent. While it might have served his own purposes and made his proposed twenty-five volume study of the Spanish empire in North America less toilsome, Bolton did not push his graduate students beyond their individual skills and interests. Bolton and Lewis settled on a pan-Indian "History of the Cattle Industry in Oklahoma, 1866–1893," as the subject of her master's thesis.[19]

The daughter of a successful Oklahoma cattle rancher who experienced many of the events recounted in her thesis, Lewis chose a study to which she was well suited. Her subject reflected national interest in cowboy culture, while providing Lewis with a professional forum through which to formulate her political views about European American encroachment. Giving a healthy nod to popular fascination with trail life, Lewis's thesis argued that European Americans used the range cattle industry to systematically encroach on Indian lands and ultimately appropriate once-sovereign domains.[20]

Lewis's argument noted the stages of western settlement outlined in Frederick Jackson Turner's Frontier Thesis, however, she did not remove American Indians from the region's history after the first stage of colonization. For Lewis, Indian history was not a thing of the past. On the matter of settler colonialism Lewis tread a careful path, "The westward movement in America was a continuous movement, beginning with the first white settlement and continuing until the winning of the last frontier." On European American and Indian frontier encounters Lewis noted, "With each advance new conflicts with the Indians were encountered, and new oppositions had to be overcome."[21]

According to Lewis, the most significant conflict between Indian and European cultures would play out in Indian Territory. In 1866 a group of desperate Texans impoverished by the Civil War devised a plan to drive approximately five million feral Longhorn cattle to markets in St. Louis, Missouri, and Sedalia, Kansas. Looking north, "The Indian territory proved a tempting field to the Texas cattlemen . . . there was an opportunity which could not remain long unnoticed and unappropriated . . . the opportunity for grazing their herds was too tempting." However, "When the cattle from

Texas continued to stream across the Indian Territory, the Indians began to resent it."[22]

By 1880 Texas cattlemen moved an annual total of 4,233,497 Longhorns onto Indian grasslands for up to a year at a time before proceeding to Kansas and Nebraska rail hubs. Standardizing these routes, cattlemen created the Great Western and Chisholm Trails. Grazing and passage were guaranteed by lease agreements with the Indian nations and Plains Indian representatives. The contentious and exploitive relationship that bound Indians to cattlemen would ultimately prove the last desperate line of defense against European American conquest of the Indian nations.[23]

Although popular Oklahoma history pitted the Boomers (non-Indian colonizers) against Indian inhabitants, Lewis contended that the most violent exchanges occurred between cattlemen determined to preserve the open range and farmers determined to settle, fence, and farm the land. Lewis identified the main Boomer protagonists as David Payne, "a convicted criminal who persist[ed] in repeating his crime," and W. L. Couch. What the followers of Payne and Couch could not accomplish by force they were finally able to achieve through popular agitation. Roused by a massive petition campaign, political negotiations were opened between the United States and the Muscogee (Creek), Seminole, and Cherokee republics for the purchase of surplus Indian Territory lands.[24]

In 1883 the Senate Committee on Indian Affairs launched an investigation of Indian Territory cattle range leases. The degree of graft, exploitation, coercion, and violence perpetrated by the range cattle operatives, most of which were organized as companies by this time, shocked Congress. Boomers used the committee's findings to advance their cause in Congress. With no effective voice to lobby in their defense, American Indians were at the mercy of Western representatives who favored opening their lands. A "bill was introduced into the House in 1886 to provide a territorial government for the Indian Territory, and to create a commission to treat with the Indians for the opening of the vacant lands to settlement." Vigorously opposed by East Coast Indian Rights proponents and the cattlemen, the bill failed. However, the colonizers and their advocates had already found a way to conquer the Indian republics.[25]

Acting with congressional authority, "President Cleveland, made treaties with the Muscogee and Seminole nations by which they agreed to convey complete title to the lands ceded in 1866." Boomers were "now to realize... [their] long cherished dream of entering the 'Promised Land.'" Lewis concluded, "Thus it was in Oklahoma as in other states of the southwest, the cattlemen paved the way for settlement." Completed in 1917, Lewis's thesis would prove a well-argued indictment of Indian betrayal through the machinations of self-serving European Americans that foreshadowed Angie Debo's exposé of European American greed in *And Still the Waters Run*.[26]

While working on her thesis, Lewis found employment at a small regional junior college in Durant, Oklahoma. Finding career prospects disagreeable in Durant, Lewis reluctantly applied for a teaching position at the new Oklahoma Industrial Institute and College for Girls in Chickasha, Oklahoma. Fearing that it was, "an institute for wayward girls" that would not offer a better deal, Lewis did not pin high hopes on the position. In 1917 the institute (later the name was changed to Oklahoma College for Women) offered Lewis a position in the history department. Lewis began a life-long career at the Oklahoma College for Women (OCW) that year. But her position was not secure, and prospects for advancement without a doctorate were slim.[27]

Although appointed college registrar, in addition to her regular duties, Lewis's position at the college remained tenuous. OCW president George Washington Austin indicated that until Lewis acquired a doctorate her position in the history department was not guaranteed. Fearing for her future, Lewis looked into pursuing a terminal degree in Oklahoma. Unfortunately, until 1929 no university in the state offered a history degree higher than a master's. Uncertain of President Austin's deadline, Lewis decided it was unwise to compromise her position by seeking a doctorate out of state. Lewis's decision to remain in Oklahoma was most likely based on conversations with Edward Everett Dale, chair of the University of Oklahoma history department, who told her about his plan to offer a doctoral degree in history.[28]

Between 1917 and 1929, Lewis collaborated with her sister Winnidell to bolster her OCW academic credentials by writing a number of articles for the *Chronicles of Oklahoma*. The material dealt exclusively with Spanish and French colonial documents detailing activities in the Arkansas River Valley. Poorly translated and documented, several of Lewis's submissions required significant editorial revision, including additional research and footnotes. Collectively, the articles revealed Lewis's growing interest in Arkansas Valley borderlands history. Echoing the work of Emma Helen Blair and Louise Phelps Kellogg—and no doubt modeled on Bolton's approach to Spanish borderlands history—Lewis's work had scholarly potential. Modest publication success aside, as an amateur translator of Spanish and French Lewis's ambition would prove to be a destructive tangent for her career. But in the short term, Lewis's *Chronicles of Oklahoma* articles placated OCW administrators and strengthened her position in the history department.[29]

After an eleven year wait Lewis received word in 1929 that the University of Oklahoma would offer the doctoral degree in history. Immediately, Lewis notified Dale, applied for permission to take the spring course, and not long afterward received an acceptance letter. For her graduate term at OU—1929 to 1930—Lewis took a one-year sabbatical from OCW, during which she completed her seminar work, passed the required doctoral exams, and wrote her dissertation. Lewis would be the University of Oklahoma's first history doctoral candidate. Unknown to her at the time, Dale would prove as detrimental to her career as Bolton had been beneficial.[30]

Where Bolton nurtured Lewis's innate intellectual talents and built on her scholarly abilities, Dale allowed her to pursue research she did not have the skill or training to engage. A lesser known Frederick Jackson Turner protégé, Dale originally planned his dissertation on "The Five Civilized Tribes and their Removal to Oklahoma" during his graduate work at Harvard. However, sometime after 1915 Dale's subject changed from Indian removal to "A History of the Range Cattle Industry in Oklahoma."[31]

Dale's decision was probably influenced by several factors, including a chance 1913 meeting with Oklahoma senator Robert L. Owen and a review of Annie Heloise Abel's work. While it cannot be stated with certainty that the idea for Dale's dissertation came from Anna Lewis's master's thesis, it is clear that his scholarship uncannily mirrored her work and sources. Suspicions are further raised by the fact that shortly after Lewis's arrival at the University of Oklahoma, Dale began to foster her interest in Spanish and French Arkansas River Valley history. Unfortunately, as revealed in the *Chronicles of Oklahoma* articles, neither Lewis nor her sister had the necessary linguistic expertise to master this material.[32]

Curiously Dale, an able translator conversant in French and German, did not find Lewis's foreign language deficiency to be a problem. Whether Dale felt that Lewis, as a promising student of Bolton and college history professor, should overcome her linguistic deficiencies in two languages within a matter of months in order to stake a position for herself in borderlands scholarship, or whether he simply wanted to preserve his own scholarly domain is not known. Either way, Dale's oversight as Lewis's committee chair contributed to an ill-fated venture that would bring public embarrassment to the woman who acquired the OU history department's first doctorate.[33]

As Angie Debo, Lewis's contemporary at the University of Oklahoma, would discover, Dale's skill as an engaging storyteller, popular classroom instructor, and published author did not translate to his work as an academic mentor. Where Lewis apparently accepted Dale's incompetence graciously, Debo bluntly challenged his often confusing (and at least on one occasion fabricated) critiques and in the end suffered his professional wrath. Neither acquiescence nor confrontation rescued either woman from Dale's lackluster performance as a doctoral adviser.³⁴

Whatever Lewis's perceptions of Dale might have been, she proceeded with her dissertation. To secure research material she employed Roland Vandergrift, a Berkeley colleague and former Bolton M.A. student, to copy several documents from the Archivo General de Indias at Seville, Spain. Although it was a great favor to Lewis, Vandergrift was immersed in his own research and did not make careful or extensive copies of the material she requested. Vandergrift's copy work mainly amounted to a small group of documents from a single *legajo* ("file"), covering the period 1768 to 1784. An examination of Vandergrift's supplemental notes reveals a confusing documentation system and a hodge-podge of random comments.³⁵

Compounding Lewis's foreign language deficiencies, the material Vandergrift gathered did not allow a full treatment of the topic. Lewis's only recourse was to have the copies translated and hope to find enough additional material to fashion a dissertation. Calling on the services of her sister Winnidell—who at that time taught high school Spanish and French in the Muskogee, Oklahoma, public school system—Lewis acquired a hasty translation sometime in 1929. Over the next few months Lewis typed a dissertation titled, "A History of the Arkansas River Region, 1541–1800," and submitted it to her committee.³⁶

On Thursday, May 8, 1930, Lewis defended her dissertation in the Oklahoma Union building before committee members Edward Everett Dale, J. L. Waller, and Carl Coke Rister. The deliberation was not recorded, but the outcome was definitive: Anna Lewis became Dr. Anna Lewis. As a Choctaw, Lewis was the first American Indian to be awarded a doctorate at the University of Oklahoma. Having earned the terminal degree Lewis assumed greater responsibly in the OCW history department, eventually becoming chair.³⁷

Following graduation, Lewis submitted a manuscript based on her dissertation to the University of Oklahoma Press for consideration. While waiting for the press's verdict, Lewis also published a daring contribution to the pedagogy of Oklahoma history. Reflecting her aversion to racial and cultural bigotry, Lewis's *Problems in Oklahoma History: A Workbook for High School Students*, coauthored with Howard Taylor, dean of the OCW Education department, guided students from Indian sovereignty through European American settler colonialism. Though a modest contribution, the preface noted that "westward movement . . . developed an inevitable conflict of European culture with that of Native Americans." Lewis and Taylor argued that Oklahoma's settlement by European Americans was destructive to the region's American

Indian peoples and cultures. In this the workbook advanced a then-radical political position. No other professional Oklahoma historian would take up this potentially career ending approach until Angie Debo published *And Still the Waters Run* in 1940.[38]

The first reader's report on Lewis's manuscript from University of Oklahoma librarian Jesse L. Rader arrived at the press on September 10, 1931, followed three months later by OU assistant history professor Alfred B. Thomas's review on December 14, 1931. Both Rader's and Thomas's reviews were negative. In his rejection letter, OU Press director Joseph Brandt apologized that "the manuscript has been in our hands for so long," adding frankly, "our readers do not recommend publication." Quoting from Rader's review Brandt advised, "The style should be more incisive and the English severely scrutinized." From Thomas's report Brandt extrapolated, "The definition of 'Arkansas Region' is inadequate . . . there is no statement of name, location and range of the Indian groups." Concluding, Brandt suggested that Lewis revise and submit to the Southwest Press in Dallas, Texas. Owned by P. L. Turner, "former manager of the Methodist Publishing House," Southwest Press had a reputation for publishing "contrarian" histories outside the academic mainstream. In terms of scholarly prestige, Southwest was considered a popular press.[39]

The critiques by Rader and Thomas reflect contradictions that suggest Lewis's manuscript did not get a fair review. While neither openly criticized ethnic and cultural identity—as did reviewers for Rachel Caroline Eaton's manuscript—Rader and Thomas largely based their conclusions on manufactured problems. In a review that critiqued the "careless and almost slipshod manner in which . . . [Lewis's manuscript] was written," Rader admitted, "I have read at least the first half of Miss Lewis's thesis with great care." Having read at least half of the manuscript Rader confidently divined, "The other more serious objection to the thesis is that it presents nothing new." Rader added, "I am positive, however, that the whole thesis should be very carefully rewritten with the idea of making a straightforward English statement of the facts." It is not clear if Rader intended to address content, syntax, or ethnicity for the half of the manuscript he actually read. Noting that he did not have the expertise to substantially address Lewis's work, Rader concluded, "There is a possibility, of course, that I may be wrong in my conclusions."[40]

Rader was not a trained historian and indicated this in his review. Alfred Thomas on the other hand was a respected scholar and emerging American Southwest history expert. Thomas submitted a blistering critique that faulted Lewis for a phantom manuscript she did not write. In a detailed review Thomas advanced a straw man argument that boldly misrepresented Lewis's scholarship. Thomas asserted, "The Arkansas River has a history in the Colorado region for 150 years (1650–1800)." Thomas continued, "This history is a record of Navajo-Ute-Pawnee-Apache-Comanche-Spanish and French relationships that should not be overlooked in a study of the Arkansas River Region."[41]

Thomas's critique is puzzling, given that Lewis clearly identified the area of her study as the country "drained by the Arkansas, Verdigris, and Canadian Rivers." Lewis further asserted, "The history of this wedge-shaped country has been heretofore treated as only secondary to that of the country to the North and South." The Verdigris River originates in southeastern Kansas and terminates in the Arkansas River at Muskogee, Oklahoma, forming the northern boundary of Lewis's triangular Arkansas River "wedge." The Canadian, Cimarron, and Verdigris Rivers join roughly between Tulsa, Oklahoma, and Fort Smith, Arkansas, forming the long terminal point of the wedge. Given that Lewis clearly stated the focus of her study was this overlooked wedge, Thomas's point was irrelevant. Furthermore, given that Lewis's manuscript examined a two hundred and fifty-nine year period spanning from 1541 to 1800, Thomas's complaint that Lewis failed to address the years 1650 to 1800 appears unfounded.[42]

The second part of Thomas's review chided Lewis for "overlooking" Arkansas River Valley Indians noting, "There is no statement of the name, location, & range of the Indian groups." It is not clear how Thomas reached this conclusion, if in fact he actually read Lewis's manuscript. Approximately one fourth of Lewis's study addressed American Indian history in the wedge area with discussions of Touacara, Zautoouy, Padouca, and Jumano villages. Other regional Indian villages were also addressed by name and location. Moreover, Lewis correctly addressed American Indian history that actually occurred in the wedge, notably "Osage," "Natchez," "Comanche," "Choctaw," and "Chickasaw."[43]

Lewis's reply to Joseph Brandt is not recorded, but it is clear she followed his advice and submitted her work to the Southwest Press. The manuscript was accepted and by 1932 it was published as *Along the Arkansas*. Lewis did not record her reaction to publication, but she no doubt felt that her hard work was finally being rewarded.[44]

As a newly published author all seemed right for Lewis, but as with Debo, she found her time with Dale would come back to haunt her. For Lewis the specter arrived in June 1933. In a devastatingly vicious and academically narrow-minded review of *Along the Arkansas*, Lansing Bartlett Bloom, former New Mexico commissioner to the Seville Spain exposition and an indefatigable scholar of documents held by the Archivo de Indias at Seville, proclaimed in the *Mississippi Valley Historical Review*, "The book leaves much to be desired in both scholarship and workmanship. . . . From preface to the brief inadequate index, the text is replete with errors." Specifically Bloom noted, "Many [errors] may be accounted for by careless proofreading, but many others are in Spanish and French names and terms."[45]

Not that Bloom's reviews were models of civility, however, his attack on Lewis seemed particularly severe and likely sexist. A survey of Bloom's reviews for publications by male authors does not reveal a comparable degree of harsh scrutiny. Furthermore, as Bolton's rival in Spanish borderland history, Bloom would not have been inclined to show sympathy for one of his rival's students in the face of obvious mistakes. The evidence indicates that for comparatively petty reasons, Bloom obscured one of the most important transitional publications in professional American Indian history.[46]

While postcolonial historical analysis was at least two decades away, *Along the Arkansas* was notable for addressing ways in which colonialism shaped the perceptions and representations of Indian peoples and cultures. Describing the ever present social, political, and economic tensions between colonizers and colonized, *Along the Arkansas* noted how the imperial gaze sculpted the social structures and daily activities of Europeans and American Indians in the Arkansas River wedge. Giving special consideration to material culture, Lewis illuminated the imperial presumptions that overvalued European commodities, and undervalued Indian material culture.[47]

Looking beyond colonial critique, Lewis also considered intertribal politics. Lewis contended that while colonialism cast a shadow across the entire wedge, intertribal politics exerted a kind of collective agency. This agency most notably manifested through controlled tension cultivated by Indian villages and tribes. By pitting the French and Spanish against each other, Arkansas River Valley Indian villages and tribes crafted autonomous cultural spaces in which they were able to live outside the imperial gaze. Without dismissing the validity of Bloom's technical points, it is important to note that Lewis's pioneering intertribal scholarship was revolutionary in its broad ethnological sensitivity, postcolonial reach, and complex "middle ground" political vision.

Considering American Indian intertribal relations in the Arkansas River wedge, Lewis looked at a number of Indian villages including Touacara, Zautoouy, Padouca, and Jumano. Examining both trade and political interactions, Lewis argued that Osage, Natchez, Comanche, Chickasaw, Choctaw, and Apache peoples in the Arkansas River wedge had successfully navigated French and Spanish imperial agendas by promoting controlled friction. This fabricated standoff ultimately worked for the colonizer and colonized, because it brought comparatively equitable profits that proved more attractive than costly campaigns of repeated conquest and reoccupation. The relative peace of this strategic equilibrium evaporated in 1803 when Napoleon sold the Louisiana Territory to the American republic. Controlled friction was replaced by unmitigated American expansion. Elaborating a kind of middle ground, Anna Lewis's *Along the Arkansas* prefigured historian Richard White's scholarship by sixty years. Clearly, while Bloom was busy parsing the trees, he missed the forest.[48]

Lewis's reaction to Bloom's public ridicule is not known. However, she obviously was not inclined to follow his advice and republish the book following extensive revisions. As a prominent expert on Spanish and French borderlands, Bloom's review of Lewis's book was definitive—it was a damning critique from which her borderlands scholarship would not recover. *Along the Arkansas* would prove to be Lewis's last comprehensive intertribal history. From 1933 Lewis renounced the academic course she and Dale plotted, primarily returning to intratribal (Choctaw) and Oklahoma history. While Lewis's first attempt at creating a scholarly niche was complicated by a project ill-suited to her talents, she nevertheless managed to reinvent herself over the next decade.[49]

Lewis's academic experience with Dale, while not ideal, was not altogether unusual for graduate school, but her unpleasant experience had a long-term effect on American Indian history. The struggles surrounding Lewis's dissertation and subsequent publication illuminate both the magnitude of her achievement and the ignobility of her historiographical invisibility. However, this difficulty should not overshadow the fact that Lewis was the first American Indian to acquire a doctorate from the University of Oklahoma and that she earned the first Ph.D. awarded by the OU history department. Apart from her early publication difficulties, Lewis went on to a distinguished thirty-nine year career as a history professor and department chair at the Oklahoma College for Women. In 1956 Lewis retired to her vacation home in the old Choctaw Nation near Clayton, Oklahoma.[50]

MURIEL H. WRIGHT, INDIAN TERMINATION, AND THE OKLAHOMA HISTORICAL SOCIETY

Like Anna Lewis, Muriel Hazel Wright was a citizen of the Choctaw Nation. Muriel Wright was born on a ranch outside Lehigh, Choctaw Nation, to Ida Belle Richards Wright and Dr. Eliphalet Nott (E. N.) Wright. Eliphalet Wright was Choctaw, son of former chief Allen Wright, and he served as physician for the Missouri-Pacific Coal Mines and president of the Choctaw Oil and Refining Company. Ida Belle Wright was a European American blue blood who traced her ancestry to the Mayflower. On her maternal side Ida Belle

Muriel H. Wright. Longtime editor of the Oklahoma Historical Society's journal, *Chronicles of Oklahoma,* and daughter of former Choctaw chief Allen Wright, Muriel Wright wielded considerable prestige as an Indigenous Indian historian. Courtesy of the Research Division of the Oklahoma Historical Society (OHSRD-13681).

claimed to be related to Captain Samuel Clinton Richards and President Chester A. Arthur.[51]

Unlike Anna Lewis, whose father was a European American married to a Choctaw woman, both Wright's Choctaw grandfather and father were married to European American missionary women. Where Lewis closely identified with her mother and the matriarchal line of Choctaw culture,

Wright identified with her father and his interest in the political and economic aspects of Choctaw national life. Ultimately the difference between how each woman defined her social and tribal roles created tension in their relationship.[52]

Muriel Wright lived a life of privilege in the Choctaw Nation, and as a young woman she benefited notably from her father's political and economic connections. Yet, as an adult Wright did not seem to profit from her allotment. During the Great Depression Wright found herself unemployed and often in desperate financial circumstances. In part this was the result of Wright's own taste for using polarizing political rhetoric.

Like her father and mother, Wright was an avid Republican who delighted in lambasting Oklahoma Democrats. Wright proudly boasted of her support for Oklahoma's only pre-suffrage congresswoman, the controversial one-term Republican representative Alice Robertson. Wright's political bent would have dire consequences for her immediate scholarly plans. In 1936 Wright tried to establish a federal Works Progress Administration Indian History program in Oklahoma. Although a worthy endeavor, Wright's proposal found little support among Oklahoma historians and anthropologists, who worried that her work would detract from their own. Wright received no support from local and national Democrats, whose frigid response ultimately doomed the proposal.[53]

The promising young daughter of elite Choctaw and European American parents, Wright like many in her position, replaced a lack of material prestige with an exaggerated pedigree. But Wrights' vocational difficulties and academic frustrations would bring this fabricated status into question. Wright's personal disappointments, particularly her failure to acquire a graduate history degree, fueled her bitter jealousy of Angie Debo's scholarly achievements. The fact that Debo, a European American, gained renown as an Indian historian made her fame all the more painful for Wright.[54]

Wright's academic venture began in 1906 when she was enrolled at Wheaton Seminary in Norton, Massachusetts. There Wright acquired notoriety as a Southern belle and assimilated Choctaw. Unable to pass as a European American and singled out as an Indian, the racial segregation, if not outright bias, that Wright experienced at Wheaton cultivated her lifelong propensity for "playing Indian." Within two years Wright was summoned to join her family in Washington, D.C., where her father served as the new Choctaw delegate to Congress. The family remained in Washington until 1910. Unlike Lewis, Wright did not return to Oklahoma immediately after the dissolution of the Five Indian nations. In Washington Wright defined herself as a cultural mediator whose use of stock Indian costumery was intended to contrast with her own genteel refinement and civilized status. One account notes that at a formal ball Wright presented herself as "an Indian girl in all the picturesque trappings of her ancestral tribe." Actually, Wright was costumed in a Cheyenne buckskin dress.[55]

At the conclusion of Eliphalet Wright's term in Washington, the family returned to their ranch outside Lehigh, Oklahoma. Responding to the new state's call for teachers in 1911, Wright studied pedagogy at East Central State College in Ada, Oklahoma. After earning her certification, Wright taught in the Wapanuka, Tishomingo, and Thompson public schools between 1912 and 1915. At the conclusion of the 1915 term, Wright applied for graduate studies at Barnard College—the women's affiliate of Columbia University, New York. Between 1916 and 1918, Wright studied United States history with popular textbook author David S. Muzzey and Latin American history with noted cartographer William R. Shepherd. At Barnard Wright moved in elite circles, rooming with Lucy Dewey, daughter of renowned educator John Dewey, and keeping company with Ellen Borden, scion of the popular dairy product family.[56]

For reasons unknown Wright dropped out of Barnard in 1918, returning home to Lehigh. Wright would never return to academia. From 1918 to 1924 Wright served as principal of the Hardwood District School not far from her family home. Thereafter, Wright served with her father on the Choctaw Advisory Committee—a controversial intratribal political organization affiliated with the Republican Party. The Advisory Committee was ostensibly formed to settle outstanding tribal land claims. In the 1930s Wright also began to publish articles on American Indian history and culture, notably that of the Five Tribes. Wright's intertribal scholarship began two decades before the publication of her book *A Guide to the Indian Tribes of Oklahoma*. Before 1943 Wright "had published eighteen articles and five book reviews" in the *Chronicles of Oklahoma*.[57]

Largely based on her publications, personal connections, and an advantageous political climate, on July 1, 1943, Wright became associate editor of the Oklahoma Historical Society's flagship journal, *Chronicles of Oklahoma*. From 1955 until her retirement in 1973, Wright served as chief editor. At a time when regional history journals were dwindling, Wright cultivated a national following. Occasionally, when submissions waned, Wright authored articles. In the years spanning her two decades as chief editor, Wright published over one hundred scholarly articles highlighting state and American Indian history. In addition to writing seven books on Oklahoma, American Indian, and Civil War history, Wright also coauthored five books on Oklahoma history. Drawn from her own experiences, family stories, and Indian lore, Wright's work incorporated genealogy with archival documentation. As an amateur historian, "Wright . . . worked to uphold the prestige and privilege of her family as she documented Choctaw Nation . . . history," particularly their prominent role in Choctaw assimilation.[58]

ANGIE DEBO, SOVEREIGNTY, AND THE HISTORY OF AMERICAN INDIAN NATIONS

Professional historian and noted scholar Angie Debo deemed herself a straightforward and objective student of history. Almost two decades before her death Debo noted, "When I start on a research project I have no idea how it will turn out . . . I simply . . . dig out the truth and record it." Debo insisted, "I am not pro-Indian, or pro-anything, unless it is pro-integrity . . . [but] sometimes I find all the truth on one side of an issue." Though the specific facts of Debo's scholarship were not known in advance, each of her nine publications bore the heavy mark of her personal and intellectual lineage.[59]

Debo's life has been well documented, but new evidence demonstrates a deep but largely constructive intellectual tension between Muriel Wright, Anna Lewis, and Angie Debo. Thoughtful and introspective, Debo's response to Wright and Lewis would ultimately take shape as her monumental indictment of assimilation, termination of the Five Indian nations, and loathsome crimes against Oklahoma Indian peoples—*And Still the Waters Run*.[60]

Angie Debo was born January 30, 1890, in Beattie, Kansas, to Edward and Lina Debo, European American homesteaders. Nine years later the Debo family moved to a new homestead near Marshall in Oklahoma Territory. Debo came of age at a time when the new territory was struggling to build the basic institutions of an emerging state. Although Marshall boasted a small grade school—from which Debo graduated in 1903—the Marshall junior high school would not be completed until 1905.[61]

During the intervening two years, Debo became a devotee of the local newspaper, revealing a particular fascination with international affairs. Debo was mesmerized by details of the 1905 Russian workers insurrection known as "Bloody Sunday." News of the Russian unrest exposed Debo to the looming question of popular sovereignty and the right of nations and peoples to decide their own fates. The next year, as a ninth grader in the new high school, Debo participated in a class debate on popular sovereignty. The contest proposed was "Resolved: That a nation or nations should interfere with and slow the barbarities that are now being perpetrated in Russia." Taking the negative side, Debo championed the Russian peasants. Questions about popular sovereignty and human rights would continue to trouble Debo for the rest of her life.[62]

Debo also developed interests in institutional tyranny and women's rights, and whatever the actualities Debo would always associate the two. Debo's

Angie Debo, exterior photograph standing in front of finely detailed front porch, ca. 1910–20. Debo was the first widely known professional historian of American Indian history. She moved the field toward a more inclusive, complex ethnological and cultural analysis that interrogated assimilationist assumptions and favored Indian sovereignty. Angie Debo Papers, Special Collections and University Archives, Oklahoma State University Libraries (B63f45-08.TIF).

first experience with gender and institutions arose from her exposure to the fiery temperance leader Carry A. Nation, recent transplant to Oklahoma Territory. A resident of Guthrie, just thirty miles from Marshall, Nation led temperance and statehood campaigns that attracted the Debo family. Nation's free journal, *The Defender*, proved welcome reading in the often cash-strapped Debo home. Believing that a new state government would abolish saloons (it did), Nation triumphantly concluded her Oklahoma residency with statehood in 1907. From her observation of Nation's work, Debo concluded that public institutions were not inherently benevolent. Institutions must be compelled to better society.[63]

However, crusading political activist Catherine Ann "Kate" Barnard wielded far more influence over young Debo. Elected the first Oklahoma Commissioner of Charities and Corrections in 1907, Kate Barnard took office at a time when Oklahoma women could not cast votes for statewide offices. Barnard immediately began agitating for a new state law banishing child labor. She also campaigned for compulsory public education and promoted the eight hour workday. Although Barnard's political fortunes would later falter, she was a hero to seventeen-year-old Angie Debo.[64]

Unfortunately for Debo, upon its completion in 1906 the Marshall high school still lacked accommodations for grades 10–12. Between 1906 and 1910 Debo taught at neighboring public schools. When Marshall finally added the terminal grades, Debo resumed her studies. As a twenty-one year old tenth grader, Debo particularly relished debate class. In one such engagement Debo argued the case for women's suffrage, contending that "power was derived from the consent of the governed—in other words the people."[65]

As Europe moved toward war in 1913, Debo graduated from Marshall high school at the age of twenty-three. Working again as a local schoolteacher in a bid to raise money for college, Debo was stricken with typhoid fever. Recurring illness and fatigue prevented her from pursuing college course work until 1915. That year Debo enrolled at the University of Oklahoma, where she majored in English.[66]

Finding that the English degree was designed to prepare students for a lifetime of grading high school essays, in 1917 Debo switched to geology and enrolled in a history course taught by Everett Edward Dale. By her senior year, Debo decided to major in history. Debo was clearly taken with Dale's American history class—she found it deeply disturbing. While Dale proved an engaging professor who skillfully presented the march of western civilization as the ultimate manifestation of progress, Debo took a decidedly dimmer view. A vocal opponent of the European war and an avowed isolationist, Debo saw U.S. Western expansion as an imperialistic usurpation that violated American Indian human rights. Debo's 1918 class essays charted her developing concept of internal imperialism—notably her essays on "Acquisition of Florida," "Acquisition of Oregon," "Acquisition of Texas," and "Acquisition of Territory, the Louisiana Purchase." Following graduation in 1918, Debo taught public school in Enid, Oklahoma, and saved for graduate school over the next five years. In 1923 Debo's application to the University of Chicago history program was accepted. Debo chose the Chicago program because of its reputation for international studies and the borderlands scholarship of Herbert Eugene Bolton's protégé, J. Fred Rippy. In addition to her master's history work, Debo minored in political science. Popular sovereignty and institutional justice were still on her mind.[67]

Styled J. (James) Fred Rippy, Debo's Chicago mentor, was a recipient of the 1917–18 Native Sons of the Golden West research fellowship. A California promotional association, Native Son's scholarships were established by historian H. Morse Stephens to encourage the study of California history "at its sources in Spain and elsewhere." Herbert Eugene Bolton served for many years as a leading figure in the organization. Under Bolton's guidance, Native Son's scholarship program focused on Mexican-American-Indian borderlands studies. Scholarship recipients were encouraged to work in Spanish and European archives and were assisted with translation work. Unfortunately for Rippy, who planned to do research in Spain, the European war made overseas travel hazardous. Dissuaded from transatlantic study, Rippy concentrated on Mexican and American Indian history.[68]

Rippy's research bore fruit in 1919 when he published "Mexican Projects of the Confederates" in the *Southwestern Historical Quarterly*. Rippy's article explored Southern efforts to forge a supply agreement with Mexico and establish a Confederate colony south of the United States border. Three months later Rippy published "The Indians of the Southwest in the Diplomacy of the United States and Mexico, 1848–1853." Likely reflecting Rachel Caroline Eaton's lingering influence, Rippy's article argued that a forgotten aspect of the Treaty of Guadalupe Hildago required U.S. constraint of "Indians ranging along the international border" and confiscation of goods brought by Indians from Mexico. The article inspired Debo's later work on southern Cherokee refugees.[69]

As Debo began her studies at Chicago she leaned toward international affairs and treaty relations. Debo found Rippy's interpretation of American imperialism, as explicated in his popular "The Americas in World Affairs" class attractive. She also found the work of Rippy's colleague, Phillip Quincy Wright—who would garner a national reputation among political scientists for his study of war and its aftermath—intriguing. It was during Wright's "American Diplomacy" class that Debo began research that culminated in her master's thesis, "The Historical Background of the American Policy of

Isolationism." Debo's pro-isolation thesis argued that United States insular policy fostered democratic development, prosperity, domestic tranquility, and cultural distinctiveness. These themes would reoccur in Debo's subsequent American Indian scholarship. Rippy proved so deeply invested in Debo's work that upon its completion, he submitted it for publication—with his name as coauthor—to the *Smith College Studies in History* journal in 1924. That spring Debo's thesis appeared as the journal's sole article.[70]

Pressed for cash and buoyed by Rippy's praise, Debo inquired about academic job prospects and was disheartened to find that leading universities, with rare exception, would not hire women historians. Debo bristled at what she considered institutional male chauvinism for the rest of her life. Debo's reaction reflected her early impressions of institutional corruption cultivated by the political rhetoric of Carry Nation and Kate Barnard.[71]

Much scholarly attention has been given Debo's effort to break into a profession "barred against women," but the actual barrier was far more subtle— an informal sexual division of labor within the history profession. Debo's career frustrations were not caused by her inability to enter the history profession, but rather by her desire to contravene the professional bias that relegated women historians to archives, historical societies, museums, and women's and teacher's colleges.[72]

Debo was already in the history profession. Like her female colleagues, she was welcomed by male academics who wanted trained historians to curate document repositories and spread interest in academic history at the secondary level. Debo found temporary employment at a Texas teacher's college in 1925 and afterward she held a museum curatorial position. While Debo seemed to ignore the subtleties of her employment situation, she knew that real professional stature came from a university position at a recognized coeducational institution. For Debo's generation of women historians, separate simply was not equal.[73]

A tremendous amount of scholarship has also focused on Debo's efforts to secure a tenured faculty position, but no attention has been given to how Debo's intellectual interaction with Anna Lewis and Muriel Wright affected the nature of her American Indian research and publication. While Debo's struggle to breach vocational segregation impacted her scholarly life, her intellectual altercations with two Indigenous women historians proved definitive for Debo's impending publications.

MUDDIED WATERS

After graduating with her master's from the University of Chicago, Debo found the only academic position available to her was as a teacher in a demonstration high school attached to the West Texas State Teacher's College (WTSTC) in Canyon, Texas. Debo worked as an instructor, mainly teaching dropouts who wanted to earn a high school diploma. Considering Debo's stellar performance at the University of Chicago and her acclaimed scholarship with Rippy, WTSTC proved a humiliating disappointment. That WTSTC history department chair, Lester Sheffy had been a fellow graduate assistant with Debo under Rippy further fueled her discontent.[74]

In 1929 Debo received an unexpected windfall from a published short story and used it to fund a leave of absence from WTSTC. During this interlude, Debo enrolled in the University of Oklahoma history doctoral program—along with Anna Lewis. Initially welcomed by her old undergraduate mentor, Edward Everett Dale, Debo embarked on preliminary coursework that she completed in 1932. However, Debo had already muddied the waters with Dale in 1931. While biographers place this tension later in the chronology, tying it to Debo's rejection of Dale's dissertation critique, the actual source was an earlier well-intended, but presumptuous "greenhorn" historiographical analysis.[75]

Written for a class taught by Dale's colleague Ralph H. Records during the 1930–31 fall term, Debo's paper was titled, "Edward Everett Dale, Historian of Progress." Superficially, the paper seemed a cloying attempt to curry favor. The first paragraph proclaimed, "It is . . . fortunate that this startling young commonwealth in the southwest has finally become articulate through the teaching and writing of a typical Oklahoman, Edward Everett Dale, dean of Oklahoma historians, and head of the state university."[76]

Dale, however, was not a university president or the dean of Oklahoma historians. Unfortunately for Debo, though affable, Dale often proved thin-skinned, especially when he was the subject of scholarly criticism. The remainder of Debo's lengthy essay took Dale's progressive ideology to task, drawing a sharp and stunningly frank distinction between her own isolationist understanding of American expansion and Dale's unshakable faith in the beneficent unfolding of Manifest Destiny.[77]

Framing Dale's graduate scholarship as a contrast between his University of Oklahoma baccalaureate thesis titled, "The Location of the Indian Tribes of Oklahoma" and his Harvard master's thesis, "The White Settlement of Oklahoma," Debo ruthlessly exposed the racial and imperialistic bias of Dale's thought. Summarizing his scholarly vision, Debo brashly rhapsodized, "The adventure of American conquest across the continent became to this son of the frontier a great heroic epic." Speculating on his personal motives, Debo added, "He had the naive unconscious imperialism of the American pioneer who went out into the wilderness with the innocent determination to own it all." Though true, Debo unwisely exposed her doctoral committee chair as a scholarly fraud, as a man incapable of contemplating or resolving his own intellectual and moral conflicts.[78]

The personal flaws so brazenly presented by Debo would be poignantly revealed in an account of Dale's work for Lewis Merriam's 1927, "Survey of Indian Affairs," featured in Merriam's final 1928–29 report, *The Problem of Indian Administration*. Unable to comprehend the social and cultural devastation wrought by the last four decades of assimilation, Dale's account did not display criticism, discomfort, or disgust for the visible failures of United States Indian policy. Dale might as well have been describing a leisurely camping trip in the American outback where for the most part everyone just got along. In summation, Dale called for the government to stay the course, pursuing more assimilation, not less. Dale's inability to see a connection between "The White Settlement of Oklahoma" and "The Location of the Indian Tribes of Oklahoma," reflected his own unwillingness to engage in scholarly criticism. In his published work Dale noted, "I have yet to be convinced, that a grouchy temper is a sure indication of scholarship."[79]

However frank her previous assessments, Debo was still not finished with Dale. Her paper continued, "[Dale's] viewpoint is limited to the frontier . . . he knows European history, but only as a series of personal narratives like an historical novel. . . . Diplomacy and the world of politics for him do not exist—he can visualize people but not peoples." Debo further asserted, "Imperialism, if he thinks of it at all, is the march of civilization across the waste plains of the earth." Summing the scope of his intellect, Debo added, "It is to be greatly feared that Dale has a philosophy of history. . . . Even more appalling is the suspicion that he does not realize the enormity of his heresy against the craft. . . . His philosophy may be summed up in one word *Progress*." Debo concluded, "Unlike Turner, who can explain the influence of the frontier but is somewhat vague about the next step, Dale regards the future as the most interesting advance of all. . . . For this reason Dale goes blithely on his way in an age of disillusionment." Starkly, Debo drew a distinction between her own ideology and Dale's. Where Debo saw true progress as the extension of human rights, she portrayed Dale's measure of progress as conformity to European American culture. Hence, Debo had branded her committee chair a crusading imperialist and perhaps a naive racist.[80]

Dale was aware of the paper, but he never revealed his displeasure to Debo. Given the precarious status of the department's doctoral program and Dale's aversion for conflict he chose to hide his sentiments. Luckily for Debo, as she began to contemplate a career in American Indian scholarship the effect of Merriam's shocking report on academic circles helped to soften Dale's reservations about critical Indian history.[81]

Adding to the sea change initiated by Merriam's report, in 1929 the American Historical Association (AHA) witnessed a stunning reversal of George Burton Adams's 1908 rejection of interdisciplinary scholarship. Newly installed AHA president James Harvey Robinson proclaimed, "Our rather solemn estimate of the orderly proceedings of mankind as recorded in documents was reinforced by a fear of what George Burton Adams called 'a new flaring up of interest in the philosophy of history.'" Robinson continued, "The same writer was also solicitous that history should retain its integrity since it was threatened with assaults from stealthy, youthful social sciences.... This fear has I trust vanished." Assessing the current state of the profession, Robinson somewhat unrealistically noted, "As we look back thirty years we find historians perhaps rather pedantic and defensive.... They are humble enough now." Dismissing Adams's earlier concerns, Robinson asserted that historians now "seek help from quarters undreamed of when I began to teach... [and] readily admit that anyone can view historically anything he wishes and we bless him for his wisdom if he does."[82]

Galvanized by this new interdisciplinary license, Debo's seminar papers departed from the staid political history of the past. In 1932 Debo penned an essay that radically challenged recent Indian history. In particular, "Southern Refugees of the Cherokee Nation" indicated the direction of her pending dissertation work. Elaborating a theme she developed while working with Rippy, Debo argued that forced alliances between the Union, Confederacy, and Cherokee Nation shattered Cherokee sovereignty during and after the Civil War. Debo concluded that in the aftermath of the renegotiated 1866 treaty, what little remained of the postbellum Cherokee Nation entered a painful period of nation building that fostered their determination to regain independence. The issue of Five Nations sovereignty would draw Debo's attention for the next decade.[83]

Completing her course work in 1932, Debo considered a dissertation topic. Inspired by the work of Annie Heloise Abel, Debo decided to address post-removal Indian history. Dale suggested she make use of unpublished Choctaw records in the University of Oklahoma's Phillips Collection. Dale also suggested research at the Bureau of Indian Affairs (BIA) archives, for which he provided a letter of recommendation. Once there, Debo perused the same BIA files that Abel had organized and consulted for her work on slaveholding Indians. While at the BIA, Debo also conducted research with Anna Lewis's brother, Choctaw principle attorney, Grady Lewis. In conjunction with his work on the pending Leased District case, Grady Lewis also researched Choctaw Nation legal and treaty history. Mr. Lewis's expertise on Choctaw political and legal history profoundly shaped the scope and ideology of Debo's dissertation. Ironically, Grady Lewis's research at the BIA signaled the rebirth of the very republic Debo would proclaim dead.[84]

As tribal attorney, Grady Lewis helped organize one of the most important events in the revival of Oklahoma Indian sovereignty—the 1930 intertribal sovereignty and claims conference. Initially promoted by the Indian Memorial Association (IMA) as part of a bid to save the old Choctaw Tribal Council House and timed to coincide with the one hundredth anniversary of the 1830 Choctaw removal treaty, The Treaty of Dancing Rabbit Creek, the event slowly transformed into an affirmation of Five Tribes sovereignty. Convoked October 22–23, 1930, at Southeastern State Teacher's College in Durant, Oklahoma, the event drew Choctaw and Chickasaw participants from across the old republics, as well as Plains Indians from the Choctaw-Chickasaw Leased District, and tribal members from the old Muscogee (Creek), Seminole, and Cherokee nations.[85]

Conference goals were twofold, the first proposed a joint effort by the IMA and Southeastern State Teacher's College (SSTC) to relocate the Choctaw Tribal Council House to the SSTC campus. At its new SSTC home the refurbished building would serve as "the Indian memorial to all Red men of Oklahoma." The second part of the conference was devoted to long-standing tribal claims against the United States. Though slated as a terminating event for Indian independence, the conference stoked interest in Oklahoma Indian history and revisited the federal government's perfidy in flagrantly violating its treaties and promises with Oklahoma Indians. Perhaps of greatest historical significance, the convocation galvanized a new generation of emerging Oklahoma Indian nationalists. The conference tone was set by a celebrity guest who did not actually attend. In a widely circulated rebuff to Choctaw chief Benjamin Dwight's invitation, Cherokee humorist Will Rogers complained, "We don't need a memorial. . . . We ain't dead yet but just getting started. . . . We could get the whole country back right now if we would just assume a second mortgage."[86]

The opening addresses were delivered by Eugene Briggs of SSTC and Anna Lewis of the Oklahoma College for Women at Chickasha. Briggs spoke on the pending Council House project and proposed concurrent work on a comprehensive history of the Five Tribes. Lewis spoke on the historical and contemporary role of women in Indian tribal life. The featured address was presented in Choctaw by Joseph Oklahombi, a World War I code talker. Concluding the morning session, Edward Gardner of Muskogee, Oklahoma, spoke on Pushmataha, father of the Choctaw republic.[87]

In the evening session, Dwight, as conference leader, initiated a discussion of "wants regarding a settlement of . . . affairs with the government." Dwight's action built on a previous statewide conference with Choctaws,

Chickasaws, and other Oklahoma Indian tribes regarding the status of their claims against the United States. After prolonged discussion, the evening session produced a list of grievances and new intertribal alliances. Participants agreed to coordinate legal advice, litigation, and claims settlement. Chief Dwight also revealed plans to seek tribal economic relief, in conjunction with the Chickasaws, through Interior department and BIA loans. In all Dwight intended to borrow 5.5 million dollars. Dwight's proposal virtually guaranteed Choctaw continuity by binding the tribe and its leadership to loan payments and litigation extending several decades.[88]

Conference agreement on widespread Indian poverty and abuse under BIA management further reinforced the desire for a collective effort to secure immediate economic relief. Intertribal discussions concerning legal costs, tribal consensus, and collective liability for loan and claims proposals demonstrated that Oklahoma Indian interests were no longer compatible with the old assimilation and termination goals. Even for nominal advocates of assimilation like Dwight, it became clear that tribal welfare could not be separated from some form of tribal sovereignty. The 1930 Five Tribes conference turned the corner on the old termination politics that had linked claims settlement and federal aid with crippling BIA oversight and the push toward tribal termination. In this emerging era of Oklahoma intertribal cooperation—partly driven by economic desperation—claims settlement, sovereignty, and federal support were deemed inseparable and inalienable Indian rights.[89]

After the conclusion of the Five Tribes conference, Grady Lewis was charged with pressing a final settlement of the old Choctaw Leased District claim. For a tribe hit hard by the Great Depression, a Leased District monetary settlement promised quick relief. To prepare for litigation Grady Lewis spent much of 1930 to 1933 in the BIA archives researching Choctaw legal and treaty rights, as well as the historical and political function of the Choctaw republic. In this capacity Grady Lewis became a leading authority on Choctaw documentation and an expert guide to the BIA archives. Grady Lewis would also be the first antiassimilationist Choctaw scholar to master this material.[90]

FROM ARCHIVE TO DISSERTATION

Although Debo did not acknowledge Grady Lewis in her dissertation or later publications, she did note his influence in a 1932 letter to Dale. Because of Debo's omission, Grady Lewis's role in the revival of Choctaw sovereignty remains unknown and little information on his life or work exists in print.

An obscure 1935 newspaper interview reveals the depth of his antiassimilationist sentiments and dangerous political leanings for the time.[91]

In a *Washington Post* article titled, "Communal Life Declared Best for Indian, Choctaw Lawyer Here to Back Thomas-Rodgers Bill," Grady Lewis stated that Indian "temperament makes it impossible for him to adapt himself to the capitalistic system and it is high time the United States government recognize this racial peculiarity." Lewis continued, "Until the twentieth century the five civilized tribes ... were happy and prosperous in the communistic republic[s] they maintained on land given them by the government." Considering Grady Lewis's "communistic" sympathies, it is reasonable to assume that even the outspoken Miss Debo approached his help with caution. Debo likely thought it wise to hide his connection to her work.[92]

Debo's time with Grady Lewis deeply influenced her own views about Indian sovereignty and the historical legitimacy of the Choctaw republic. Reflecting Grady Lewis's own research, Debo's dissertation would unwittingly place her in the midst of the century-long Choctaw assimilation-sovereignty dispute. Muriel Wright and Anna Lewis would find themselves representative voices of each faction, Wright offering the pro-assimilation and Lewis the antiassimilation critique of Debo's scholarship. Presented as an objective history of the Choctaw republic, Debo's work came to play a central role in validating the emerging renaissance of Oklahoma Indian sovereignty.[93]

In addition to her work with Grady Lewis, other research took Debo to the office of the superintendent of the Five Civilized Tribes in Muskogee, Oklahoma, where she met amateur historians Grant and Caroline Foreman. As a former Dawes Commission fieldworker and local antiquarian, Grant provided Debo with valuable insight into the political and economic machinations of assimilation and allotment. Though Debo would later question Grant's treatment of Indian Civil War history, the two remained on amicable terms. Early in 1932, with research in hand, Debo began writing her dissertation.[94]

Later that year Debo submitted her first two chapters to Dale. His response initiated the public face of their now notorious scholarly tussle. Dale claimed to have read her chapters with "a great deal of care," however his critique clearly revealed he hardly bothered to look at her work. Ironically, for a "raconteur, who recycled his previous experiences into his endeavors as a historian," Dale complained that the first chapter was too long, relied too heavily on secondary sources, and made use of too many "life sketches" and Indian voices (ethnology). Debo found Dale's response disingenuous. Firing back, Debo noted that of the first chapter's one hundred and twenty-eight citations, only six were from secondary sources. She further contended that inclusion of material on "those who figured very prominently in the diplomatic or political life of the tribe" was necessary for clarity, but she agreed to remove much of the introductory ethnological material. Dale did not take kindly to Debo's tone, noting that in the future she should expect his reviews to be brief and uncontested. According to Richard Lowitt, "[Dale] rarely if ever willingly stated or defended in a public setting the courage of his convictions," but by refusing to address Debo's legitimate concerns Dale had "literally . . . abrogated part of his role as a graduate student mentor."[95]

In spite of Debo's well-developed thought on popular sovereignty, "History of the Choctaw Nation from the End of the Civil War to the Close of the Tribal Period," carefully navigated assimilationist sentiment and Indian independence. Contending that Choctaws had developed a hybrid civilization that was eventually dismantled by European American land lust, Debo noted, "The merging of tribal history into the composite life of the state of Oklahoma may be said to have ended the separate history of this gifted people."[96]

Having moved beyond the political history of long-dead Indians, Debo found it impossible to address the national history of a living people without mentioning their culture. Accordingly, Debo's first draft contained detailed ethnographic information. In response to Dale's antiquated Turnerian contempt for ethnological scholarship, Debo shortened the first chapter to a few sentences explaining Choctaw and Chickasaw stories of tribal origins from the brothers Chahtah and Chikasah. Confident in her own objectivity and scrupulous in her research, Debo corrected this deletion a few months later.[97]

In May 1933, Debo successfully defended her dissertation and became Dr. Angie Debo. Unfortunately as an instructor on leave, her position at West Texas State Teacher's College was precarious. Following a round of budget cuts, Debo's position was terminated. Upon appeal, Debo was reassigned to an affiliated facility—the Panhandle-Plains Museum. Simultaneous with her dismissal from WTSTC, Debo received word that the University of Oklahoma Press would publish her dissertation as part of its Civilization of the American Indian series.[98]

Although Debo and Dale had a tense professional relationship, Dale favorably reviewed her dissertation for publication—it was in his own professional interest. Afterwards, in preparing the draft manuscript, Debo restored the deleted ethnological material and expanded it to encompass three additional chapters. Debo again came into conflict with Dale. Reviewing the manuscript Dale suggested, as he had before, that Debo use more primary source material. At first Debo refused given her dire financial situation, but she finally agreed to conduct additional research in the University of Oklahoma Phillips Collection.[99]

In the end Debo persevered, keeping her ethnological chapters. Whether knowingly or unknowingly, Debo's book also struck a stinging blow against Dale—her acknowledgments failed to mention him. Within the context of Debo's struggle to find employment and Dale's disinterest in her predicament, her oversight is revealing. When brought to her attention by the university press, Debo quickly wrote Dale, "I seem to have a positive genius for doing things wrong." For his part Dale responded with a cold absolution, "I think you are troubling yourself quite unnecessarily with respect to the acknowledgments which you did not make in your preface." For Debo the waters were about to become even more muddied.[100]

THE "DODO" BOOK

In the summer of 1934 Debo's revised dissertation was published as *The Rise and Fall of the Choctaw Republic*. Reviews were good and mirrored R. N. Richardson's assessment that Debo had successfully turned the corner on the old ethnological taboo in American Indian history. Richardson noted, "There is . . . a pronounced tendency for students of American history to regard the Indian as something . . . whose subjugation or destruction opened the way for a superior people." Instead Richardson affirmed, there are "those who contend that [American Indians] ha[ve] profoundly affected American civilization and made some substantial contributions to it." Richardson identified Debo's book as exemplary of "this point of view."[101]

Yet all was not exactly well for Debo. Relieved of her position at WTSTC and now serving as curator of the isolated Panhandle-Plains Museum, she hoped her publication would launch a new phase in her career. Little did she realize that trouble was brewing among Choctaw assimilationists in Oklahoma. The first hint came in a 1934 book review by her old graduate school colleague and chair of the Oklahoma College for Women's history department, Anna Lewis. Given Lewis's own humiliation at the hands of Lansing Bartlett Bloom, coupled with knowledge of her brother's role in Debo's scholarship, it seems that Lewis tried to diffuse assimilationist discontent with diplomatic criticism.[102]

Lewis noted, "Miss Debo has written her history from documents and other printed sources. . . . Had she known more about Choctaws her volume would have been a more comprehensive history of the Choctaw people." Notably, Lewis's concern was with the quantity of ethnological sources, not Debo's conclusions. Reflecting her own sense of isolation from Choctaw culture at the hands of a cold and culturally insensitive European American stepmother, Lewis concurred with Debo's overall analysis noting, "Miss Debo's observations show a sympathy and a realization of the vital problems of the Choctaw." In a cruel twist of fate, Lewis's critique in the *Mississippi Valley Historical Review* was preceded by Lansing Bartlett Bloom's cloying review of Louisa Frances Gillmore's *Traders to the Navajos*.[103]

Positive reviews aside in 1935 Muriel Wright published an analysis of *The Rise and Fall of the Choctaw Republic* that would haunt Debo for the rest of her life. A dedicated Choctaw assimilationist, Wright jealously guarded her heritage, particularity the larger than life legacies of her father and grandfather. Debo's book asserted that Chief Allen Wright, Muriel Wright's grandfather had accepted a "kickback" for his part in the 1866 "Reconstruction" treaty. Wright was outraged. Family lore held that rumors of her grandfather's misdeed were politically motivated. For Wright, Debo's assertion was a manifold slight—not only was it deemed personally unforgivable it was also counted as an example of Debo's flawed understanding of Choctaw culture.

Wright's 1935 review of Debo's book in the *Chronicles of Oklahoma* was singularly the most historically flawed and unprofessional critique of her career. Obscuring the political turmoil surrounding the minority election of her grandfather as Choctaw chief, Wright also misrepresented her father's role in the Atoka Agreement and Supplemental Agreement, particularly his hell-bent determination to drag the Choctaw republic down the termination path.

Refuting the accuracy of both Debo and her empathetic reviewer Anna Lewis, Wright proclaimed, *The Rise and Fall of the Choctaw Republic* "contains much that is interesting and informative, [but] has errors in statement, half-truths, and refutations that destroy its value as authentic history of the Choctaws." Significantly, Wright argued, "The title of the book is a misnomer itself. . . . The Choctaw republic rose but *it did not fall*." Wright insisted, "From its inception over a century ago, it was planned as a training ground for the Choctaw people, in preparation for the time when they of their own volition would become citizens of their protector republic, the United States." Arguing that the Choctaw Nation achieved this goal when it was incorporated into the state of Oklahoma in 1907, Wright asserted, "Thus, the Choctaw nation as a republic did not fall, it attained its objective."[104]

It is hard to tell what astonished Debo more, Wright's brash disregard for the history of Choctaw nationalism or the fact that she seemed to passionately believe her own self-serving narrative. Moreover, Wright's critique advanced an outlook that was far more disturbing, the idea that as a European American Debo was an "essential" outsider who could not fathom real Choctaw history. Debo had to go no farther than the well-respected Choctaw historian Anna Lewis to find an "essential" Indian who did not agree with Wright.[105]

Equally damning was Wright's behind the scenes effort to besmirch Debo's reputation among Choctaw assimilationists and Wright's political allies. Evidenced in two separate, previously unpublished letters written on April 22, 1936—one to Wright's aunt and another to an unidentified relative "Svnnih" (Sonny)—Wright voiced a blistering indictment of Debo intended for malicious repetition. In her note to Svnnih, Wright asked, "Did aunt Anna or anyone else write you about Debo's flourishes in the press?" Wright pressed on, informing Svnnih, "She was awarded a prize for her "Rise and Fall of the Choctaw Republic" at Chattanooga last December.... But the award does not make her book an authentic history.... She is 'a climber' for position." Wright added, "I wonder if it will sustain her to the end of a *successful* career ... I doubt it." Wright concluded, "Aunt Anna calls her volume the *'Dodo Book'* ... I think that very amusing and quite appropriate."[106]

Wright's letter to Aunt Anna posted the same day also revealed a bitter jealousy, not only of Debo as an historian, but as a successful writer. As a college dropout who aspired to a career in academic history, Wright found Debo's success as a European American historian of the Choctaws unacceptable. Wright's missive noted, "You spoke of the Debo biography appearing in the Sunday paper not long since.... Of course she has her backers but that does not make her book correct." Wright noted, "I cannot be worried about her achievement.... Let her go, I say." Emphasizing the point Wright concluded, "No, I do not intend to let the flashes of other writers trouble me ... I valued your comment along those lines."[107]

Debo's reaction to Wright's family gossip campaign is not known, if indeed she knew about it. Wright's review was read by Debo, who claimed to have put it aside and out of mind, but Debo was not honest in this assertion. Over the next few months Debo completed work on a book that defended her Choctaw scholarship by extending its thesis to all of the Five Tribes. That publication, *And Still the Waters Run: The Betrayal of the Five Civilized Tribes* proved a devastatingly sharp, clear refutation of Wright's critique. Using both European American and American Indian primary sources, Debo struck at both ends of Wright's argument. Where Wright claimed the Choctaw republic had been fabricated as a tutelage state, Debo proved that it, along with the four other Indian nations, was legally established as a sovereign republic in perpetuity. While Wright argued that three generations of select European Americans and elite Indians selflessly worked to acculturate American Indians, Debo irrefutably proved that many used the ruse of philanthropic assimilation to defraud and cheat Indian citizens out of land, possessions, money, cultural autonomy, tribal identity, and independence. For Debo the matter was personal, and while she claimed to have embarked on a publication career for financial support, her motives were actually far more complex.[108]

ANGIE DEBO AND THE NEW ETHNO-POLITICAL CONSCIOUSNESS

Wright's negative review aside, in 1935 the American Historical Association awarded Debo's book the John H. Dunning Prize. Hailed as, "The most important contribution to American historical studies in 1934," *The Rise and Fall of the Choctaw Republic* was officially added to the cannon of professional American history. Most important for the struggling author, the Dunning award served as a springboard for her anticipated scholarship.[109]

While Dale occasionally mentioned a history of the Five Tribes since removal during his doctoral seminars, the subject proved too controversial for his own scholarship. Restrained in part by his aversion for conflict and concern for his own faculty position, Dale avoided the potentially contentious issue of Five Tribes post-removal history but it remained his pet pipe dream. In 1935 Dale's anticipated subject was taken up by Debo.[110]

Using part of the Dunning award cash prize of two hundred dollars and a grant from the Social Science Research Council, Debo began preliminary investigation for a book on the termination of Five Tribes sovereignty. Building on her dissertation sources, Debo expanded her research to archives in Oklahoma City and Muskogee, Oklahoma, and Washington, D.C. During the course of her investigation, Debo paid special attention to Wright's contention that the Choctaw republic—and the other four Indian nations—were devised as tutelage states. Debo believed this interpretation was patently false and found evidence that several Indian elites abused positions of trust for their own enrichment. Among the long list of crimes committed against Five Tribes citizens, Debo uncovered the names of Oklahoma perpetrators who sullied Dale's notion of civilized frontier progress. One bright spot for Debo was the work of Oklahoma's first commissioner of Charities and Corrections, Kate Barnard. Late in her career Barnard launched an effort to prevent well-placed European American and elite Indian grafters from defrauding American Indian minors and orphans out of their allotments. In large part, as a result of her attempted exposé, Barnard was driven from office and soon fell into obscurity. Within a few years the former commissioner of Charities died alone and penniless in an Oklahoma City flophouse. Barnard's fate gave Debo pause. Rather than surrendering to fear, Debo proceeded to make Kate Barnard's heroic stand a feature of her developing manuscript.[111]

Debo's draft was submitted to Joseph Brandt at the University of Oklahoma Press in fall 1936. Wright's caustic 1935 review of her first book made a lasting impression on Debo and directly shaped "As Long As the Waters Run: The Betrayal of the Five Civilized Tribes," her original manuscript title. Replying directly to Wright's criticism Debo's introduction stated, "The policy of the United States in liquidating the institutions of the Five Tribes was a gigantic blunder that... destroyed a unique civilization, and degraded thousands of individuals."[112]

Initially Brandt praised Debo's manuscript, noting a positive review from reader D' Arcy McNickle, administrative assistant to John Collier at the Bureau of Indian Affairs. As a BIA employee McNickle felt Debo's book would buoy efforts to extend coverage of the 1935 Indian Reorganization Act to the Cherokees, Choctaws, Muscogees (Creeks), Chickasaws, Seminoles, and other tribes. However, to avoid political backlash, McNickle suggested that much of the Indian testimony and the names of the accused be removed. Brandt concurred. Debo was incensed. While she agreed to some minor editing, Debo specifically refused to remove the names of American Indian and European American conspirators. Those names would vindicate Debo against Wright's damning 1935 charges. Debo intended to strike Wright and her cadre with the very words and actions of those for whom Wright claimed to speak.[113]

Debo's ongoing dispute with the University of Oklahoma Press led to a special review by former history professor and assistant to the president of the University of Oklahoma, Morris Wardell. It is unfortunate that Debo never learned of Wardell's role, because he raised unsavory questions about her character. Secret charges are difficult to address. Like McNickle, Wardell also raised the issue of libel. Fearing the book would offend university friends and anti-intellectual penny-pinchers at the state capitol, higher powers eventually forced Brandt to back out of Debo's publication contract. Equally frustrated with the turn of events, Debo concurred.[114]

Within two years Brandt found his own position at the University of Oklahoma Press untenable. Brandt believed that honest peer review and academic excellence were being subverted by an overbearing and politicized administration. In July 1938 Brandt left Oklahoma to become director of Princeton University Press. From his new position, Brandt wrote Debo asking for another chance to review her manuscript. Following a slight change to avoid duplication of a recent publication title, *And Still the Waters Run* was sent to Brandt. Again reviewers raised libel concerns. Strapped for cash, Debo acquiesced on many points, but insisted on retaining key names. This time Brandt championed Debo's position and garnered administration support. The book was published in the fall of 1940, bringing Debo's "long night" to a close.[115]

In spite of her difficulties, Debo did not seem to fully appreciate the inflammatory nature of her new ethno-political scholarship. A year after publishing *And Still the Waters Run*, Debo contemplated a far more incendiary treatise on the perils of American imperialism. In an unpublished draft titled, "Indian Policy as a Problem in Colonial Administration," Debo used strikingly modern terminology to describe her evolving views on Indian assimilation. Regarding American imperialism she noted, "Our real colonial policy is found in our dealings with the Indians, and that it touches on every aspect of our national lives." In ascribing a motive, Debo found "the age-old economic object, the determination of a strong race to exploit the property of a weaker one." Sadly, Debo also discovered a disturbing end, "the liquidation of . . . subject nationalities, leaving a racial minority to be assimilated by the dominant group."[116]

Anticipating research support from Collier, Debo forwarded a copy and prepared a corollary piece titled, "Communism in the Indian Service." At the time Collier was under attack by Red-baiting political opponents, who believed his Indian Reorganization Act was communistic. Debo thought a passionate defense of the Indian Service might curry Collier's favor. Whatever Collier's initial thoughts, his response dated December 8, 1941—just a day after the attack on Pearl Harbor—reflected the new realities of a nation at war. A survivor of World War I Red hysteria, Collier had no desire to make waves. While foreseeing a book-length treatment, Collier strongly suggested a broad politically neutral ethnological study, rather than "the narrow thesis of imperialism." Scolding Debo, Collier added, "The treatment of our own Government should be set in the context of national development, with more than a bow to the inevitableness of much that happened." Debo's response, if sent, was not recorded. Apparently taking Collier's harsh criticism to heart, Debo did not pursue her imperialism book. Notably, she also filed away her defense of Collier and the BIA.[117]

Where Collier found Debo's work too provocative, another old scholar who admired the Oklahoma historian from afar found her work fulfilling. More importantly, this champion embraced Debo's new interpretation of American internal imperialism. Mirroring the argument in Debo's unpublished "Indian Policy as a Problem in Colonial Administration," Annie Heloise Abel's 1941 review of *And Still the Waters Run* concluded, "The author proceeds to investigate the most colossal of all the subterfuges that have been used . . . to attain their own selfish and sinister ends under guise of bestowing inestimable benefits upon a weaker people hopelessly at their mercy."[118]

Unaware of Collier's response to Debo, Abel added, "The brightest spot of all finds a place in the concluding chapters which concern themselves with the Indian policy of more recent days and notably with the John Collier reforms." Courageously, for a woman historian who so carefully dodged the ethno-political taboo, Abel added, "It is to be hoped that this story of the stupendous wrong done to the Five Civilized Tribes will commend itself to a larger reading public than is usual with books of similar sort."[119]

BREAKING THROUGH

As a scholar Debo dared to reexamine United States assimilation policy and conjoin it with a biting critique of American imperialism. Before the horrors of Nazi concentration camps and Stalin's gulag were widely publicized—helping make contemporary critiques of American imperialism publicly tolerable—Debo dared to address the exploitation and brutality of United States Indian assimilation policy. To the horror of European Americans, Debo conclusively demonstrated that westward expansion proceeded with a savage, often deadly attempt to colonize American Indians. Although Debo's new construction of American Indian history in part vented her frustration with institutional tyranny, her scholarship achieved the rare status of transcending the historian's own narrow interests and time. In large measure this is why *And Still the Waters Run* remains a key text in American Indian history.

Notably, the sexual division of labor so hated by Debo accounted in large part for her public fame and scholarly renown. Had Debo held a comprehensive university position it is likely that *And Still the Waters Run*—in its incendiary and most valuable form—would not have been published. While Debo felt it lacked the prestige of tenured academic employment, her work as a public historian and freelance author was in large part responsible for her brutally honest scholarship.

After 1941 women historians began to make steady gains in the academy. This new development in turn eroded the unique niche of women American Indian historians that had been nurtured by the profession's sexual division of labor and enduring sexism since the late 1890s. This dispersion also meant the end of European American women's control over a scholarship that defined American Indian history as pan-Indian history for a little over a century. Angie Debo would continue to publish Indian history after *And Still the Waters Run*, as would other professional European American women historians, however, 1941 signaled the culminating phase in European American women's long hegemony over the specialized field of American Indian history.

Conclusion

Women Historians, American Indian History, and Gender Politics

The intellectual and scholarly tensions that linked Angie Debo, Anna Lewis, and Muriel Wright signaled a culminating phase in European American women's hegemony over American Indian history. Lasting for a little over a century, this historical trajectory first emerged with Transcendentalist and evangelical European American women, who took up the cause of American Indian assimilation as a marginal social and political interest. For these women, American Indians were to be pitied, as the occasional object of evangelical affection and social activism.

The antebellum slavery debate would turn women's nascent assimilation concerns away from the Five Tribes and their perceived tolerance for slavery toward western and Plains Indians. However, most of these women considered American Indians a weak, lazy, ignorant, and impotent people destined for extinction—hardly social or political equals. In contrast, African American slaves became powerful metaphors for the unequal status of women in American society. Through abolition activities women were able to publicly advance their own political goals at a time when women's rights agitation was less welcome in the public sphere than abolitionism. As they demanded immediate emancipation and full civil rights for slaves, they artfully advanced their own rights. The success of the slave metaphor would marginalize women's scholarly interest in American Indians until after the Civil War.

With the decline of the postbellum radical civil rights movement, the lateral diffusion of the Washington women's rights movement, and the rise of American Darwinism, American Indians became powerful political subjects for European American maternal patriots. Everyday women's rights proponents and women on the margins of that movement were able to increase their own stature in American society by taking up the cause of Indian assimilation. While some women advocates of Indian assimilation once worked for the abolition cause, most like Amelia Quinton, Mary Bonney, Helen Hunt Jackson, and Alice Fletcher were novices at racial politics.

For women who were of marginal importance to the women's rights movement (if at all), unlocking the evolutionary secrets of American Indians promised social and political influence at a time when they were barred from the voting booth, many vocations, and political office. While much of this work showed an ethno-political bent, a small portion of it also attempted to address some of the historical facts surrounding American Indian treaties and federal Indian policy. Two women scholars—Helen Hunt Jackson and Alice Fletcher—would build on this tradition to craft the first comprehensive, document-driven pan-Indian histories. Notably, Jackson and Fletcher's skillful mastery of archives and deft application of primary source documents complicates, if not actually contradicts, existing scholarship on the gender of history.

With the new Indian scholarship also came real power. Jackson and Fletcher would use their two published Indian histories to exercise a considerable degree of influence over the lives and property of American Indians. Based largely on her fame as the author of *A Century of Dishonor*, Jackson was named a special Indian agent for the Interior department and empowered to investigate conditions among southern California Indians. While Fletcher's *Indian Education and Civilization* report would become an important source of information for the federal allotment effort.

Discovery of secrets included political prescriptions and that medicine ultimately proved irritating at best and deadly at worst. As European American women's ethno-political understanding of Indians came into question, interest in their scholarship faded. Women scholar's work in American Indian history once bestowed a degree of political and personal power, but ultimately their efforts proved intellectually fleeting and destructive to American Indian peoples and cultures.

The preprofessional generation of women scholars was able to fashion a body of Indian work that drew on anthropology, ethnology, and history, but as the fields of anthropology and history were professionalized, women's preprofessional Indian scholarship became increasingly marginalized. Frederick Jackson Turner's cadre of Frontier historians and other members of the profession shunned the ethnological and American Darwinist sentiments that undergirded American Indian studies penned by preprofessional women scholars. The history profession's distaste for ethnology and American Darwinism was further buttressed by the discovery of genetics in 1900 and the rise of the American eugenics movement. Displaced by academic professionals and new scientific discoveries, preprofessional women's American Indian scholarship largely passed into the twilight. Deemed peripheral to American history, American Indians would play only a tangential role in emerging frontier scholarship. Consequently, male historians were not interested in pursuing specialized American Indian history.

The division of anthropology and history into distinct professions during the latter half of the twentieth century also saw a marked increase in women historians. Reflecting attitudes prevalent in contemporary society, few faculty positions at comprehensive universities were awarded to women historians. Practicality and prejudice combined to direct many women historians toward employment in museums, archives, historical societies, women's colleges, and high schools. By the early 1900s a handful of women historians would take up Indian history in a bid to generate professional visibility and scholarly acknowledgement. Publications on American Indians offered these women a way to acquire professional recognition and scholarly status, while rebelling against the academic presumptions and gender prejudices of the history profession. As the national Indian assimilation movement withered, Indian history would be used to further the professional and institutional aspirations of women scholars. Women historian's efforts to navigate professional and institutional politics replaced preprofessional women's quest for national prestige and political influence through scholarship on American Indians.

Although encouraged by Frederick Jackson Turner and Reuben Gold Thwaites, professional women historians' venture into Indian history proved tricky. Ethno-political scholarship was discredited in the academy and anthropology and ethnology were essentially taboo in the history profession. Women historians avoided these scholarly sanctions by confining their work to document-driven nonpartisan histories of Indian politics, treaties, and United States statutes relating to Indian affairs. Two of Turner's students, Emma Helen Blair and Louise Phelps Kellogg, would publish Indian histories based on translated archival documents. In the years after Blair's death in 1911, Kellogg would give American Indian history a conspicuous presence through her impressive cache of acclaimed publications. Annie Heloise Abel, the only early professional Indian historian to have held a faculty position at a coeducational institution, pushed this scholarship deep into the American West and to the doorstep of contemporary American Indian history. Although the historical profession became more tolerant of ethnological and anthropological sources, professional politics kept Abel from piercing the old taboo and addressing postbellum Indian history.

Breaching the old cultural and academic barriers that limited Indigenous women's access to public and government documents, prevented them from publishing recognized Indian scholarship, and also discouraged them from entering the academy, Rachel Caroline Eaton became the first Indian woman to earn an American history doctorate and the first Indigenous woman historian to publish a document-driven American Indian history. While a laudable achievement, Eaton's work did not reach beyond the intratribal focus of previous Indigenous women's publications or move Indian history beyond the Civil War era. Intertribal Indian history would be taken up at the University of Oklahoma by Anna Lewis.

In a bid to secure her career and gain greater academic visibility, Lewis conducted research on Arkansas River valley Indian tribes and their interactions with the French and Spanish empires. Lewis's findings were published in her seminal intertribal Indian history, *Along the Arkansas*. Lewis's book proved innovative not only for its middle-ground-like approach, but also for its ethnological and anthropological sensitivities. Ravaged by a small-minded book review, Lewis turned from intertribal Indian history to focus on intratribal and Oklahoma history for the remainder of her career. Ethnological and anthropological sources would be united with document-driven Indian history by Anna Lewis's contemporary at the University of Oklahoma Angie Debo.

Fighting for her own professional credibility and rebelling against institutional gender bias, Angie Debo authored a study of the Choctaw republic. Debo's effort embraced anthropology and ethnology and raised the ire of two Oklahoma Choctaw scholars, Anna Lewis, a professional historian, and Muriel Wright, a public historian. Both women felt Debo had misrepresented Choctaw culture. Wright further argued that the Choctaw republic was founded as a tutelage state. Debo ultimately responded to this criticism with *And Still the Waters Run*, contending that all five of the Indian republics were established to exist in perpetuity. Moreover, Debo argued that the failure of the Five Nations was not planned, rather they were eviscerated by an unconscionable orgy of unfettered criminal outrages perpetrated by European Americans and American Indian elites. By engaging modern Indian history, Debo inadvertently engaged modern Indigenous historians.

Conflict with Lewis and Wright made Debo a better historian—it sharpened and expanded her scholarship. However, it also brought into question European American women's hegemony over Indian history. Debo's experience with Lewis and Wright demonstrated that European American women historians could no longer dominate the scholarship of American Indians for their own personal and political agendas. Too many diverse voices were emerging in the history profession and, as with Anna Lewis and Muriel Wright, American Indians were now examining the history of Indian scholarship and asking uncomfortable questions about the legacy of assimilation.

Though epic in its influence, *And Still the Waters Run* proved a culminating publication. With the social turn, new ideas about who could write minority history began to emerge and women's new political agendas would be cast in increasingly predictable molds. In 1972, ninety-one years after Helen Hunt Jackson's *A Century of Dishonor* set in motion the trajectory that would solidify into women historians' first specialized field, American Indian history, Gerda Lerner initiated the modern discipline of women's history. Where Blair, Kellogg, Abel, and Debo deployed American Indian history in part to advance their personal and professional aspirations, a new generation of women historians would take up the scholarship of gender and women's history in part to advance their own personal, social, political, and institutional rights.

Over time women historians would be confronted with the increasingly insistent professional presumption that their work must illuminate some aspect of socially constructed gender, sexuality, and the historical patterns of women's lives. When women wished to work outside these analytical modes their scholarship would find its most receptive audience when beamed through the lens of gender studies and women's history. As women historians took up this new field, American Indian history largely slipped off their radar. European American women in particular shunned Indian history in favor of gender studies and women's history.

During this period of scholarly transition from 1945 to 1980, a handful of Indigenous women scholars began work that linked Indian history with a heightened anthropological and ethnological sensitivity to American Indian peoples and cultures. But just as Ella Cara Deloria, Beatrice Medicine, Ruth Muskrat Bronson, and other Indigenous women historians were venturing into a culturally rich "thick" Indian scholarship, they were challenged. What seemed a fringe interest for male historians since the development of the profession, became a quite attractive subject for Americanists marginalized within the exponentially expanding cohort of new doctors of history and an uncertain academic job market.

Highlighted by the Frontier Thesis's diminished post-WWII status and a concurrent rise in nonelite scholarly interests sparked by the social turn, minority history increasingly came to foreground male historical interests. For a new generation of predominantly European American male historians, a reformulated form of ethno-political Indian history became the conduit to professional distinction. Once again American Indian history created a professional niche for European American historians.

Representatives of this approach expanded to include a more diverse body of historians, yet scholars of American Indians continued to struggle with the contentious issues of ossified professional gender roles, the politics of Indian identity and cultural understanding, and professional versus "essentialized" credentials. Moreover, new women Indian historians were often corralled by the profession's penchant for cloaking their scholarship in the tropes of sexuality and gender. Typecasting aside, women historians of American Indians still play a prominent role in the field. American Indian, African American, Asian American, Latino-Latina, LGBTQ, and European American historians now openly contribute to a far more diverse and informative, but equally contested, body of American Indian scholarship.

In the final analysis, what makes the history of women's Indian scholarship so compelling is the social prestige and political influence it bestowed at a time when women were generally barred from the voting booth, the professions, political office, and academia. Even after women gained the right to vote and greater access to professions and the academy, a new generation of marginalized women historians fashioned a constructed Indian history that they used to advance their own professional status. For women who penned American Indian history during its first formative century, it truly was a field of their own.

NOTES

PREFACE

1. Louise Newman, Gloria Jean Watkins (Bell Hooks), and others have noted that gender does not automatically level racial and cultural differences nor spontaneously create political alliances.

2. Wooten, *Women Tell the Story*, pref., intro., 39–42, 145–49. During the course of researching and writing *A Guide to the Indian Tribes of Oklahoma*, Wright began to question her assimilationist beliefs.

INTRODUCTION

1. Debo, *And Still the Waters Run*, ix; Turner, Review of *The Winning of the West*, 71–73.

2. For the ongoing process of Indian cultural and historical "commodification," see Castile, "Commodification," 743–49; Shanley, "Indians America Loves," 675–702; Gidley, *Edward S. Curtis*, passim; Black, "'Mascotting,'" 605–22; Harding, "Cultural Commodification," 137–55.

3. See Clifton, *Prairie People*; Berkhoffer, *White Man's Indian*; Batille and Silet, eds., *Pretend Indians*; Drinnon, *Facing West*; Stedman, *Shadows*; Dippy, *Vanishing American*; Bieder, *Science Encounters*; Deloria, *Playing Indian*; Clifton, ed., *Invented Indian*.

4. Notable among these are Hoxie, *Final Promise* and Adams, *Education for Extinction*. For European American women's use of American Indian imagery, see Landsman, "The 'Other,'" 247–84.

5. Novick, *That Noble Dream*, 25, 30, 44–45. Amateur historian Grant Foreman complicates this distinction. An attorney, Foreman came to Indian Territory in 1899 where he served as a Dawes Commission field-worker until 1903. Foreman's intimate knowledge of the Dawes Commission and its work made him an attractive prospective author for the University of Oklahoma Press's Civilization of the American Indian series, for which he eventually wrote five volumes. Foreman was not a professional historian or academician, but in 1932 the University of Tulsa awarded him an honorary Ph.D. in English literature. See Wiesendanger, *Grant and Carolyn Foreman*, 5–14.

6. Des Jardins, *Women and Historical Enterprise*, 13–51; Novick, *That Noble Dream*, 367.
7. Hounshell, "Edison," 612–17; Kevles, Sturchio, and Carrol, "Sciences in America," 26–32.
8. Mark, "Francis La Flesche," 497–510.
9. Mark, *A Stranger*, 29–42; Stevenson, *Zuni and the Zunians*, 3, 6, 30; Jackson, *Century of Dishonor*; Fletcher, *Indian Civilization*.
10. Militello, "Horatio Nelson Rush," 1–57.
11. Smith, B. G., *Gender of History*, chaps. 1–4; Militello, "Horatio Nelson Rush," 1–57.
12. Stubbs, *Discourse Analysis*, chaps. 8–9; Blommaert, *Discourse*, 39–66; Foucault, *Archeology of Knowledge*, chaps. 3–6; Underhill, *Creating Worldviews*, passim.
13. Mari Sandoz is not included in this study because she does not belong to the historiography or historical trajectory in question since she did not write a document-driven Indian history. Sandoz's most prominent work on Indians, *Crazy Horse: The Strange Man of the Oglalas*, published in 1940, contains fictionalized material, no citations, and no bibliography. Awarded an honorary doctorate in English literature later in life, Sandoz cannot be placed among either the preprofessional women scholars or the professional women historians of American Indians. See Stauffer, *Mari Sandoz*, 1–53; Bristow, "Enduring Mari Sandoz," 1–8; Sandoz, *Crazy Horse*.

CHAPTER 1

1. *Hearing before the Committee on Woman Suffrage of the United States Senate, December 17, 1904*, 10; "For Women's Suffrage," *Salt Lake Tribune* (Utah), 18 December 1904, 2.
2. Stanton, ed., *History of Woman Suffrage*, vol. 5, 435. Thomas and Clara Bewick adopted a young Lakota girl named Zintkala Numi. See Garraty and Carnes, eds. *American National Biography*, 194–96.
3. McMillen, *Seneca Falls*, chaps. 3–6; Stanton, ed., *History of Woman Suffrage*, vol. 5, passim.
4. Lincoln, *Speeches and Writings*, 536. For more on new nation thought and women's rights, see Peabody, "Letter to the Editor," 745–48; Woodhull, *Arguments*, 7; Des Jardins, *Women*, 118–44; Smith, B. G., *Gender of History*, 37–68.
5. Griffith, *In Her Own Right*, 220–22; Buhle, *Concise History*, 277.
6. For women's preprofessional historical credentials, see Des Jardins, *Women*, 13–51; Smith, B. G., *Gender of History*, 37–68, 157–70, 238–40.
7. Jackson was surprised by the generally high praise *A Century of Dishonor* garnered from reviewers. Even the dean of preprofessional male historians, Francis Parkman, called her volume, "An honest and valuable record." See Kate Phillips, *Helen Hunt Jackson*, 235. Academic trivialization of *A Century of Dishonor* stemmed from biting criticism published by Theodore Roosevelt in 1889—four years after Jackson's death. Roosevelt branded her book an "hysterical polemic" that is "dishonest" and of "fictitious value." See Roosevelt, *The Winning of the West*, 334. Herbert Eugene Bolton to Frederick Webb Hodge, 14 January 1907, Records of the Bureau of American Ethnology, Letters received 1907, box 119, National Anthropological Archives, Smithsonian Institution, Washington, D.C. Although Fletcher's voluminous body of scholarship appeared in many of the leading anthropological and ethnological publications of her day, Bolton informed Hodge, "In a few cases I may find it easier to re-write than to modify [her] articles."
8. Mark, *A Stranger*, 19–26; Phillips, K., *Helen Hunt Jackson*, 140–42; "Bancroft's Banquet," *Washington Post*, 11 January 1878, 4.
9. Mead, *How Vote Was Won*, chaps. 1–2; Kodumthara, "Anti-Suffragists," chaps. 1–2.
10. Norgren, *Belva Lockwood*, 94, 204–13; Garraty and Carnes, eds., *American National Biography*, 194–96; Pascoe, *Relations of Rescue*, 112–45; Jacobs, M. D., *White Mother*, chaps., 2–3.

11. Clark, E. "Religion, Rights . . . in Early," 29–57; Hewitt, *No Permanent Wave*, 3; Cole, *Mary Moody Emerson*; Wayne, *Woman Thinking*, chap. 1–3. For scholarship suggesting that political rhetoric about women's new expanded role in American society was shaped by itinerant evangelical women preachers of the Second Great Awakening, see Brekus, "Female Preaching," 20–29; Botting and Houser, "Drawing the Line, 265–78; Brekus, "Harriet Livermore," 389–404; Billington, L., "Female Laborers," 369–94.

12. Boller, *American Transcendentalism*, xix, xxi; "The Unitarian Movement in New England," 409–43; Boller, *American Transcendentalism*, 79–92, 99–138; Dall, *Transcendentalism*, 24.

13. "Transcendentalism," 382–86; Rose, *Transcendentalism*, passim; Gura, *American Transcendentalism*, chap. 3–7; Gohdes, *Periodicals Transcendentalism*,17–37, 143–51, 210–28; Greenstone, "Dorothea Dix," 527–59; Robinson, "Margaret Fuller," 83–98; Wallace, J. D., "Hawthorne," 201–22; Cole, "Stanton, Fuller," 533–59; Rogers and Dykeman, "Introduction," viii–xxxiv; Dall, *Historical Pictures*, 249. Dall was off by a year in her citation according to Fuller, "The Great Lawsuit," 1–47; Dall, *Transcendentalism*, 6; Caroline Wells Healey Dall Papers, correspondence 1834–1917, Caroline Wells Healey Dall Papers, Massachusetts Historical Society.

14. Williams, D. R. "Wilderness Rapture," 1–16; Marshall, "Elizabeth Palmer Peabody," 1–15; Wach, "Boston Vindication," 3–35; Wayne, *Women Thinking*, passim; Mott, *Biographical Dictionary*, 44, 60–63, 79–80, 103–107, 199–201, 219–20; Barton, *Transcendental Wife*, passim. For Paulina Wright Davis, see Weissbourd, "Women's Rights," 7–20; Jones, D. B., "Elizabeth Palmer Peabody," 195–207; Myerson, "Calendar," 197–207; Smith, H. N., "Scribbling Women," 47–70; Robinson, D. M., "New Epoch," 557–77; Capper, "Margaret Fuller," 509–28; Myerson, *New England Transcendentalists*, 121–25, 192–97, 201–203, 206–208.

15. Yellin, *Women*, 1–26; Williams, C., "Female Antislavery Movement," 159–77; Cott, *Bonds of Womanhood*, xix, 9–12, 92–111, 136; Ryan, *Cradle*, 83–98, 108–16, 186–87; Rosenberg, *Beyond Separate Spheres*, chaps. 1–2; English, "Revealing Accounts," 100–10, 110n244.

16. Acts 2:17; Clark, E. B., "Religion, Rights . . . Origins," 1–53; Clark, E. B. "Religion, Rights . . . Early," 29–57; Isenberg, "'Co-equality," passim; Jürisson, "Federalist, Feminist," passim; Hatch, *Democratization*, 3–17, 49–78; Hewitt, "Feminist Friends," 27–49; Brekus, *Strangers*, 123; Weisbrod, "Family, Church," 3; Fiorenza, *In Memory*, 344–45; Isenberg, "'Pillars," 98–128; Birdsall, "Second Great Awakening," 345–64; Cott, "Young Women," 15–29; Mathews, "Second Great Awakening," 23–43; Shiels, "Scope," 223–46; Brekus, *Strangers*, chaps. 3–6; Billington, L., "Female Laborers," 378–79.

17. Towle, *Vicissitudes*, 8–9, intro.

18. Livermore, *Narrative*, 15–16; Chase, "Harriett Livermore," 16–23; "Harriett Livermore," 64; Parker, *More Than Petticoats*, 36–47; "A Large Audience Listened with a Good Deal of Interest," *New-Hampshire Statesman* (Concord), 20 June 1825; "Miss Livermore," *Daily National Intelligence*, 12 January 1827; "From Our Correspondent," *New-York Spectator*, 16 January 1827; "Miss Livermore the Preacher," *Maryland Gazette*, 18 January 1827; "Miss Harriet Livermore Is Expected to Preach Next Sabbath at the Capital," *The Globe* (Washington, D.C.), 26 May 1832; "Miss Livermore, the Distinguished Quakeress Preacher," *Dover Gazette & Strafford Advertiser* (N.H.), 5 July 1836; "Women's Rights," *The Emancipator* (New York), 21 June 1838; "Harriet Livermore," *New-York Spectator*, 24 October 1840.

19. The scope of Second Awakening women preacher's ministries can be approximated from Towle and Livermore's writings. See Towle, *Vicissitudes*, 1–100; Livermore, *A Narrative*, 1–17; Brekus, *Strangers*, 119–126; Billington, L., "Female Laborers," 378–79; Davis, A. H., *Female Preacher*, 12–19, 34; Livermore, *Scriptural Evidence*, passim; Pierce, D., *Scriptural Vindication*, passim; Dow, *Eccentric Preacher*, 182–204.

20. One of the largest organized evangelical sects, the Freewill Baptist General Conference gave women laity full voting privileges on church matters and held that even male deacons were not allowed to baptize or officiate at communion. Regarding evangelical sacraments,

this would seem a moot point given that baptism and communion were largely considered symbolic, whereas leading souls to acceptance of Christ (being "saved") comprised the only recognized medium by which God dispensed grace. See *Minutes of the General Conference of the Freewill Baptist Connection*, 62, 65, 80, 142; Billington, L., "Female Laborers," 380–88;. Barrett, *Memoirs*, 143–45, 188, 285–86. For links between early Evangelical abolitionist churches and women abolitionist and women's rights lecturers, see "Proceedings of the Boston Female Anti-Slavery Society," *The Liberator* (Boston), 28 December 1838, 209.

21. Brekus, *Female Preaching*, 267–306; Billington, L., "Female Laborers," 391–94.

22. Non-evangelical women preachers continued ministries within other Christian movements. Brekus, *Stranger*, 305–46; Collier-Thomas, *Daughters of Thunder*, 41–68; Haywood, *Prophesying Daughters*, 1–13; Hunter, *Women Preachers*, 43–98; Hanaford, *Daughters of America*, 415–76; Billington, L., "Female Laborers," 391–94; Brekus, "Female Preaching," 27–29.

23. Most liberal women did not actively evangelize. However, it would be a mistake to label them as secular in that personal faith and a general sense of religious mission permeated their activities. Wilbanks, ed., *Walking by Faith*, chaps. 7–10; Palmer, ed., *Selected Letters*, passim; Karcher, *First Woman of Republic*, chaps. 8–9. Ellen DuBois privileges suffrage within the women's rights movement, distinguishing between "secular" and "religious" divisions. See DuBois, "Radicalism Woman Suffrage," 63–71. In contrast Elizabeth Clark argues the evidence revealed a more permeable set of women's rights goals. See Clark, "Religion, Rights . . . Early," 29–57.

24. Towle, *Vicissitudes*, 21–25; Clark, "Religion, Rights . . . Early," 29–57.

25. DuBois, "Radicalism Woman Suffrage," 63–71; Bailey, J. B., "Nancy Towle," passim; Solomon, C. J. "From Pulpits," 1–18.

26. Towle, *Vicissitudes*, 18, 85; Billington, L. "Female Laborers," 189; Bailey, "Nancy Towle," chaps. 1–2.

27. Towle, *Vicissitudes*, 286; Sanborn, *Sixty Years of Concord*, 12; Sanborn and Cameron, ed., *Transcendental Eye*, 8, 19–26. In the concluding paragraph of *Vicissitudes*, Towle refers to Mary Wollstonecraft's work, *A Vindication of the Rights of Woman* (London: J. Johnston, 1796). See Bailey, J. B., "Nancy Towle," conclusion.

28. Towle, *Vicissitudes*, 256. A brief survey reveals that *Vicissitudes* has remained in the public domain and of continuing intellectual engagement since 1833. See *Catalogue of the Private Library . . . Albert Gorton Greene*, 489; *Catalogue of Recently Added Books, Library of Congress*, 145; *Catalogue of the Private Library Samuel Gardner Drake*, 515; *Catalogue American History Library Alfred S. Manson*, 215; *Bulletin of Books Added Public Library of Detroit*, 174; *Bulletin New York Public Library*, 223; and "Books Wanted—Shepard Book Co." Towle's encounter with early Mormon faithful in Missouri made *Vicissitudes* a subject of interest for Church of Latter-day Saints writers and historians. See Marquardt, *Rise of Mormonism*, 309–10; Bailey, J. B., "Nancy Towle," introduction.

29. Livermore, *Harp of Israel*, 1–12, 169–80; Boudinot, *Star in the West*, passim; Wolff, *Travels and Adventures*, 512, 518. In 1831 Livermore tied her version of the Jewish-Indian theory to Wolff's millennial eschatology. See Livermore, *Millennial Tidings*, vol. 1, 58–59; Livermore, *Millennial Tidings*, vol. 2, 91–106.

30. Given Ga-la-gi-noh's Eastern lecture tour and sojourns to Washington during the Cherokee removal crisis it is likely that he and Livermore first met sometime in 1830 or 1831. See Dale, "Letters Two Boudinots," 333–34. For the 1834 meeting, see Livermore, *Counsel of God*, 222–23. For the Indian-Jewish theory, see Boudinot, *Star in West*, 23–31, 279–301. By 1823 Ga-la-gi-noh publicly advanced the argument that American Indians were descended from ancient Jews. See "Letter from an Indian," *New-Hampshire Repository*, 31 March 1823, 49. Ga-la-gi-noh was well acquainted with the ideas of Joseph Wolff. See "A Christian Jew," *Cherokee Phoenix*, 10 April 1828; "Latest From Mr.Wolff," *Cherokee Phoenix*, 4 June 1828.

31. Livermore encountered the *Book of Mormon* in 1830, but was not convinced of its validity. Hoxie, E. F., "Harriet Livermore," 44. Livermore utilized a philological list compiled from the works of Boudinot, Adair, and Johnson. See Livermore, *Harp of Israel,* 171–72. For a discussion of the Jewish-Indian theory's nineteenth-century prominence, see Dahl, "Mound-Builders," 187–88n10; Mann, *Native Americans,* 9–20. By the late 1840s the Jewish-Indian theory fell out of archeological and popular favor.

32. Livermore, *Counsel of God,* 170, 176–84, 195, 220–24; Livermore, *Harp of Israel,* 89, 96, 171–72; Livermore, *Millennial Tidings,* vol. 1, 3–7, 59, 71; Livermore, *Millennial Tidings,* vol. 4, 4–7, 91–106.

33. For Joseph Wolff's millennial views, see Wolff, *Narrative*; Wolff, *Travels.* For how Wolff's ideas influenced Livermore's millennial theology, see Livermore, *Millennial Tidings,* vol. 1–4, passim; "Miss Harriet Livermore," 381. For more on the era's millennial craze, see Oren, *Power,* 1–148; Obenzinger, "Holy Land," 241–67; Whalen, "'Christians" 225–59; Elliot, *Daniel Deronda,* chaps. 52–70.

34. "Miss Livermore's Second Letter," 409; Hoxie, E. F., "Harriet Livermore," 44. For the term *wahconda's* [sic] *wakko,* see Livermore, *Counsel of God,* 184. For Livermore's robbery at Fort Leavenworth, see Adams, C. F., ed., *Memoirs John Quincy Adams,* vol. 10, 6–8.

35. Sears, *Days of Delusion,* introduction. Both Pennsylvania and Washington would become hotbeds for Indian benevolence work among liberal and evangelical women by the late 1860s. See "The Original Indian Association," *Christian Union,* 6 October 1887, 346.

36. Davis, R. I., *Gleanings,* 326–27; "Brooklyn, L. I." 436–37; "Harriet Livermore, Diseases," 29–30; "Harriet Livermore," 675–76. As an interdenominational organization attracting the support of both evangelical and nonevangelical abolitionists, the AMA foreshadowed the interdenominational Indian Treaty-Keeping and Protective Association. See Beard, *Crusade,* chaps. 1–2; "The Original Indian Association," 346.

37. Livermore, *Addresses,* 1–268.

38. A complete list of Livermore's publications can be found in Brekus, *Strangers,* 426–27. Contemporary religious and secular literature was rife with the Jewish-Indian association. Livermore's Jewish-Indian assertion was far from eccentric or outside the mainstream of mid-nineteenth century evangelical thought. See Sigourney, *Traits,* 17–18.

39. Bartlett, *Liberty,* 38–52; Kolmerten, *American Life,* 28, 42–43, 60–99, 154–55, 207–53; Karcher, *First Woman,* 123, 216–17; Palmer, ed., *Selected Letters,* 417; Beecher, *Essay* on Slavery, 98–105; Karcher, *First Woman,* 320–55; Croly, *Miscegenation,* 16–65; "Letter from Mr. Tappan," *The Liberator* (Boston), 14 September 1833, 147; "Refuge of Oppression," *The Liberator* (Boston), 20 July 1835, 121.

40. Beecher, *Essay on Slavery,* 102–103.

41. Ceplair, ed. *Public Years,* 338. Portnoy, *Their Right,* chap. 1–3; Deese, ed., *Daughter of Boston,* 93, 106–107, 240–41, 244.

42. John Quincy Adams made a distinction between the radical rights endorsed by liberal women and conservative women's petitioning. Though Adams supported liberal women's antislavery petition work, he did not endorse their larger women's rights agenda. See Isenberg, *Sex and Citizenship,* 64–74; Portnoy, "'Female Petitioners,'" 573–610. Conservative women initially claimed the right to petition based on an older tradition. See Rohrs, "'Public Attention,'" 107–23.

43. Portnoy, *Their Right,* 87–113.

44. "By Authority, James Monroe," *City of Washington Gazette,* 30 December 1817, 2; "Memorial of the Representatives of the Religious Society of Friends," 1–3; An Act Making Provision for the Civilization of the Indian Tribes, 516–17; Andrew, *From Revivals to Removal,* 95–100. For more on the ABCFM, see Phillips, C. J., *Protestant America.*

45. Andrew, *From Revivals to Removal,* 96–97; "Chronology of Major Events," 2.

46. Andrew, *From Revivals to Removal,* 133–99; Hershberger, "Mobilizing Women," 15–40.

47. Since conservative benevolent women avoided public speaking, the women's Anti-removal campaign relied on a network of male speakers and activists. Though liberal women activists relied on male cohorts, they increasingly moved away from male collusion. See Zaeske, *Signatures*, 24–25; Sklar, *Catharine Beecher*, 98–99; Hershberger, "Mobilizing Women," 17n5, 25; Sigourney, *Letters*; Sigourney, *Traits*.

48. Beecher also campaigned through anonymous editorials. See "To the Editor of the Phoenix," *Cherokee Phoenix*, 12 February 1831; Hershberger, "Mobilizing Women," 27; "Circular Addressed to Benevolent Ladies," 65–66.

49. Kerber, "Abolitionist Perception," 271–95; Magliocca, "Cherokee Removal," 879–919; "The Late Jeremiah Evarts, Esq." *Cherokee Phoenix*, 28 May 1831; "We Insert Today Some Accounts of this Great and Good Man," *Cherokee Phoenix*, 2 July 1831; "The Late Mr. Evarts," *Cherokee Phoenix*, 2 July 1831. The Ladies Association for Supplicating Justice and Mercy Toward the Indians (LASJMTI) disappeared from historical view after 1830. The last known public mention of LASJMTI was in "Congressional Senate," *Hudson Western Intelligencer* (Ohio), 12 March 1830, 3. See Portnoy, *Their Right*, 95–96; Hershberger, "Mobilizing Women," 26–28; Andrew, *From Revivals to Removal*, 251–62.

50. For a broader view of the various conservative, moderate, liberal, and radical abolitionist factions, see Mayer, *All on Fire*. For women abolitionists, see Yellin and Van Horne, *Abolitionist Sisterhood*; "Mandate!" *The Liberator* (Boston), December 19, 1835, 203; Sarah M. Grimké, "Equal Rights," *The Liberator* (Boston), February 16, 1838, 28.

51. Yellin and Van Horne, *Abolitionist Sisterhood*, xv–xvii, passim; Brown, I. V., "Am I Not a Woman?" 1–19; Sterling, *Turning the World*, introduction, passim. In Philadelphia the Progressive Friends sect was established in 1854, the American Indian Aid Association was founded in 1859, the evangelical (Episcopal) Indian's Hope Association in 1868, and the interdenominational Indian Treaty-Keeping and Protective Association in 1879.

52. Yellin, *Women*, 3, 5, 21, 25, chaps. 1–4; Karcher, ed., *A Lydia Maria Child Reader*, 71–94.

53. Brantlinger, *Dark Vanishings*, 45–68; Portnoy, *Their Right*, 87–159.

54. Portnoy, *Their Right*, chap. 5; Yellin, *Women*, 29–77; Adams, *Speech of John Quincy Adams*, 1–121; Wheelan, *Mr. Adams Last Crusade*, 97–152; Ceplair, ed., *Public Years*, chaps. 3–5; Karcher, *First Woman*, 151–95; "Rights of Women," *New-Hampshire Statesman and State Journal* (Concord), 28 July 1838; "Political Support of Slavery," 412–15; "Miss Grimke," *The Liberator* (Boston), 9 March 1838; Wheelan, *Mr. Adams*, chaps. 9–12; Mitchell, M., "'I Held,'" 221–29; "The Following Notice of Mr. John Q. Adams' Remarks upon the Petitions for the Abolition of Slavery in the District of Columbia Which Have Poured into Congress," *United States Telegraph* (Washington, D.C.), 18 January 1836, 138; "Abolition in the District of Columbia," *The Globe* (Washington, D.C.), 3 May 1836.

55. Green, C. M., *Secret City*, 46; Wheelan, *Mr. Adams*, 225–44, 247–52.

56. Portnoy, "Female Petitioners," 573–10; Hershberger, "Mobilizing Women," 15–40; Ann Royall, "Anti-Slavery Convention," *Paul Pry*, 31 October 1835, 2; Ann Royall, "Lo! The Poor Indians," *Paul Pry*, 9 September 1836, 2; Ann Royall, "Church and State and the Western States," *The Huntress*, 2 December 1836, 2; Ann Royall, "Speech of Mr. Bynum of North Carolina," *The Huntress*, 11 March 1837, 1; Ann Royall, "*The Globe* and Church and State," *The Huntress*, 6 May 1837, 2; Ann Royall, "The Abolitionists," *The Huntress*, 28 April 1838, 2; Ann Royall, "Abolitionists' Worlds Convention and *Baltimore Sun*," *The Huntress*, 12 September 1840, 2; Ann Royall, "John Quincy Adams," *The Huntress*, 15 October 1842, 1. For Tyler, see Yellin, *Women*, 3. On petitioning, see Wheelan, *Mr. Adams*., 107–30, 145–46, 160, 256; Beecher, *Essay on Slavery*, 102–104.

57. *American Slave Almanac* 1, no. 3, 20–21, 26–27, 29; *American Slave Almanac* 1, no. 4, 7. Although a later publication, the citations show the historical toleration or indifference toward slavery shown by Baptist, Presbyterian, and Methodist churches.

58. "We Give the Constitution of the 'American Missionary Association,'" *Ohio Observer*, 18 November 1846; "American Missionary Association," *The Emancipator*, 7 June 1848;

"American Missionary Association," *Emancipator and Free Soil Press*, 20 September 1848; "American Missionary Association," *The Weekly Herald*, 13 May 1854; "The *New York Post* Says at a Meeting of the American Missionary Association," *The Daily Scioto Gazette* (Chillicothe, Ohio), 12 October 1854; Tappan, *History*, 67–96; Prucha, *Great Father*, 152–79; Waugh, *U. S. Grant*, 134–35; Smith, T., "Grant's Peace Policy," 1–204; Lewit, "Indian Missions," 39–55; "Appeal of the American Missionary Association," *Vermont Chronicle* (Bellows Falls), 13 August 1861; "Since the Abolition of Slavery," *Lowell Citizen News* (Lowell, Mass.), 29 October 1866; "American Missionary Association," *Vermont Chronicle* (Bellows Falls), 30 September 1865; "The American Missionary Association," *Lowell Daily Citizen and News* (Lowell, Mass.), 24 May 1869; "Secretary Strieby," *The Congregationalist*, 20 August 1874, 4.

59. Andrew, *From Revivals to Removal*, 164–78, 206–39, 331; Ray, *Southern Baptist*, 33–36, Tracy, *History American Missions*, 360–64.

60. Tappan, *History*, 1–96; McCoy, *History Baptist Missions*, 397; "Memorial of the Board of Managers," House Document 73, 1–6; Andrew, *From Revivals to Removal*, 123, 150, 154, 156–58, 177–78, 206–208, 212–13, 238–39, 242–45; McLoughlin, *Champions of Cherokees*, 226. A careful reading of the following sources reveals an historic flow of money and support from the Northern/abolitionist Baptists to the AMA. See *American Missionary*, 122–32; *American Annual Cyclopedia*, 67. For the ITKPA, see Quinton, "Original Indian Aid Organization," 346.

61. Beeson, *Plea*, 106–33; Prucha, *Great Father*, 468–69, 499; Prucha, *American Indian Policy*, 34–38; Mardock, *The Reformers*, 9–12, 112–34, 208–10. For AIAA founding, see "Integral Reform Association," *New York Daily Tribune* 30 January 1857, 7; "Meeting in Behalf of the American Indian," *New York Times*, 9 November 1858, 5.

62. Tappan Townsend presented a petition to Congress based on AIAA goals in 1857. Many of the petition's objectives were incorporated into Grant's 1869 Peace Policy. See *Petition to Congress for the Preservation and Elevation of American Indians*. For AIAA influence see "Yearly Meeting of the Progressive Friends," *The Liberator* (Boston), 17 June 1859, 96; "Important Meeting of Friends of the Indian Tribes," *The Liberator* (Boston), 28 December 1860, 208. AIAA idealism also spread through the pages of *Calumet*, official organ of the AIAA. See "Exchange Gleanings," *Mystic Pioneer* (Mystic, Conn.) 17 December 1859, 153. For AIAA Indian reservation oversight, see Beeson, *Plea*, 126–27; "The Red Men," *New York Herald*, 11 November 1874, 3; "Memorial of John Beeson," 8.

63. Foster, "Imperfect Justice, 246–87; "Universal Peace Union," *New York Times*, 11 May 1875; "Pennsylvania Peace Society," 702. Quaker organizations linked liberal women and early Indian assimilationists. See *Pennsylvania Yearly Meeting of Progressive Friends*; *Friend's Intelligencer*, 8–12; "The Indian," 87–89. Lucretia Motts's relationship with the AIAA and John Beeson's temperance activities bridged Indian assimilationists and liberal women. See "Indian Aid Association," *The Liberator* (Boston), 15 April 1859, 60; "Indians and Intoxicating Drinks," *Daily Inter Ocean* (Chicago), 23 September 1879, 3. For John Beeson's interaction with the women's rights movement, see "The Woman Suffrage Society," *New York Times*, 8 March 1878, 2.

64. For objectivity and the history profession, see Novick, *That Noble Dream*, 21–86. Although Francis Parkman, Hubert Howe Bancroft, and Henry Schoolcraft have been labeled early Indian historians, their Indian scholarship was largely based on hearsay, anecdote, personal observation, and ethnological/anthropological reports. Parkman, Bancroft, and Schoolcraft did not write objective document-driven Indian history.

CHAPTER 2

1. DuBois, *Feminism and Suffrage*, 77–104; Moldow, "All Qualified Persons," 19–26. Women's higher education significantly contributed to their postbellum entry into the traditional

professions and the formation of autonomous professions that also attracted women to Washington. See Woody, *History*, chaps. 5–9; Eschbach, *Higher Education*, chaps. 4–5, 9.

2. Green, C. M., *Washington*, 65–68, 96–97, 168–69; Moldow, "Gilded Age," 217–49. For the vanguard's radical thought, see *"The Revolution* Will Discuss," *The Revolution*, 30 April 1868, 272; "New York Woman Suffrage Association," *Woman's Journal*, 11 January 1873, 16; "Miss Anthony's Defense," *Woman's Journal*, 15 February 1873, 51; "The Washington Convention," *Woman's Journal*, 31 January 1874; Norgren, *Belva Lockwood*, 155–68; Hanaford, *Daughters of America*, 353–57.

3. Johnson, T. R., "Reconstruction Politics,"180–90; "The District of Columbia to Have a Territorial Government," *Newark Advocate* (Ohio), 27 January 1871; Public Law 419; "Inflation," 12–15; Chipman, "The Appendix," 1–21; "District of Columbia," 12–15; Whyte, "District of Columbia," 87–102.

4. Green, C. M., *Secret City*, chaps. 5–6; House Report 7.

5. For 1877–79 economic distress, see Lubetkin, *Jay Cooke's Gamble*, chaps. 1–3; House Report 627, 1–11; Senate Report 479, 1–5; "Good Day's Work," *New York Herald Tribune* 18 June 1874, 1; "The District of Columbia," *Bangor Daily Whig & Courier* (Me.), 14 December 1874; Crane, *The Washington Ring*, passim; Crane, *More About Washington*, passim. While dismissed by opponents as a disgruntled grafter and racist, Crane was an abolitionist and early whistleblower. Crane's publications were donated to Harvard College Library by Charles Sumner.

6. Green, C. M., *Secret City*, chaps. 5–6; "Failure of Negro Suffrage," *New York Herald*, 28 November 1874, 4; "The Washington Ring," *Pomeroy's Democrat*, 19 December 1874, 2; "Going Back on the Negro," *Georgia Weekly Telegraph*, 22 December 1874, 3.

7. "The Woman's Congress," *New York Times*, 16 October 1874, 1; "Woman Suffrage Debate," *Morning Oregonian*, 4 June 1874, 4; Miller, F. *Argument before the Judiciary Committee*, passim; *Arguments in Behalf of a Sixteenth Amendment*, passim. The women's Sixteenth Amendment campaign was stymied by a rival desegregated school effort. "Constitutional Amendment," *The Christian Recorder*, 31 August 1876; Horowitz, "Victoria Woodhull," 403–34.

8. Liberal, moderate, and conservative definitions are gleaned from several sources. Ginzberg, *Women and Work*, chaps. 1–4; Hewitt, "From Seneca Falls," passim; Vapnek, "Staking Claims," 15–38, 305–28; Geer, "Lucy W. Hayes and the New Woman," 18–26; Geer, "Lucy W. Hayes and Woman's Home Mission," 5–14; Niemtzow, "Marriage and New Woman," 377–95.

9. For a later example of lateral diffusion, see Hartman, *Other Feminists*, 4–13, 207–16; *Elizabeth Cady Stanton*, chaps. 5–6.

10. Newman, *White Women's Rights*, 116–31; Pascoe, *Relations of Rescue*, 59–60, 69, 102–103, 110, 141–42.

11. Quinton, "Original Indian Organization," 349.

12. Janiewski, "Giving Women a Future," 325–40; Riley, *Confronting Race*, 1–10.

13. Mary Bonney and Amelia Quinton used the terms "Oklahoma Indians" and "Indians in/of Oklahoma" when referencing American Indians in the geographical boundary that would later become the state of Oklahoma. See Quinton, *Indian's Friend*, 1883–1906, passim. From Indian removal to Oklahoma statehood in 1907, the new homeland of the Five Tribes and other Indians was routinely labeled "Indian Territory." After "Oklahoma Territory" was established in the western half of present-day Oklahoma by the 1890 Oklahoma Organic Act, only the eastern section of the future state was called Indian Territory. In reality, no actual "Indian Territory" was ever legally created by Congress. Given common use and well-established scholarly convention this book uses the term "Indian Territory." See, Rhea, "Creating a Place," 46n50. The Union Agency consolidated the functions of the old Cherokee, Choctaw, Chickasaw, Muscogee (Creek), and Seminole United States Indian agencies. See Goble, *Progressive Oklahoma*, 70; Women's Baptist Home Mission Society Minutes, 1 May 1877, First Baptist Church, Philadelphia Record Group, box 10.21–22, American Baptist

Historical Society; *Annual Report American Home Mission Society, 1876,* 10; Davis, S. P., ed., *History of Nevada,* 1225–26.

14. Women's Baptist Home Mission Society Minutes, 17, 18 May 1877, 1 October 1877, First Baptist Church, Philadelphia Record Group, box 10.21–22, American Baptist Historical Society; Keen, *Bi-centennial,* 391; *Baptist Home Missions,* 519–20, 573; Cozzens, *Eyewitnesses,* 428; "Baptist-Third Day Convention at Providence," *Boston Evening Journal,* 25 May 1877, 4; "Women's Work in Home Missions," *Boston Daily Adviser,* 20 June 1877, 4; *Annual Report American Home Mission Society 1876,* 23. Philadelphia First Baptist was one of the most significant WBHMS branches. Lauback, *To Think,* 4; *Baptist Home Missions,* 514–23; Keen, *Bi-centennial,* 391–92; Cathcart, *Baptist Encyclopedia,* 541.

15. Mrs. H. L. Wayland, "Women's Home Mission Union," 245–46; H. L. Wayland, "First— The Women's Home Mission Society," *National Baptist,* 15 May 1879, 5; H. L. Wayland, "Woman's Baptist Home Mission Union," *National Baptist,* 22 May 1879, 4.

16. The author is completing a forthcoming anthology chapter that examines the WBHMS-ABHMS conflict and WNIA origins.

17. Crawford, I., *Kiowa,* 7; Lindley and Stebner, eds., *Westminster Handbook,* 51; "Civilized Indians," *The Daily Gazette* (Kalamazoo, Mich.), 20 July 1879, 3; Prucha, *American Indian Policy,* 134–38; "Constitution of the Indian Treaty-Keeping and Protective Association." For an analysis of formative ITKPA/WNIA history (1876–1881) and a detailed discussion of the issues outlined above see Rhea, forthcoming article.

18. Mielke, *Moving Encounters,* 1–13, 194–95; Wexler, *Tender Violence,* 1–14, 15–52. Amelia Quinton specifically addressed early ITKPA sentimentality. See Farmer, ed., *National Exposition Souvenir,* 298–99. Other Indian assimilation groups existed, but they were not women's organizations or national. See "The Welfare of the Indians," *New York Times,* 20 March 1878, 2; Mardock, *The Reformers,* 160–61, 208.

19. "Rural Pennsylvania Quakers," *Springfield Daily Republican,* 2 August 1879, 3; "The Universal Peace Union," *Evening Star,* 3 May 1879, 8.

20. "Work among the Indians. The Episcopalians," 90–91; Tullidge, *Evangelical Church,* xi–xlvi; Whittaker, ed., *Protestant Episcopal Almanac,* passim; Slattery, *Felix Reville Brunot,* 126–36; "Indian's Hope Mission," *Philadelphia Inquirer,* March 17, 1877, 2; "The Aborigines," *Philadelphia Inquirer,* March 23, 1882, 2; Keen, *Bi-Centennial,* 303; Welsh, W., Jr. "Sketch," 11–12; Wright, E. R.,"A Sketch of the Life of Mrs. William Welsh," 18–26; Wanken, " 'Woman's Sphere,' " 7; Welsh, W. *Women Helpers,* passim.

21. Welsh. W., Jr., "Sketch," 12; "William Welsh Sudden Death," *North American* (Philadelphia) 12 February 1878; Hagan, *Indian Rights Association,* chaps. 1–3; Candidus, "Herbert Welsh," 18–23; "Personal," *New York Herald Tribune,* 11 June 1879, 4; "The S. P. C. C." *Philadelphia Inquirer,* 17 January 1882, 8; "Germantown's Workingman's Club," *Philadelphia Inquirer,* 11 May 1882, 2; "A Plea for the Indians," *New York Herald Tribune,* 13 November 1882, 5; "William Welsh," *Philadelphia Inquirer,* 12 February 1878, 4; "The Indian Hope Association," *Philadelphia Inquirer,* 30 November 1880, 3; Prucha, *American Indian Policy,* 134–38.

22. Whipple, *Taopi,* 73–87, passim; Hoxie, *Final Promise,* 55; Fritz, *Movement,* 198–99; H. L. Wayland, "Women's Baptist Home Mission Society, Chicago," *National Baptist,* 5 June 1879, 5; *Women's Baptist Home Mission Society,* 4–5; H. L. Morehouse, "Women's Baptist Home Mission Society," 201–202; "Indian Treaties," *Philadelphia Inquirer,* 14 February 1881, 3; Wanken, " 'Woman's Sphere,' " 21–32nn185–89.

23. Willard and Livermore, *American Women,* 595; "Prof. R. L. Quinton," *Delaware Daily Times,* 6 June 1880, 4; "Lectures at Haverford College," 537; Logan, *Part Taken,* 407; Zaeske, *Signatures,* 1–30.

24. Merging Indian treaty history with ITKPA political rhetoric was a feature of Quinton's tact that distinguished the ITKPA from other Indian movements. Quinton, "Small Request,"

2; Welsh, *Four Weeks*, 1–31; Welsh, *Apache Prisoners*, 1–62; Welsh, *Brief Statement*, 1–43; *Women's Baptist Home Mission Society*, 15; "A Century of Dishonor," *National Baptist*, 9 June 1881, 6.

25. H. L. Wayland penned an earlier factually flawed petition with Bonney and submitted it to the 1879 WBHMS annual meeting in her stead. This petition was almost immediately withdrawn. I use first "public" petition to distinguish Bonney and Quinton's "first" collaborative petition from this first failed petition. It is also important to note that while WNIA scholars focus on the first three petitions, in fact many were penned and circulated over the years. See H. L. Wayland, "Women's Baptist Mission Society, Chicago," *National Baptist*, 6 June 1879, 5; *Women's Baptist Home Mission Society*, 4–5; Morehouse, "Women's Baptist," 201–202; Bonney, "Historical Sketch," 10–11; Quinton, *Official Pamphlet*, 7–5; Quinton, "Care of Indian," 379.

26. Jackson was a popular poet and author whose Indian reform writings impressed Quinton. Wanken, "'Woman's Sphere,'" 17–22, 23–25; Quinton, "Care of Indian," 374–75; "Mrs. Helen Hunt Jackson," *Boston Daily Advertiser*, 6 February 1880, 2.

27. Quinton, "Care of the Indian," 380–81.

28. Wanken, "'Woman's Sphere,'" 28–29; Ross, "Awakened Interest," *Cherokee Advocate*, 17 March 1882, 1; Quinton, "They Are for Justice," *Cherokee Advocate*, 19 May 1882, 2.

29. Farmer, *National Exposition*, 298–99; Wanken, "'Woman's Sphere,'" 32.

30. Wanken, "'Woman's Sphere,'" 31–34.

31. *Congressional Record*, 1326–30.

32. *Congressional Record*, 1326–30.

33. Farmer, *National Exposition*, 298–99; Quinton, "Original Indian Association," 346; Quinton, "Care of Indian," 374–75.

34. Farmer, *National Exposition*, 299; Quinton, "Original Indian Association," 346. Sources are not clear on when Fletcher began her association with the ITKPA or when she became a nominal member of the organization. She may have joined sometime in 1882. Like Helen Hunt Jackson, Fletcher was only an honorary member.

35. Quinton, "Care of Indian," 378–85. Although scholarship almost universally references the organization as the WNIA from 1879, this practice obscures important ideological developments. While the same organizational structure, the ITKPA was not ideologically identical to the WNIA. Each name change corresponded to important ideological and historical shifts.

36. Marsden, "A Dedication,"109–12; Phillips, K., *Helen Hunt Jackson*, 1–39.

37. Livermore, "Helen Hunt Jackson," 67–70; Phillips, K., *Helen Hunt Jackson*, 14–15.

38. Barnard, "Memoir," 33–38; Phillips, K., *Helen Hunt Jackson*, 78.

39. Phillips, K. *Helen Hunt Jackson*, 15–16.

40. Hunt, *Union Foundations*, 13–16, 48–49.

41. Barnard, "Memoir," 35–38.

42. Keysor, "Helen Hunt Jackson," 60–61; Bolton, S. K., *Lives of Girls*, 18–31.

43. Mathes, *Indian Reform Letters*, 56. The extent of Helen Hunt Jackson's concern with brain health can be seen in subsequent publications. See Jackson, *Hettie's*, 182, 192, 251, 275, 279; Jackson, *Bits of Talk*, 10, 43, 51–54, 57, 75, 173, 186–87, 209, 223, 239; Jackson, *Zeph*, 112, 181, 191, 228.

44. Quinton, "Care of Indian," 374; Quinton, "Original Indian Association," 346. Marsden, "A Dedication," 110; Bolton, S. K., *Lives of Girls*, 18–31.

45. Mathes, ed., *Indian Reform Letters*, 1–43, 51, 57, 60, 73–77, 81, 86, 88, 90, 99, 114–15; Tibbles, *Buckskin*, 8, 216.

46. Mark, *A Stranger*, 3–4.

47. Ibid., 4–8.

48. Ibid., 8–42.

49. "Miss Alice C. Fletcher Lectures on Ancient America," *Cincinnati Daily Star*, 28 November 1879, 1; "The Archeological Lectures by Miss Alice C. Fletcher," *Cincinnati Daily Star*,

1 December 1879, 5; "Miss Alice C. Fletcher Lectures this Afternoon," *Cincinnati Daily Star*, 4 December 1879, 8; Mark, *A Stranger*, 32.

50. Gacs, et al., eds., *Women Anthropologists*, 995–96.

51. Browman and Williams, *New Perspectives*, 222–23; Gacs, et al., eds., *Women Anthropologists*, 95–96.

52. Mark, *A Stranger*, 42–79.

CHAPTER 3

1. Newman elaborates on this point, adding that passage of the fourteenth and fifteenth amendments and African American citizenship also contributed to political change in the postbellum women's rights movement. Newman, *White Women's Rights*, 3–17, 56–85.

2. Newman, *White Women's Rights*, 57; Pascoe, *Relations of Rescue*, 69; Simonsen, *Making Home Work*, 2–12, 59–60; Janiewski, "Giving Women Future," 325–40; Geer, "Lucy W. Hayes and the New Woman," 18–26. Simonsen's treatment of "Social Darwinism" does not consider the conflation of biological and cultural traits common to nineteenth-century American Darwinist racial theory.

3. "Scientific Washington," 158–59; Flack, "Scientific Societies," 430–42; "National Public Museum," *New York Times*, 19 February 1882, 5; "A Great Museum," *New York Times*, 24 October 1886, 12; "How Great Schools Came," *New York Times*, 1 September 1890, 2. Historians have not given sufficient weight to the fact that many early women assimilationists were well versed in the academic arts and scientific analysis before they engaged in fieldwork. See *Biographical Memoirs*, 29–41. For other scientifically minded women who made the westward trek, see Bonta, *American Women Afield*, 9–16, 17–32, 33–44, 45–54, 84–94, 95–105; Des Jardins, *Women*, 3–18, 40–46; Smith, B. G., *Gender of History*, 37–69, 113–16, 164, 185–212; Ginzberg, *Women and Work*, chaps. 4–6.

4. Adams, J. Q., *History of United States*, 83–84; Adams, H., *Life of Albert Gallatin*, 5, 45, 126, 167–69, 303, 644–652; Martin, *Languages of Difference*, 66–90; Bancroft, G., *History of Colonization*, 98–112; Parkman, *Oregon Trail*, 134, 138, 192, 236, 290; Bancroft, H. H., ed., *Native Races*, 1–81; Morgan, "Montezuma's Dinner," 265–308; Royce, *California*, 3–18, 40–46; Winsor, *The Colonies*, 27–31, 94–95, 383, 489, 522; Winsor, ed., *Narrative and Critical History*, 369–411, 413–15, 421–28; Roosevelt, *Winning of West*, passim. Des Jardins, *Women*, 13–51.

5. Mark, *A Stranger*, 397–404; Weeks, *Library Daniel G. Brinton*, 90–99, 160–61; Baker, "Daniel G. Brinton's Success," 394–423. For Helen Hunt Jackson as historian, see Bienstock, "Helen Hunt Jackson," 148–52; Cook-Lynn, *Notebooks*, 163.

6. Catlin, *Letters and Notes*; Dodge, *Our Wild Indians*; Northrop, *Indian Horrors*; Vanderwerth, *Indian Oratory*; and Johannsen, *House of Beadle and Adams*.

7. Jackson, *Glimpses*, 355; Phillips, K., *Helen Hunt Jackson*, 230.

8. Fletcher, Omaha Field Diary 1881 (Sept. to Nov.), 18, 21, 30 Sept., Alice Fletcher and Francis La Flesche Papers, National Anthropological Archives, Smithsonian Institution, series 9, box 11; Fletcher, "Camping with the Sioux," book 1, 1887, Alice Fletcher and Francis La Flesche Papers, National Anthropological Archives, Smithsonian Institution, series 5, box 7. Both Fletcher's 1881 field diary and book 1 of her fictionalized account of this period, "Camping with the Sioux," were consulted. For convenience, the pages of her unnumbered diary are referenced by month and day.

9. For extinction narratives, see Brantlinger, *Dark Vanishings*, 68–93; Burlin, *Indians' Book*, xxix.

10. Rhea, "Women and Construction Indian Scholarship," 138–69; Rhea, "Frontiers of Mind," 180–86; Byrd and Clayton, *American Health Dilemma*, 249; Pierce, "Making White Man's West," 39–40; Harris, *Rise Anthropological Theory*, 90–98.

11. Bannister, *Social Darwinism*, 26–29; Lorimer, "Theoretical Racism," 405–30; Cravens, *Triumph Evolution*, 3–11, 89–121.

12. Powell, *Sketch of Mythology*, 9; Haller, *Outcasts*, xii–xiv; Powell, "From Barbarism," 97–123; Tooker, "Lewis H. Morgan," 357–75; "Major Powell's Bureau," *Washington Post*, 12 April 1885, 2.

13. Powell, *Sketch of the Mythology*, 9; Haller *Outcasts*, xii–xiv; Powell, "From Barbarism," 97–123; Tooker, "Lewis H. Morgan," 357–75; "Major Powell's Bureau," *Washington Post*, 12 April 1885, 2; Baker, *From Savage*, 44–53; Martin, *Languages of Difference*, 36–42; "Our Duty Toward Dependent Races," *Christian Union*, 12 March 1891, 341–42.

14. Martin, *Languages of Difference*, preface, 53. The third national ITKPA petition signaled a significant shift in the organization's assimilation views. With the third petition Bonney and Quinton (and the ITKPA as a whole) embraced legally mandated, coercive assimilation, particularly forced allotment of Indian lands. See Farmer, *National Exposition*, 299; Quinton, "Original Indian Association," 346.

15. Hunt, "Fretting," 271; Jackson, *Father Junipero*, 66.

16. Fletcher, *Indian Story and Song*, 120.

17. Kevles, et al., "Sciences in America," 26–32; Hounshell, "Edison," 612–17; Schoolcraft, *Historical and Statistical Information*; Domenech, *Seven Years' Residence*; Gill, "Edward Drinker Cope," 831–63; Fowler, *A Laboratory*, 71–91; Renehan, *Transcontinental Railroad*, 59–80. Richard White argues the transcontinental railroads were built before there was an actual need. See White, *Railroaded*, 460–66. It can be argued that modern American anthropology emerged in part as a response to the "Indian problem." See Fowler, *A Laboratory*, 81.

18. Romer, "Cope versus Marsh," 201–207; Bowler, "Edward Drinker Cope," 249–65; Wheeler, "The Uintatheres," 1171–76; Davidson, "Send the Fossils," 243–54; Jaffe, *Gilded Dinosaur*, passim; Wallace, D. R., *Bone Hunter's Revenge*, passim; Debus, *Dinosaurs*, chaps. 2–7.

19. "Missing Link Found," *New York Times*, 24 December 1881, 1; Cope, "Occurrence of Man," 593; Hubrecht, *Descent of Primates*, 18–25.

20. Fowler, *A Laboratory*, 15–30; Hinsley, "Drab Doves," 2–20; Meltzer, *First Peoples*, 64–94; Darnell, "Toward Consensus," 23–24; Baker, *From Savage*, 41–42; Baker, *Anthropology*, 11.

21. Darnell, "Toward Consensus," 29–35; Rapp and Hill, *Geoarchaeology*, 8. Over the next three decades (from 1879–1900) Powell and his colleagues would continue to identify anthropology and ethnology as a new kind of history. Powell would go so far as to identify the development of anthropology as a sign of higher racial evolution. Powell, "Human Evolution," 176–208; Powell, Review of *Evolution of To-day*, 264–65; Stuart-Glennie, "Desirability of Treating History," 229–40; Laguna and Hallowell, *American Anthropology*, 25; Patterson, *Social History*, 31. Teresa Militello addresses the ease with which pre-professional American anthropologists and ethnologists labeled themselves "historians," or "new historians." See Militello, "Horatio Nelson Rush," 1–57.

22. Judd, *Bureau*, 34.

23. Judd, *Bureau*, 3–4; Rapp and Hill, *Geoarchaeology*, 8. Powell likely based his classification on an 1850 proposal by his professional rival, Daniel G. Brinton. See Brinton, *Proposed Classification*, 1–5.

24. "Bureau of Ethnology," *New York Times*, 23 April 1882, 7; Powell, *U.S. Geological Survey*, passim; Powell, *Introduction to Study*, passim; Powell, *On Primitive Institutions*, passim; Crawford, J., "On Language," 1–9; Holmes, *Twenty-Seventh Annual Report*, 14, 35, 639–40.

25. For the role of language in racial evolution, see Richards, R. J., "Linguistic Creation," 21–48; Taub, "Evolutionary Ideas," 171–93; Hale, "Language as a Test," 413–55; Brinton, *Language Palaeolithic Man*, 1–26; "The Origin and Development of Language," 145–46; Brinton, *On Polysythesis*, 1–35.

26. *Proceedings of Eighth Annual Meeting*, 16. For James McCosh, see "James M'Cosh," 1496. McCosh's sentiments were given a wider audience when his 1890 Lake Mohonk speech was published in the 1891 Interior department report to Congress. See *Executive Documents of the House of Representatives*, 844.

27. *Proceedings of Eighth Annual Meeting*, 152.

28. Powell, *Introduction to Study*, passim; Powell, *Philology*, passim; Judd, *Bureau*, 4, Mark, *A Stranger*, 397–99.

29. Franceschi, "On the Margins," 267–68; King, "Unsung Visionary," 40; Mark, *A Stranger*, 397–99.

30. Powell, *Canyons of Colorado*, 24, 27–30, 49, 51, 71, 120, 303–11; Mathes and Lowitt, *Standing Bear Controversy*, 89–90; Mark, *A Stranger*, 253.

31. Sligh, *A Study*, 13–14.

32. Zanjani, *Sarah Winnemucca*, 63–68; Canfield, *Sarah Winnemucca*, 29–32.

33. Zanjani, *Sarah Winnemucca*, 89–97, 102. The letter was reprinted in Jackson's *A Century of Dishonor*, 395–96. For more on "culture brokers," see Szasz, *Between Indian and White Worlds*, 5–20.

34. Zanjani, *Sarah Winnemucca*, 146–83; Canfield, *Sarah Winnemucca*, 135–49.

35. Hopkins (Winnemucca), *Life Among the Piutes*, 244–47; Zanjani, *Sarah Winnemucca*, 197, 226–27.

36. "Indian Agents to be Renounced," *New York Times*, 18 December 1881, 5; Hopkins (Winnemucca), *Life Among the Piutes*, 76.

37. Zanjani, *Sarah Winnemucca*, 201–203; Hopkins (Winnemucca), *Life Among the Piutes*, 52–53.

38. Quinton, "Care of Indian," 382; Hopkins (Winnemucca), *Life Among the Piutes*, 147.

39. Zanjani, *Sarah Winnemucca*, 257–60; Canfield, *Sarah Winnemucca*, 232–42; Peabody, *Sarah Winnemucca's Practical Solution*, 5–6; "Princess Winnemucca Dead," *New York Times*, 27 October 1891, 1.

40. Callahan, *Wynema*, xiii–viv.

41. Foreman, "S. Alice Callahan," 311.

42. "Harrell Institute Locals," *Our Brother in Red*, 1 February 1887, 4; "Locals," *Our Brother in Red*, 24 September 1887, 3; "Locals," *Our Brother in Red*, 15 June 1888, 5; "Locals," *Our Brother in Red*, 14 July 1888, 5; "Report of Rev. W. A. Duncan," *Our Brother in Red*, 2 November 1889, 2; Joshua Ross, "Indian International Agricultural Society and Fair Association," *Our Brother in Red*, 22 June 1889, 4.

43. Callahan, *Wynema*, xvi–xvii, xix; "Post Office Book Store," *Cherokee Telephone*, 26 February 1891, 2; "Horace O'Donoghue's Suicide," *New York Times*, 19 April 1893, 2.

44. Meacham, *Wi-ne-ma*, passim.

45. Meacham, *Wi-ne-ma*, 20–28; Callahan, *Wynema*, xxv–xxvi.

46. Van Dyke, "An Introduction to *Wynema*," 123–28.

47. Callahan, *Wynema*, 50–53; Tatonetti, "Behind the Shadows," 1–31.

48. Callahan, *Wynema*, 50, 54, 72–74, 97.

49. Mark, *A Stranger*, 67, 125; Hickey, *Nebraska Moments*, 11; Day, *The Mortons*, 17; Giffen and La Flesche (Tibbles), *Oo-mah-ha Ta-wa-tha*, 11–21, 28–40; Swetland, "Make-Believe White-Men," 211, 216–29.

50. *City of Elizabeth, New Jersey*, 107; Senate Misc. Doc. 46–49, 46th Congress, 2nd session, 1880, 20, 26–28.

51. Mathes and Lowitt, *Standing Bear Controversy*, 83–98; Tibbles, *Ponca Chiefs*, vii–viii; Harsha, *Ploughed Under*, 3–6; Mark, *A Stranger*, 122–38.

52. *Trans-Mississippi International Exposition*, 20, 21.

53. Giffen and La Flesche (Tibbles), *Oo-mah-ha Ta-wa-tha*, 53–56.

54. Brightman, "Cultures and Culture Theory," 381; Castile, "Commodification," 743–49; Algeo, "Indian for a Night," 1–17. A notable exception was Tonawanda Seneca leader and Office of Indian Affairs commissioner Ely Samuel Parker, who had access to public and government documents but did not write an Indian history. See Genetin-Pilawa, *Crooked Paths*, 73–93.

CHAPTER 4

1. Phillips, K., *Helen Hunt Jackson*, 125–26, 141–42, 144–46.
2. Mathes and Lowitt, *Standing Bear Controversy*, 93–98; Helen Hunt Jackson, "An Appeal for the Indians," *New York Tribune*, 9 December 1879, 5; Trefousse, *Carl Schurz*, 12–13.
3. Mathes, *Indian Reform Letters*, 65, 68, 86; Mathes and Lowitt, *Standing Bear Controversy*, 93–98.
4. "Helen Hunt," *Omaha Herald*, 17 July 1881, 1; Tibbles, *Buckskin*, 8, 216; Mathes, *Indian Reform Letters*, 114–15; Jackson, *Century of Dishonor*, 205, 370–71.
5. *Fourth Annual Report of Women's National Indian Association*, 8; Jackson, *Century of Dishonor*, 337; Mrs. A. S. Quinton, "Home Mission Concert," *National Baptist*, 5 May 1881, 12; "A Century of Dishonor," *National Baptist*, 9 June 1881, 6; Tibbles, *Buckskin*, 216.
6. Jackson, *Century of Dishonor*, xiv, xv; Roosevelt, *Winning of West*, 334.
7. Jackson, *Century of Dishonor*, xiv, xv; Roosevelt, *Winning of West*, 334.
8. Quinton, "Care of Indian," 379, 381; Jackson, *Century of Dishonor*, 340. Jackson certainly did not share the post 1882 WNIA demand for legally mandated, coercive Indian assimilation, but it is also not correct to depict her as a strict "hands off" proponent. Neither approach accurately reflects Jackson's complex Indian policy sentiments. "Gradual" assimilation, as coined and later rejected by the early ITKPA (WNIA) is a fair compromise that reflects Jackson's advocacy for Indian tutelage, Indian education, fair treatment, land and treaty rights, and voluntary, but nevertheless *encouraged* Indian assimilation into European American society. Jackson's sentiments mirrored those of other lesser known contemporary gradualists like Thomas A. Bland, founder of the National Indian Defense Association. As C. Joseph Genetin-Pilawa reminds us, "Alternative reformers urged lawmakers to consider other approaches . . . that would allow tribal nations and individuals time and opportunities to assimilate on their own terms and timelines." Genetin-Pilawa, *Crooked Paths*, 2, 118–33.
9. Jackson, *Century of Dishonor*, xix–xxiv, 1–5, 340; Mark, *A Stranger*, 73.
10. Pagden, *Lords of All World*, chaps. 1–2; Cohen, *Felix S. Cohen's Handbook*, chaps. 1–3, passim; Jackson, *Century of Dishonor*, 32–46.
11. Jackson, *Century of Dishonor*, 46–56.
12. Ibid., 47–65.
13. Eight nonvoting members of the forty-seventh Congress are included in the number of Congressmen who received a copy of *A Century of Dishonor*. Given Jackson's contacts in Washington, it would be reasonable to assume she was aware of the California Mission Indian bill working its way through Congress in 1879. Bueler, *Colorado's Colorful Characters*, 96; Mathes, *Helen Hunt Jackson*, 38, 43; Turner, F. W., "Century after *A Century of Dishonor*," 715–31; Padget, "Travel Writing," 838.
14. Mathes, *Helen Hunt Jackson*, 38–54; Padget, "Travel Writing," 838.
15. Akins, "Lines on Land," 1–77; Mathes, *Divinely Guided*, 177–203.
16. Mathes, *Indian Reform Letters*, 206–207; Akins, "Lines on Land," 1–77.
17. Mathes, *Indian Reform Letters*, 230–31.
18. Valerie Sherer Mathes's excellent biographical works on Jackson meticulously document her life. Mathes, *Indian Reform Letters*, 55–75, 204–15, 244; Mathes, *Helen Hunt Jackson*, 48–75.
19. Mathes, *Helen Hunt Jackson*, 69–73.

20. Jackson and Kinney, *Report on the Condition*, 9; Mathes, *Indian Reform Letters*, 262–64.
21. Mathes, *Helen Hunt Jackson*, 72–75.
22. Jackson, *Mercy Philbrick's Choice*, 33, 99, 129, 134, 205, 215, 248; Jackson, *Hettie's*, 182, 192, 251, 275, 279; Jackson, *Bits of Travel*, 30, 266, 417; Jackson, *Bits of Talk*, 10, 43, 51, 53–54, 57, 75, 173, 186–87, 209, 223, 237, 239; Jackson, *Zeph*, 112, 181, 191, 228.
23. Jackson, "Father Junipero," 3–18, 199–215; Jackson, "Present Condition," 515–29; Jackson, *Father Junipero*, 9, 10–13, 20–25, 33–34, 66–69; Bolton, H. E., "Spanish Mission," 42–61.
24. Jackson, *Father Junipero*, 66–69.
25. Phillips, K., *Helen Hunt Jackson*, 240–64; Brigandi and Robinson, "Killing of Juan Diego," 1–24; Davis and Alderson, *True Story of Ramona*, chaps. 1–4; Mathes, *Indian Reform Letters*, 258; Padget, "Travel Writing," 836.
26. Jackson, *Ramona*, 403. This section is informed by the work of Daneen Wardrop and Carl Gutiérrez-Jones. Wardrop and Gutiérrez-Jones link Alessandro's mental illness to displacement and loss of dignity prompted by European American settler prejudice and abrupt removal from his cultural community. See Wardrop, "Jouissant Politics," 27–38; Gutiérrez-Jones, *Rethinking Borderlands*, 50–79.
27. Jackson, *Ramona*, 426, 427–90.
28. Martin Padget argues that Jackson's *Ramona* was actually a complex critique of Indian assimilation, and he rejects interpretations of *Ramona* that advance the idea of an idealistic American colony. Padget, "Travel Writing," 833–76.
29. James, *Through Ramona's Country*, 167–72; Phillips, K., *Helen Hunt Jackson*, 273; DeLyser, *Ramona Memories*, 31–64, passim.
30. Mathis, *Indian Reform Letters*, xiv; Byers, "Helen Hunt Jackson," 143–48; Byers and Byers, "Helen Hunt Jackson," 196–42.

CHAPTER 5

1. Fletcher, Omaha Field Diary 1881 (Sept. to Nov.), 16 September, Alice Fletcher and Francis La Flesche Papers, series 9, box 11, National Anthropological Archives, Smithsonian Institution, Washington, D.C. (hereafter cited as Alice Fletcher and Francis La Flesche Papers); "Camping with the Sioux," book 1, 1887, Alice Fletcher and Francis La Flesche Papers, series 5, box 7.
2. Mark, *Four Anthropologists*, 62; Mark, *A Stranger*, 122–38, 157–68, 169–203, 265–77. Notably, E. Jane Gay, Fletcher's expedition companion referred to the allotment process as the march of "civilization against barbarism. . . . The throes of evolution." See Gay, *With the Nez Perces*, 87.
3. For compulsory education, see Fletcher, *Life Among the Indians*, 36–40, 243–50, 311–14; Mark, *A Stranger*, 79, 84–85; Hoxie, *Final Promise*, 147–210; Adams, *Education for Extinction*, 97–206. For Oglala Lakotas, see Stacy Makes Good, "Sioux is Not Even a Word," *Lakota Country Times*, 12 March 2009, 5.
4. Mathes and Lowitt, *Standing Bear Controversy*, 83–98; Mark, *A Stranger*, 38–39.
5. Annual Report of the Association for the Advancement of Women, 1880, 7–8; Annual Report of the Association for the Advancement of Women, 1881, 7.
6. Janiewski, "Giving Women a Future," 325–26; Janiewski, "Gendered Colonialism, 57–76. The field notebook is mislabeled as, "1881 Omaha Allotment Notebook." Actually it is a detailed historical and cultural record, Alice Fletcher and Francis La Flesche Papers, Incoming Correspondence, 1881 Omaha Allotment Field Notebook, box 3 (hereafter OAFN; for convenience, the pages of this unnumbered notebook are referenced as 1–391). Alice Fletcher to John Wesley Powell, 11 August 1881, Alice Fletcher and Francis La Flesche Papers, series 1, box 69, Correspondence, 1879–1887.

7. Alice Fletcher to John Wesley Powell, 11 August 1881, Alice Fletcher and Francis La Flesche Papers, series 1, box 69, Correspondence 1879–1887.

8. Mark, *A Stranger*, 34–36. Fletcher, *Brief Memories*, 6–8; Carr, *Notes on Crania*, frontis. Alice Fletcher to John Wesley Powell, 16 November 1881, Alice Fletcher and Francis La Flesche Papers, series 1, box 69, Correspondence, 1879–1887.

9. Mark, *A Stranger*, 49, 53; Fletcher, Omaha Field Diary 1881 (Sept. to Nov.), 18, 25 September, 4, 15 October, Alice Fletcher and Francis La Flesche Papers, series 9, box 11; "Camping with the Sioux," book 1, 1887, Alice Fletcher and Francis La Flesche Papers, series 5, box 7.

10. By the time Thomas H. Tibbles agreed to a western trip with Fletcher he had already written a book on the U.S. violation of Ponca treaty rights and another on corruption in the Indian Bureau. Tibbles felt Fletcher was exploiting Indian peoples. Tibbles, *Ponca Chiefs*; Tibbles, *Hidden Power*.

11. Tibbles, *Buckskin*, 238–39, 241, 256, 257, 261, 267, 269, 278, 279, 289; Fletcher and La Flesche, *The Omaha*, 2; Fletcher, Omaha Field Diary 1881 (Sept. to Nov.), 26, 29 October, Alice Fletcher and Francis La Flesche Papers, series 9, box 11; "Camping with the Sioux," book 1, 1887, Alice Fletcher and Francis La Flesche Papers, series 5, box 7.

12. Fletcher, OAFN, 92–98.

13. Mark, *A Stranger*, 52–53; Barnes, *Two Crows Denies It*, 12–14.

14. Tibbles, *Buckskin*, 246, 256. The "tent" mentioned by Tibbles on page 256 is the same teepee noted on page 246; Laubin and Laubin, *Indian Tipi*, 57–63.

15. Tibbles, *Buckskin*, 257–58.

16. Fletcher, Omaha Field Diary 1881 (Sept. to Nov.), 27–30 October, Alice Fletcher and Francis La Flesche Papers, series 9, box 11; "Camping with the Sioux," book 1, 1887, Alice Fletcher and Francis La Flesche Papers, series 5, box 7; Mark, *A Stranger*, 62–64.

17. Fletcher, Omaha Field Diary 1881 (Sept. to Nov.), 5, 9 September, 27 October, Alice Fletcher and Francis La Flesche Papers, series 9, box 11; "Camping with the Sioux," book 1, 1887, Alice Fletcher and Francis La Flesche Papers, series 5, box 7.

18. Woodruff, "On Our Indian Question," 293–303. See also Gibbon, "On Our Indian Question," 101–22; Wood, "On Our Indian Question," 123–82; Butler, "On Our Indian Question," 183–277.

19. Swetland, "Make-Believe White-Men," 204–205.

20. Swetland, "Make-Believe White-Men," 205; Fletcher, OAFN, 1.

21. Mark, *A Stranger*; Fletcher and La Flesche, *Omaha Tribe*; Powell, "James Owen Dorsey," 53–54; Dorsey, *Omaha Sociology*. Dorsey encouraged Fletcher to take an interest in linguistics and philology, but Fletcher never complied. J. Owen Dorsey to Alice Fletcher December 1882, National Anthropological Archives, Smithsonian Institution, Alice Fletcher and Francis La Flesche Papers, Incoming Correspondence. 1881–1882, box 1; Fletcher, OAFN.

22. Kappler, *Indian Affairs*, vol. 2, 611–14; Swetland, "Make-Believe White-Men," 207–209.

23. Kappler, *Indian Affairs*, vol. 2, 872–75; Fletcher, *Historical Sketch Omaha Tribe*, 6–7; Swetland, "Make-Believe White-Men," 209–10.

24. House Doc. 509, 56th Congress, 2nd session, 1901, 210–19; Deloria and Demallie, *Documents*, 233–48; Kinney, *Continent Lost*, 137–60.

25. Fletcher, *Historical Sketch*, 8–9; Rinella, *American Buffalo*, 81–86.

26. Fletcher, *Historical Sketch*, 7–8; Swetland, "Make-Believe White-Men," 213.

27. Kappler, *Indian Affairs*, vol. 1, 270–76; Fletcher, *Historical Sketch*, 1.

28. Fletcher, *Historical Sketch*, 8–10; Swetland, "Make-Believe White-Men," 213; Giffin and La Flesche (Tibbles), *Oo-mah-ha Ta-wa-tha*, 3, 53–56.

29. "A Boston Girl Joins an Indian Tribe to Learn Their Traditions," *Boston Journal* 10 February 1882, 3; George W. Wilkinson was appointed as the new Omaha-Winnebago agent on October 17, 1881. His tenure began the following month. see Andreas, *History State of Nebraska*.

30. Fletcher, Omaha Field Diary 1881 (Sept. to Nov.), 25–26 September, Alice Fletcher and Francis La Flesche Papers, series 9, box 11; "Camping with the Sioux," book 1, 1887, Alice Fletcher and Francis La Flesche Papers, series 5, box 7; Mark, *A Stranger*, 62–64; *Proceedings of the Twenty-Fifth Annual Meeting of the Lake Mohonk Conference*, 88, 178–79.
31. For a list of Win-dja'-ge residents (1855), see Swetland, "Make-Believe White-Men," 212.
32. Fletcher, OAFN, 8.
33. Ibid., 8.
34. Ibid., 10.
35. Ibid., 34; Swetland, "Make-Believe White-Men," 212; *Senate Misc. Doc.* 31, 47th Congress, 1st session, 1882, 1–14; Alice Fletcher to Hon. John Morgan, 31 December 1881, Alice Fletcher and Francis La Flesche Papers, Outgoing Correspondence, box 2.
36. Senate Misc. Doc. 31, 47th Congress, 1st session, 1882, 3–4. Fletcher, OAFN, 34–50. Virtually the same material is contained in OAFN, but the Senate document is more accessible.
37. Senate Misc. Doc. 79, 54th Congress, 1st session, 1896, 3–8.
38. Ibid., 4.
39. Fletcher, OAFN, 34–391. These names are also listed on the 1882 petition Fletcher presented to Congress. See Senate Misc. Doc. 31, 47th Congress, 1st session, 1882, 1–14.
40. Senate Misc. Doc. 26, 47th Congress, 1st session, 1888, 1–6.
41. "Hon. A. M. Clapp's Speech," *New York Times*, 9 July 1877, 2; "Hon. A. M. Clapp's Golden Wedding," *Washington Post*, 20 April 1882, 1.
42. Alice Fletcher to Mrs. Clapp, 1 December 1882, Alice Fletcher and Francis La Flesche Papers, Outgoing Correspondence, box 2. Dolores Janiewski notes that when addressing women's rights proponents Fletcher represented her work as the study of Indian women. See Janiewski, "Giving Women a Future," 326–32.
43. Alice Fletcher to John Morgan, 31 December 1881, Alice Fletcher and Francis La Flesche Papers, Outgoing Correspondence, box 2. For Morgan, see Hoxie, *Final Promise*, 72, 160. Other sources have misidentified John Tyler Morgan as Commissioner of Indian Affairs in 1881. Roland E. Trowbridge served from 1880–81, Hiram Price from 1881–93. *The Commissioners of Indian Affairs*, 1–2; Spotford, ed. *American Almanac*, 145; Leonard, *Who's Who*, 506; Alice Fletcher to John Morgan, 31 December 1881, Alice Fletcher and Francis La Flesche Papers, Outgoing Correspondence, box 2.
44. Alice Fletcher to John Morgan, 31 December 1881, Alice Fletcher and Francis La Flesche Papers, Outgoing Correspondence, box 2. For petition debates among Citizen's Party Omaha, see Fletcher, OAFN, 362, 364–68, 370. For the first draft of the petition see Fletcher, OAFN, 100.
45. Alice Fletcher to Henry L. Dawes, 4 February 1882, in Mathes and Lowitt, "'I Plead For Them," 36–41; Alice Fletcher to Henry L. Dawes, 4 February 1882, Alice Fletcher and Francis La Flesche Papers, Outgoing Correspondence, box 2; Alice Fletcher to S. J. Kirkwood, 8 February 1882, Alice Fletcher and Francis La Flesche Papers, Outgoing Correspondence, box 2.
46. Kappler, *Indian Affairs*, 212–14; "The Rights of Indians," *Omaha Daily Bee*, 30 December 1882, 1.
47. Mark, *A Stranger*, 75; *Proceedings of the Twenty-Fifth Annual Meeting of the Lake Mohonk Conference*, 178; Alice Fletcher to John Morgan, 12 January 1882, Alice Fletcher and Francis La Flesche Papers, Incoming Correspondence, 1881–1882, box 1.
48. Alice Fletcher to John Morgan, 4 February 1882, Alice Fletcher and Francis La Flesche Papers, Outgoing Correspondence, box 2; Alice Fletcher to Henry L. Dawes, 4–8 February 1882, Alice Fletcher and Francis La Flesche Papers, Outgoing Correspondence, box 2; Laura Sunderland to Alice Fletcher, 31 May 1882, Alice Fletcher and Francis La Flesche Papers, Incoming Correspondence, 1881–1882, box 1; Sarah Crapo to Alice Fletcher, 1 June 1882, Alice

Fletcher and Francis La Flesche Papers, Incoming Correspondence, 1881–1882, box 1. For Sarah Crapo, see Bacon, E. M., *Men of Progress*, 212; for Laura Sunderland, see "Death of Miss Laura Sunderland," *Evening Star* (Washington, D.C.), 24 February 1890, 2.

49. Electra S. Dawes to Alice Fletcher, 24 April 1882, Alice Fletcher and Francis La Flesche Papers, Incoming Correspondence, 1881–1882, box 1; M. S. to Alice Fletcher, Alice Fletcher and Francis La Flesche Papers, Incoming Correspondence, 1881–1882, box 1; Emily Talbot to Anna Dawes, 13 May 1882, Alice Fletcher and Francis La Flesche Papers, Incoming Correspondence, 1881–1882, box 1; Anna Laurens Dawes to Alice Fletcher, 16 May 1882, Alice Fletcher and Francis La Flesche Papers, Incoming Correspondence, 1881–1882, box 1.

50. D. H. Ross, "Awakened Interest in the Indian Question," *Cherokee Advocate*, 17 March 1882, 1.

51. Amelia Quinton, "They Are for Justice, a Splendid Letter from a Woman," *Cherokee Advocate*, 19 May 1882, 2.

52. "The Army of the James," *New York Times*, 8 June 1876, 1; Sarah Crapo to Alice Fletcher, 15 May 1882, Alice Fletcher and Francis La Flesche Papers, Incoming Correspondence, 1881–1882, box 1; Mr. & Mrs. Jos. R. Hawley to Alice Fletcher, May 1882, Alice Fletcher and Francis La Flesche Papers, Incoming Correspondence, 1881–1882, box 1; Harriet W. Hawley to Alice Fletcher, 15 May 1882, Alice Fletcher and Francis La Flesche Papers, Incoming Correspondence, 1881–1882, box 1; D. Lathrop to Alice Fletcher, 16 March 1882, Alice Fletcher and Francis La Flesche Papers, Incoming Correspondence, 1881–1882, box 1. A WNIA "committee" was less formal than a WNIA branch. See Quinton, "Our Association's Chronology, Number Four," 2, 12.

53. W. G. Wilkinson to Alice Fletcher, 25 May 1882, Alice Fletcher and Francis La Flesche Papers, Incoming Correspondence, 1881–1882, box 1; R. H. Pratt to Alice Fletcher, 25 May 1882, Alice Fletcher and Francis La Flesche Papers, Incoming Correspondence, 1881–1882, box 1; Alice M. Robertson to Alice Fletcher, 30 May 1882, Alice Fletcher and Francis La Flesche Papers, Incoming Correspondence, 1881–1882, box 1; C. L. Hall to Alice Fletcher, 30 May 1882, Alice Fletcher and Francis La Flesche Papers, Incoming Correspondence, 1881–1882, box 1; W. C. Wade to Alice Fletcher, 13 October 1882, Alice Fletcher and Francis La Flesche Papers, Incoming Correspondence, 1881–1882, box 1; Joseph La Flesche to Alice Fletcher, 22 October 1882, Alice Fletcher and Francis La Flesche Papers, Incoming Correspondence, 1881–1882, box 1; Rosalie La Flesche to Alice Fletcher, 24 October 1882, Alice Fletcher and Francis La Flesche Papers, Incoming Correspondence, 1881–1882, box 1.

54. Mark, *A Stranger*, 75; Henry M. Teller to Alice Fletcher, 19 May 1882, Alice Fletcher and Francis La Flesche Papers, Incoming Correspondence, 1881–1882, box 1; *Proceedings of the Twenty-Fifth Annual Meeting of the Lake Mohonk Conference*, 178–79.

55. Mark, *A Stranger*, 73–78, 116–18. The gradual assimilation approach—slowly dissolving reservations over the course of several years, if not decades, reflected the early WNIA position. In this respect, at least until 1887 Senator Dawes and Secretary Teller were more in line with Helen Hunt Jackson's sentiments than with Fletcher. For WNIA gradual assimilation, see *Annual Report of the Women's National Indian Association, 1885*, 8–10, 34.

56. *Proceedings of the Twenty-Fifth Annual Meeting of the Lake Mohonk Conference*, 178–79; Teller to Fletcher, 19 May 1882, Alice Fletcher and Francis La Flesche Papers, Incoming Correspondence, 1881–1882, box 1.

57. Wanken, "'Woman's Sphere,'" 25–39; Kappler, *Indian Affairs*, 212–14; U.S. Statutes at Large, 341 (1882): 168; Charles F. Aldrich to Alice Fletcher, 5 August 1882, Alice Fletcher and Francis La Flesche Papers, Incoming Correspondence, 1881–1882, box 1. Charles F. Aldrich was Senator Dawes's secretary. Dawes's congratulations were forwarded in a note Aldrich sent to Fletcher. Hiram Price to Alice Fletcher, 20 April 1883, Alice Fletcher and Francis La Flesche Papers, Omaha Allotment Incoming Correspondence, 1883–1884, box 3. For Helen Hunt Jackson, see Jackson, *Century of Dishonor*, xv.

58. In a retrospective of her work Fletcher only briefly noted her years allotting. She placed a far greater value on her OAFN, ethnological publications, the 1882 and 1887 Congressional allotment acts, and her 1888 *Indian Education and Civilization* report. See *Proceedings of the Twenty-Fifth Annual Meeting of the Lake Mohonk Conference*, 178–79; Judd, *Bureau*, 53; Wanken, "'Woman's Sphere,'" 153–81.

59. BIA Commissioner Price stipulated that the Omahas could not lease their lands or become U.S. citizens without special congressional legislation. Nevertheless, Ed Farley was allowed to lease and farm acreage on the reserved land and break land for allotted Indians. Hiram Price to Alice Fletcher, February 21, 1884, Alice Fletcher and Francis La Flesche Papers, box 69; Statement of Edwood [sic] Farley, 12 July 1884; George F. Hull and Ed Farley contract, 2 June 1884; Alice Fletcher [on behalf of Omaha petitioners] to Hiram Price, 1887; D. L. Hawkins to Henry L. Dawes, 2 May 1887; Alice Fletcher [on behalf of Omaha petitioners] to the Congress of the United States, 17 December 1887; Shon gai ska, Sinde ha ha, and Louis Saunsoci to Hiram Price, 10 January 1888, Alice Fletcher and Francis La Flesche Papers, Correspondence: Omaha Indians and U.S. Government, 1884–1887, box 3.

60. Frederic Ward Putnam's promotion of women in the sciences is well documented. See Browman, "Frederic Ward Putnam," 209–41; Alice Fletcher to Frederic Ward Putnam, 7 June 1884, Alice Fletcher and Francis La Flesche Papers, 1884, box 2; Alice Fletcher to Caroline Dall, 7 July 1884, Massachusetts Historical Society, Caroline Wells Healey Dall Papers, Dall 323, reel 13, box 9, file 1-c.

61. A complete Fletcher bibliography can be found in Mark, *A Stranger*, 397–403; Amatniek, "Women's Anthropological Society," 5–32.

62. Judd, *Bureau*, 53.

63. Mark, *A Stranger*, 346; Judd, *Bureau*, 52–53.

64. Brickhouse, *Unsettlement of America*, 232–34; Tonkovich, *Allotment Plot*; 20–25; Newman, *White Women's Rights*, 121–22.

65. Genetin-Pilawa, *Crooked Paths*, 112–55; Mathes and Lowitt, *Standing Bear Controversy*, 112–60; Mark, *A Stranger*, 101–22.

66. Vore, "The Omahas," 180; "A Suggestion from a Western Friend," 156.

67. "An American Historical Association in Contemplation," 188; *Proceedings of the American Association for the Advancement of Science*, 654–65; Fletcher, *Lands in Severalty*, 1–14.

68. *Second Annual Address to the Public of the Lake Mohonk Conference*, 5.

69. *Second Annual Address to the Public of the Lake Mohonk Conference*, 7–11; William J. Potter, "An Oasis in the Political Desert," *The Index* (Boston), 23 October 1884, 194.

70. "For the Coming Expositions," *New York Times*, 16 August 1884, 3; Fletcher, *Report of Alice C. Fletcher*, 1–3; Fletcher, *Historical Sketch Omaha Tribe*, 1–33; Mark, *A Stranger*, 109–14.

71. *Special Report of the Bureau of Education*, 42–42. This catalog clearly lists twenty-three photographs. Washington Matthews suggested in a 1902 article that some or all of the photographs might date to 1883. Fletcher stated that all were commissioned in 1885. Mathews, "The Earth Lodge," 188; Fletcher, *Report of Alice C. Fletcher*, 1; "The Red Men's Friends," *National Republican*, 9 January 1885, 3; *Sixteenth Annual Report of the Bureau of Indian Commissioners, 1884*, 55, 59–66.

72. *Special Report of the Bureau of Education*, 41–43, 48–49; Fletcher, *Report of Alice C. Fletcher*, 2–3.

73. Fletcher, *Report of Alice C. Fletcher*, 2–3; *Special Report of the Bureau of Education*, 215.

74. Clark, S. N., "Are Indians Dying Out?" 1–42; U.S. Statutes at Large 24 (1886): 388–91; Fletcher, *Indian Education and Civilization*, 9–10; Holm, *Great Confusion*, 9–13; Mark, *A Stranger*, 109–15.

75. *Annual Report of the Department of the Interior, 1887*, 1209; Mark, *A Stranger*, 115–16.

76. *Proceedings of the Third Annual Meeting of the Lake Mohonk Conference*, 34–45, 48–50, 71; *Seventeenth Annual Report of the Board of Indian Commissioners*, 6, 9–11, 34–35, 69, 86, 93–94,

104–105; "The Indian Question," *Boston Daily Advertiser*, 10 October 1885, 5; A. P. F., "The Indian Conference at Lake Mohonk," *Congregationalist*, 15 October 1885, 1.
77. Mark, *A Stranger*, 115–17; Fletcher, *Indian Education and Civilization*.
78. Mark, *A Stranger*, 115–17; Fletcher, *Indian Education and Civilization*.
79. Mark, *A Stranger*, 129–133. See Joseph La Flesche to Alice Fletcher, 13 March 1886; Lucy La Flesche to Alice Fletcher, 14 March 1886; Rosalie La Flesche to Alice Fletcher, 16 March 1886, Alice Fletcher and Francis La Flesche Papers, microfilm 4558, box 2, Correspondence; D. L. Hawkins to Henry L. Dawes, 2 May 1887, Alice Fletcher and Francis La Flesche Papers, Correspondence: Omaha Indians and U.S. Government, 1884–1887, box 3; Alice Fletcher to J. E. Rhodes, 7 April 1887, Records of the Bureau of Indian Affairs, Correspondence, 1879–1887, box 69, National Anthropological Archives, Smithsonian Institution, Washington, D.C.
80. *Annual Meeting and Report of the Women's National Indian Association, 1885*, 54; *Annual Meeting and Report of the Women's National Indian Association, 1886*, 28–29, 34; *Annual Meeting and Report of the Women's National Indian Association, 1887*, 8, 27; *Annual Meeting and Report of the Women's National Indian Association, 1888*, 54; Hagan, *Indian Rights Association*, 65, 131.
81. Mark, *A Stranger*, 105–22; Gay, *With the Nez Perces*, passim; Josephy, *Nez Perce Indians*, 634–44; Greenwald, *Reconfiguring the Reservation*, 27, 32, 60–89, 116, 144–49.
82. Fletcher, *Indian Education and Civilization*, 1–11, 22, 48, 63, 70, 78, 80, 84, 111, 167–68, 171, 549, 658, 683; Prucha, *Americanizing the Indians*, 63; Mark, *A Stranger*, 200–201; Case and Voluck, *Alaska Natives*, 104–105.

CHAPTER 6

1. After 1913 Fletcher continued to publish, her last piece appearing in 1920. These works included a non–peer reviewed book published by C. C. Birchard and articles for the popular *Journal of Art and Archeology*, published by the Archeological Institute of America. A 1934 publication is occasionally listed as Fletcher's publication, but the citation is actually for a short piece by Frances Densmore that references a Fletcher conference paper published in 1915. "Women Who Serve Science," *Evening Star*, 6 July 1889, 7; Cravens, "Abandonment of Evolutionary Social Theory," 5–20; Mark, *A Stranger*, 397–403
2. Mark, *A Stranger*, 223–45; Miller, *Matilda Coxe Stevenson*, 88–77, 101–102.
3. Currell and Codell, *Popular Eugenics*, 269–307; Stern, *Eugenic Nation*, 27–115; Kevles, *In Name of Eugenics*, 64; Powell, "Evolution of Music," 244–49n1; Hoxie, *Final Promise*, 124–26; Powell, *Physiographic Regions*, 70–72, 84–85.
4. Mark, *A Stranger*, 168–202; Fletcher, "Dr. Spofford," 40; Nicolay, *Sixty Years*, 23–35. Current scholarship describes Fletcher's fellowship as a "salary" that conferred professional status. It was an open-ended benevolent stipend that carried no academic or professional requirements. See Mark, *A Stranger*, 203–16.
5. Powell, "The Humanities," 410–22.
6. Rhea, "Frontiers of Mind," 181, 184–86.
7. Haller, *Outcasts*, 100; Fletcher, *Indian Story and Song*, 120; Lomawaima, "Estelle Reel," 5–32.
8. Browman, "Peabody Museum," 510–11; Browman, "Frederic Ward Putnam," 217–24.
9. Des Jardins, *Women and Historical Enterprise*, 30–38; Patterson, *Social History*, 50–51; MacCurdy, "Anthropology at the Chicago Meeting," 401–405.
10. Solomon, B. M., *In the Company*, chaps. 1–4; McCandless, *Past in Present*, chaps. 1–5.
11. Browman, "Frederic Ward Putnam," 222–24.
12. Bernstein, "First Recipients," 551–64. Harvard, Johns Hopkins, and Clark were barred to women in 1890. See Rossiter, "Doctorates for Women," 159–83. By 1905 twenty-two women had been awarded history doctorates. See Des Jardins, *Women and Historical Enterprise*, 30–38.

13. Lepowsky, "Charlotte Gower," 164–65; Nurge, "Renewed Interest," 487–96; Jennings, "Growing Partnership," 87–104; McKay, "Historians, Anthropology," 185–241.
14. By 1890 Otis T. Mason was so sure of the distinction between professional historians and archaeologists (including anthropologists) that he informed the American Historical Association that little more than a complimentary "border land" existed between each. Mason, "Border Land," 113.
15. "German Universities," 258–72; "Why Our Science Students," 463–66; Adams, H. B., "Leopold von Ranke," 101–33; Novick, *That Noble Dream*, 21–48; Mark, *A Stranger*, 243–83.
16. Jameson, *John Franklin Jameson*, 274–75; Novick, *That Noble Dream*, 25, 47–49; Smith, B. G., *Gender of History*, 102–56.
17. Adams, H. B., *Methods Historical Study*, 1–23, 64–78.
18. Adams, H. B., "Leopold von Ranke," 104–105; Smith, B. G., *Gender of History*, 133–46; Novick, *That Noble Dream*, 40–54.
19. Jameson, "American Historical Association" 1–20; Link, "American Historical Association," 7.
20. Jameson, "American Historical Association," 2–3.
21. The most notable version is Angie Debo's assertion that the history profession was "barred to women." Rhea, "Creating a Place," 26–51.
22. Hurtado, *Herbert Eugene Bolton*, chap. 10.
23. Some women graduates gravitated toward women's colleges and the K-12 system from the beginning. See Novick, *That Noble Dream*, 366–67; Goggin, "Challenging Sexual Discrimination," 769–802; Smith, B. G., *Gender of History*, chaps. 3–5; Scott, *Gender and Politics*, 178–98; Riley, "Frederick Jackson Turner," 59–71; Leckie, *Angie Debo*, 3–10.
24. Goggin, "Challenging Sexual Discrimination," 772–75. The progressive moniker has been applied to early male historians in this context and advanced in several sources. Link, "American Historical Association," 1–17; Bogue, *Frederick Jackson Turner*, 55–56, 123, 235–37.
25. Link, "American Historical Association," 5; Des Jardins, *Women and Historical Enterprise*, 77–78, 108–18.
26. Bernstein, "First Recipients," 551–64; Rossiter, "Doctorates for Women," 769–802.
27. Browman, "Origins Stratigraphic Excavations," 242–64; Browman, "Peabody Museum," 513–16; Darnell, *Along Came Boas*, chaps. 6–9. Even the fieldwork of professional anthropologists depended on holding a university position in an anthropology department. Snead, "Science, Commerce," 256–71. Alice Fletcher made a desperate bid to create a private anthropological institution along the lines of American history societies, and in the process she created a lasting and definitive rift between the earlier preprofessional anthropologists and the professional academic anthropologists. "School of American Archeology," 401; Lorini, "Alice Fletcher," 1–25; Mark, *A Stranger*, 319–24. For professional American history, see Novick, *That Noble Dream*, 47–60; Scott, *Gender and Politics*, 103–12. Frederick Jackson Turner was zealous in his promotion of history at the elementary and secondary school levels. See Clifford and Guthrie, *Ed School*, 129–30.
28. Lunbeck, *Status of Women*, 15–16; Jardine, "Women in Humanities," 9–19; Novick, *That Noble Dream*, 133–67; Goggin, "Confronting Sexual Discrimination," 771–92; "War Makes Inroads," 22; Mitchell, M. J., "Correspondence Study," 400–401.
29. Jameson, *John Franklin Jameson*, 5–10.
30. Adams, H. B. *American Historical Association*, frontis; Jameson, *John Franklin Jameson*, 12–13; Tyler, "Neglect and Destruction," 20–22.
31. Adams, H. B., "Report of the Organization," 5–44.
32. Bogue, *Frederick Jackson Turner*, 123, 235–37; Jacobs, W. R., *Historical World*, 194–95.
33. Bannon, *Herbert Eugene Bolton*, 283–89; Rhea, "Creating a Place," 26–50; Leckie, *Angie Debo*, 43–59.

34. Turner, Review of *The Winning of the West*, 71–72; Turner, *Frontier in American History*, 293.
35. Bogue, *Frederick Jackson Turner*, 113.
36. Turner, "Significance of the Frontier," 3, 11, 15.
37. Ibid., 11–15.
38. Williams, W. A., "Brooks Adams," 217–32; Williams, W. A., "The Frontier Thesis," 379–95; LaFeber, *New Empire*, 63–101; Ambrosius, "Turner's Frontier Thesis," 332–39; Jacobs, W. R., "Natural Frontiers," 261–70; Ridge, "Significance," 2–13. Turner was cautious about a benevolent American expansion, and outside of Emma Helen Blair's comparatively brief involvement with *The Philippine Islands* publications most of Turner's female students focused on Indian political history. Historical voices that compared Indian assimilation to American Pacific expansion spoke from within a diverse national narrative, but they did not comprise the narrative.
39. Turner, "Social Forces," 122–39; Turner, "The West and American Ideas," 145–48; Turner, "Middle Western Pioneer Democracy," 176–80.
40. Marble, "The Ethical Element in Patriotism," 142–46; Smith, "Triumph of Nationalism," *New York Times*, 9 November 1900, 6; Gildemeister, "Teaching of Patriotism," 438–41.
41. Hagan, *Indian Rights Association*, 65–66, 101–103; Mark, *A Stranger*, 101–22; Newman, *White Women's Rights*, 116–31.
42. *Proceedings of the Tenth Annual Meeting of the Lake Mohonk Conference*, 80–88.
43. Gay, *With the Nez Perces*, 81; Mark, *A Stranger*, 95.
44. Mark, *A Stranger*, 211.
45. Gay, *With the Nez Perces*, xxxiv–xxxv, 164–67; Mark, *A Stranger*, 213–15.
46. Mark, *A Stranger*, 223–40.
47. Ibid., 233–45; Miller, *Matilda Coxe Stevenson*, 101–102.
48. Miller, *Matilda Coxe Stevenson*, 183–84, 191, 193–95,196–230; Mark, *A Stranger*, 267–68.
49. McKenzie, "Assimilation American Indian," 761–72; Sholtz, *Negotiating Claims*, 5, 24–26, 164.
50. Shurz, *American Imperialism*, 4; Love, *Race over Empire*, 1–15.
51. Williams, W. L., "United States Indian Policy," 815–17; Roosevelt, "Copperheads," 338.

CHAPTER 7

1. Williams, W. L., "United States Indian Policy," 810–31. See also Slotkin, *Fatal Environment* and Slotkin, *Gunfighter Nation*. Others have disagreed with the Indian assimilation–Philippine premise. See Wertheim, "Reluctant Liberator," 494–18. For Roosevelt and Philippines occupation, see Jones, *Honor in Dust*, chaps. 24–25.
2. Blair, Robertson, and Bourne, *The Philippine Islands*, 1–3; Miller, *"Benevolent Assimilation,"* chaps. 1–4; Kaplan, "Frederick Jackson Turner," 12–16.
3. Bogue, *Frederick Jackson Turner*, 55–56, 235–37; Coughlin, "Women and History," 471–79; Goggin, "Challenging Sexual Discrimination," 769–802; Riley, "Frederick Jackson Turner," 216–30. Riley argues that Turner overlooked women as a subject in his scholarship, more so than as colleagues.
4. At least Kellogg was better documented in historiographical scholarship on Turner. "Emma Helen Blair," *Madison Democrat*, 26 September 1911; "Emma Helen Blair," *Wisconsin State Journal*, 25 September 1911; Blair, *The Indians*, vol. 1; "The Late Emma Helen Blair," back cover insert, *Ripon College Catalogue 1917*, 166; *University of Wisconsin Catalogue, 1892–93*, 221; *University of Wisconsin Catalogue, 1905–1906*, 408, *University of Wisconsin Catalogue, 1909–1910*, 212.
5. Thwaites, ed. *Jesuit Relations*, vol. 1, vii–xiii, 1–45.

6. Turner, *Reuben Gold Thwaites*, 18, 30; Thwaites, ed. *Jesuit Relations*, vol. 1, vii–xiii, 1–45.
7. Cano, "Blair and Robertson's *The Philippine Islands*," 10–11; Grivas, "Arthur H. Clark," 67–68; Turner, *Reuben Gold Thwaites*, 18, 30; Thwaites, *Jesuit Relations*, vol. 1, 1–44; Blair, "Osage Indians in France," 780.
8. Thwaites, ed., *New Discovery*, ix–xiv; Thwaites, ed., *Original Journals*, pref.; "Emma Helen Blair," *Madison Democrat*, 26 September 1911; "Emma Helen Blair," *Wisconsin State Journal*, 25 September 1911.
9. Cano, "Blair and Robertson's *The Philippine Islands*," 3–46; Lockwood, *Life Edward E. Ayer*, chaps. 1–4; Wilgus, "James Alexander Robertson," 3–10. Robertson's highest degree was a postgraduate Bachelor of Philosophy (Ph.B.) from Western Reserve University, Cleveland, Ohio, and an honorary Doctor of Humane Letters degree (LHD).
10. Grivas, "Arthur H. Clark," 63–78.
11. Ibid.; Wilgus, "Life James Alexander Robertson," 3–4.
12. Grivas, "Arthur H. Clark Company," 67–68.
13. Cano, "Blair and Robertson's *The Philippine Islands*," 4–6.
14. Blair, Robertson, and Bourne, *The Philippine Islands*, vol. 1, pref., historical intro., 15, 19, 20–37, 38–86; Cano, "Blair and Robertson's *The Philippine Islands*," 6–8.
15. LeRoy (and Taft) was not against colonialism, only the way it was carried out by Spain in the Philippines. See LeRoy, "Our Spanish Inheritance," 330–47; Robertson and Bourne, Review of *The Philippine Islands*, 359–60; LeRoy, Review of *The Philippine Islands*, *AHR* 9: 149–54; LeRoy, Review of *The Philippine Islands*, *AHR* 10: 168–70.
16. Robertson and Bourne, Review of *The Philippine Islands*, 359–60; Blair, "Correspondence," 414–15.
17. Gates, "Official Historian," 57–67; Cano, "Blair and Robertson's *The Philippine Islands*," 8–9.
18. Leroy's political interests prevented him from formulating a coherent positon on Spanish colonialism in his published work. Cano, "Blair and Robertson's *The Philippine Islands*," 9–18.
19. Bourne, *Spain in America*.
20. Turner, *Rise of the New West*.
21. Years later Turner remarked, "My interest in the Indians helped (along with Dr. Thwaites' influence) to produce Miss Helen Blair's *Indian Tribes of the Upper Miss. Valley*," Billington, *The Genesis*, 212; Cano, "Blair and Robertson's *The Philippine Islands*," 11–17; Jacobs, *Historical World*, 59. Robertson would later serve as chief of the Philippine library, a position recommended by LeRoy and affirmed by President Taft. For LeRoy's death, see Coleman, "James Alfred LeRoy," xiii–xxviii.
22. Cano, "Blair and Robertson's *The Philippine Islands*," 34. Clark's support is verified by the fact that he published the series. See Blair, *Indian Tribes*, publication credits. After 1913 Turner routinely referenced "Dr. Thwaites" leading to confusion over Thwaites's professional credentials as an historian. Thwaites was awarded an honorary "Doctor of Laws" degree by the University of Wisconsin in 1913. See Woodburn, "Reuben Gold Thwaites," 298–301.
23. "State Obituaries," *Milwaukee Sentinel*, 26 September 1911, 2; "Librarians," 604; Blair, *Indian Tribes*, vol. 1, 19–20.
24. Blair, *Indian Tribes*, dedication.
25. Blair, *Indian Tribes*, vol. 2, 355; Sapir, "Paul Radin," 65–67.
26. Blair, *Indian Tribes*, vol. 1, 21, 25–274, 275–372; Blair, *Indian Tribes*, vol. 2, 13–138, 139–82, 183–248, 249–56.
27. Blair, *Indian Tribes*, vol. 2, 249–56, 257–83, 284–98.
28. Blair, *Indian Tribes*, vol. 1, 18–21. The evidence suggests that Blair was affiliated with a cadre of Indian rights activists in Ripon and Madison, Wisconsin. Notable among these were Sister Lillian, an Episcopal "nun" who helped run the Oneida Indian Reservation

lace-weaving works, and Edward Kremers, a Madison pharmacologist who actively promoted a wintergreen plantation and distillery scheme for Indian employment. See, "Visiting in Oneida," 273–74; Curtiss, *History of the Diocese*, 25; McLester and Skenadore, "Saving Lace," 4, 9; Quinton, "News and Notes," 4.

29. "Emma Helen Blair," 43–44; Review of *The Indian Tribes*, 839–40.

30. Blair, "The Problem," 196–99.

31. The first being Kate A. Everest in 1893. Bogue, *Frederick Jackson Turner*, 66–65; Billington, R. A., *Frederick Jackson Turner*, 96–97, 135; Kinnett, "Miss Kellogg's," 266–99; James, *Notable American Women*, 321–22.

32. James, *Notable American Women*, 320–21; Kinnett, "Miss Kellogg's," 273; Thwaites, *University of Wisconsin*, 345; Nettles, Doane, and Alexander, "Louise Phelps Kellogg," 6–7; Smith, B. G., *Gender of History*, 185–207; James, *Notable American Women*, 321. The high number of women awarded Ph.D. degrees between 1890 and 1935 and their specialized work with documents suggests a modification to the gender of history.

33. Smith, B. G. *Gender of History*, 185–207.

34. Des Jardins, *Women and Historical Enterprise*, 35; Goggin, "Challenging Sexual Discrimination," 772–76; Kinnett, "Miss Kellogg's," 274–75.

35. Kinnett, "Miss Kellogg's," 269–92; Turner, *Reuben Gold Thwaites*, 21–28; James, *Notable American Women*, 321.

36. Turner, *Reuben Gold Thwaites*, 18, 30.

37. Kinnett, "Miss Kellogg's," 276–77; Kellogg, "The Fox Indians," 142–88.

38. Kellogg, "The Fox Indians," 142–43, 146–48, 177–85, 186–88.

39. Kinnett, "Miss Kellogg's," 221–73, 279.

40. Ibid., 275–79. Thwaites died before completion of the *Early Western Travels* series. James, *Notable American Women*, 320–21.

41. Kinnett, "Miss Kellogg's," 277; "Migrations of Wisconsin Indians, Member of State Historical Staff Tells of Early Scenes," *Baraboo Daily News* (Wisc.), 20 April 1912; "Extract from an Old Letter, Visit to a Winnebago Indian Village on the Baraboo River in 1833," *Baraboo Daily News* (Wisc.), 13 May 1912; Kellogg, "Glory of the Morning and the Decorah Family," *Madison Democrat* (Wisc.), 21 February 1912; Kellogg, *Indian Diplomacy*.

42. James, *Notable American Women*, 320–21; Kinnett, "Miss Kellogg's," 275, 277; "Louise Phelps Kellogg," 6; "Marquette University," 231.

43. James, "Indian Diplomacy," 125–42.

44. Kinnett, "Miss Kellogg's," 279–99.

45. Anderson, "Annie Heloise Abel," 1–7, 8–21. Anderson's dissertation is a comprehensive biography of Abel, however I have given precedence to biographical information on Abel contributed by Suzanne Julin in Leckie and Parezo's, *Their Own Frontier*. See Julin, "Annie Heloise Abel," 45–63.

46. Ibid., 22–24.

47. Ibid., 26; Malin, "Frank Heywood Hodder," 115–21; Speer, "Accuracy in History," 60–69. The history of the Kansas slavery debate remained a hot-button issue into the early twentieth century. See Woods, "Integration, Exclusion," 181–98.

48. Malin, "Frank Haywood Hodder," 115–16; Anderson, "Annie Heloise Abel," 26; Julin, "Annie Heloise Abel," 47–48.

49. Abel's sentiments on a corollary between British and American imperialism were elaborated in later writings, notably her collaboration with noted American historian of the British Empire Frank J. Klingberg. See Abel and Klingberg, *A Side-Light on Anglo-American Relations*, v–vi, 1–51. For North American British colonial heritage mirroring the Imperialist or Anglo-Saxionist school of Abel's dissertation mentor, Edward Gaylord Bourne, see Anderson, "Annie Heloise Abel," 62–67. For British nineteenth-century popular and political juxtaposition of British imperialism and American Manifest Destiny, see Tuttle, "Forerunners of

Frederick Jackson Turner," 219–27. For an overview of the humanitarian view of British imperialism, see Ferguson, *Empire*.

50. Julin, "Annie Heloise Abel," 47.

51. Abel, "Indian Reservations in Kansas," 1.

52. Ibid., 1–4, 10, 15–16, 38, and 38n.1. Abel was invited to read her thesis before a meeting of the Kansas State Historical Society in 1902, and it was published by the society's *Transactions* 8. Shortly after, it was submitted to the Yale University Bulkley award committee.

53. Stoke, *Yale University Endowments*, 79; Caughey, et al., "Frank J. Klingberg," 3–7; Anderson, "Annie Heloise Abel," 271; Abel, "Indian Reservations." There is some discrepancy between the Anderson and Abel sources, but much of the confusion stems from equating Abel's bachelor's degree earned in 1898 with the master's degree she earned in 1900. The Kansas State Historical Society editor mistakenly referenced Abel's master's thesis as an article.

54. Julin, "Annie Heloise Abel," 48–49.

55. Anderson, "Annie Heloise Abel," 118, 271; Aeschbacher, "Mississippi Valley Historical Association," 339–53; Billington, R. A., "Tempest in Clio's Teapot," 348–69.

56. Billington, R. A., "Tempest in Clio's Teapot," 348–69. West Coast historians organized a Pacific Coast Branch of the AHA in 1904, largely due to the difficulty and cost of traveling across county to attend AHA meeting on the East Coast. See Garver, "Forty Years," 237–67; Shambaugh, *Proceedings*, 287–316. For a detailed analysis of the early AHA sectional crisis, see Rhea, "Women and Construction Indian Scholarship," 329–38.

57. Des Jardins, *Women and Historical Enterprise*, 97; Jameson, *John Franklin Jameson*, 74–75; Abel, "History of Events," 233–450.

58. Novick, *That Noble Dream*, 57–60, 200–202. For Turner's role in soothing sectional tensions, see Billington, R. A., *Genesis of Frontier Thesis*, 6, 29, 235–36; Billington, R. A., *Frederick Jackson Turner*, 245–47.

59. Anderson, "Annie Heloise Abel," 62–67.

60. Ibid., 65–66.

61. Ibid., 65–66.

62. Ibid., 66; Farrand, "Compromises of Constitution," 479–89.

63. Farrand, "Compromises of Constitution," 483–84. Edward Gaylord Bourne was a principle editor of the *Yale Review*, and the Farrand article used in his Madison-Jefferson seminar cited material used in the Bacon article. See Bacon, N. T., "Some Insular Questions," 159–78. In 1789 the Congress of the republic revised the Northwest Ordinance giving certain powers previously reserved by the old league Congress to the Executive branch. The "federal government" as used here indicates this change.

64. Abel, "History of Events," 233–413, 244.

65. Ibid., 296–321.

66. Ibid., 412.

67. Ibid., 332–43.

68. Anderson, "Annie Heloise Abel," 97–98. Anderson does not identify the author of this criticism, but given that Jameson was editor of AHA publications and the critical phrase exactly mirrors his documented private comments to Andrew C. McLaughlin, it is clear that Jameson was the anonymous critic. Jameson, *John Franklin Jameson*, 74–75.

69. Abel, "Proposals for Indian State," 87–104.

70. Rhodes, *Historical Essays*, 191–200.

71. Adams, G. B. "History and Philosophy," 221–36.

72. Ibid., 224–29, 235–36.

73. Ibid., 236; Abel, "History of Events," 237.

74. Abel, *American Indian as Slaveholder*; Wolgemuth, "Woodrow Wilson," 158–73; Sosna, "South in the Saddle," 30–49; O'Reilly, "Jim Crow Policies," 117–19.

75. Abel, *Indian as Slaveholder*, 14.

76. Ibid., 14–15.

77. Abel, *Official Correspondence James S. Calhoun*, x–xi.

78. Anderson, "Annie Heloise Abel," 271–72; Kelsey, "Annie Heloise Abel-Henderson," 2–3.

79. For Rodman Wanamaker, Joseph Dixon, and the Americanization plan, see Lindstrom, "'Not from the Land Side," 209–27; Barsh, "War and Reconfiguring," 3, 371–410. For Cato Sells and the campaign to allow Indian WWI service, see Tate, "From Scout to Doughboy," 417–32; Barsh, "American Indians," 276–303.

80. Blight, *Race and Reunion*, 1–25, 359–61, chaps. 7–10; Abel, *American Indian As Participant*, 113–98, 210–72, 300–28, 334–35.

81. Novick, *That Noble Dream*, 74–77; Foner, *Forever Free*, xxii–xxviii; Abel, *American Indian under Reconstruction*, passim.

82. Abel, ed., *Chardon's Journal*; Abel, ed., *Tabeau's Narrative*.

83. Eaton, *John Ross*, pref.; "In Hall of Fame, Pioneer," *The Oklahoman*, 7 July 1936, 2.

84. Wright, "Rachel Caroline Eaton," 509; Ken Willhoite, "War Changed Future of G. W. Eaton," *Claremore Daily Progress*, 20 October, 2014; Starr, *History Cherokee Indians*, 666; Benedict, *Muskogee*, vol. 2, 405.

85. "Death of Col. Morgan," *Democrat-Voice* (Coleman, Tex.), 14 March 1924, 6; "Funeral of Capt. Milton M. Boggess," *Waco Weekly News* (Tex.), 4 August 1893, 4; Wright, "Rachel Caroline Eaton," 509.

86. "More About Cattle," *Indian Chieftain*, (Vinita, IT.), 20 August 1885, 2; "Radium Town, the Smell of Success," *Claremore Daily Progress*, 22 March 2008; Ken Willhoite, "War Changed Future of G. W. Eaton," *Claremore Daily Progress*, 20 October 2014; Hayes, *Contributions to Economic Geography*, 227; "Much Was Accomplished, Road to Radium Wells," *Claremore Daily Progress*, 16 February 1907, 1.

87. Wright, "Rachel Caroline Eaton," 509; Eaton, "Legend of Battle," 369.

88. Shirk, *Oklahoma Place Names*, 52; "Historical Notes, Park Hill," 99; Wright, "Notes on Life," 348–55.

89. "Death of Dr. Emmet Starr," 129–32; Starr, *History Cherokee Indians*, 235; Wright, *Rachel Caroline Eaton*, 509–10.

90. "Christmas Wedding," *Claremore Daily Messenger*, 23 December 1901, 1; "Burns-Eaton," *Claremore Daily Messenger*, 26 December 1901, 1; Starr, *History Cherokee Indians*, 235; "Prof. J. A. Burns," *Claremore Daily Messenger*, 19 January 1895, 3; "New Principal Selected," *Claremore Daily Messenger*, 4 June 1898, 3; Benedict, *Muskogee*, 601, 639; Richards, W. B., *Oklahoma Red Book*, 501; "Reunion Prompts Look Back," *Nowata Star* (Okla.), 9 June 2010, 1; "Sageeyah Items," *Claremore Daily Messenger*, 21 October 1917, 3; "Citizen's Hotel Company of Nowata," *Daily Oklahoman*, 1 April 1911, 1.

91. The chronology of events spanning the period from 1905 to 1914 is difficult to follow and requires careful cross-referencing with the following sources: "Mr. and Mrs. J. A. Burns of the Nowata Schools," *Coffeyville Weekly Journal* (Kans.), 28 July 1905, 5; "Prof. J. A. Burns," *Claremore Daily Messenger*, 19 June 1895, 3; Benedict, *Muskogee*, vol. 2, 405–406; *Annual Register of the University of Chicago, 1912–1913*, 461; *Annual Register of the University of Chicago, 1920–1921*, 520; Rowland, *Official and Statistical Register*, 223; Eaton, "John Ross," 1; Eaton, *John Ross and the Cherokee Indians* (1914), 210.

92. Benedict, *Muskogee*, vol. 2, 405–406; Winslow, "Dormitory Discipline," 112; "Mrs. J. A. Burns," *Tulsa World*, 4 June 1916, 7; "Nowata," *Tulsa World*, 21 October 1917, 41; "Mrs. Lawson Appoints Vice Chairman for Defense Council Work," *Oklahoma State Register*, 26 July 1917, 4; Benedict, *Muskogee*, vol. 2, 406; "Obituary, Joel Merrit Eaton," *Claremore Progress*, 30 March 1922, 4.

93. Benedict, *Muskogee*, vol. 2, 405–406; "The Claremore Schools Open," *Claremore Messenger*, 19 September 1919, 1; Eaton, *John Ross and the Cherokees* (1914), 1–213; Eaton, *John Ross and the Cherokees* (1921), 1–153.

94. Benedict, *Muskogee*, vol. 2, 406; "Democratic Convention Held Here Saturday," *Claremore Daily Progress*, 5 February 1920, 1; Mills, "Head of Rogers County Schools Raised in State," *Tulsa World*, 10 September 1922, 2; *School District no. 17 v. Eaton Co. Supt.* 1924 OK 184, 223 P. 857, 97 Okla. 177.

95. Wright, "Rachel Caroline Eaton," 509–10; "In Hall of Fame," *Daily Oklahoman*, 7 July 1936, 2; Matthews, *Twenty Thousand Mornings*, intro., xxxvi n. 39; John M. Oskison Rejection, John Ross Story, 1933, box 17, folder 6, University of Oklahoma Libraries, Western History Collections, University of Oklahoma Press Collection (hereafter OU WHC UOP Collection); Rachel Caroline Eaton Rejection, "A History of the Cherokee," 1935, box 9, folder 10, OU WHC UOP Collection.

96. "Prof. Edward Martin Sheppard," 273–75.

97. Eaton, "John Ross," 1–52; Eaton, *John Ross and the Cherokees* (1914), 4–5; Eaton, *John Ross and the Cherokees* (1921), 3–4.

98. Foreman, "Aunt Eliza," 53; "Sequoyah Historical Society," *Claremore Messenger*, 3 April 1908, 1; "Historical Society," *Claremore Progress*, 9 February 1912, 5; Eaton, *John Ross and the Cherokees* (1914, 1921), pref.

99. Eaton, "John Ross;" "Ivey Is Compiling Cherokee History," *Tahlequah Arrow*, 17 August 1911, 2; Quinton, "Col. Gus Ivey," 1; Parins, *Literacy and Intellectual Life*, 145–49; Posey, *Fus Fixico Letters*, 30, Gideon, *Indian Territory*, 143. Between August and September 1911 the following Oklahoma newspapers published notices about Ivey's publication plan: *Calumet Weekly, Harold Sentinel, New Era, Eldorado Courier, Hollis Tribune, Lexington Leader, Sayre Headlight, Stroud Democrat*.

100. "Historical Society," *Claremore Messenger*, 9 February 1912, 5; "Mrs. Caroline Eaton," *Claremore Messenger*, 3 October 1913, 5; "John Ross and the Cherokees," *Claremore Messenger*, 18 December 1914, 1.

101. Eaton, *John Ross and the Cherokee Indians*, dedication, passim.

102. Des Jardins, *Women and Historical Enterprise*, 97; Dodd, *Expansion and Conflict*, 328; Eaton, *John Ross and the Cherokees*, 209.

103. Eaton, "John Ross"; Eaton, *John Ross and the Cherokees* (1914); Eaton, *John Ross and the Cherokees* (1921).

104. Wright, "Rachel Caroline Eaton," 510; author's correspondence with family of Dr. Rachel C. Eaton, 27 March 2015.

105. Savoie Lottinville to Rachel Caroline Eaton, 26 June 1935, box 17, folder 6, OU WHC UOP Collection, 1928–38; "Will Go to Pittsburg," *Cleveland Enterprise*, 29 March 1917, 1.

106. Rachel Caroline Eaton to Savoie Lottinville, 28 June 1935, box 17, folder 6, OU WHC UOP Collection, 1928–38.

107. Savoie Lottinville to Rachel Caroline Eaton, July 1, 1935, box 17, folder 6, OU WHC UOP Collection, 1928–38.

108. Rachel Caroline Eaton to Savoie Lottinville, 9 August 1935, box 17, folder 6, OU WHC UOP Collection, 1928–38.

109. Joseph A. Brandt to Rachel Caroline Eaton, 10 August 1935, box 17, folder 6, OU WHC UOP Collection, 1928–38.

110. Joseph A. Brandt to Rachel Caroline Eaton, 8 October 1935, box 17, folder 6, OU WHC UOP Collection, 1928–38.

111. Joseph A. Brandt to Rachel Caroline Eaton, 18 November 18, 1935, box 17, folder 6, OU WHC UOP Collection, 1928–38.

112. Leckie, *Angie Debo*, 60–70.

113. Morris L. Wardell, *Political History of the Cherokee Nation*, 1938, box 52, folder 3, OU WHC UOP Collection, 1928–38; materials relating to *A Political History of the Cherokee Nation*, record group 7, University of Oklahoma Libraries, Western History Collections, Morris L. Wardell Collection; Litton, Review of *A Political History of the Cherokee Nation*, 378–80; Joseph A. Brandt to Rachel Caroline Eaton, 18 November 1935, box 17, folder 6, OU WHC UOP Collection, 1928–38.

114. John M. Oskison, "Unconquerable, the Story of John Ross, Chief of the Cherokees, 1828–1866," Jesse Bartley Milam Papers, University of Tulsa, Special Collections; M. L. Wardell, reader report for John M. Oskison manuscript, 7 January 1933; Grant Foreman to Joseph A. Brandt, 27 February 1933; James J. Hill, reader report for John M. Oskison manuscript, 15 March 1933; John M. Oskison to Joseph A. Brandt, 20 May 1933, box 9, folder 23, OU WHC UOP Collection, 1928–38.

115. J. M. Oskison, regarding rejection of John Ross manuscript, box 9, folder 9–10, OU WHC UOP Collection, 1928–38.

116. M. L. Wardell, reader report for John M. Oskison manuscript, 7 January 1933, box 9, folder 23, OU WHC UOP Collection, 1928–38; Joseph A. Brandt to Rachel Caroline Eaton, 18 November 1935, box 17, folder 6, OU WHC UOP Collection, 1928–38.

117. Joseph A. Brandt to Rachel Caroline Eaton, 18 November 1935, box 17, folder 6, OU WHC UOP Collection, 1928–38. Based on a comparative review of Eaton's 1914 and 1921 publications and John Oskison's 1933 manuscript, Eaton's was by far the better text.

118. Abel, Review of *John Ross and the Cherokee Indians*, 672–73; Dodd (unsigned), Review of *John Ross and the Cherokee Indians*, 293–94. Author's correspondence with Rachel Caroline Eaton family, 19 October 2013.

119. Debo, "Southern Refugees," 255–66.

CHAPTER 8

1. "Cherokee Nation Dissolved," 237–39.

2. Much of the material on Anna L. Lewis came from an earlier published article. The author would like to thank Dr. Lynn Musslewhite, editor of the *Great Plains Journal* for his gracious permission to reuse this material. Rhea, "Creating a Place," 26–51; Winnidell Gravitt Wilson, "Anna Lezola Lewis, Ph.D. 1885–1961," Anna Lewis Collection, Nash Library, University of Science and Arts of Oklahoma, Chickasha, Oklahoma (hereafter USAO). The Wilson piece is a short unpublished biography of Anna Lewis written by her niece, Mrs. Wilson. Mrs. Wilson devoted much of her time and energy to documenting and promoting Anna Lewis's legacy. See also Semple and Gravitt, "Grady Lewis," 301.

3. "Indian Relics and Early Pictures Contained in the College Museum," clipping, n.d.; Lewis, "Lecture on Creek Indians"; Lewis, "Native Americans Places in History," Anna Lewis Collection, Nash Library, USAO; Lewis, "Nunih Waiya," 214–20.

4. This is reflected in several of Lewis's surviving history lectures from her days at the Oklahoma College for Women. See Lewis, "The Historic Struggle for Equality between the Sexes," "Women's Role in Democracy," "Democracy and Education," "Women's Achievements and Responsibilities," all in the Anna Lewis Collection, Nash Library, USAO; Spear, "Choctaw Indian Education," 183–84.

5. It is not clear whether Lewis received financial support from the Choctaw Nation for her studies at Mary Connor Junior College, however, even with out of state costs, tuition at Mary Connor Junior College would have been more economical than tuition at either of the Oklahoma territorial universities. See Morris, Goins, and McReynolds, *Historical Atlas of Oklahoma*, 64; Spear, "Choctaw Indian Education," 154–55; *Why Home-Seekers and Investors Should Come to Lamar County and Paris, Texas*; Connor, ed. *Dear America*, 14–21, 90–93, 117–25; Neville, *History Lamar County*, 1–95; Connor, *Dear America*, passim; Wilson, "Anna Lezola Lewis." Anna Lewis Collection, Nash Library, USAO.

6. Wilson, "Anna Lezola Lewis," Anna Lewis Collection, Nash Library, USAO; Gravitt, "Anna Lewis," 326–29; Goins, Goble, *Historical Atlas of Oklahoma*, 118–20, 190; Spear, "Choctaw Indian Education."

7. Wilson, "Anna Lezola Lewis," Anna Lewis Collection, Nash Library, USAO; Don Miller, Stroup-Lewis Family Archive; Pauline Stroup Hoyle, Stroup-Lewis Family Archive.
8. Debo, *Rise and Fall*, 271–90; Hastain, *Choctaw-Chickasaw Deeds*, 807.
9. Contradictory evidence obscures when Lewis sold her allotment and for how much her land was sold. Wilson, "Anna Lezola Lewis," Anna Lewis Collection, Nash Library, USAO.
10. Kidwell, *Choctaws in Oklahoma*, 148; Morris, Goins, McReynolds, *Historical Atlas of Oklahoma*, 71; Wilson, "Anna Lezola Lewis," Anna Lewis Collection, Nash Library, USAO.
11. Wilson, "Anna Lezola Lewis," Anna Lewis Collection, Nash Library, USAO; *Kentucky College for Women; Danville in the Blue Grass; History of Kentucky College for Women*, Kentucky College for Women, Special Collections, Grace Doherty Library, Centre College, Danville, Ky.; Lewis, A. F., *History Higher Education Kentucky*, 247–49.
12. Dennis, *Lessons in Progress*, 1–42; Breckinridge, *An Address Delivered*; Young, *Fourth Annual Report of the Kentucky Colonization Society*; *A Year in the Life of Caldwell College*; Wilson, *Fifty Years*, 3–6, 64–107, 108–67, 233–59, 269–80; Sims, *Natural History*, 79–94.
13. Wilson, "Anna Lezola Lewis," Anna Lewis Collection, Nash Library, USAO.
14. A common misconception holds that Oklahoma, or a portion thereof, officially existed as Indian Territory. The lands of the Five Nations (Choctaw, Chickasaw, Cherokee, Muskogee [Creek], and Seminole) did not comprise a legally recognized territory of the United States, although the region was commonly known as "Indian Territory." See Shirk, *Oklahoma Place Names*, vii–viii; Scales and Goble, *Oklahoma Politics*, 3–20; Kappler, ed., *Indian Treaties*, 910–14, 918–29, 931–36, 942–46; Goble, *Progressive Oklahoma*, 43–114, 187–202; and Lewis, "Creek Indians," "Native American's Place in History," "Oklahoma Women Pioneers," "Women's Achievements and Responsibilities," all in the Anna Lewis Collection, Nash Library, USAO.
15. Wilson, "Anna Lezola Lewis," Anna Lewis Collection, Nash Library, USAO; Gravitt, "Anna Lewis," 328.
16. Anna Lewis's niece Winnidell Gravitt Wilson, writing some fifty years after the fact, understandably presented conflicting dates and events that must be put into chronological order. Through intertextual comparisons and cross-textual analysis most of the contradictions can be resolved. Wilson, "Anna Lezola Lewis," Anna Lewis Collection, Nash Library, USAO.
17. The A.B. degree is for classical studies majors, see *Studies in Classical Philology*.
18. Hastain, *Choctaw-Chickasaw Deeds*, 818; Bannon, *Herbert Eugene Bolton*, 97–98.
19. Bannon, *Herbert Eugene Bolton*, app. B, 88–89; Lewis, "History of the Cattle Industry in Oklahoma."
20. Aldridge, *Life on a Ranch*; Hough, *Story of Cowboy*; Paxson, *Last American Frontier*; von Richthofen, *Cattle Raising on the Plains*; and Siringo, *A Texas Cowboy*; Lewis, "History of the Cattle Industry," 1–17, 38–55, 84–89.
21. Lewis, "History of the Cattle Industry,"18.
22. Ibid., 3–4, 12–17.
23. Ibid., 38–55.
24. Ibid., 56–83.
25. Ibid., 83–85.
26. Ibid., 86–87, 89.
27. Wilson, "Anna Lezola Lewis," Anna Lewis Collection, Nash Library, USAO.
28. Gittinger, *University of Oklahoma*, 140. Lewis officially received her master's degree from Berkeley in 1918. See Gravitt, "Anna Lewis," 326–29; Edward Everett Dale, handwritten roster of personal friends listing "Lewis, Anna, Okla. College for Women Chickasha, Okla." ca. 1917, University of Oklahoma Libraries, Western History Collections, Edward Everett Dale Collection. Notably, Angie Debo does not appear on Dale's list.

29. Lewis, "La Harpe's," 331–49; Lewis, "French Interests," 253–68; Lewis, "Oklahoma As Part," 45–58; Lewis, "Du Tisne's Expedition," 319–23. Lewis's access to publication through the *Chronicles of Oklahoma* was facilitated by her friend and fellow Choctaw citizen Muriel Wright, who later served as the *Chronicles* editor. Wright's blessing proved necessary for publication or favorable mention in the Oklahoma Historical Society's flagship monthly publication—as Angie Debo would find a few years later. See Leckie, *Angie Debo*, 55–57; and Fisher, "Muriel H. Wright," 2–29.

30. Cowgill, "Alumnae Leaders," 288–89.

31. Anna Lewis to Dr. E. E. Dale, 11 January 1929, University of Oklahoma Libraries, Western History Collections, Edward Everett Dale Collection; Gibson, *West Wind*, 126, 264.

32. As Angie Debo would note in *And Still the Waters Run*, Robert L. Owen was one of the principal Cherokee conspirators implicated in fraudulent Indian land deals. Ever conscious of political ramifications, Dale would not have taken up a subject that might offend Owen. More so, given Abel's publication and Dale's sensitivity to gender roles, it seems likely that he would not have written on the subject after finding the scholarship dominated by women historians. Dale, "History Live Stock Industry." Dale's first draft was completed in 1920. Unlike Lewis, Dale interpreted the Oklahoma cattle industry as one of several beneficial stages in the state's march toward civilization. See also Dale, *Range Cattle Industry*, chaps. 1–2.

33. Gibson, *West Wind*, 142, 153–54, 176–77. Dale translated and edited a volume of French correspondence. See Dale, *Lafayette Letters*.

34. Gibson, *West Wind*, 402–403.

35. Lewis apparently hired Vandergrift on earlier excursions to bring back copies for her *Chronicles of Oklahoma* articles. Lewis, "Early History of Arkansas," pref.; Ogden and Sluiter, *Greater America*, app. A, 667; Bloom, Review of *Along the Arkansas*, 117. See also Vandergrift notes for Anna Lewis on the *legajo* copies made in Seville, Spain, Anna Lewis Collection, Nash Library, USAO.

36. *Sooner Magazine*, 392; Wilson, "Anna Lezola Lewis," Anna Lewis Collection, Nash Library, USAO.

37. Theses for M.A. and Ph.D. Degrees in the OU Department of History, 1912–1933, A. K. Christian, University of Oklahoma, personal library of David W. Levy, A. K. Christian Collection; Savage, "Oklahoma College for Women," 176–78; Wilson, "Anna Lezola Lewis." Anna Lewis Collection, Nash Library, USAO; Shafer, "USAO—The Impossible Dream," 91–115.

38. Lewis and Taylor, *Problems in Oklahoma History*, pref.

39. Joseph A. Brandt to Anna L. Lewis, 16 December 1931, box 9, folder 2, University of Oklahoma Libraries, WHC, University of Oklahoma Press Collection (hereafter OU WHC UOP Collection), 1928–38; Tinkle, *American Original*, 123–31.

40. Jesse L. Rader to Joseph A. Brandt, 10 September 1931, box 2, folder 9, OU WHC UOP Collection, 1928–38.

41. Alfred B. Thomas, reader report, 14 December 1931, box 2, folder 9, OU WHC UOP Collection, 1928–38.

42. Goins and Goble, *Historical Atlas of Oklahoma*, 6–7; Lewis, *Along the Arkansas*, pref., 6–7.

43. Alfred B. Thomas, reader report, 14 December 1931, box 2, folder 9, OU WHC UOP Collection, 1928–38; Lewis, *Along the Arkansas*, 7, 14, 18, 21, 35–36, 40, 43, 45–46, 61–86, 48–49, 50, 55–59, 63–66, 75, 81–88, 98–99, 106, 109, 112, 128, 140–49, 150–55, 175, 190.

44. See introduction and publication information, Anna Lewis, *Along the Arkansas*.

45. "Books Recently Added to Library," 226; Walter, "Lansing Bartlett Bloom," 93–94; Bloom, Review of *Along the Arkansas*, 16–117.

46. Bloom, Review *Forgotten Frontiers*, 277–79; Bloom, Review of *Companions on the Trail*, 595–96; Bloom, Review of *Oklahoma*, 597–98.

47. Anna Lewis provided a short overview of her "post-colonial" thesis in a 1931 article. See Cowgill, "Alumnae Leaders," 287–89.

48. Lewis, *Along the Arkansas*, pref., 21–33, 171–93.
49. Bloom, Review of *Along the Arkansas*, 117.
50. In the early decades of professionalization academic historians often called on their students to conduct research and occasionally appropriated their scholarship. See Novick, *That Noble Dream*, 47–86; Wilson, "Anna Lezola Lewis," Anna Lewis Collection, Nash Library, USAO; Gravitt, "Anna Lewis"; Newspaper clipping, n.d., McAlester, Oklahoma, Anna Lewis Collection, Nash Library, USAO.
51. Laughlin, *Hidden Treasures*, 23–24.
52. Wright, "Brief Review," 267–86; Muriel Wright to Mr. Ponce Jemison, 19 November 1936, Muriel H. Wright Collection, USAO; Loughlin, *Hidden Treasures*, 23–24; Lewis, "Native Americans Place in History," "Oklahoma Women Pioneers," "Role of Historian, History and Education in Preventing War and Racial Hatred," "The Teaching of History," "Historical Struggle for Equality Between the Sexes," "Women's Achievements and Respectability," all in the Anna Lewis Collection, Nash Library, USAO.
53. Muriel Wright to Elise D. Hand, 21 January 1936; Elise D. Hand to Muriel Wright, 19 February 1936, Muriel H. Wright Collection, USAO.
54. Muriel Wright to Ponce Jemison, 19 November 1936; Muriel Wright to W. N. P. Dailey, 19 November 1936; Muriel Wright to Susie Peters, 2 October 1936; Muriel Wright to Miss Gibbons, 22 August 1936; Muriel Wright to James Brooks Wright, 22 April 1936; Muriel Wright to Joe Sprague, 20 January 1936; Lee L. Harkins to Muriel Wright, n.d., Muriel H. Wright Collection, USAO.
55. Loughlin, *Hidden Treasures*, 27–29; Muriel Wright to Lee Harkins, 8 April 1936; Muriel Wright to W. N. P. Dailey, 19 November 1936; Sarah Gertrude Knott to Mr. Logan, 5 October 1936; Muriel Wright to Sarah Gertrude Knott, 21 April 1936; Muriel Wright to Peter J. Hudson, 17 September 1936, Muriel H. Wright Collection, USAO. For "playing Indian," see Deloria, *Playing Indian*, 95–153; Fischer, "Muriel H. Wright," 5–7; Loughlin, *Hidden Treasures*, 27–29.
56. Ellen Borden was "an avid student of Indian history and culture." See Fischer, "Muriel H. Wright," 6–10; Kammen, *Mystic Cords of Memory*, 8.
57. Fischer, "Muriel H. Wright," 11–13. According to Patricia Loughlin, Wright blamed her academic disappointments on the outbreak of WWI. See Loughlin, *Hidden Treasures*, 58.
58. Fischer, "Muriel H. Wright," 12–13, 22–23; Loughlin, *Hidden Treasures*, 25.
59. Debo, "To Establish Justice," 405.
60. Schrems and Wolff, "Politics and Libel," 184, 203.
61. Ibid., 186; Leckie, *Angie Debo*, 17–18.
62. Leckie, *Angie Debo*, 18–19.
63. Nation, *Use and Need*, 319–32; Leckie, *Angie Debo*, 20.
64. Leckie, *Angie Debo*, 21–22; Musslewhite and Crawford, *One Woman's*, chaps. 2–4, 7–10, 12.
65. Leckie, *Angie Debo*, 22–23; Schrems and Wolff, "Politics and Libel," 186.
66. Leckie, *Angie Debo*, 24–25, 29; Schrems and Wolff, "Politics and Libel," 186.
67. Leckie, *Angie Debo*, 30–31; Angie Debo American History Papers, 1915–1918, box 6 folder 25–47, Angie Debo Papers, Special Collections and University Archives, Oklahoma State University Libraries.
68. Chapman, C. E., "The Native Sons," 398–94; Bushnell and Coatsworth, "J. Fred Rippy," 103–104.
69. Rippy, "Mexican Projects," 291–317; Rippy, "Indians ofSouthwest," 363–96.
70. Debo, "Class Notes, Dr. Rippy, The Americas in World Affairs," box 6, folder 25–47, Angie Debo Papers, Special Collections and University Archives, Oklahoma State University Libraries; Debo, "Class Notes, Dr. Quincy Wright, American Diplomacy 64," box 6, folder 48 and box 7, folder 6, Angie Debo Papers, Special Collections and University Archives,

Oklahoma State University Libraries; Rippy and Debo, "Historical Background," 71–169; Leckie, *Angie Debo*, 32–38.

71. Leckie, *Angie Debo*, 36–38.
72. Rhea, "Creating a Place," 27–28.
73. Lowitt, "Dear Miss Debo," 374–75; Leckie, *Angie Debo*, 38–42.
74. Leckie, *Angie Debo*, 38–44.
75. Lowitt, "Dear Mrs. Debo," 376–77; Leckie, *Angie Debo*, 50–51.
76. Angie Debo, "Edward Everett Dale, Historian of Progress," box 6, folder 48 and box 7, folder 6, Angie Debo Papers, Special Collections and University Archives, Oklahoma State University Libraries.
77. Author's discussion with Dale biographers, Richard Lowitt, 8 February 2009, and David Levy, 9 March 2009.
78. Angie Debo, "Edward Everett Dale, Historian of Progress," box 6, folder 48 and box 7, folder 6, Angie Debo Papers, Special Collections and University Archives, Oklahoma State University Libraries.
79. Ibid. Gibson, *West Wind*, 287–336.
80. Angie Debo, "Edward Everett Dale, Historian of Progress," box 6, folder 48 and box 7, folder 6, Angie Debo Papers, Special Collections and University Archives, Oklahoma State University Libraries.
81. Dale, *Tales of the Tepee*, iii–v, 62–65. In this children's book Dale revealed a range of assimilationist attitudes. The story of "Wynema," the tireless peacemaker, reflected Dale's own sentiments on the "Indian Question."
82. Robinson, J. H., "Newer Ways," 245–55.
83. Debo, "Southern Refugees," 255–66; Leckie, *Angie Debo*, 46.
84. Reese, "Dr. Anna Lewis," 428–49. Leckie did not mention Grady Lewis or his effect on Debo.
85. "Old Choctaw Capitol to get New Life," *Daily Oklahoman*, 19 December 1928, 11; "Choctaws to Talk Capitol Removal," *Daily Oklahoman*, 23 February 1929, 19; "The Old Choctaw Council House," *Daily Oklahoman*, 16 June 1929, 65; "Indians Call State Parley, Choctaw Tribesmen Moved to Observe Anniversary of Removal to West," *Daily Oklahoman*, 28 August 1930, 17; "Choctaw Indians to Hold Meetings, Final Action on Affairs of Tribe Slated," *Daily Oklahoman*, 8 September 1930, 12; "Choctaw Indians to Meet in Durant, Ben Dwight, New Chief Calls Meeting, Oct. 22," *Daily Oklahoman*, 21 September 1930, 96; "Indian Delegates to Session Named, Choctaws, Chickasaws Observe Treaty Anniversary," *Daily Oklahoman*, 28 September 1930, 12.
86. "Indians Need No Memorial Will Believes," *Daily Oklahoman*, 21 October 1930, 9.
87. "Five Tribes Meet Today," *Daily Oklahoman*, 22 October 1930, 4. On October 27, 1930, Briggs sent a letter to former Oklahoma U.S. congresswoman Alice Robertson asking for assistance in securing funds for a comprehensive history of the Five Tribes. Eugene S. Briggs to Alice Robertson, 27 October 1930, Alice M. Robertson Collection, McFarlin Library, Special Collections, University of Tulsa.
88. Thoburn, *Standard History*, 1362–63; *Survey of Conditions of the Indians*, 5367–71.
89. "Five Tribes Meet Today; Durant Indian Host as U.S. Settlement Is Talked; Two Sessions Set," *Daily Oklahoman*, 22 October 1930, 4; "Federal Loan Is Tribal Aim, Relief Fund of $5,500,000 Sought by Choctaws, Chickasaws," *Daily Oklahoman*, 18 December 1930, 11. The Choctaw sovereignty renaissance was also visible in Anna Lewis's purchase of the old Tuskahoma Female Seminary remains. Lewis hired workmen to salvage the stone and build a retirement home. Kelly Brown to author, 10 March, 2009; "Former Pupil Buys Indian School Site," *Daily Oklahoman*, 20 January 1932, 1.
90. Kidwell, *Choctaws in Oklahoma*, 151–61. Grady Lewis's research into Choctaw tribal history began in the 1920s; his research spanning 1930–33 reflected preparation for the Leased

District case. See Semple and Gravitt, "Grady Lewis," 301–305; Chapman, B. B.," Day in Court," 1–21.

91. Reese, "Dr. Anna Lewis," 428–49.

92. Virginia Lee Warren, "Communal Life Declared Best for Indian, Choctaw Lawyer Here to Back Thomas-Rodgers Bill," *Washington Post*, 25 April 1935, 14.

93. Reese, "Dr. Anna Lewis," 442. Over the next three decades Grady Lewis continued to litigate the Leased District claim. In 1951 Lewis won a final settlement. See Chapman, B. B., "Day in Court," 1–21.

94. Debo, *Rise and Fall*, x; Angie Debo, "Personal Diary, January 1941," box 2, folder 27, and box 5, folder 5, Angie Debo Papers, Special Collections and University Archives, Oklahoma State University Libraries; Debo, " Dedication to Memory," 215–18; Clark, "Grant Foreman," 226–42; Leckie, *Angie Debo*, 46–47.

95. Lowitt, "Dear Miss Debo," 374–78.

96. Debo, "History of the Choctaw Nation," pref.

97. Lowitt, "Dear Miss Debo," 376.

98. Leckie, *Angie Debo*, 31–34; Lowitt, "Dear Miss Debo," 370–78.

99. Debo, *Rise and Fall*, 1–58; Lowitt, "Dear Miss Debo," 377–88.

100. Lowitt, "Dear Miss Debo," 387.

101. Richardson, Review of *Rise and Fall*, 229–30.

102. Lewis, Review of *Rise and Fall*, 409–10.

103. Ibid.; Lewis, "History of Cattle Industry," 1–14.

104. Wright, Review of *Rise and Fall*, 108–20.

105. See Lewis, "History of Cattle Industry," and Lewis, Review of *Rise and Fall*.

106. Muriel Wright to Svnnih, 22 April 1936, Muriel H. Wright Collection, USAO. Pronounced "Sănny," Svnnih was a pet name that translates into English as Sonny. Author interview with Mrs. Eleanor Caldwell, 14 November 2012, Choctaw School of Language, Choctaw Nation of Oklahoma.

107. Muriel Wright to Aunt Anna, 22 April 1936, Muriel H. Wright Collection, USAO.

108. Angie Debo, "Personal Diary, 16 January 1941," box 2, folder 27 and box 5, folder 5, Angie Debo Papers, Special Collections and University Archives, Oklahoma State University Libraries.

109. Leckie, *Angie Debo*, 60–61, "Angie Debo," 14.

110. Gibson, *West Wind*, 126.

111. Schrems and Wolff, "Politics and Libel," 184–200.

112. Debo, *And Still the Waters Run*, x, xi; Leckie, *Angie Debo*, 60–70.

113. Leckie, *Angie Debo*, 66–76.

114. Schrems and Wolff, "Politics and Libel," 184–203.

115. Ibid., 197–202.

116. Angie Debo, "Indian Policy as a Problem in Colonial Administration," box 22, folder 47–77, Angie Debo Papers, Special Collections and University Archives, Oklahoma State University Libraries.

117. John Collier to Angie Debo, 8 December 1941, box 2, folder 27 and box 5, folder 5, Angie Debo Papers, Special Collections and University Archives, Oklahoma State University Libraries.

118. Abel, Review of *And Still the Waters Run*, 464–66.

119. Ibid., 466.

BIBLIOGRAPHY

PRIMARY SOURCES

Manuscript and Archival Sources

American Baptist Historical Society, Atlanta, Georgia
    Women's Baptist Home Mission Society Minutes, First Baptist Church, Philadelphia
Don Miller, Stroup-Lewis Family Archive, Ardmore, Oklahoma
Kentucky College for Women, Centre College, Grace Doherty Library Special Collections, Danville, Kentucky
Massachusetts Historical Society, Boston, Massachsuetts
    Caroline Wells Healey Dall Papers
National Anthropological Archives, Smithsonian Institution, Washington, D.C.
    Alice Fletcher and Francis La Flesche Papers
    Records of the Bureau of American Ethnology
    Records of the Bureau of Indian Affairs
Oklahoma State University Library, Stillwater, Oklahoma
    Angie Debo Collection
Pauline Stroup Hoyle, Stroup-Lewis Family Archive, Warren, Arkansas
University of Oklahoma, Norman, Oklahoma
  Dr. David Levy, A. K. Christian Collection
  Western History Collections
    Angie Debo Collection
    Edward Everett Dale Collection
    University of Oklahoma Press Collection
    Morris L. Wardell Collection
University of Science and Arts of Oklahoma, Chickasha, Oklahoma
  Anna Lewis Collection
  Mary Jane Brown Collection
  Muriel H. Wright Collection
University of Tulsa, Tulsa, Oklahoma, McFarlin Library, Special Collections

John M. Oskison Collection
Alice M. Robertson Collection

Books

Abel, Annie Heloise. *The American Indian As Participant in the Civil War.* Cleveland, Ohio: The Arthur H. Clark Company, 1919.

———. *The American Indian As Slaveholder and Secessionist: An Omitted Chapter in the Diplomatic History of the Southern Confederacy.* Cleveland, Ohio: The Arthur H. Clark Company, 1915.

———. *The American Indian under Reconstruction.* Cleveland, Ohio: The Arthur H. Clark Company, 1925.

Adams, Charles Francis, ed. *Memoirs of John Quincy Adams.* Vol. 10. Philadelphia: J. B. Lippencott, 1876.

Adams, Henry. *The Life of Albert Gallatin.* Philadelphia: J. B. Lippencott, 1879.

Adams, John Quincy. *Speech of John Quincy Adams, Upon the Right of People to Petition.* New York: Arno Press & The New York Times, 1969.

———. *History of the United States of America.* Vol. 1–2. New York: Charles Scribner's Sons, 1889.

Adams, Herbert Baxter. *American Historical Association: Officers, Act of Incorporation, Constitution, List of Members, Historical Societies in the United States.* Washington, D.C.: American Historical Association, 1894.

American Annual Cyclopedia and Register of Important Facts, The. New York: D. Appleton and Company, 1869.

Andreas, Alfred Theodore. *History of the State of Nebraska.* Chicago: Western Historical Co., 1882.

Annual Catalogue of Ripon College for the Graduate Year 1916–1917. Ripon, Wisc.: Ripon College, 1917.

Annual Meeting and Report of the Women's National Indian Association. Philadelphia: Grant & Faires, 1883.

Annual Meeting and Report of the Women's National Indian Association. Philadelphia: Grant & Faires, 1884.

Annual Meeting and Report of the Women's National Indian Association. Philadelphia: Grant & Faires, 1885.

Annual Meeting and Report of the Women's National Indian Association. Philadelphia: Royal Printing, 1886.

Annual Meeting and Report of the Women's National Indian Association. Philadelphia: Royal Printing, 1887.

Annual Meeting and Report of the Women's National Indian Association. Philadelphia: J. A. Wilbour, 1888.

Annual Register of the University of Chicago, 1912–13. Chicago: University of Chicago Press, 1912.

Annual Register of the University of Chicago, 1920–21. Chicago: University of Chicago Press, 1920.

Annual Report of the American Home Mission Society, 1876. New York: American Home Mission Society, 1877.

Annual Report of the Association for the Advancement of Women, 1880. Dedham, Mass.: W. L. Wardle, 1880.

Annual Report of the Association for the Advancement of Women, 1881. Boston: Cochrane & Sampson, 1882.

Bacon, Edwin Monroe. *Men of Progress: One Thousand Biographical Sketches.* Boston: New England Magazine, 1896.

Bancroft, George. *History of the Colonization of the United States of America.* New York: D. Appleton and Company, 1898.

Bancroft, Hubert Howe, ed. *Native Races of the Pacific States.* San Francisco: A. L. Bancroft & Company, 1882.

Baptist Home Missions, 1832–1882. New York: Baptist Home Mission Rooms, 1883.
Barrett, Selah Hibbard. *Memoirs of Eminent Preachers of the Free Will Baptist Denomination*. Rutland, Ohio: Selah Hibbard Barrett, 1874.
Beard, Augustus Field. *A Crusade of Brotherhood: A History of the American Missionary Association*. Boston: The Pilgrim Press, 1909.
Beecher, Catherine E. *An Essay on Slavery and Abolition, with Reference to the Duty of American Females*. Freeport, N.Y.: Books for Libraries Press, 1970.
Beeson, John. *A Plea for the Indians, with Facts and Features of the Late War in Oregon*. New York: Pudney & Russell, 1857.
Benedict, John Downing. *Muskogee and Northeastern Oklahoma*. 3 vols. Chicago: S. J. Clark Publishing, 1922.
Biographical Memoirs. Washington, D.C.: Judd & Detweiler, 1895.
Blair, Emma Helen. *The Indian Tribes of the Upper Mississippi Valley and Region of the Great Lakes*. Vol 1–2. Cleveland, Ohio: The Arthur H. Clark Company, 1911.
Blair, Emma Helen, James A. Robertson, and Edward Gaylord Bourne. *The Philippine Islands, 1493–1803*. Vol 1–5. Cleveland, Ohio: The Arthur H. Clark Company, 1903.
Bolton, Sarah Knowles. *Lives of Girls Who Became Famous*. New York: Thomas Y. Crowell, 1886.
Boudinot, Elias. *Star in the West; or, a Humble Attempt to Discover the Long Lost Ten Tribes of Israel*. Trenton, N.J.: D. Fenton, S. Hutchinson, and J. Dunham, 1816.
Bourne, Edward Gaylord. *Spain in America*. New York: Harper and Brothers, 1904.
Breckinridge, Robert J. *An Address Delivered before the Colonization Society of Kentucky*. Frankfort, Ky.: A. G. Hodges, 1831.
Brinton, Daniel G. *On Polysynthesis and Incorporation As Characteristics of American Languages*. Philadelphia: Press of MacCalla, 1885.
———. *The Language of Palaeolithic Man*. Philadelphia: Press of MacCalla, 1888.
Bulletin of Books Added to the Public Library of Detroit. N.p., 1899.
Bulletin of the New York Public Library, vol. 13. N.p., 1909.
Burlin, Natalie Curtis. *The Indians' Book: Songs and Legends of the American Indians*. New York: Harper and Brothers, 1907.
Caldwell College Yearbook: A Year in the Life of Caldwell College. N.p., 1910.
Callahan, S. Alice. *Wynema: A Child of the Forest*, ed. A. LaVonne Brown Ruoff. Lincoln: University of Nebraska Press, 1997 [1891].
Carr, Lucien. *Notes on the Crania of New England Indians*. Boston: Boston Society of Natural History, 1880.
Catalogue of the American History Library of Alfred S. Manson. Boston: The Libbie Snow Print, 1899.
Catalogue of the Private Library of the Late Hon. Albert Gorton Greene. New York: n.p., 1869.
Catalogue of the Private Library of Samuel Gardner Drake, A. M. Boston: Alfred Mudge & Son, 1876.
Cathcart, William. *The Baptist Encyclopedia*. Vol 2. Philadelphia: Louis H. Evarts, 1881.
Catlin, George. *Letters and Notes on the Manners, Customs, and Conditions of the North American Indians*. Vol. 1–3. London: Tilt and Bogue, 1841.
City of Elizabeth, New Jersey, Illustrated. Elizabeth, N.J.: Elizabeth Daily Journal, 1889.
Connor, Seymour V., ed. *Dear America: Some Letters of Orange Cicero and Mary America (Aikin) Connor*. Austin: Jenkins Publishing Company, 1971.
Crane, John H. *More about the Washington Tammany*. Washington, D.C.: n.p., 1873.
———. *The Washington Ring*. Washington, D.C.: n.p., 1872.
Crawford, Isabel. *Kiowa: A Woman Missionary in Indian Territory*. London: Fleming H. Revell, 1915.
Croly, David Goodman. *Miscegenation: The Theory of the Blending of the Races Applied to the White and Negro*. New York: H. Dexter, Hamilton & Co., 1864.
Curtiss, Alonzo Parker. *History of the Diocese of Fond Du Lac and Its Several Congregations*. Madison, Wisc.: Haber Printing Company, 1925.

Dall, Caroline H. *Transcendentalism in New England:* A Lecture Delivered Before the Society for Philosophical Equality, Washington, D.C., May 7, 1895. Boston: Roberts Brothers, 1897.
Dall, Caroline Wells Healey. *Historical Pictures Retouched: A Volume of Miscellanies.* Boston: Walker, Wise and Company, 1860.
Danville in the Blue Grass. Danville, Ky.: Chamber of Commerce, n.d.
Davis, Almond H. *The Female Preacher, or Memoir of Salome Lincoln.* Boston: A. B. Kidder, 1843.
Davis, Rebecca Ingersoll. *Gleanings from Merrimac Valley.* Portland, Maine: Hoyt, Fogg & Donham, 1881.
Debo, Angie. *And Still the Waters Run: The Betrayal of the Five Civilized Tribes.* Princeton, N.J.: Princeton University Press, 1940.
———. *The Rise and Fall of the Choctaw Republic.* Norman: University of Oklahoma Press, 1934.
Dodge, Richard Irving. *Our Wild Indians: Thirty-Three Years Personal Experience among the Red Men of the Great West.* Hartford, Conn: A. D. Worthington, 1882.
Domenech, Abbé Em. *Seven Years' Residence in the Great Deserts of North America.* Vol. 1–2. London: Longman, Green, Longman, and Roberts, 1860.
Dow, Lorenzo. *The Eccentric Preacher: or A Sketch of the Life of the Celebrated Lorenzo Dow.* Lowell, Mass.: E. A. Rice, 1841.
Eaton, Rachel Caroline. *John Ross and the Cherokee Indians.* Menasha, Wisc.: George Banta Publishing Company, 1914.
———. *John Ross and the Cherokee Indians.* Muskogee, Okla.: Star Printery, 1921.
Elliot, George. *Daniel Deronda.* Oxford, Eng.: Oxford University Press, 1984.
Farmer, Lydia Hoyt, ed. *The National Exposition Souvenir: What America Owes to Women.* Buffalo, N.Y.: Charles Wells Moulton, 1893.
Fletcher, Alice Cunningham. *Historical Sketch of the Omaha Tribe of Indians in Nebraska.* Washington, D.C.: Judd & Detweiller, 1885.
———. *Indian Story and Song: From North America.* Boston: Small Maynard & Company, 1900.
———. *Lands in Severalty to Indians; Illustrated by Experiences with the Omaha Tribe.* Salem, Mass.: Salem Press, 1885.
———. *Report of Alice C. Fletcher to the Honorable Commissioner of Indian Affairs.* Carlisle, Penn.: Indian School Print, 1885.
———. Joanna C. Scherer and Raymond J. DeMallie, eds. *Life among the Indians: First Fieldwork among the Sioux and Omahas.* Lincoln: University of Nebraska Press, 2013.
———, and Francis La Flesche. *The Omaha Tribe.* 2 vols. Lincoln: University of Nebraska Press, 1992 [1911].
Fletcher, Robert. *Brief Memories of Colonel Garrick Mallery.* Washington, D.C.: Judd & Detweiler, 1895.
Fourth Annual Report of the Women's National Indian Association. Dedham, Mass.: W. L. Wardle, 1884.
Gay, E. Jane. *With the Nez Perces: Alice Fletcher in the Field, 1889–1892.* Lincoln: University of Nebraska Press, 1981.
Gideon, D. C. *Indian Territory: Descriptive, Biographical, and Genealogical.* New York: Lewis Publishing Company, 1901.
Giffen, Fannie Reed, and Susette La Flesche Tibbles. *Oo-mah-ha Ta-wa-tha: Omaha City.* Lincoln: F. B. Festner, 1898.
Grimké, Angelina Emily. *Letters to Catherine E. Beecher.* Freeport, N.Y.: Books for Libraries Press, 1971.
Harsha, William Justin. *Plowed Under: The Story of an Indian Chief.* New York: Fords, Howard, & Hulbert, 1881.
Hastain, E. *Choctaw-Chickasaw Deeds and Allotments.* Muskogee, Oklahoma: E. Hastain, 1910.
History of Kentucky College for Women. N.p., n.d.

Hopkins, Sarah Winnemucca. *Life Among the Piutes*. Boston, Mass.: Cupples, Upham & Co., 1883.
Hubrecht, A. A. W. *The Descent of the Primates*. New York: Charles Scribner's Sons, 1897.
Hunt, E. B. *Union Foundations: A Study of American Nationality a Fact of Science*. New York: D. Van Nostrand, 1863.
Jackson, Helen Hunt. *A Century of Dishonor*. Norman: University of Oklahoma Press, 1995 [1881].
———. *Bits of Talk about Home Matters*. Boston, Mass.: Robert's Brothers, 1879.
———. *Bits of Travel at Home*. Boston, Mass.: Roberts Brothers, 1878.
———. *Father Junipero and the Mission Indian of California*. Boston: Little, Brown, 1902.
———. *Glimpses of Three Coasts*. Boston, Mass.: Roberts Brothers, 1886.
———. *Hettie's Strange History*. Boston, Mass.: Roberts Brothers, 1877.
———. *Mercy Philbrick's Choice*. Boston, Mass.: Roberts Brothers, 1876.
———. *Ramona: A Story*. Boston, Mass.: Roberts Brothers, 1884.
———. *Zeph: A Posthumous Story*. Boston, Mass.: Roberts Brothers, 1885.
James, George Wharton. *Through Ramona's Country*. Boston, Mass.: Little, Brown and Company, 1909.
Judd, Neil Merton. *The Bureau of American Ethnology: A Partial History*. Norman: University of Oklahoma Press, 1967.
Kappler, Charles J., ed. *Indian Treaties: 1778–1883*. Mattituck, N.Y.: Amereon House, 1972 [1904].
Keen, William Williams. *The Bi-centennial Celebration of the Founding of the First Baptist Church of the City of Philadelphia*. Philadelphia: American Baptist Publication Society, 1899.
Kellogg, Louise Phelps. *Indian Diplomacy during the Revolution in the West*. Springfield, Ill.: Journal Print, 1920.
Kentucky College for Women. N.p., n.d..
Leonard, John W. *Who's Who in America, 1899–1900*. Chicago: A. N. Marquis & Company, 1899.
Lewis, Anna L. *Along the Arkansas*. Dallas, Tex.: Southwest Press, 1932.
Lewis, Anna, and Howard Taylor. *Problems in Oklahoma History: A Workbook for High School Students*. Oklahoma City: Economy Company, 1931.
Lewis, Alvin Fayette. *History of Higher Education in Kentucky*. Washington, D.C.: Government Printing Office, 1899.
Livermore, Harriet. *Addresses to the Dispersed of Judah*. Philadelphia: L. R. Bailey, 1844.
———. *A Narrative of the Religious Experience in Twelve Letters*. Concord, N.H.: Jacob B. Moore, 1826.
———. *Millennial Tidings*, vol. 1–4. Philadelphia: Harriet Livermore, 1831–39.
———. *Scriptural Evidence in Favor of Female Testimony in Meetings for Christian Worship*. Portsmouth, N.H.: n.p., 1843.
———. *The Counsel of God, Immutable and Everlasting*. Philadelphia: n.p., 1844.
———. *The Harp of Israel, to Meet the Loud Echo in the Wilds of America*. Philadelphia: J. Rakestraw, 1835.
Lockwood, Frank C. *The Life of Edward E. Ayer*. Chicago: A. C. McClurg, 1929.
Logan, Mary Simmerson. *The Part Taken by Women in History*. Wilmington, Del.: Perry Nalle Publishing, 1912.
McCoy, Isaac. *History of the Baptist Indian Missions: Embracing Remarks on the Former and Present Condition of the Aboriginal Tribes; Their Settlement within the Indian Territory, and Their Future Prospects*. Washington, D.C.: William M. Morrison, 1840.
Meacham, A. B. *Wi-ne-ma: The Woman Chief and Her People*. Hartford, Conn: American Publishing Company, 1876.
Miller, Frances. *Argument before the Judiciary Committee of the House of Representatives Upon the Petition of 600 Citizens Asking for the Enfranchisement of the Women of the District of Columbia, Jan. 21, 1874*. Washington, D.C.: Gibson Brothers, 1874.
Minutes of the General Conference of the Freewill Baptist Connection. Dover, N.H.: William Burr, 1859.

Nation, Carry Amelia. *The Use and Need of the Life of Carry A. Nation.* Topeka, Kans.: F. M. Stevens & Sons, 1908.
Neville, Alexander White. *The History of Lamar County.* Paris, Tex.: North Texas Publishing, 1937.
Nicolay, Helens. *Sixty Years of the Literary Society.* Washington, D.C.: n.p., 1934.
Northrop, Henry Davenport. *Indian Horrors: Or, Massacres by the Red Men.* Philadelphia: W. B. Benford, 1891.
Parkman, Frances. *The Oregon Trail: Sketches of Prairie and Rocky-Mountain Life.* Boston: Little, Brown and Company, 1872.
Pierce, Deborah. *A Scriptural Vindication of Female Preaching, Prophesying, or Exhortation.* Auburn, N.Y.: N. Roberts, E. Burroughs, 1817.
Peabody, Elizabeth P. *Sarah Winnemucca's Practical Solution of the Indian Problem.* Cambridge, Mass.: John Wilson and Son, 1886.
Pennsylvania Yearly Meeting of Progressive Friends. N.p.: 1854.
Petition to Congress for the Protection and Elevation of American Indians. New York: Varney Steam Print, 1857.
Powell, John Wesley. *On Primitive Institutions.* Philadelphia: Dando Printing and Publishing, 1896.
———. *Sketch of the Mythology of the North American Indians.* Rockville, Md.: Wildside Press, 2007.
———. *The Physiographic Regions of the United States.* New York: American Book Company, 1895.
Proceedings of the Eighth Annual Meeting of the Lake Mohonk Conference of the Friends of the Indian. Boston: Frank Wood, 1890.
Proceedings of the Nineteenth Annual Meeting of the Lake Mohonk Conference of Friends of the American Indian. Lake Mohonk, N.Y.: The Lake Mohonk Conference, 1902.
Proceedings of the Tenth Annual Meeting of the Lake Mohonk Conference of Friends of the American Indian. Lake Mohonk, N.Y.: The Lake Mohonk Conference, 1892.
Proceedings of the Twenty-Fifth Annual Meeting of the Lake Mohonk Conference of the Friends of the American Indian and Other Dependent Peoples. Lake Mohonk, N.Y.: Lake Mohonk Conference, 1907.
Proceedings of the Twenty-Third Annual Lake Mohonk Friends of the American Indian and Other Dependent Peoples. Lake Mohonk, N.Y.: The Lake Mohonk Conference, 1905.
Quinton, Amelia S. *Official Pamphlet of the National Indian Association, with Suggestions and Facts for Its Helpers.* Philadelphia: National Indian Association, 1882.
Rhodes, James Ford. *Historical Essays.* New York: The Macmillan Company, 1909.
Richards, W. B. *The Oklahoma Red Book.* Vol. 12. Oklahoma City, Okla.: n.p., 1912.
Rowland, Dunbar. *The Official and Statistical Register of the State of Mississippi.* Nashville, Tenn.: Brandon Printing Company, 1912
Roosevelt, Theodore. *The Winning of the West.* Vol. 1–5. New York: P. F. Collier, 1889.
Royce, Josiah. *California from the Conquest of 1846 to the Second Vigilance Committee in San Francisco: A Study in American Character.* Boston: Houghton Mifflin, 1888.
Sanborn, Franklin Benjamin. *Sixty Years of Concord, 1855–1915.* Hartford, Conn: Transcendental Books, 1976.
Schoolcraft, Henry Rowe. *Historical and Statistical Information, Respecting the History, Condition, and Prospects of the Indian Tribes of the United States: Collected and Prepared under the Direction of the Bureau of Indian Affairs per Act of Congress of March 3rd, 1847.* Vol. 1–6. Philadelphia: Lippencott, Grambo, 1851–57.
Sears, Clara Endicott. *Days of Delusion: A Strange Bit of History.* Boston: Houghton Mifflin, 1924.
Second Annual Address to the Public of the Lake Mohonk Conference. Philadelphia: Executive Committee of the Indian Rights Association, 1884.

Shambaugh, Benjamin F. *The Proceedings of the Mississippi Valley Historical Society.* Vol 1–15. Cedar Rapids, Iowa: The Torch Press, 1909–13.
Shurz, Carl. *American Imperialism.* N.p., 1899.
Sigourney, Lydia Huntley. *Letters to Young Ladies.* New York: Harper & Brothers, 1837.
———. *Traits of the Aborigines of America: A Poem.* Cambridge, Mass.: Hilliard and Metcalf Printers, 1822.
Slattery, Charles Lewis. *Felix Reville Brunot, 1820–1898.* New York: Longmans, Green, and Co., 1901.
Spotford, Ainsworth R., ed. *An American Almanac and Treasury of Facts, Statistical, Financial and Political for the Year 1882.* New York: The American News Company, 1882.
Starr, Emmet. *History of the Cherokee Indians and Their Legends and Folklore.* Oklahoma City, Okla.: Warden Company, 1921.
Stevenson, Matilda Coxe. "The Zuni Scalp Ceremonial." In *The Congress of Women, Held in the Women's Building World's Columbian Exposition, Chicago, U.S.A., 1893.* Ed. Mary Kavanaugh Oldham, 484–87. Chicago: Monarch Book Company, 1894.
Stevenson, Matilda Coxe Evans. *The Zuni and the Zunians.* Washington, D.C.: n.p., 1881.
Stoke, Anson Phelps. *Yale University Endowments: A Description of Various Gifts and Bequests Establishing Permanent University Funds.* New Haven, Conn: Tuttle, Morehouse and Taylor Company, 1917.
Tappan, Lewis. *History of the American Missionary Association: Its Constitution and Principles, Etc.* New York: n.p., 1855.
Tatum, Lawrie. *Our Red Brothers and the Peace Policy of President Ulysses S. Grant.* Philadelphia: John C. Winston, 1899.
Thwaites, Reuben Gold, ed. *A New Discovery of a Large Country in America by Father Louis Hennepin.* Chicago: A. C. McClurg, 1903.
———. *France in America, 1497–1763.* New York: Harper & Brothers, 1905.
———, ed. *Original Journals of the Lewis and Clark Expedition, 1804–1806.* New York: Dodd, Mead, 1904.
———, ed. *The Jesuit Relations and Allied Documents.* Cleveland, Ohio: The Imperial Press, 1896.
———, ed. *The University of Wisconsin: Its History and Its Alumni.* Madison, Wisc.: J. N. Purcell, 1900.
Tibbles, Thomas Henry. *Buckskin and Blanket Days.* Lincoln: University of Nebraska Press, 1969.
———. *Hidden Power: A Secret History of the Indian Ring.* New York: G. W. Carlton, 1881.
———. *The Ponca Chiefs: An Indian's Attempt to Appeal from the Tomahawk to the Courts.* Boston: Lockwood, Brooks, 1879.
Towle, Nancy. *Vicissitudes Illustrated: In the Experience of Nancy Towle in Europe and America.* Portsmouth, N.H.: James L. Burges, 1833.
Trans-Mississippi and International Exposition, 1898. St. Louis: n.p., 1898.
Tullidge, Henry. *The Evangelical Church: A Series of Discourses by Ministers of Different Denominations, Illustrating the Spiritual Unity of the Church of Christ.* New York: Thomas Whittaker, 1879.
Turner, Frederick Jackson. *The Frontier in American History.* Mineola, N.Y.: Dover Publications, 2010 [1920].
———. *Rise of the New West, 1819–1829.* New York: Harper & Brothers, 1906.
———. *Reuben Gold Thwaites: A Memorial Address.* Chicago: Lakeside Press, 1914.
Wisconsin University Catalogue. Madison: University of Wisconsin, 1893, 1906, 1910.
Welsh, Herbert. *A Brief Statement of the Objects, Achievements and Needs of the Indian Rights Association.* Philadelphia: Indian Rights Association, 1887.
———. *Four Weeks among Some of the Sioux Tribes of Dakota and Nebraska.* Philadelphia: Horace F. McCann, 1882.

———. *The Apache Prisoners in Fort Marion, St. Augustine, Florida.* Philadelphia: Indian Rights Association, 1887.
Welsh, William. *Women Helpers in the Church: Their Sayings and Doings.* Philadelphia: J. B. Lippincott & Co., 1872.
Willard, Francis Elizabeth, and Mary Ashton Rice Livermore. *American Women.* New York: Mast, Crowell and Kirkpatrick, 1897.
Women's Baptist Home Mission Society, 1877–1882. Chicago: R. R. Donnelley & Sons, 1883.
Whipple, Henry B. *Taopi and His friends, or the Indians' Wrongs and Rights.* Philadelphia: Claxton, Remsen & Haffelfinger, 1869.
Whittaker, Thomas, ed. *Protestant Episcopal Almanac and Church Directory.* New York: T. Whittaker, 1876.
Why Home-Seekers and Investors Should Come to Lamar County and Paris, Texas. St. Louis, Mo.: Woodward & Tiernan Printing Company, 1888–89.
Wilson, Elizabeth. *Fifty Years of Association Work Among Young Women, 1866–1916: A History of Young Women's Christian Associations in the United States of America.* New York: National Board of the Young Women's Christian Associations of the United States of America, 1916.
Winsor, Justin, ed. *Narrative and Critical History of America.* Vol. 1–8. Boston: Houghton, Mifflin, 1884–89.
———. *The Colonies and the Republic West of the Alleghenies, 1763–1798.* Boston: Houghton, Mifflin & Company, 1897.
Wolff, Joseph. *Narrative of a Mission to Bokhara.* N.p.,: Harrison and Co., 1845.
———. *Travels and Adventures of Rev. Joseph Wolff.* London: Saunders, Otley and Co., 1861.
Woodhull, Victoria C. *The Argument for Woman's Electoral Rights Under Amendments XIV and XV of the Constitution of the United States: A Review of My Work at Washington, D.C. in 1870–1871.* London: G. Norman & Son, 1887.
Wooten, Mattie Lloyd. *Women Tell the Story of the Southwest.* San Antonio, Tex.: Naylor Company, 1940
Young, John Clarke. *Fourth Annual Report of the Kentucky Colonization Society.* N.p., 1833.

Articles

Abel, Annie Heloise. Review of *John Ross and the Cherokee Indians*, by Rachel Caroline Eaton. *American Historical Review* 20, no. 3 (April 1915): 672–73.
Abel-Henderson, Annie Heloise. Review of *And Still the Waters Run*, by Angie Debo. *Pacific Northwest Quarterly* 32, no. 4 (October 1941): 464–66
Adams, George Burton. "History and the Philosophy of History." *American Historical Review* 14, no. 2 (January, 1909): 221–36.
Adams, Herbert Baxter. "Leopold von Ranke." In *Papers of the American Historical Association*, vol. 3, ed. Herbert Baxter Adams, 101–33. New York: G. P. Putnam's Sons, 1889.
"Report of the Organization and Proceedings, Saratoga, 9–10 September 1884." In *Papers of the American Historical Association*, vol. 1, 5–44. New York: G. P. Putnam and Sons, 1886.
American Missionary 14, no. 6 (June 1870): 122–32.
American Slave Almanac, The 1, no. 3 (1839): 20–21, 26–27, 29.
American Slave Almanac, The 1, no. 4 (1840): 7.
"An American Historical Association in Contemplation." *Magazine of American History* 12, no. 2 (August 1884): 188.
Bacon, Nathaniel T. "Some Insular Questions." *Yale Review* 10, no. 1 (May 1901): 159–78.
Barnard, F. A. P. "Memoir of Edward B. Hunt, 1822–1863." In *Biographical Memoirs; National Academy of Sciences* 3, N. A., 29–41. Washington, D.C.: Judd & Ditweiler, 1895.

Beale, Anne. "Our Tractarian Movement." In *The Girl's Outdoor Book*, ed. Charles Peters, 497–505. Philadelphia: J. B. Lippencott Company, 1889.
Blair, Emma Helen. "Correspondence: The Philippine Island Series." *The Nation* 76, no. 1977 (May 1903): 414–15.
———. "Osage Indians in France." *American Anthropologist* 2, no. 4 (Oct.–Dec. 1900): 780.
Bloom, Lansing B. Review of *Along the Arkansas*, by Anna Lewis. *The Mississippi Valley Historical Review* 20, no. 1 (June 1933): 117.
Boas, Franz. "The Bureau of American Ethnology." *Science* 16, no. 412 (November 1902): 828–31.
Bonney, Mary L. "A Historical Sketch." *The Indian's Friend* 9, no. 2 (October 1896): 9–11.
"Books Wanted—Shepard Book Co., Salt Lake City, Utah." *The Publishers Weekly* 79 (1911): 60.
Brinton, Daniel G. "Proposed Classification and International Nomenclature of the Anthropological Sciences." In *Proceedings of the American Association for the Advanced Science* 41, 257–58. Salem, Mass.: Salem Press Publishing and Printing Company, 1892.
"Brooklyn, L. I., July 27th, 1842." *Brother Jonathan* 2, no. 16 (1842): 436–37.
Butler, E. "On Our Indian Question." *Journal of the Military Service Institution of the United States* 2, no. 5–8 (1881): 183–277.
Chase, C. C. "Harriett Livermore." *Contributions of the Old Residents Historical Association, Lowell, Mass.* 4, no. 1 (August 1888): 16–23.
"Cherokee Nation Dissolved, The." *The Quarterly Journal of the Society of American Indians* 2, no. 3 (July–September 1914): 237–39.
Chipman, Norton P. "The Appendix." *The Republic* 2 no. 4 (April 1874): 1–21.
"Circular Addressed to the Benevolent Ladies of the United States." *Christian Advocate and Journal* (December 1829): 65–66.
Cope, Edward Drinker. "The Occurrence of Man in the Upper Miocene of Nebraska." In *Proceedings of the American Association for the Advancement of Science*, ed. Frances Ward Putnam, 593. Salem, Mass.: The Salem Press, 1885.
Cowgill, Elizabeth King. "Alumnae Leaders." *Sooner Magazine* 3, no.8 (May 1931): 288–89, 304–305.
Crawford, John. "On Language as a Test of the Races of Man." *Transactions of the Ethnological Society of London* 3 (1865): 1–9.
"Death of Dr. Emmet Starr." *Chronicles of Oklahoma* 8, no. 1 (March 1930): 129–32.
Debo, Angie. "To Establish Justice." *Western Historical Quarterly* 7, no. 4 (October 1976): 405–12.
"District of Columbia, The." *The Republic* 2, no. 1 (January 1874): 12–15.
Dodd, William E. (unsigned). Review of *John Ross and the Cherokee Indians*, by Rachel Caroline Eaton. *The Mississippi Valley Historical Review* 2, no. 2 (September 1915): 293–94.
Eastman, Charles A. "The Indian Health Problems." *Popular Science Monthly* 86, no. 1 (January–June 1915): 49–55.
"Emma Helen Blair," *Book Review Digest* 18 no.12 (December 1912): 43–44.
Farrand, Max. "Compromises of the Constitution." *American Historical Review* 9 (April 1904): 479–89.
Fletcher, Alice C. "Dr. Spofford as a Member of the Literary Society." In *Annual Meeting of the Library of Congress*, ed. Herbert Putnam, 40–45. New York: Webster Press, 1909.
Foreman, Carolyn Thomas. "Aunt Eliza of Tahlequah." *Chronicles of Oklahoma* 9, no. 1 (March 1931): 43–55.
Friend's Intelligencer 16 (Mar. 1859): 8–12.
Fuller, Margaret. "The Great Lawsuit." *The Dial* 2, no. 1 (July 1843): 1–47.
"German Universities." *Atlantic Monthly* 7, no. 41 (March, 1861): 258–72.
Gibbon, John. "On Our Indian Question." *Journal of the Military Service Institution of the United States* 2, nos. 5–8 (1881): 101–22.

Gildemeister, Theda. "The Teaching of Patriotism." In *Addresses and Proceedings of the National Education Association of the United States*, 438–41. Chicago: University of Chicago Press, 1920.

Gill, Theodore. "Edward Drinker Cope, Naturalist—A Chapter in the History of Science." *The American Naturalist* 31, no. 370 (October, 1897): 831–63.

Hale, Horatio. "Language as a Test of Mental Capacity." *Journal of the Anthropological Institute of Great Britain and Ireland* 21 (1892): 413–55.

"Harriet Livermore." *Contributions of the Old Resident's Historical Association, Lowell, Massachusetts* 4 (August 1888): 30.

"Harriett Livermore." *Little's Living Age* 10 (July, August, September 1868): 64.

"Harriet Livermore." *Southern Literary Messenger* 6, no. 9 (September 1840): 675–76.

"Harriet Livermore, Diseases." *Boston Weekly Magazine* 3, no. 4 (October 1840): 29–30.

Hunt, Helen. "Fretting." In *The Study: Helps for Preachers*, ed. R. D. Dickinson, 271–73. London: Folkard and Sons, 1875.

Indian's Friend 15, no. 10 (June 1903): 4.

"Indian, The." *Friend's Intelligencer* 16 (April 1859): 87–89.

"Inflation." *The Republic* 3, no. 4 (April 1874): 12–15.

Jackson, Helen Hunt. "Father Junipero Serra and His Work: A Sketch of the Foundation, Prosperity, and Ruin of the Franciscan Missions." *Century Magazine* 26, no. 11 (May 1883): 3–18, 199–215.

———. "The Present Condition of the Mission Indians in Southern California." *Century Magazine* 26, no. 4 (August 1883): 515–29.

James, James Alton. "Indian Diplomacy and the Opening of the Revolution in the West." In *Proceedings of the State Historical Society of Wisconsin* (1909): 125–42.

"James M'Cosh." *The Interior* 25, no. 1278 (November 1894): 1496.

Jameson, J. Franklin. "The American Historical Association." *American Historical Review* 15, no. 1 (October 1909): 1–20.

Kellogg, Louise Phelps. "The Fox Indians During the French Regime." In *Proceedings of the State Historical Society of Wisconsin at its 55th Annual Meeting Held Nov. 7, 1907.* (1908): 142–88.

Keysor, Jennie E. "Helen Hunt Jackson, 1831–1885." *Popular Educator* 16, no. 2 (October 1898): 60–61.

"Lectures at Haverford College." *Friends Review* 34, no. 34 (April 1881): 532.

"Lectures of Prof. R. L. Quinton, at Association Hall, The." *The Christian Recorder* 23, no. 5 (January 1880): 2.

LeRoy, James A. "Our Spanish Inheritance in the Philippines." *Atlantic Monthly* (March 1905): 330–47.

———. Review of *The Philippine Islands, 1493–1803*, by Emma Helen Blair, James A. Robertson, and Edward Gaylord Bourne. *The American Historical Review* 9, no. 1 (October, 1903): 149–54.

———. Review of *The Philippine Islands*, by Emma Helen Blair, James A. Robertson, and Edward Gaylord Bourne. *American Historical Review* 10, no. 1 (October–July, 1903–1904): 168–70.

Lewis, Anna. "Du Tisne's Expedition into Oklahoma, 1719." *Chronicles of Oklahoma* 3, no. 4 (December 1925): 319–23.

———. "French Interests and Activities in Oklahoma," *Chronicles of Oklahoma* 2, no. 3 (1924): 253–68.

———. "La Harpe's First Expedition in Oklahoma, 1718–1719." *Chronicles of Oklahoma* 2, no. 3 (1924): 331–49.

———. "Nunih Waiya." *Chronicles of Oklahoma* 16, no. 2 (June 1938): 214–20.

———. "Oklahoma As Part of the Spanish Dominion, 1763–1803." *Chronicles of Oklahoma* 3, no. 1 (March 1925): 45–58.
Lewis, Anna L. Review of *The Rise and Fall of the Choctaw Republic*, by Angie Debo. *The Mississippi Valley Historical Review* 21, no. 3 (December 1934): 409–10.
Lewit, Robert T. "Indian Missions and Antislavery Sentiment: A Conflict of Evangelical and Humanitarian Ideals." *Mississippi Valley Historical Review* 50 (1963–64): 39–55.
"Librarians," *Library Journal* 36, no.11 (November 1911): 604.
Livermore, Mary A. "Helen Hunt Jackson." *The Perry Magazine* 3, no. 1 (September 1900): 67–70.
MacCurdy, George Grant. "Anthropology at the Chicago Meeting." *Science* 27, no. 689 (March 1908): 401–405.
Marble, A. P. "The Ethical Element in Patriotism." In *National Education Association Journal of Proceedings and Addresses*, 142–46. St. Paul: Pioneer Press, 1895.
Matthews, Washington. "The Earth Lodge in Art." *American Anthropologist* 4, no. 1 (January–March 1902): 1–12.
McKenzie, Fayette Avery. "The Assimilation of the American Indian." *American Journal of Sociology* 19, no. 6 (May 1914): 761–72.
Mitchell, Margaret J. "Correspondence Study." *University of Oklahoma Bulletin* (1918–19): 400–401.
"Miss Harriet Livermore." *Brother Jonathan* 2, no. 14 (July 1842): 381.
"Miss Higgin's School." In *The City of Elizabeth New Jersey, Illustrated*, 107. Elizabeth, N.J.: Elizabeth Daily Journal, 1889.
"Miss Livermore's Second Letter." *Brother Johnathan* 2, no. 15 (August 1842): 409.
Morehouse, H. L. "Women's Baptist Home Mission Society." *The Home Mission Monthly* 1, no. 13 (July 1879): 201–202.
"Mrs. Mary L. Bonney," *The Indian's Friend* 12, no. 12 (August 1900): 8.
"Origin and Development of Language, The." *Science* 12, no. 295 (September 1888): 145–46.
"Pennsylvania Peace Society." *Friends Intelligencer* 42, no. 44 (December 1885): 702.
Peabody, Elizabeth Palmer. "A Letter to the Editor of *The Radical*." *The Radical* 2 (August 1867): 745–48.
"Political Support of Slavery." *Quarterly Anti-Slavery Magazine* 8 (July 1837): 412–15.
Powell, John Wesley. "Evolution of Music from Dance to Symphony." *Science* 14, no. 349 (October 1889): 244–49
———. "From Barbarism to Civilization." *American Anthropologist* 1, no. 2 (April 1888): 97–123.
———. "Human Evolution. Annual Address of the President, J. W. Powell, Delivered November 6, 1883." *Transactions of the Anthropological Society of Washington* 2 (February–May 1882–83): 176–208.
———. "Humanities, The." *The Forum* 10 (1890): 410–22.
———. Review of *Evolution of To-day*, by H. W. Conn. *Science* 58, no. 189 (September 1886): 264–65.
"Prof. Edward Martin Sheppard," *Drury College Bulletin* 35, no. 2 (June 1934): 273–75.
Quinton, Amelia. "A Small Request to Pastors," *The Christian Recorder* 19, no. 5 (December 1881): 2.
———. "Care of the Indian." In *Woman's Work in America*, ed. Annie Nathan Meyer, 357–91. New York: Henry Holt, 1891.
———. "Col. Gus Ivey." *Indian's Friend* 24, no. 2 (October 1911): 1.
———. "News and Notes." *Indian's Friend* 24, no. 4 (December 1911): 4.
———. "Original Indian Association, The." *Christian Union* 36, no. 14 (October 1884): 346.
———. "Our Association's Chronology, Number Four," *Indian's Friend* 9, no. 8 (April 1897): 2, 12.

———. "Through Southern California: Letter Number Seven." *Indian's Friend* 7 (October 1891): 5.
Review of *The Indian Tribes of the Upper Mississippi Valley*, by Emma Helen Blair. *American Historical Review* 17, no. 4 (July 1912): 839–40.
Richardson, R. N. Review of *The Rise and Fall of the Choctaw Republic*, by Angie Debo. *Southwestern Historical Quarterly* 38, no. 3 (January 1935): 229–30.
Robertson, James A., and Edward Gaylord Bourne. Review of *The Philippine Islands*, by Emma Helen Blair. *The Nation* 76, no. 1974 (April 1903): 359–60.
Roosevelt, Theodore. "The Copperheads of 1900." In *The Works of Theodore Roosevelt: Campaigns and Controversies*, vol. 14, 334–41. New York: Charles Scribner's Sons, 1925.
"Scientific Washington." *Science* 23, no. 581 (March 1894): 158–59.
School Journal, The 63 (1901): 445.
"School of American Archeology." *Science* 34, no. 874 (September 1911): 401.
Semple, William F. Review of *Pushmataha, an American Patriot*, by Anna Lewis. *Chronicles of Oklahoma* 3, no. 2 (1959): 255–56.
Sooner Magazine 2, no. 10 (July 1930): 392.
Speer, John. "Accuracy in History." In *Transactions of the Kansas State Historical Society*, ed. George W. Martin, 60–69. Topeka, Kans.: W. Y. Morgan, 1900.
"Statement by Commissioner of Indian Affairs, Glenn L. Emmons on Policy Governing Sales of Individually-Owned Indian Lands." *Smoke Signals, Colorado River Indian Tribes* 2, no. 12 (June 1958): 1.
Stuart-Glennie, J. S. "The Desirability of Treating History as a Science of Origins." *Transactions of the Royal Historical Society* 5 (1891): 229–40.
Studies in Classical Philology 1 [University of Chicago] (1895).
"Suggestion from a Western Friend, A." *Council Fire and Arbiter* 7, no. 10 (October 1884): 156.
"Suggestions for Christmas." *Home and Garden* 13, no. 1 (January–June 1908): 12–13.
Thayer, James Bradley. "A People Without Law." *The Atlantic Monthly* 68 (1891): 676–87.
Thwaites, Reuben Gold. "Black Hawk War, The." *Magazine of the Western History* 5, no. 2 (December 1886): 181–95.
"Transcendentalism." *The Dial* 2, no. 3 (January 1841): 382–86.
Turner, Frederick Jackson. "The Character and Influence of the Indian Trade in Wisconsin: A Study of the Trading Post as an Institution." *Johns Hopkins University Studies in Historical and Political Science* 11–12 (November–December 1891): 547–615.
———. "Middle Western Pioneer Democracy." In *Rereading Frederick Jackson Turner*, ed. John Mack Faragher, 159–80. New York: Henry Holt and Company, 1994.
———. "Problems in American History." In *Congress of Arts and Sciences Universal Exposition, St. Louis, 1904*, ed. Howard J. Rogers, 183–94. Boston: Houghton, Mifflin and Company, 1904.
———. Review of *The Winning of the West*, by Theodore Roosevelt. *The Dial* 10, no. 112 (August 1889): 71–73.
———. "Significance of History, The." In *Rereading Frederick Jackson Turner*, by John Mack Faragher, 11–30. New York: Henry Holt and Company, 1994.
———. "Significance of the Frontier in American History, The." In *Rereading Frederick Jackson Turner*, by John Mack Faragher, 31–60. New York: Henry Holt and Company, 1994.
———. "Social Forces in American History." In *Rereading Frederick Jackson Turner*, ed. John Mack Faragher, 119–39. New York: Henry Holt and Company, 1994.
———. "The West and American Ideas." In *Rereading Frederick Jackson Turner*, ed. John Mack Faragher, 145–58. New York: Henry Holt and Company, 1994.
Tyler, Moses Coit. "The Neglect and Destruction of Historical Materials in This Country." In *Papers of the American Historical Association*, ed. Herbert Baxter Adams, 20–22. New York: G. P. Putnam's Sons, 1887.

"Unitarian Movement in New England, The." *The Dial* 1, no. 4 (April 1841): 409–43.
"Visting Oneida," *Spirit of Missions* 77 no.346–47 (1913): 273–74.
Vore, Jacob. "The Omahas—An Unhopeful Outlook." *Council Fire and Arbitrator* 7, no. 12 (December 1884): 180.
"War Makes Inroads upon List of Faculty Members." *University of Oklahoma Magazine* 17, no. 1 (October 1917): 22.
Wayland, Mrs. H. L. "Women's Home Mission Union." *The Home Mission Monthly* 12, no. 12 (December 1880): 245–46.
Welsh, William, Jr. "A Sketch of the Life of William Welsh." *Papers Read Before the Historical Society of Frankford* 1, no. 6 (1908): 11–12.
"Why Our Science Students Go to Germany." *The Atlantic Monthly* 63 (April 1889): 463–66.
Winslow, Ada. "Dormitory Discipline." *High School Quarterly* 6, no. 2 (January 1918): 112–16.
Wood, C. E. S. "On Our Indian Question." *Journal of the Military Service Institution of the United States* 2, no. 5–8 (1881): 123–82.
Woodruff, Thomas M. "On Our Indian Question." *Journal of the Military Service Institution of the United States* 2, no. 5–8 (1881): 293–303.
"Work among the Indians. The Episcopalians." *Missionary Herald* 73 (1878): 90–91.
Wright, Eleanore R. "A Sketch of the Life of Mrs. William Welsh." *Papers Read Before the History Society of Frankford* 1, no. 6 (1908): 18–26.
Wright, Muriel. Review of *The Rise and Fall of the Choctaw Republic*, by Angie Debo. *Chronicles of Oklahoma* 13, no. 1 (1935): 108–20.

Government Documents

MISCELLANEOUS

"Address by Glenn L. Emmons, Commissioner of Indian Affairs, Before the Governor's Interstate Indian Council, Sheridan, Wyoming, August 6, 1956," Department of the Interior, Information Service, 6 August 1956.
Congressional Record. 47th Cong., 1st sess., 1882, 13, pt. 83: 1326–30.
"Constitution of the Indian Treaty-Keeping and Protective Association." Adopted June 3rd, 1881. N.p., 1881.
"Glenn L. Emmons Nominated for Indian Post." Department of the Interior, Information Service, July 15, 1953.
Petition to Congress for the Preservation and Elevation of American Indians (N.p., 1858). *School District no. 17 v. Eaton Co. Supt.* 1924 OK 184 223 p.857 97 Okla. 177.

HOUSE OF REPRESENTATIVES

House Document 509, 56th Cong., 2nd session, 1901: 210–19.
House Report 7, 42nd Cong., 3rd sess., 1872: 1–10.
House Report 22, 41st Cong., 3rd sess., 1871: 1–17.
House Report 627, 43rd Cong., 1st sess., 1874: 1–11.
"Memorial of the Board of Managers of the American Indian Association, January 13, 1846." 29th Cong., 1st sess., 1846, House Document 73, 1–6.

SENATE

"Memorial of John Beeson." 43rd Cong., 1st sess., 1874, Senate Document no. 94, serial 1584, 4.
"Memorial of the Omaha Tribe of Indians for a Grant of Land in Severalty," Senate Miscellaneous Document 31, 47th Cong., 1st sess., 1882: 3.

"Memorial of the Representatives of the Religious Society of Friends, in the States of Ohio, Indiana, and Illinois, Praying the Adoption of Measures for Civilization and Improvement of the Indians." 15th Cong., 2nd sess., 1818, Senate Document no. 47, 1–3.
Senate Document 31, 20th Cong., 2nd sess., 1829: 1.
Senate Miscellaneous Document, 36th Cong., 1st sess., 1860: 249–70.
Senate Miscellaneous Document, 36th Cong., 2nd sess., 1861: 38–42, 284–343.
Senate Miscellaneous Document 16, 41st Cong., 3rd sess., 1871: 1–2.
Senate Miscellaneous Document 31, 47th Cong., 1st sess., 1882: 1–14.
Senate Miscellaneous Document 26, 47th Cong., 1st sess., 1888: 1–6.
Senate Miscellaneous Document 46–49, 46th Cong., 2nd sess., 1880: 20, 26–28.
Senate Miscellaneous Document 79, 54th Cong., 1st sess., 1896: 3–8.
Senate Report 479, 43rd Cong., 2nd sess., 1874: 1–5.
Senate Report 523 [part 1], 45th Cong., 3rd sess., 1878: 1–2.
Senate Report 523 [part 2], 45th Cong., 3rd sess., 1878: 1–9.
Senate Report 670 [Testimony Relating to the Removal of the Ponca Indians], 46th Cong., 2nd sess., 1880: 1–501.

STATUTES

An Act Making Provision for the Civilization of the Indian Tribes Adjoining the Frontier Settlements, U.S. Statutes at Large 3 (1819): 516–17.
Public Law 419, 41st Cong., 3rd sess. (21 February 1871): 419–29.
U.S. Statutes at Large 24 (1886): 388–91.
U.S. Statutes at Large 341 (1882): 168.

PUBLISHED DOCUMENTS

Abel, Annie Heloise. *The History of Events Resulting in Indian Consolidation West of the Mississippi*. Washington, D.C.: Government Printing Office (GPO), 1908.
———. *The Official Correspondence of James S. Calhoun while Indian Agent at Santa Fé and Superintendent of Indian Affairs in New Mexico*. Washington, D.C.: GPO, 1915.
———. "Proposals for an Indian State, 1778–1878." In *Annual Report of the American Historical Association* 1 (1907): 87–104. Washington, D.C.: GPO, 1909.
———. "The History of Events Resulting in Indian Consolidation West of the Mississippi." In *Annual Report of the American Historical Association*, 233–450. Washington, D.C.: GPO, 1908.
Adams, Herbert Baxter. *The Study of History in American Colleges and Universities*. Washington, D.C.: GPO, 1887.
Annual Report of the American Historical Association for 1910. Washington, D.C.: GPO, 1912.
Annual Report of the Department of the Interior, vol. 12 Washington D.C.: GPO, 1887.
Arguments in Behalf of a Sixteenth Amendment to the Constitution of the United States, Prohibiting the Several States from Disfranchising United States Citizens on Account of Sex. Washington, D.C.: GPO, 1878.
Catalogue of Recently Added Books, Library of Congress, 1873–1875. Washington, D.C.: GPO, 1876.
Clark, S. N. "Are the Indians Dying Out? Preliminary Observations Relating to Indian Civilization and Education." In *Annual Report of the Commissioner of Indian Affairs to the Secretary of the Interior*. E. A. Hyatt, 485–520. Washington, D.C.: GPO, 1877.
Commissioners of Indian Affairs, The. Washington, D.C.: U.S. Department of the Interior/GPO, 2008.

BIBLIOGRAPHY   255

Dorsey, James Owen. *Omaha Sociology.* Washington, D.C.: GPO, 1885.
Executive Documents of the House of Representatives for the Second Session of the Fifty-First Congress, 1890–1891, The. Washington, D.C.: GPO, 1891.
"Federation of Women's Clubs." In *Annual Report of the Commissioner of Indian Affairs to the Secretary of the Interior.* Washington, D.C.: GPO, 1921.
Fletcher, Alice C. *Indian Education and Civilization* report. Washington, D.C.: GPO, 1888.
Fletcher, Alice, and Francis La Flesche. *The Omaha Tribe.* Washington, D.C.: GPO, 1911.
Hayes, C. W., and Waldemar Lindgren. *Contributions to Economic Geography, 1907: Metals and Nonmetals, Except Fuels.* Washington, D.C.: GPO, 1908.
Hearing before the Committee on Woman Suffrage of the United States Senate, December 17, 1904. Washington, D.C.: GPO, 1905.
Hodges, Frederick Webb. *Handbook of American Indians North of Mexico.* Washington, D.C.: GPO, 1911.
Holmes, William H. *Twenty-Seventh Annual Report of the Bureau of American Ethnology, 1905–1906.* Washington, D.C.: GPO, 1911.
Jackson, Helen Hunt, and Abbot Kinney. *Report on the Condition and Needs of the Mission Indians of California.* Washington, D.C.: GPO, 1883.
Kappler, Charles J. *Indian Affairs: Laws and Treaties.* Vol. 2. Washington, D.C.: GPO, 1903.
Lewis, Alvin Fayette. *History of Higher Education in Kentucky.* Washington, D.C.: GPO, 1899.
Lindgre, Waldemar, and others. *Contributions to Economic Geology 1907.* Washington. D.C.: GPO, 1908.
Mason, Otis T. "The Border Land Between the Historian and Archaeologist." In *Annual Report of the American Historical Association for 1890,* 113. Washington, D.C.: GPO, 1891.
Powell, John Wesley. *Introduction to the Study of Indian Languages with Words, Phrases and Sentences to be Collected.* Washington, D.C.: GPO, 1880.
———. "James Owen Dorsey." In *Annual Report of the Board of Regents of the Smithsonian Institution,* 53–54. Washington, D.C.: GPO, 1896.
———. *On the Organization of Scientific Work of the Central Government,* vol. 1 and 2. Washington, D.C.: GPO, 1886.
———. *Philology, or The Science of Activities Designed for Expression.* Washington, D.C.: GPO, 1903.
———. *U.S. Geological Survey of the Rocky Mountain Region.* Washington, D.C.: GPO, 1877.
Reel, Estelle. *Report of the Superintendent of Indian Schools.* Washington, D.C.: GPO, 1904.
Sixteenth Annual Report of the Bureau of Indian Commissioners, 1884. Washington, D.C.: GPO, 1885.
Special Report of the Bureau of Education: Education Exhibits and Conventions at the World's Industrial and Cotton Exposition, New Orleans, 1884–85. Washington, D.C.: GPO, 1886.
Survey of Conditions of the Indians in the United States. Washington, D.C.: GPO, 1931.

Newspapers, 1830–1941

American Advocate (Hallowell, Maine)
Augusta Chronicle (Ga.)
Baltimore Gazette and Daily Advertiser (Md.)
Baltimore Sun (Md.)
Baraboo Daily News (Wisc.)
Boston Daily Advertiser (Mass.)
Boston Evening Journal (Mass.)
Bangor Daily Whig & Courier (Maine)
Brattelboro Messenger (Vt.)
Calumet Weekly (Okla.)
Cherokee Advocate (Tahlequah, Cherokee Nation [present-day Tahlequah, Okla.])

Cherokee Phoenix (New Echota, Ga.)
Cherokee Telephone (Cherokee Nation)
Christian Union (New York)
Christian Recorder (Philadelphia)
Cincinnati Commercial Tribune (Ohio)
Cincinnati Daily Enquirer (Ohio)
Cincinnati Daily Gazette (Ohio)
Cincinnati Daily Star (Ohio)
City of Washington Gazette (D.C.)
Claremore Daily Messenger (Okla.)
Claremore Daily Progress (Okla.)
Cleveland Morning Daily Herald (Ohio)
Coffeyville Weekly Journal (Kans.)
Concord Observer (N.H.)
Congregationalist (Boston)
Critic (Washington, D.C.)
Daily Atlas (Boston)
Daily Critic (Washington, D.C.)
Daily Evening Bulletin (San Francisco)
Daily Gazette (Kalamazoo, Mich.)
Daily Inter Ocean (Chicago)
Daily National Intelligencer (Washington, D.C.)
Daily Oklahoman (Oklahoma City)
Daily Rocky Mountain News (Denver)
Daily Scioto Gazette (Chillicothe, Ohio)
Delaware Daily Time (Chester, Penn.)
Dover Gazette & Strafford Advertiser (N.H.)
Eastern Argus (Portland, Maine)
Eldorado Courier (Okla.)
Emancipator and Free Soil (Boston)
Emancipator (New York)
Evening Star (Washington, D.C.)
Farmer's Cabinet (N.H.)
Georgia Weekly Telegraph (Macon)
Globe (Washington, D.C.)
Gloucester Telegraph (Gloucester, Mass.)
Harold Sentinel (Okla.)
Hollis Tribune (Okla.)
Hudson Western Intelligencer (Ohio)
Huntress (Washington, D.C.)
Illustrated Police News (Boston, Mass.)
Index (Boston)
Indian Chieftain (Vinita, Okla.)
Inter Ocean (Chicago)
Lakota Country Times (Oglala Sioux Tribe, Rosebud Sioux Tribe, Shannon and Bennett Counties, S.Dak.)
Lexington Leader (Okla.)
Liberator (Boston)
Literary Port Folio (Worcester, Mass.)
Lowell Citizen News (Mass.)
Lowell Daily Citizen and News (Mass.)

Madison Democrat (Wisc.)
Maryland Gazette
Morning Oregonian
Mystic Pioneer (Conn.)
National Baptist (Philadelphia)
National Gazette (Philadelphia)
Newark Advocate (Ohio)
Newburyport Herald (Mass.)
New Bedford Mercury (Mass.)
New Day (New York)
New Hampshire Patriot (Concord)
New Hampshire Patriot and State Gazette (Concord)
New Hampshire Repository (Concord)
New-Hampshire Statesman and State Journal (Concord)
New Hampshire Statesman (Concord)
New York Daily Tribune
New York Herald
New York Herald Tribune
New York Times
New York Tribune
New York Spectator
New York Sun
North American (Philadelphia)
Nowata Star (Okla.)
Observer and Telegraph (Hudson, Ohio)
Ohio Observer (Hudson)
Oklahoma State Register (Guthrie)
Omaha Daily Bee (Nebr.)
Omaha Herald (Nebr.)
Oregon Statesman (Salem)
Our Brother in Red (Muskogee, Muscogee Nation)
Paul Pry (Washington, D.C.)
Pensacola Gazette (Pensacola, Fla.)
Pomeroy's Democrat (Chicago)
Revolution (New York)
Philadelphia Inquirer (Penn.)
San Francisco Bulletin (Calif.)
Sayre Headlight (Okla.)
Southwestern Christian Advocate (New Orleans)
Springfield Daily Republican (Mo.)
Stroud Democrat (Okla.)
Sun (Baltimore, Md.)
Sun (Washington, D.C.)
Tahlequah Arrow (Okla.)
Troy Weekly Times (New York)
Tulsa World (Okla.)
United States Telegraph (Washington, D.C.)
Vermont Chronicle (Bellows Falls)
Vermont Gazette (Bennington)
Voice of Peace (Worcester, Mass.)
Waco Daily News (Texas)

Washington Post (Washington, D.C.)
Weekly Herald (New York)
Wheeling Register (W.Va.)
Wisconsin Sentinel (Madison)
Wisconsin State Journal (Madison)
Wisconsin State Register (Portage)
Woman's Journal (Boston)
Worcester Daily Spy (Mass.)

SECONDARY SOURCES

Books

Abel, Annie Heloise, ed. *Chardon's Journal at Fort Clark, 1834–1839.* Lincoln: University of Nebraska Press, 1997.

———, ed. *Tabeau's Narrative of Loisel's Expedition to the Upper Missouri.* Norman: University of Oklahoma Press, 1968.

Abel, Annie Heloise, and Frank J. Klingberg. *A Side-Light on Anglo-American Relations 1839–1858.* Lancaster, Pa.: The Association for the Study of Negro Life and History, 1927.

Adams, David Wallace. *Education for Extinction: American Indians and the Boarding School Experience, 1875–1928.* Lawrence: University of Kansas Press, 1995.

Adams, Herbert Baxter. *Methods of Historical Study.* Vol. 2. Baltimore, Md.: John Murphy, 1884.

———. *The Germanic Origins of New England Towns.* Baltimore, Md.: Johns Hopkins University Press, 1882.

Aldridge, Reginald. *Life on a Ranch: Ranch Notes in Kansas, Colorado, the Indian Territory and Northern Texas.* New York: D. Appleton and Company, 1884.

Andreas, A. T. *History of the State of Nebraska.* Chicago: Western Historical Company, 1882.

Andrew, John A. III. *From Revivals to Removal: Jeremiah Evarts, the Cherokee Nation, and the Search for the Soul of America.* Athens, Ga.: University of Georgia Press, 1992.

Bailey, Garrick A., ed. *The Osage and the Invisible World: From the Works of Francis La Flesche.* Norman: University of Oklahoma Press, 1995.

Baker, Lee D. *Anthropology and the Racial Politics of Culture.* Durham, N.C.: Duke University Press, 2010.

———. *From Savage to Negro: Anthropology and the Construction of Race, 1896–1954.* Berkeley: University of California Press, 1998.

Bannister, Robert C. *Sociology and Scientism: The American Quest for Objectivity, 1880–1940.* Chapel Hill: University of North Carolina Press, 1987.

———. *Social Darwinism: Science and Myth in Anglo-American Social Thought.* Philadelphia: Temple University Press, 1979.

Bannon, John Francis. *Herbert Eugene Bolton: The Historian and the Man.* Tuscon: University of Arizona Press, 1978.

Barnes, Robert Harrison. *Two Crows Denies It: A History of Controversy in Omaha Sociology.* Lincoln: University of Nebraska Press, 1984.

Barton, Cynthia H. *Transcendental Wife: The Life of Abigail May Alcott.* Lanham, Mass.: University Press of America, 1996.

Bartlett, Elizabeth Ann. *Liberty, Equality, Sorority: Origins and Interpretations of American Feminist Thought.* Minneapolis: University of Minnesota Press, 1981.

Batille, Gretchen M., and Charles L. P. Silet, eds. *The Pretend Indians: Images of Native Americans in the Movies.* Ames: Iowa State University Press, 1980.

Berkhofer, Robert F. *The White Man's Indian: Images of the American Indian from Columbus to the Present.* New York: Random House, 1979.

Bieder, Robert E. *Science Encounters the Indian, 1820–1880*. Norman: University of Oklahoma Press, 1986.
Billington, Ray Allen. *Frederick Jackson Turner: Historian, Scholar, Teacher*. New York: Oxford University Press, 1973.
———. *The Genesis of the Frontier Thesis: A Study in Historical Creativity*. San Marino, Calif.: The Huntington Library, 1971.
Blight, David W. *Race and Reunion: The Civil War in American Memory*. Cambridge, Mass.: Harvard University Press, 2001.
Blommaert, Jan. *Discourse: A Critical Introduction*. New York: Cambridge University Press, 2005.
Blumin, Stuart. *The Emergence of the Middle Class: Social Experience in the American City, 1790–1900*. Cambridge, Eng.: Cambridge University Press, 1989.
Bogue, Allen G. *Frederick Jackson Turner: Strange Roads Going Down*. Norman: University of Oklahoma Press, 1998.
Boller, Paul F. *American Transcendentalism, 1830–1860*. New York: G. P. Putnam's Sons, 1974.
Bonta, Marcia Myers. *American Women Afield: Writings by Pioneering Women Naturalists*. College Station: Texas A&M University Press, 1995.
Boritt, Gabor. *The Gettysburg Gospel: The Lincoln Speech that Nobody Knows*. New York: Simon & Schuster, 2006.
Bowler, Peter J. *Evolution: The History of an Idea*. Berkeley: University of California Press, 1983.
———. *Life's Splendid Drama: Evolutionary Biology and the Reconstruction of Life's Ancestry, 1860–1940*. Chicago: University of Chicago Press, 1996.
———. *The Non-Darwinian Revolution: Reinterpreting a Historical Myth*. Baltimore, Md.: Johns Hopkins University Press, 1988.
———. *Theories of Human Evolution: A Century of Debate, 1844–1944*. Baltimore, Md.: Johns Hopkins University Press, 1986.
Brantlinger, Patrick. *Dark Vanishings*. Ithaca, N.Y.: Cornell University Press, 2003.
Brekus, Catherine A. *Strangers and Pilgrims: Female Preaching in America, 1740–1845*. Chapel Hill: University of North Carolina Press, 1998.
Brickhouse, Ann. *The Unsettlement of America: Translation, Interpretation, and the Story of Don Luis de Velasco, 1560–1945*. New York: Oxford University Press, 2015.
Brophy, William A., and Sophie A. Aberle. *The Indian: America's Unfinished Business*. Norman: University of Oklahoma Press, 1966.
Browman, David L., and Stephen Williams. *New Perspectives on the Origins of Americanist Archaeology*. Tuscaloosa: University of Alabama Press, 2002.
Buhle, Mari Jo, and Paul Buhle, eds. *The Concise History of Woman Suffrage*: Selections from the Classic Works of Elizabeth Cady Stanton, Susan B. Anthony, Matilda Joslyn Gage, and the National Woman Suffrage Association. Urbana: University of Illinois Press, 1978.
Bueler, Gladys R. *Colorado's Colorful Characters*. Boulder, Colo.: Smoking Stack Press, 1981.
Butler, Judith. *Gender Trouble: Feminism and the Subversion of Identity*. New York: Routledge, 1990.
Byrd, W. Michael, and Linda A. Clayton. *An American Health Dilemma: A Medical History of African Americans and the Problem of Race, Beginnings to 1900*. New York: Routledge, 2000.
Campbell, Karlyn Kohrs. *Women Public Speakers in the United States, 1800–1925: A Bio-Critical Source Book*. Westport, Conn.: Greenwood Press, 1993.
Canfield, Gae Whitney. *Sarah Winnemucca of the Northern Paiutes*. Norman: University of Oklahoma Press, 1983.
Case, David S, and David Avraham Voluck. *Alaska Natives and American Laws*. Fairbanks: University of Alaska Press, 2002.
Ceplair, Larry, ed. *The Public Years of Sarah and Angelina Grimké: Selected Writings, 1835–1839*. New York: Columbia University Press, 1989.

Clifford, Geraldine Joncich, and James W. Guthrie. *Ed School: A Brief for Professional Education*. Urbana: University of Illinois Press, 1988.
Clifton, James A., ed. *The Invented Indian: Cultural Fictions and Government Policies*. New Brunswick, N.J.: Transaction Publishers, 1990.
———. *The Prairie People: Continuity and Change in Potawatomi Indian Culture, 1665–1965*. Lawrence: University of Kansas Press, 1977.
Cohen, Felix S. *Felix S. Cohen's Handbook of Federal Indian Law*. Ed. Rennard Strickland. Charlottesville, Va.: Michie, 1982.
Cole, Phyllis. *Mary Moody Emerson and the Origins of Transcendentalism: A Family History*. New York: Oxford University Press, 1998.
Collier-Thomas, Bettye. *Daughters of Thunder: Black women Preachers and Their Sermons, 1850–1979*. San Francisco: Jossey-Bass, 1998.
Cook-Lynn, Elizabeth. *Notebooks of Elizabeth Cook-Lynn*. Tuscon: University of Arizona Press, 2007.
Cott, Nancy F. *The Bonds of Womanhood: "Woman's Sphere" in New England, 1780–1835*. New Haven, Conn.: Yale University Press, 1977.
Cozzens, Peter. *Eyewitnesses to the Indian Wars, 1865–1890: The Army and the Indians*. Vol. 5. Mechanicsburg, Pa.: Stackpole Books, 2005.
Cravens, Hamilton. *The Triumph of Evolution: The Heredity-Environment Controversy, 1900–1941*. Baltimore, Md.: Johns Hopkins University Press, 1988.
Currell, Susan, and Christina Codell, eds. *Popular Eugenics: National Efficiency and American Mass Culture in the 1930s*. Athens: Ohio University Press, 2006.
Dale, Edward Everett. *The Range Cattle Industry: Ranching on the Great Plains from 1865 to 1925*. Norman: University of Oklahoma Press, 1930.
———. *Tales of the Tepee*. New York: D.C. Heath & Company, 1920.
———, ed. *Lafayette Letters*. Oklahoma City: Harlow Publishing Company, 1925
Darnell, Regna. *And Along Came Boas: Continuity and Revolution in Americanist Anthropology*. Amsterdam, Neth.: John Benjamins Publishing Company, 1998.
Davis, Carlyle Channing, and William A. Alderson. *The True Story of "Ramona": Its Facts, Fictions, Inspiration and Purpose*. New York: Dodge Publishing, 1914.
Davis, Sam P., ed. *The History of Nevada*. Vol 2. Reno, Nev.: The Elms Publishing Co., 1913.
Day, Bess Eileen. *The Mortons of Arbor Lodge: Their Early Years in Nebraska*. Lincoln, Nebr.: Writer's Club Press, 2001.
Debus, Allen A. *Dinosaurs in Fantastic Fiction: A Thematic Survey*. Jefferson, N.C.: McFarland and Company, 2004.
Deese, Helen R., ed. *Daughter of Boston: The Extraordinary Diary of a Nineteenth-Century Woman, Caroline Healey Dall*. Boston: Beacon Press, 2005.
Deloria, Philip J. *Playing Indian*. New Haven, Conn.: Yale University Press, 1998.
Deloria, Vine, Jr., and Raymond J. DeMallie, eds. *Documents of American Indian Diplomacy: Treaties, Agreements, and Conventions, 1775–1979*. Vol. 1. Norman: University of Oklahoma Press, 1999.
DeLyser, Dydia. *Ramona Memories: Tourism and the Shaping of Southern California*. Minneapolis: University of Minnesota Press, 2005.
Dennis, Michael. *Lessons in Progress: State Universities and Progressivism in the New South, 1880–1920*. Urbana: University of Illinois Press, 2001.
Des Jardins, Julie. *Women and the Historical Enterprise in America: Gender, Race, and the Politics of Memory, 1880–1945*. Chapel Hill: University of North Carolina Press, 2003.
Dippy, Brian W. *The Vanishing American: White Attitudes and U.S. Indian Policy*. Middletown, Conn.: Wesleyan University Press, 1980.
Dodd, William E. *Expansion and Conflict*. Cambridge, Mass.: The Riverside Press, 1914.

Drinnon, Richard. *Facing West: The Metaphysics of Indian-Hating and Empire-Building*. Minneapolis: University of Minnesota Press, 1980.
DuBois, Ellen Carol. *Feminism and Suffrage: The Emergence of an Independent Women's Movement in America, 1848–1869*. Ithaca, N.Y.: Cornell University Press, 1978.
———. *Woman Suffrage and Women's Rights*. New York: New York University Press, 1998.
Ertman, Martha M., and Joan C. Williams. *Rethinking Commodification: Case and Readings in Law and Culture*. New York: New York University Press, 2005.
Eschbach, Elizabeth Seymour. *The Higher Education of Women in England and America, 1865–1920*. New York: Garland Publishing, 1993.
Faragher, John Mack, ed. Rereading Frederick Jackson Turner: "The Significance of the Frontier in American History" and Other Essays. New York: Henry Holt and Company, 1994.
Ferguson, Niall. *Empire: The Rise and Demise of the British World Order and the Lessons for Global Power*. New York: Basic Books, 2002.
Fine, William F. *Progressive Evolution and American Sociology, 1890–1920*. Ann Arbor: UMI Research Press, 1976.
Fiorenza, Elisabeth Schüssler. *In Memory of Her: A Feminist Theological Reconstruction of Christian Origins*. New York: Crossroad, 1983.
Foner, Eric. *Forever Free: The Story of Emancipation and Reconstruction*. Ed. Joshua Brown. New York: Vintage, 2006.
Foucault, Michel. *Archeology of Knowledge*. New York: Vintage Books, 2010.
Fowler, Don D. *A Laboratory for Anthropology: Science and Romanticism in the American Southwest, 1846–1930*. Albuquerque: University of New Mexico Press, 2000.
Fritz, Henry E. *The Movement for Indian Assimilation, 1860–1890*. Philadelphia: University of Pennsylvania Press, 1963.
Gabriel, Ralph Henry, ed. *The Pageant of America: A Pictorial History of the United States*. New Haven, Conn.: Yale University Press, 1929.
Gacs, Ute, Aisha Khan, Jerrie McIntyre, and Ruth Weinberg, eds. *Women Anthropologists: Selected Bibliographies*. Urbana: University of Illinois Press, 1989.
Garraty, John A., and Mark C. Carnes, ed. *American National Biography*. Vol 5. New York: Oxford University Press, 1999.
Genetin-Pilawa, Joseph C. *Crooked Paths to Allotment: The Fight over Federal Indian Policy after the Civil War*. Chapel Hill: University of North Carolina, 2012.
Gibson, Arrell Morgan. *The West Wind Blows: The Autobiography of Edward Everett Dale*. Oklahoma City: Oklahoma Historical Society, 1984.
Gidley, Mick. *Edward S. Curtis and the North American Indian, Incorporated*. Cambridge, Eng.: Cambridge University Press, 2000.
Ginzberg, Lori D. *Elizabeth Cady Stanton: An American Life*. New York: Hill and Wang, 2009.
———. *Women and the Work of Benevolence: Morality, Politics, and Class in the Nineteenth-Century United States*. New Haven, Conn.: Yale University Press, 1990.
Gittinger, Roy. *The University of Oklahoma, 1892–1942*. Norman: University of Oklahoma Press, 1942.
Goble, Danny. *Progressive Oklahoma: The Making of a New Kind of State*. Norman: University of Oklahoma Press, 1980.
Gohdes, Clarence L. F. *The Periodicals of American Transcendentalism*. Durham, N.C.: Duke University Press, 1931.
Goins, Charles Robert, and Danny Goble. *Historical Atlas of Oklahoma*. Norman: University of Oklahoma, 2006.
Goodwin, Joan. *The Remarkable Mrs. Ripley: The Life of Sarah Alden Bradford Ripley*. Boston: Northeastern University Press, 1998.

Green, Constance McLaughlin. *The Secret City: A History of Race Relations in the Nation's Capital.* Princeton, N.J.: Princeton University Press, 1967.
———. *Washington: Capital City 1879–1950.* Princeton, N.J.: Princeton University Press, 1963.
Green, Richard. *Te Ata: Chickasaw Storyteller, American Treasure.* Norman: University of Oklahoma Press, 2002.
Greenwald, Emily. *Reconfiguring the Reservation: The Nez Perces, Jicarilla Apaches, and the Dawes Act.* Albuquerque: University of New Mexico Press, 2002.
Griffith, Elizabeth. *In Her Own Right: The Life of Elizabeth Cady Stanton.* London: Oxford University Press, 1985.
Gura, Philip F. *American Transcendentalism: A History.* New York: Hill & Wang, 2007.
Gutiérrez-Jones, Carl. *Rethinking the Borderlands: Between Chicano Culture and Legal Discourse.* Berkeley: University of California Press, 1995.
Hagan, William T. *The Indian Rights Association: The Herbert Welsh Years, 1882–1904.* Tucson: University of Arizona Press, 1985.
Haller, John S. *Outcasts from Evolution: Scientific Attitudes of Racial Inferiority, 1859–1900.* Urbana: University of Illinois Press, 1971.
Halttunnen, Karen. *Confidence Men and Painted Women: A Study of Middle-Class Culture in America, 1830–1870.* New Haven, Conn.: Yale University Press, 1982.
Hanaford, Phebe A. *Daughters of America, or Women of the Century.* Augusta, Me.: True and Company, 1883.
Harris, Marvin. *The Rise of Anthropological Theory: A History of Theories of Cultures.* Walnut Creek, Calif.: Alta Mira Press, 2001.
Hartman, Susan M. *The Other Feminists: Activists in the Liberal Establishment.* New Haven, Conn.: Yale University Press, 1998.
Hatch, Nathan O. *The Democratization of American Christianity.* New Haven, Conn.: Yale University Press, 1989.
Haywood, Chanta M. *Prophesying Daughters: Black Women Preachers and the Word, 1823–1913.* Columbia: University of Missouri Press, 2003.
Hewitt, Nancy A. *No Permanent Wave: Recasting Histories of U.S. Feminism.* New Brunswick, N.J.: Rutgers University Press, 2010.
———. *Women's Activism and Social Change: Rochester, New York, 1822–1872.* Ithaca, N.Y.: Cornell University Press, 1984.
Hickey, Donald R, Susan A. Wunder, and John R. Wunder. *Nebraska Moments.* Lincoln: University of Nebraska Press, 2007.
Holm, Tom. *The Great Confusion in Indian Affairs: Native Americans and Whites in the Progressive Era.* Austin: University of Texas Press, 2005.
Hough, Emerson. *The Story of the Cowboy.* New York: D. Appleton and Company, 1884.
Hoxie, Frederick E. *A Final Promise: The Campaign to Assimilate the Indians, 1880–1920.* Cambridge, Eng.: Cambridge University Press, 1984.
Hunter, Fannie McDowell. *Women Preachers.* Dallas, Texas: Berachah Printing Co., 1905.
Hurtado, Albert L. *Herbert Eugene Bolton: Historian of the American Borderlands.* Berkeley: University of California Press, 2012.
Isenberg, Nancy. *Sex and Citizenship in Antebellum America.* Chapel Hill: University of North Carolina Press, 1998.
Jacobs, Margaret D. *White Mother to a Dark Race: Settler Colonialism, Maternalism, and the Removal of Indigenous Children in the American West and Australia, 1840–1940.* Lincoln: University of Nebraska Press, 2009.
Jacobs, Wilbur R. *The Historical World of Frederick Jackson Turner.* New Haven, Conn.: Yale University Press, 1968.
Jaffe, Mark. *The Gilded Dinosaur: The Fossil War between E. D. Cope and O. C. Marsh and the Rise of American Science.* New York: Crown Publishers, 2000.

James, Edward T., Janet Wilson Ames, Paul S. Boyer, eds. *Notable American Women, 1607–1950: A Biographical Dictionary.* Vol. 1. Cambridge, Mass.: Belknap Press of Harvard University, 1974.
Jameson, John Franklin. *John Franklin Jameson and the Development of Humanistic Scholarship in America.* 3 vols. Ed. Morey Rothberg and Jacqueline Anne Goggin. Athens: University of Georgia Press, 1998–2001.
Johannsen, Albert. *The House of Beadle and Adams and Its Dime and Nickel Novels.* Vols. 1–3. Norman: University of Oklahoma Press, 1950.
Jones, Gregg. *Honor in the Dust: Theodore Roosevelt, War in the Philippines, and the Rise and Fall of America's Imperial Dream.* New York: New American Library, 2012.
Josephy, Alvin M., Jr. *The Nez Perce Indians and the Opening of the Northwest.* New Haven, Conn.: Yale University Pres, 1965.
Judd, Neil M. *The Bureau of American Ethnology: A Partial History.* Norman: University of Oklahoma Press, 1967.
Kammen, Michael. *Mystic Cords of Memories: The Transformation of Tradition in American Culture.* New York: Knopf Doubleday, 2011.
Karcher, Carolyn L., ed *A Lydia Maria Child Reader.* Durham, N.C.: Duke University Press, 1997.
———. *The First Woman in the Republic: A Cultural Biography of Lydia Maria Child.* Durham, N.C.: Duke University Press, 1998.
Keller, Robert H., Jr. *American Protestantism and United States Indian Policy, 1869–1882.* Lincoln: University of Nebraska Press, 1983.
Keller, Rosemary Skinner, and Rosemary Radford Ruether, eds. *Encyclopedia of Women and Religion in North America.* 3 vols. Bloomington: Indiana University Press, 2006.
Kevles, Daniel J. *In the Name of Eugenics: Genetics and the Uses of Human Heredity.* New York: Knopf, 1985.
Kidwell, Clara Sue. *The Choctaws in Oklahoma: From Tribe to Nation, 1855–1970.* Norman: University of Oklahoma Press, 2007.
Kinney, Jay P. *A Continent Lost, a Civilization Won: Indian Land Tenure in America.* Baltimore, Md.: Johns Hopkins Press, 1937.
Kolmerten, Carol A. *The American Life of Ernestine L. Rose.* Syracuse, N.Y.: Syracuse University Press, 1999.
Kunhardt, Philip B. *A New Birth of Freedom: Lincoln at Gettysburg.* Boston: Little, Brown, 1983.
LaFeber, Walter. *The New Empire: An Interpretation of American Expansion, 1860–1898.* Ithaca, N.Y.: Cornell University Press, 1963.
Laguna, Frederica de, and A. Irving Hallowell. *American Anthropology, 1888–1920: Papers from the American Anthropologist.* Lincoln: University of Nebraska Press, 2002.
Lauback, David Charles. *To Think That It Happened on Mulberry Street.* Valley Forge, Penn.: National Ministries American Baptist Churches USA, 2007.
Laubin, Gladys, and Reginald Laubin. *The Indian Tipi: Its History, Construction, and Use.* Norman: University of Oklahoma Press, 1989.
Lears, Jackson. *Rebirth of a Nation: The Making of Modern America, 1877–1920.* New York: Harper Collins, 2009.
Leckie, Shirley A. *Angie Debo: Pioneering Historian.* Norman: University of Oklahoma Press, 2000.
Leckie, Shirley A., and Nancy J. Parezo, eds. *Their Own Frontier: Women Intellectuals Re-Visioning the American West.* Lincoln: University of Nebraska Press, 2008.
Lincoln, Abraham. *Speeches and Writings, 1859–1865.* New York: Library of America, 1989.
Lindley, Susan Hill, and Eleanor J. Stebner, eds. *The Westminster Handbook to Women in American Religious History.* Westminster, UK: John Knox Press, 2008.
Loughlin, Patrica. *Hidden Treasures of the American West: Muriel H. Wright, Angie Debo, and Alice Marriott.* Albuquerque: University of Albuquerque Press, 2005.

Love, Eric T. L. *Race over Empire: Racism and U.S. Imperialism, 1865–1900*. Chapel Hill: University of North Carolina Press, 2004.
Lubetkin, John M. *Jay Cooke's Gamble: The Northern Pacific Railroad, the Sioux, and the Panic of 1873*. Norman: University of Oklahoma Press, 2006.
Lunbeck, Elizabeth. *The Status of Women in the Historical Profession*. Washington, D.C.: American Historical Association, 2005.
Mann, Barbara Alice. *Native Americans, Archaeologists, and the Mounds*. New York: Peter Lang, 2003.
Mardock, Robert Winston. *The Reformers and the American Indian*. Columbia: University of Missouri Press, 1971.
Mark, Joan. *A Stranger in Her Native Land: Alice Fletcher and the American Indians*. Lincoln: University of Nebraska Press, 1988.
———. *Four Anthropologists: An American Science in its Early Years*. New York: Science History Publications, 1980.
Marquardt, H. Michael. *The Rise of Mormonism, 1816–1844*. Longwood, Fla.: Xulon Press, 2005.
Martin, Ronald E. *The Languages of Difference: American Writers and Anthropologists Reconfigure the Primitive, 1878–1940*. Newark: University of Delaware Press, 2005.
Mathes, Valerie Sherer. *Divinely Guided: The California Work of the Women's National Indian Association*. Lubbock: Texas Tech University Press, 2012.
———. *Helen Hunt Jackson and Her Indian Reform Legacy*. Austin: University of Texas Press, 1990.
———, ed. *The Indian Reform Letters of Helen Hunt Jackson, 1879–1885*. Norman: University of Oklahoma Press, 1998.
Mathes, Valerie Sherer, and Richard Lowitt. *The Standing Bear Controversy: Prelude to Indian Reform*. Urbana: University of Illinois Press, 2003.
Matthews, John Joseph. *Twenty Thousand Mornings: An Autobiography*. Norman: University of Oklahoma Press, 2012.
Mayer, Henry. *All on Fire: William Lloyd Garrison and the Abolition of Slavery*. New York: St. Martin's Press, 1989.
McCandless, Amy Thompson. *The Past in Present: Women's Higher Education in the Twentieth-Century American South*. Tuscaloosa: University of Alabama, 1999.
McLoughlin, William G. *Champions of the Cherokees: Evan and John B. Jones*. Princeton, N.J.: Princeton University Press, 1990.
McMaster, John Bach. *The Acquisition of Political, Social, and Industrial Rights of Man in America*. Cleveland, Ohio: The Arthur H. Clark Company, 1903.
McMillen, Sally G. *Seneca Falls and the Origins of the Women's Rights Movement*. London: Oxford University Press, 2009.
Mead, Rebecca J. *How the Vote Was Won: Woman Suffrage in the Western United States, 1868–1914*. New York: New York University Press, 2004.
Meltzer, David J. *First Peoples in a New World: Colonizing Ice Age America*. Berkeley: University of California Press, 2009.
Mielke, Laura L. *Moving Encounters: Sympathy and the Indian Question in Antebellum Literature*. Amherst: University of Massachusetts Press, 2008.
Miller, Darlis A. *Matilda Coxe Stevenson: Pioneering Anthropologist*. Norman: University of Oklahoma Press, 2007.
Miller, Stuart Creighton. *"Benevolent Assimilation": The American Conquest of the Philippines, 1899–1903*. New Haven, Conn.: Yale University Press, 1984.
Morris, John W., Charles R. Goins and Edwin C. McReynolds. *Historical Atlas of Oklahoma*. Norman: University of Oklahoma Press, 1986
Mott, Wesley T. *Biographical Dictionary of Transcendentalism*. Westport, Conn.: Greenwood Press, 1996.

Musslewhite, Lynn, and Crawford, Suzanne Jones. *One Woman's Political Journey: Kate Barnard and Social Reform, 1875–1930.* Norman: University of Oklahoma Press, 2003.

Myerson, Joel. *The New England Transcendentalists and the Dial.* Rutherford, N.J.: Fairleigh Dickinson University Press, 1980.

Newman, Louise Michele. *White Women's Rights: The Racial Origins of Feminism in the United States.* New York: Oxford University Press, 1999.

Norgren, Jill. *Belva Lockwood: The Woman Who Would Be President.* New York: New York University Press, 2007.

Novick, Peter. *That Noble Dream: The "Objectivity Question" and the American Historical Profession.* Cambridge, Eng.: Cambridge University Press, 1998.

Ogden, Adele, and Engel Sluiter. *Greater America: Essays in Honor of Herbert Eugene Bolton.* Berkeley: University of California Press, 1945.

Oren, Michael B. *Power, Faith, and Fantasy: America in the Middle East, 1776 to the Present.* New York: W.W. Norton & Company, 2007.

Pagden, Anthony. *Lords of All the World: Ideologies of Empire in Spain, Britain and France, c. 1500–c. 1800.* New Haven, Conn: Yale University Press, 1995.

Palmer, Beverly Wilson, ed. *Selected Letters of Lucretia Coffin Mott.* Urbana: University of Illinois Press 2002.

Parker, Gail Underwood. *More Than Petticoats: Remarkable New Hampshire Women.* Kearney, Nebr.: Morris Book Publishing, 2009.

Parins, James W. *Literacy and Intellectual Life in the Cherokee Nation, 1820–1906.* Norman: University of Oklahoma Press, 2013.

Pascoe, Peggy. *Relations of Rescue: The Search for Female Moral Authority in the American West, 1874–1939.* New York: Oxford University Press, 1990.

Patterson, Thomas Carl. *A Social History of Anthropology in the United States.* New York: Berg, 2001.

Paxson, Frederic Logan. *The Last American Frontier.* New York: McMillian, 1910.

Phillips, Kate. *Helen Hunt Jackson: A Literary Life.* Berkeley: University of California Press, 2003.

Phillips, Clifton Jackson. *Protestant America and the Pagan World: The First Half Century of the American Board of Commissioners for Foreign Missions, 1810–1869.* Cambridge, Mass.: East Asian Research Center Harvard University, 1969.

Portnoy, Alisse. *Their Right to Speak: Women's Activism in the Indian and Slave Debates.* Cambridge, Mass.: Harvard University Press, 2005.

Posey, Alexander Lawrence. *The Fus Fixico Letters: A Creek Humorist in Early Oklahoma.* Norman: University of Oklahoma Press, 2002.

Prucha, Francis Paul. *American Indian Policy in Crisis: Christian Reformers and the Indian, 1865–1900.* Norman: University of Oklahoma Press, 1976.

———. *Americanizing the Indians: Writings by the "Friends" of the Indian, 1880–1900.* Lincoln: University of Nebraska Press, 1973.

———. *The Great Father: The United States Government and the American Indians.* Vol 1–2. Lincoln: University of Nebraska Press, 1984.

Radin, Margaret Jane. *Contested Commodities: The Trouble with Trade in Sex, Children, Body Parts and Other Things.* Cambridge, Mass.: Harvard University Press, 1996.

Rapp, George R., and Christopher L. Hill. *Geoarchaeology: The Earth-Science Approach to Archaeological Interpretation.* New Haven, Conn.: Yale University Press, 2006.

Ray, T. B., *Southern Baptist Foreign Missions.* Nashville, Tenn.: Sunday School Board, Southern Baptist Convention, 1910.

Renehan, Edward J., Jr. *The Transcontinental Railroad: The Gateway to the West.* New York: Chelsea House, 2007.

Riley, Glenda. *Confronting Race: Women and Indians on the Frontier, 1815–1915.* Albuquerque: University of New Mexico Press, 2004.

———. *Women and Indians on the Frontier, 1825–1915*. Albuquerque: University of New Mexico Press, 1984.
Rinella, Steven. *American Buffalo: In Search of a Lost Icon*. New York: Spiegel & Grau, 2008.
Ronda, Bruce A. *Elizabeth Palmer Peabody: A Reformer on Her Own Terms*. Cambridge, Mass.: Harvard University Press, 1999.
Rose, Anne C. *Transcendentalism as a Social Movement, 1830–1850*. New Haven, Conn.: Yale University Press, 1981.
Rosenberg, Rosalind. *Beyond Separate Spheres: Intellectual Roots of Modern Feminism*. New Haven, Conn.: Yale University Press, 1982.
Ryan, Mary P. *Cradle of the Middle Class: The Family in Oneida County, New York, 1790–1865*. New York: Cambridge University Press, 1981.
Sanborn, F. B., and Cameron, Kenneth Walter, eds. *The Transcendental Eye: Historical Papers Concerning New England and Other Points on a Great Circle*. Hartford, Conn.: Transcendental Books, 1980
Sandoz, Mari. *Crazy Horse: The Strange Man of the Oglalas*. New York: Knopf, 1942.
Scales, James R., and Danny Goble. *Oklahoma Politics: A History*. Norman: University of Oklahoma Press, 1982.
Scott, Joan Wallach. *Gender and the Politics of History*. New York: Columbia University Press, 1999.
Senier, Siobhan. *Voices of American Indian Assimilation and Resistance: Helen Hunt Jackson, Sarah Winnemucca, and Victoria Howard*. Norman: University of Oklahoma Press, 2001.
Shetrone, Henry Clyde. *The Mound-Builders*. Tuscaloosa: University of Alabama Press, 2004.
Shirk, George H. *Oklahoma Place Names*. Norman: University of Oklahoma Press, 1965.
Sholtz, Christa Sieglinde. *Negotiating Claims: The Emergence of Indian's Land Claim Negotiation Policies in Australia, Canada, New Zealand, and the United States*. New York: Routledge, 2006.
Silverberg, Robert. *Mound Builders of Ancient America*. Greenwich, Conn.: New York Graphic Society, 1968.
Sims, Mary S. *The Natural History of a Social Institution: The Young Women's Christian Association*. New York: The Women's Press, 1936.
Simonsen, Jane E. *Making Home Work: Domesticity and Native American Assimilation in the American West*. Chapel Hill: University of North Carolina Press, 2006.
Siringo, Charles A. *A Texas Cowboy; or Fifteen Years on the Hurricane Deck of a Spanish Pony*. Chicago: Siringo & Dobson, 1886.
Sklar, Kathryn Kish. *Catharine Beecher: A Study in American Domesticity*. New Haven, Conn.: Yale University Press, 1973.
Sligh, Gary Lee. *A Study of Native American Women Novelists: Sophia Alice Callahan, Mourning Dove, and Ella Cara Deloria*. Lewiston, N.Y.: Edwin Mellon Press, 2003.
Slotkin, Richard. *Gunfighter Nation: The Myth of the Frontier in Twentieth-Century America*. New York: Harper Perennial, 1993.
———. *The Fatal Environment: The Myth of the Frontier in the Age of Industrialization, 1800–1890*. New York: Atheneum, 1985.
Smith, Bonnie G. *The Gender of History: Men, Women and Historical Practice*. Cambridge, Mass.: Harvard University Press, 1998.
Solomon, Barbara Miller. *In the Company of Educated Women: A History of Women and Higher Education in America*. New Haven, Conn.: Yale University Press, 1986.
Stanton, Elizabeth Cady, Susan Brownell Anthony, Matilda Joslyn Gage, and Ida Husted Harper. *The History of Woman Suffrage*. 6 vols. New York: J. J. Little & Ives Company, 1922.
Stauffer, Helen Winter. *Mari Sandoz*. Boise, Idaho: Boise State University, 1984.
Stedman, Raymond William. *Shadows of the Indian: Stereotypes in American Culture*. Norman: University of Oklahoma Press, 1982.
Sterling, Dorothy. *Turning the World Upside Down: The Anti-Slavery Convention of American Women*. New York: The Feminist Press at the City University of New York, 1987.

Stern, Alexandra Minna. *Eugenic Nation: Faults and Frontiers of Better Breeding in Modern America*. Berkeley: University of California Press, 2005.
Stubbs, Michael. *Discourse Analysis: The Sociolinguistic Analysis of Natural Language*. Chicago: University of Chicago Press, 1983.
Szasz, Margaret Connell. *Between Indian and White Worlds: The Cultural Broker*. Norman: University of Oklahoma Press, 1994.
Thoburn, Joseph B. *A Standard History of Oklahoma*. 5 vols. Chicago: American Historical Society, 1916.
Thomas, Marcia L. *John Wesley Powell: An Annotated Bibliography*. Westport, Conn.: Praeger Press, 2004.
Tinkle, Lon. *An American Original: The Life of J. Frank Dobie*. Boston: Little, Brown, 1978.
Tonkovich, Nicole. *The Allotment Plot: Alice C. Fletcher, E. Jane Gay, and Nez Perce Survivance*. Lincoln: University of Nebraska Press, 2012.
Tracy, Joseph. *History of American Missions to the Heathen*. Worcester, Mass.: Spooner & Howland, 1840.
Trefousse, Hans Louis. *Carl Schurz: A Biography*. New York: Fordham University Press, 1998.
Ulan, Edward. *The Rogue of Publisher's Row: Confessions of a Publisher*. New York: Exposition Press, 1956.
Ulrigh, Roberta. *American Indian Nations from Termination to Restoration, 1953–2006*. Lincoln: University of Nebraska Press, 2010.
Underhill, James W. *Creating Worldviews: Metaphor, Ideology and Language*. New York: Cambridge University Press, 2011.
Vanderwerth, W. C. *Indian Oratory: Famous Speeches by Noted Indian Chieftains*. Norman: University of Oklahoma Press, 1971.
von Richthofen, Walter, Baron. *Cattle-Raising on the Plains of North America*. New York: Appleton, 1885
Wallace, David Rains. *The Bone Hunter's Revenge: Dinosaurs, Greed, and the Greatest Scientific Feud of the Gilded Age*. Boston: Houghton Mifflin, 1999.
Waugh, Joan. *U. S. Grant: American Hero, American Myth*. Chapel Hill: University of North Carolina Press, 2009.
Wayne, Tiffany K. *Woman Thinking: Feminism and Transcendentalism in Nineteenth-Century America*. Lanham, Md.: Lexington Books, 2005.
Weeks, John M. *The Library of Daniel G. Brinton*. Philadelphia: University of Pennsylvania Museum of Anthropology, 2003.
Wexler, Laura. *Tender Violence: Domestic Visions in an Age of U.S. Imperialism*. Chapel Hill: University of North Carolina Press, 2000.
Wheelan, Joseph. *Mr. Adams's Last Crusade: John Quincy Adams's Extraordinary Post- Presidential Life in Congress*. New York: Public Affairs, 2008.
Wheeler, Mark Richard, and William Anthony Nericcio, ed. *150 Years of Evolution: Darwin's Impact on Contemporary Thought and Culture*. San Diego, Calif.: San Diego State University Press, 2011.
White, Richard. *Railroaded: The Transcontinentals and the Making of Modern America*. New York: W. W. Norton, 2011.
Wiesendanger, Martin W. *Grant and Carolyn Foreman: A Bibliography*. Tulsa, Okla.: University of Tulsa, 1948.
Wilbanks, Charles, ed. *Walking by Faith: The Diary of Angelina Grimké, 1828–1835*. Columbia: University of South Carolina Press, 2003.
Williams, Lucy Fowler, William Wierzbowski, and Robert W. Preucel, eds. *Native American Voices on Identity, Art, and Culture: Objects of Everlasting Esteem*. Philadelphia: University of Pennsylvania Museum of Archaeology and Anthropology, 2005.

Wills, Garry. *Lincoln at Gettysburg: The Words that Remade America*. New York: Simon & Schuster, 1992.
Wishart, David J. *An Unspeakable Sadness: The Dispossession of the Nebraska Indians*. Lincoln: University of Nebraska Press, 1994.
Woody, Thomas. *A History of Women's Education in the United States*. New York: The Science Press, 1929.
Worster, Donald. *A River Running West: The Life of John Wesley Powell*. New York: Oxford Press, 2001.
Wrobel, David M. *The End of American Exceptionalism: Frontier Anxiety from the Old West to the New Deal*. Lawrence: University of Kansas Press, 1993.
Yellin, Jean Fagan. *Women and Sisters: The Antislavery Feminists in American Culture*. New Haven, Conn.: Yale University Press, 1989
Yellin, Jean Fagan, and John C. Van Horne. *The Abolitionist Sisterhood: Women's Political Culture in Antebellum America*. Ithaca, N.Y.: Cornell University Press, 1994.
Zaeske, Susan. *Signatures of Citizenship: Petitioning, Antislavery, and Women's Political Identity*. Chapel Hill: University of North Carolina Press, 2003.
Zanjani, Sally. *Sarah Winnemucca*. Lincoln: University of Nebraska Press, 2001.

Articles

Aeschbacher, William D. "The Mississippi Valley Historical Association, 1907–1965." *Journal of American History* 54, no. 2 (September 1967): 339–41.
Algeo, Katie. "Indian for a Night: Sleeping with the 'Other' at Wigwam Village Tourist Cabins." *Material Culture* 41, no. 2 (Fall 2009): 1–17.
Ambrosius, Lloyd E. "Turner's Frontier Thesis and the Modern American Empire: A Review Essay." *Civil War History* 17, no. 4 (December 1971): 332–39.
"Angie Debo," AHA *Perspectives* (1988): 14.
Ayala, Francisco J. "Teleological Explanations in Evolutionary Biology," *Philosophy of Science* 37, no. 1 (March 1970): 1–15.
Baker, Lee D. "Daniel G. Brinton's Success on the Road to Obscurity." *Cultural Anthropology* 15, no. 3 (August 2000): 394–423.
Barsh, Russel Lawrence. "American Indians in the Great War." *Ethnohistory* 38, no. 3 (Summer 1991): 276–303.
———. "War and the Reconfiguring of American Indian Society." *Journal of American Studies* 35 (2001): 3, 371–410.
Bernstein, Jay H. "First Recipients of Anthropology Doctorates in the United States, 1891–1930." *American Anthropologist* 104, no. 2 (June 2002): 551–64.
Bienstock, Barry W. "Helen Hunt Jackson." In *American Historians, 1866–1912*, ed. Clyde N. Wilson, 148–52. Detroit, Mich.: Bruccoli Clark, 1986.
Billington, Louis. "Female Laborers in the Church: Women Preachers in the Northeastern United States, 1790–1840." *Journal of American Studies* 19, no. 3 (December 1985): 369–94.
Billington, Ray Allen. "Tempest in Clio's Teapot: The American Historical Association Rebellion of 1915." *American Historical Review* 78, no. 2 (April 1973): 348–69.
Birdsall, Richard D. "The Second Great Awakening and the New England Social Order." *Church History* 39, no. 3 (September 1970): 345–64.
Black, Jason Edward. "The 'Mascotting' of Native America: Construction, Commodity, and Assimilation." *American Indian Quarterly* 26, no. 4 (Autumn 2002): 605–22.
Blegen, Theodore C. "Our Widening Province." *The Mississippi Valley Historical Review* 31, no. 1 (June 1944): 3–6, 13.

Bloom, Lansing B. Review of *Companions on the Trail: A Literary Chronicle*, by Hamlin Garland. *The Mississippi Valley Historical Review* 18, no. 4 (March 1932): 595–96.

———. Review of *Forgotten Frontiers: A Study of the Spanish Indian Policy of Don Juan Bautista de Anza, Governor of New Mexico, 1777–1787, from the Original Documents in the Archives of Spain, Mexico and New Mexico*, by Alfred B. Thomas. *The Mississippi Valley Historical Review* 19, no. 2 (September 1932): 277–79.

———. Review of *Oklahoma*, by Victor E. Harlow. *The Mississippi Valley Historical Review* 21, no. 4 (March 1935): 597–98.

———. Review of *Traders to the Navajos: The Story of the Wetherills of Kayanta*, by Louisa Frances Gillmore and Wade Wetherill. *The Mississippi Valley Historical Review* 21, no. 3 (December 1934): 408–409.

Bolton, Herbert Eugene. "The Spanish Mission as a Frontier Institution." *American Historical Review* 25, no. 1 (October 1917): 42–61.

"Books Recently Added to Library." *Chronicles of Oklahoma* 12, no. 2 (June 1934): 226.

Bourne, Edward Gaylord. "The Philippine 'Situado' From the Treasury of New Spain." *American Historical Review* 10, no. 2 (October–July 1903–1904): 459–61.

Bowler, Peter J. "Edward Drinker Cope and the Changing Structure of Evolutionary Theory." *Isis* 68, no. 2 (June 1977): 249–65.

———. "The Changing Meaning of 'Evolution.'" *Journal of the History of Ideals* 36, no. 1 (January–March 1975): 95–114.

Botting, Eileen Hunt, and Sarah L. Houser. "Drawing the Line of Equality: Hannah Mather Crocker on Women's Rights." *American Political Science Review* 100, no. 2 (May 2006): 265–78.

Brekus, Catherine A. "Female Preaching in Early Nineteenth-Century America." *Center for Christian Ethics at Baylor University* (2009): 20–29.

———. "Harriet Livermore, the Pilgrim Stranger: Female Preaching and Biblical Feminism in Early Nineteenth-Century America." *Church History* 65, no. 3 (September 1996): 389–404.

Brigandi, Phil and John W. Robinson. "The Killing of Juan Diego: From Murder to Mythology." *Journal of San Diego History* 40, no. 1–2 (Winter/Spring 1994): 1–22.

Brightman, Robert A. "Culture and Culture Theory in Native North America." In *New Perspectives on Native North America: Cultures, Histories, and Representations*, ed. Sergei A. Kan, Pauline Turner Strong, and Raymond D. Fogelson, 331–94. Lincoln: University of Nebraska Press, 2006.

Bristow, David L. "The Enduring Mari Sandoz." *Nebraska Life* (January–February 2001): 1–8.

Browman, David L. "Frederic Ward Putnam: Contributions to the Development of Archeological Institutions and Encouragement of Women Practitioners." In *New Perspectives on the Origins of Americanist Archaeology*, eds. David L. Browman and Stephen Williams, 209–41. Tuscaloosa: University of Alabama Press, 2002.

———. "Origins of Stratigraphic Excavations in North America: The Peabody Museum Method and the Chicago Method." In *New Perspectives on the Origins of Americanist Archaeology*, eds. David L. Browman and Stephen Williams, 242–64. Tuscaloosa: University of Alabama Press, 2002.

———. "Peabody Museum, Frederic W. Putnam, and the Rise of U.S. Anthropology, 1866–1903, The," *American Anthropologist* 104, no. 2 (June 2002): 508–19.

Brown, David S. "Historical Landscapes of Frederick Jackson Turner and Henry Adams. The," In *Cultural Landscapes: Religion and Public Life*, ed. Gabriel R. Ricci, 40. Piscataway, N.J.: Transaction Publishers, 2006.

Brown, Ira V. "'Am I Not a Woman and a Sister?' The Anti-Slavery Convention of American Women, 1837–1839." *Pennsylvania History* 50 (January 1983): 1–19.

Buffalohead, W. Roger, and Paulette Fairbanks Molin. "'A Nucleus of Civilization': American Indian Families at Hampton Institute in the Late Nineteenth Century." *Journal of American Indian Education* 35, no. 3 (May 1996): 59–94.

Bushnell, David, and John H. Coatsworth. "J. Fred Rippy, 1892–1977." *Hispanic American Historical Review* 68, no. 1 (February 1988): 103–104.

Byers, John. "Helen Hunt Jackson," *American Literary Realism* 2, no. 2 (Summer 1969): 143–48.

Byers, John, and Elizabeth S. Byers. "Helen Hunt Jackson, 1830–1885," *American Literary Realism* 6, no. 3 (Summer 1973): 196–242.

Capper, Charles. "Margaret Fuller as Cultural Reformer: The Conversations in Boston." *American Quarterly* 39, no. 4 (Winter 1987): 509–28.

Candidus, Shelly. "Herbert Welsh: Walking Crusader." *Soo Nipi Magazine* (Summer 2004): 18–23.

Cano, Gloria. "Blair and Robertson's *The Philippine Islands, 1493–1898*: Scholarship or Imperialist Propaganda?" *Philippine Studies* 56, no. 1 (2008): 10–11.

Castile, George Pierre. "The Commodification of Indian Identity." *American Anthropologist* 98, no. 4 (December 1996): 743–49.

Caughey, John W. and others. "Frank J. Klingberg, History: Los Angeles." University of California, *In Memoriam* (May 1969): 3–7.

Chapin, Bradley. "Written Rights: Puritan and Quaker Procedural Guarantees." *Pennsylvania Magazine of History and Biography* 114, no. 3 (July 1990): 323–48.

Chapman, Berlin B. "The Day in Court for the Kiowa, Comanche and Apache Tribes." *Great Plains Journal* 2, no. 1 (Fall 1962): 1–21.

Chapman, Charles E. "The Native Sons' Fellowships." *The Southwestern Historical Quarterly* 21, no. 4 (April 1918): 398–94.

"Cherokee Nation Dissolved," *The Quarterly Journal* (Society of American Indians) 2, no. 3 (July–September 1914): 237–39.

"Chronology of Major Events in the History of Friends and Native Americans: Accompanied by a Brief Bibliography, A." Friends Committee on National Legislation (2007): 1–2.

Clark, Elizabeth B. "Religion, Rights, and Difference in the Early Women's Rights Movement." *Wisconsin Women's Law Journal* 3 (1987): 29–57.

Clark, Elizabeth Battelle. "Religion, Rights and Difference: The Origins of American Feminism, 1848–1869." *Institute for Legal Studies Working Papers* 2, no. 2 (February 1987): 1–53.

Clark, J. Stanley. "Grant Foreman." *Chronicles of Oklahoma* 31, no. 3 (Autumn 1953): 226–42.

Cole, Phyllis. "Stanton, Fuller, and the Grammar of Romanticism." *The New England Quarterly* 73, no. 4 (December 2000): 533–59.

Coleman, Harry. "James Alfred LeRoy." In *The Americans in the Philippines*, by James A. LeRoy, xiii–xxviii. Boston: Houghton Mifflin Company, 1914.

Cott, Nancy F. "Young Women in the Second Great Awakening in New England." *Feminist Studies* 3, no. 1/2 (Autumn 1975): 15–29.

Coughlin, Mimi. "Women and History: Outside the Academy." *The History Teacher* 40, no. 4 (August 2007): 471–79

Cravens, Hamilton. "The Abandonment of Evolutionary Social Theory in America: The Impact of Academic Professionalization upon American Sociological Theory, 1890–1920," *American Social Studies Journal* 12, no 2 (Fall 1971): 5–20.

Dahl, Curtis. "Mound-Builders, Mormons, and William Cullen Bryant." *New England Quarterly* 34, no. 2 (June 1961):187–88 n. 10.

Dale, Edward Everett. "Letters of the Two Boudinots." *Chronicles of Oklahoma* 6 (September 1928), 333–34.

Damien, Elin C., and Eleanor M. King. "Unsung Visionary: Sara Yorke Stevenson and the Development of Archaeology in Philadelphia." In *Philadelphia and the Development of*

Americanist Archaeology, ed. Don D. Fowler and David R. Wilcox, 32–40. Tuscaloosa: University of Alabama Press, 2003.
Darnell, Regna. "Toward Consensus on the Scope of Anthropology." In *Philadelphia and the Development of Americanist Archaeology*, ed. Don D. Fowler and David R. Wilcox, 23–24. Tuscaloosa: University of Alabama Press, 2003.
Davidson, Jane P. "Send the Fossils to Me in Philadelphia: Support for Early Kansas Paleontology by United States Geological Survey of the Territories." *Transactions of the Kansas Academy of Science* 110, no. 3/4 (Fall 2007): 243–54.
Debo, Angie. "A Dedication to the Memory of Caroline Thomas Foreman, 1872–1967." *Arizona and the West* 16, no. 3 (Autumn 1974): 215–18.
———. "Southern Refugees of the Cherokee Nation." *Southwestern Historical Quarterly* 35, no. 4 (April 1932): 255–66.
DuBois, Ellen C. "The Radicalism of the Woman Suffrage Movement: Notes toward the Reconstruction of Nineteenth-Century Feminism." *Feminist Studies* 3, no. 3 (1975): 63–71.
Eaton, Rachel Caroline. "The Legend of the Battle of Claremore Mound," *Chronicles of Oklahoma* 8, no. 4 (December 1930), 369–76.
Ellis, Clyde. " 'More Real Than the Indians Themselves': The Early Years of the Indian Lore Movement in the United States." *Montana: The Magazine of Western History* 58, no. 3 (Autumn 2008): 3–22.
Fisher, LeRoy H. "Muriel H. Wright, Historian of Oklahoma," *Chronicles of Oklahoma* 52 (Spring 1974): 2–29.
Flack, J. Kirkpatrick. "Scientific Societies in Gilded Age Washington." *Records of the Columbia Historical Society* 49 (1973/1974): 430–42.
Foreman, Carolyn Thomas. "S. Alice Callahan: Author of *Wynema: A Child of the Forest*." *Chronicles of Oklahoma* 33, no. 3 (1955): 306–15.
Foster, Doug. "Imperfect Justice: The Modoc War Crimes Trial of 1873." *Oregon Historical Quarterly* 100, no. 3 (Fall 1999): 246–87.
Franceschi, Zelda Alice. "On the Margins of the Margins: Awareness and Delay." In *Writing about Lives in Science: (Auto) Biography, Gender, and Genre*, ed. Paolo Govoni and Zelda Franceschi, 264–76. Goettingen, Ger.: V & R Press, 2014.
Galloway, Patricia. "Archives, Power, and History: Dunbar Rowland and the Beginning of the State Archives of Mississippi, 1902–1936." *American Archivist* 69, no. 1 (Spring–Summer 2006): 83–91.
Garver, Frank Harmon. "Forty Years of Pacific Coast Branch History." *Pacific Historical Review* 16, no. 3 (August 1947): 237–67.
Gates, John M. "The Official Historian and the Well-Placed Critic: James A. LeRoy's Assessment of John R. M. Taylor's 'The Philippine Insurrection Against the United States.'" *Public Historian* 7, no. 3 (Summer 1985): 57–58.
Geer, Emily Apt. "Lucy W. Hayes and the New Woman of the 1880s." *Hayes Historical Journal* 3, no. 1–2 (Spring–Fall 1980): 18–26.
———. "Lucy W. Hayes and the Woman's Home Mission Society." *Hayes Historical Journal* 4, no. 4 (Fall 1984): 5–14.
Goggin, Jacqueline. "Challenging Sexual Discrimination in the Historical Profession: Women Historians and the American Historical Association, 1890–1940." *American Historical Review* 97, no. 3 (June 1992): 769–802.
Gray, Susan E. "Miengun's Children: Tales from a Mixed-Race Family." *Frontiers: A Journal of Women's Studies* 29, no. 2/3 (2008): 146–85.
Gravitt, Winnie Lewis. "Anna Lewis: A Great Woman of Oklahoma," *Chronicles of Oklahoma* 40 (Winter 1962–63): 326–29.
Greenstone, J. David. "Dorothea Dix and Jane Addams: From Transcendentalism to Pragmatism in American Social Reform." *Social Service Review* 53, no. 4 (December 1979): 527–59.

Grivas, Theodore. "The Arthur H. Clark Company, Publisher of the West: A Review of Sixty Years of Service, 1902–1962." *Arizona and the West* 5, no. 1 (Spring 1963): 67–68.
Haines, Valerie A. "Is Spencer's Theory an Evolutionary Theory?" *American Journal of Sociology* 93, no. 5 (March 1988): 1200–23.
Harding, Sarah. "Cultural Commodification and Native American Cultural Patrimony." In *Rethinking Commodification: Cases and Readings in Law and Culture*, ed. Martha M. Ertman and Joan C. Williams, 37–155. New York: New York University Press, 2005.
Heads, Michael. "Darwin's Changing Views on Evolution: From Centres of Origin and Teleology to Vicariance and Incomplete Lineage Sorting." *Journal of Biogeography* 36 (2009): 1018–26.
Hershberger, Mary. "Mobilizing Women, Anticipating Abolition: The Struggle against Indian Removal in the 1830s." *Journal of American History* 86, no. 1 (June 1999): 15–40.
Hewitt, Nancy A. "Feminist Friends: Agrarian Quakers and the Emergence of Women's Rights in America." *Feminist Studies* 12, no. 1 (Spring 1986): 27–49.
———. "From Seneca Falls to Suffrage? Reimagining a 'Master' Narrative in U. S. Women's History." In *No Permanent Waves: Recasting Histories of U.S. Feminism*, ed. Nancy A. Hewitt, 15–38. New Brunswick, N.J.: Rutgers University Press, 2010.
Hinsley, Curtis M. "Drab Doves Take Flight: The Dilemmas of Early Americanist Archaeology in Philadelphia, 1889–1900." In *Philadelphia and the Development of Americanist Archaeology*, ed. Don D. Fowler and David R. Wilcox, 2–20. Tuscaloosa: University of Alabama Press, 2003.
"Historical Notes, Park Hill." *Chronicles of Oklahoma* 9, no. 1 (March 1941): 99.
Hoffman, Tess. "Miss Fuller Among the Literary Lions: Two Essays Read at 'The Coliseum' in 1838." *Studies in the American Renaissance* (1988): 37–53.
Horowitz, Helen Lefkowitz. "Victoria Woodhull, Anthony Comstock, and the Conflict over Sex in the United States in the 1870s." *Journal of American History* 87, no. 2 (September 2000): 403–34.
Hounshell, David A. "Edison and the Pure Science Ideal in 19th-Century America." *Science* 207, no. 4431 (February 1980): 612–17.
Hoxie, Elizabeth F. "Harriet Livermore: 'Vixen and Devotee.'" *New England Quarterly* 18, no. 1 (1945): 40.
Hurtado, Albert L. "Bolton and Turner: The Borderlands and American Exceptionalism." *Western Historical Quarterly* 44, no. 1 (Spring 2013): 5–20.
Isenberg, Nancy. "'Pillars in the Same Temple and Priests of the Same Worship': Woman's Rights and the Politics of Church and State in Antebellum America." *Journal of American History* 85, no. 1 (June 1998): 98–128.
Jacobs, Wilbur R. "Natural Frontiers, Great World Frontiers, and the Shadow of Frederick Jackson Turner." *International History Review* 7, no. 2 (May 1985): 261–70.
Janiewski, Delores E. "Gendered Colonialism: The 'Woman Question' in Settler Society." In *Nation, Empire, Colony: Historicizing Gender and Race*, ed. Ruth Roach Pierson, Nupur Chaudhuri, and Beth McAuley, 57–76. Bloomington: Indiana University Press, 1998.
———. "Giving Women a Future: Alice Fletcher, the 'Woman Question,' and 'Indian Reform.'" In *Visible Women: New Essays on American Activism*, eds. Nancy A. Hewitt and Suzanne Lebsock, 325–47. Urbana: University of Illinois Press, 1993.
Jardine, Lisa. "Women in the Humanities: The Illusion of Inclusion." *Women & Performance: A Journal of Feminist Theory* 6, no. 1 (1993): 9–19.
Jennings, Francis. "A Growing Partnership: Historians, Anthropologists, and American Indian History." *History Teacher* 14, no. 1 (November 1980): 87–104.
Johnson, Helen Kendrick. "Woman Suffrage and Education." *Appleton's Popular Science Monthly* 51 (May–October 1897): 222–31.

Johnson, Thomas R. "Reconstruction Politics in Washington: 'An Experimental Garden for Radical Plants.'" *Records of the Columbia Historical Society* 50 (1980): 180–90.
Jones, Diane Brown. "Elizabeth Palmer Peabody's Transcendental Manifesto." *Studies in the American Renaissance* 16 (1992): 195–207.
Julin, Suzanne. "Annie Heloise Abel." In *Their Own Frontier: Women Intellectuals Re-Visioning the American West*, ed. Shirley A. Leckie and Nancy J. Parezo, 47–48. Lincoln: University of Nebraska Press.
Kaplan, Lawrence S. "Frederick Jackson Turner and Imperialism." *Social Science* 27 (January 1952): 12–16.
Kevles, Daniel J., Jeffrey L. Sturchio, and P. Thomas Carrol. "The Sciences in America, Circa 1880." *Science* 209, no. 4452 (July 1980): 26–32.
Kelsey, Harry. "Annie Heloise Abel-Henderson, 1873–1947." *Arizona and the West* 15, no. 1 (Spring 1973), 2–3.
Kerber, Linda K. "The Abolitionist Perception of the Indian." *Journal of American History* 62, no. 2 (September 1975): 271–95.
Kinnett, David. "Miss Kellogg's Quiet Passion." *Wisconsin Magazine of History* 62, no. 4 (Summer 1979): 266–99.
Kotlowski, Dean J. "Limited Vision: Carl Albert, the Choctaws, and Native American Self Determination." *American Indian Culture and Research Journal* 26, no. 2 (2002): 17–43
La Flesche-Tibbles, Susette. "Perils and Promises of Indian Citizenship," In *Our Day: A Record and Review of Current Reform, Vol. 5*, ed. Joseph Cook and Hazlitt Alva Cuppy, 460–71. Boston: Our Day Publishing, 1890.
Landsman, Gail H. "The 'Other' as Political Symbol: Images of the Indian in the Woman Suffrage Movement." *Ethnohistory* 39, no. 3 (1992): 247–84.
Lepowsky, Maria. "Charlotte Gower and the Subterranean History of Anthropology." In Excluded Ancestors, Inventible Traditions: Essays Toward a More Inclusive History of Anthropology, ed. Richard Handler, 164–65. Madison: University of Wisconsin Press, 2000.
Lindstrom, Richard. "'Not from the Land Side, but from the Flag Side': Native American Responses to the Wanamaker Expedition." *Journal of Social History* 30, no. 1 (Autumn 1996): 209–27.
Link, Arthur S. "The American Historical Association, 1884–1984: Retrospect and Prospect." *American Historical Review* 90, no. 1 (February 1985): 7.
Litton, Gaston L. Review of *A Political History of the Cherokee Nation*, by Morris L. Wardell. *Chronicles of Oklahoma* 16, no. 3 (September 1938): 378–80.
Lomawaima, K. Tsianina. "Estelle Reel, Superintendent of Indian Schools, 1898–1910: Politics, Curriculum, and Land." *Journal of American Indian Education* 35, no. 3 (May 1996): 5–32.
Lorimer, Douglas. "Theoretical Racism in Late-Victorian Anthropology, 1870–1900." *Victorian Studies* 31, no. 3 (Spring 1988): 405–30.
Lorini, Alessandra. "Alice Fletcher and the Search for Women's Public Recognition in Professionalizing American Anthropology." *Cromohs* 8 (2003): 1–25
"Louise Phelps Kellogg." *Wisconsin Magazine of History* 26, no. 1 (September 1942): 6.
Lowitt, Richard. "'Dear Miss Debo': The Correspondence of E. E. Dale and Angie Debo." *Chronicles of Oklahoma* 77, no. 4 (1999): 374–75.
Magliocca, Gerard N. "The Cherokee Removal and the Fourteenth Amendment." *Duke Law Journal* 53, no. 3 (December 2003): 879–919.
Malin, James C. "Frank Heywood Hodder, 1860–1935." *Kansas Historical Quarterly* 5, no. 2 (May 1936): 115–21.
Mark, Joan. "Francis La Flesche: The American Indian as Anthropologist." *Isis* 73, no. 4 (December 1982): 497–510.
"Marquette University." *Catholic Historical Review* 23 no.1 (April 1937): 231.

Marsden, Michael T. "A Dedication to the Memory of Helen Hunt Jackson, 1830–1885." *Arizona and the West* 21, no. 2 (Summer 1979): 109–12.

Marshall, Megan. "Elizabeth Palmer Peabody: The First Transcendentalist?" *Massachusetts Historical Review* 8 (2006): 1–15.

Mathes, Valerie Sherer, and Phil Brigandi, "The Mischief Record of 'La Gobernadora': Amelia Stone Quinton, Charles Fletcher Lummis, and the Warren Ranch Indian Removal." *Journal of San Diego History* 57, no. 1–2 (Winter/Spring 2011): 69–96.

Mathes, Valerie Sherer, and Richard Lowitt, eds. "'I Plead For Them': An 1882 Letter from Alice Fletcher to Senator Henry L. Dawes." *Nebraska History* 84 (2003): 36–41.

Mathews, Donald G. "The Second Great Awakening as an Organizing Process, 1780–1830: An Hypothesis." *American Quarterly* 21, no. 1 (Spring 1969): 23–43.

McKay, Ian. "Historians, Anthropology, and the Concept of Culture." *Labour* 819 (Autumn 1981): 185–241.

Michaels, Mark A. "Indigenous Ethics and Alien Laws: Native Traditions and the United States Legal System." *Fordham Law Review* 66, no. 4 (January 1998): 1564–84.

Mihesuah, Devon A. "Rachel Caroline Eaton." In *Native American Women: A Biographical Dictionary*, eds. Gretchen M. Bataille and Laurie Lisa, 101. New York: Routledge, 2001.

Militello, Teresa. "Horatio Nelson Rush and His Contributions to the Development of American Archaeology." *Pacific Coast Archaeological Society Quarterly* 41, no. 1 (April 2009): 1–57.

Mitchell, Mary. "'I Held George Washington's Horse': Compensated Emancipation in the District of Columbia." *Records of the Columbia Historical Society* 63/65 (1963/1965): 221–29.

Moldow, Gloria. "All Qualified Persons: Washington Women, a Century Ago." In *Women in the District of Columbia: A Contribution to Their History*, by Sharon Harley, Inabel B. Lindsay (Washington, D.C.: D.C. International Women's Year Coordinating Committee, 1977): 19–26.

Mood, Fulmer. "The Development of Frederick Jackson Turner as a Historical Thinker." *Transactions of the Colonial Society of Massachusetts* 36 (December 1943): 283–352.

Morgan, Lewis Henry. "Montezuma's Dinner." Review of *Native Races of the Pacific States*, by Hubert Howe Bancroft. *The North American Review* 122, no. 251 (April 1876): 265–308.

Myerson, Joel. "A Calendar of Transcendental Club Meetings." *American Literature* 44, no. 2 (May 1972): 197–207.

Nettles, Curtis P., Gilbert H. Doane, and Edward P. Alexander. "Louise Phelps Kellogg, 1862–1942." *Wisconsin Magazine of History* 26, no. 1 (September 1942): 6–7.

Niemtzow, Annette "Marriage and the New Woman in *The Portrait of a Lady*." *American Literature* 47, no. 3 (November 1975): 377–95.

"Notes and News." *American Anthropologist* 2, no. 4 (October–December 1900): 780.

Nurge, Ethel. "A Renewed Interest in History among Some American Anthropologists." *Anthropos* 62 (1967): 487–96.

Obenzinger, Hilton. "Holy Land Narrative and American Covenant: Levi Parsons, Pliny Fisk and the Palestine Mission." *Religion and Literature* 35, no. 2/3 (Summer–Autumn 2003): 241–67.

O' Reilly, Kenneth. "The Jim Crow Policies of Woodrow Wilson." *Journal of Blacks in Higher Education*, no. 17 (Autumn 1997): 117–19.

Padget, Martin. "Travel Writing, Sentimental Romance, and Indian Rights Advocacy: The Politics of Helen Hunt Jackson's *Ramona*." *Journal of the Southwest* 42, no. 4 (Winter 2000): 833–76.

Pewewardy, Cornel. "Renaming Ourselves on Our Own Terms: Race, Tribal Nations, and Representation in Education," *Indigenous Nations Studies Journal* 1, no. 1 (Spring 2000): 11–28.

Pickens, Donald K. "Westward Expansion and the End of American Exceptionalism: Sumner, Turner, and Webb." *Western Historical Quarterly* 12, no. 4 (October 1981): 409–18.

Portnoy, Alisse Theodore. "'Female Petitioners can be Lawfully Heard': Negotiating Female Decorum, United States Politics, and Political Agency, 1829–1831." *Journal of the Early Republic* 23, no. 4 (Winter 2003): 573–610.
Reese, Linda. "Dr. Anna Lewis, Historian at the Oklahoma College for Women." *Chronicles of Oklahoma* 84, no. 4 (Winter 2004–2005): 428–49
Rhea, John Mark. "Creating a Place for Herself in History: Anna Lewis's Journey from Tuskahoma to the University of Oklahoma, 1903–1930." *Great Plains Journal* 45 (2009): 26–51.
———. "Frontiers of the Mind: American Culture, Darwinism and Frederick Jackson Turner's Frontier Thesis." In *150 Years of Evolution, Darwin's Impact on Contemporary Thought and Culture*, ed. Mark Richard Wheeler and William Anthony Nericcio, 163–203. San Diego, Calif.: San Diego State University Press, 2011.
Richards, Robert J. "The Linguistic Creation of Man: Charles Darwin, August Schleicher, Ernst Haeckel, and the Missing Link in Nineteenth-Century Evolutionary Theory." In *Experimenting in Tongues: Studies in Science and Language*, ed. Matthias Dörres, 21–48. Palo Alto, Calif.: Stanford University Press, 2002.
Ridge, Martin. "The Significance of Frederick Jackson Turner's Frontier Thesis." *Montana: The Magazine of Western History* 41, no. 1 (Winter 1991): 2–13.
Rippy, J. Fred. "The Indians of the Southwest in the Diplomacy of the United States and Mexico, 1848–1853. *Hispanic American Historical Review* 2, no. 3 (August 1919): 363–396.
———. "Mexican Projects of the Confederates." *Southwestern Historical Quarterly* 22, no. 4 (April 1919): 291–317.
Rippy, J. Fred, and Angie Debo. "The Historical Background of the American Policy of Isolation." *Smith College Studies in History* 9, no. 3 (April–July 1924): 71–169.
Riley, Glenda. "Frederick Jackson Turner Overlooked the Ladies." In *Does the Frontier Experience Make America Exceptional?* ed. Richard W. Eutlain, 3–10. Boston: Bedford/St. Martins, 1999.
Robinson, David M. "Margaret Fuller and the Transcendental Ethos: Woman in the Nineteenth Century." *PMLA* 97, no. 1 (January 1982): 83–98.
———. "'The New Epoch of Belief': The Radical and Religious Transformation in Nineteenth-Century New England." *New England Quarterly*, 79, no. 4 (December 2006): 557–577.
Robinson, James Harvey. "Newer Ways of History." *American Historical Review* 35, no. 2 (1929): 245–55.
Rogers, Dorothy, and Therese B. Dykeman. "Introduction: Women in the American Philosophical Tradition, 1800–1930." *Hypatia* 19, no. 2 (Spring 2004): viii–xxxiv.
Rohrs, Richard C. "'Public Attention . . . Essentially Private Matters': Women Seeking Assistance from President James K. Polk." *Journal of the Early Republic* 24, no. 1 (Spring 2004): 107–23.
Romer, Alfred S. "Cope versus Marsh." *Systematic Zoology* 13, no. 4 (December 1964): 201–207.
Rossiter, Margaret W. "Doctorates for Women, 1868–1907." *History of Education Quarterly* 22, no. 2 (Summer 1982): 159–83.
Sapir, J. David. "Paul Radin, 1883–1959." *Journal of American Folklore* 74, no. 291 (January–March 1961): 65–67.
Savage, Cynthia. "Oklahoma College for Women: Oklahoma's Only State Supported Women's School." *Chronicles of Oklahoma* 80, no. 2 (Summer 2002): 176–78.
Schrems, Suzanne H., and Cynthia J. Wolff. "Politics and Libel: Angie Debo and the Publication of *And Still the Waters Run*." *Western Historical Quarterly* 22, no. 2 (May 1991): 184–203.
Sellers, James L. "Before We Were Members—The MVHA." *The Mississippi Valley Historical Review* 40, no. 1 (June 1953): 3, 10.
Semple, W. F., and Winnie Lewis Gravitt. "Grady Lewis, Choctaw Attorney." *Chronicles of Oklahoma* 33, no. 3 (1955): 301–305.

Shafer, Ingrid. "USAO—The Impossible Dream: A Love Story." In *Chickasha, Oklahoma 1892–1992: Our First Hundred Years* (1992): 91–115.
Shanley, Kathryn W. "The Indians America Loves to Love and Read: American Indian Identity and Cultural Appropriation." *American Indian Quarterly* 21, no. 4 (Autumn 1997): 675–702.
Shiels, Richard D. "The Scope of the Second Great Awakening: Andover, Massachusetts, as a Case Study." *Journal of the Early Republic* 5, no. 2 (Summer 1985): 223–46.
Sklar, Katheryn Kish. "American Female Historians in Context." *Feminist Studies* 3, no. 1/2 (Autumn 1975): 171–84.
Smith, Henry Nash. "The Scribbling Women and the Cosmic Success Story." *Critical Inquiry* 1, no. 1 (September 1974): 47–70.
Snead, James E. "Science, Commerce, and Control: Patronage and the Development of Anthropological Archaeology in the Americas." *American Anthropologist* 101, no. 2 (1999): 256–71.
Solomon, Cindy J. "From Pulpits to Polls: How Female Preachers Birthed the Women's Rights Movement." *Undergraduate Research Journal at UCCS* 2.1 (Spring 2009): 1–18.
Sosna, Morton. "The South in the Saddle: Racial Politics during the Wilson Years." *Wisconsin Magazine of History* 51, no. 1 (Autumn 1970): 30–49.
Stocking, George W., Jr. "Lamarckianism in American Social Science." *Journal of the History of Ideas* 23, no. 2 (April–June 1962): 239–56.
Strong, Pauline Turner, and Barrik Van Winkle. "'Indian Blood': Reflections on the Reckoning and Refiguring of Native American Identity." *Cultural Anthropology* 11, no. 4 (November 1996): 547–76.
Swetland, Mark J. "'Make-Believe White-Men' and the Omaha Land Allotments of 1871–1900." *Great Plains Research* 4 (August 1994): 201–36.
Tate, Michael L. "From Scout to Doughboy: The National Debate over Integrating Indians into the Military, 1891–1918." *Western Historical Quarterly* 17, no. 4 (October 1986): 417–32.
Taub, Lisa. "Evolutionary Ideas and 'Empirical' Methods: The Analogy between Language and Species in Works by Lyell and Schleicher." *British Journal for the History of Science* 26, no. 2 (June 1993): 171–93.
Tatonetti, Lisa. "Behind the Shadows of Wounded Knee: The Slippage of Imagination in *Wynema: A Child of the Forest*." *Studies in American Indian Literature* 16, no. 1 (Spring 2004): 1–31.
Tetrault, Lisa. "The Incorporation of American Feminism: Suffragists and the Postbellum Lyceum." *Journal of American History* 26, no. 4 (2010): 977, 1027–56.
Tooker, Elisabeth. "Lewis H. Morgan and His Contemporaries." *American Anthropologist* 94, no. 2 (June 1992): 357–75.
Turner, Frederick W., III. "The Century after *A Century of Dishonor*: American Conscience and Consciousness." *Massachusetts Review* 16, no. 4 (Autumn 1975): 715–31.
Tuttle, William M., Jr. "Forerunners of Frederick Jackson Turner: Nineteenth-Century British Conservatives and the Frontier Thesis." *Agricultural History* 141, no. 3 (July 1967): 219–27.
Vapnek, Lara. "Staking Claims to Independence: Jennie Collins, Aurora Phelps, and the Boston Working Women's League, 1865–1877." In *No Permanent Waves: Recasting Histories of U.S. Feminism*, by Nancy A. Hewitt, 305–28. New Brunswick, N.J.: Rutgers University Press, 2010.
Van Dyke, Annette. "An Introduction to *Wynema: A Child of the Forest*." *Studies in American Indian Literature* 4, no. 2/3 (Summer/Fall 1992): 123–28.
Wach, Howard M. "A Boston Vindication: Margaret Fuller and Caroline Dall Read Mary Wollstonecraft." *Massachusetts Historical Review* 7 (2005): 3–35.

Wallace, James D. "Hawthorne and the Scribbling Women Reconsidered." *American Literature* 62, no. 2 (June 1990): 201–22.
Walter, Paul A. F. "Lansing Bartlett Bloom." *New Mexico Historical Review* 21 no. 2 (April 1946): 93–94.
Wardrop, Daneen. "The Jouissant Politics of Helen Hunt Jackson's *Ramona*: The Ground that is 'Mother's Lap.'" In *Speaking the Other Self: American Women Writers*, ed. Jeanne Campbell Reesman, 27–38. Athens: University of Georgia Press, 2011.
Weisbrod, Carol. "Family, Church, and State: An Essay on Constitutionalism and Religious Authority." (University of Wisconsin–Madison, Institute for Legal Studies) *Legal History Program: Working Papers* 1, no. 2 (1986): 3.
Weissbourd, Jenny. "Women's Rights and Women's Health in the Providence Physiological Society, 1850–1851." *Brown Journal of History* (Spring 2008): 7–20.
Wertheim, Stephen. "Reluctant Liberator: Theodore Roosevelt's Philosophy of Self-Government and Preparation for Philippine Independence." *Presidential Studies Quarterly* 39, no. 3 (September 2009): 494–518.
Whalen, Robert K. "'Christians Love the Jews!' The Development of American Philo-Semitism, 1790–1860." *Religion and American Culture: A Journal of Interpretation* 6, no. 2 (Summer 1996): 225–59.
Wheeler, Walter H. "The Uintatheres and the Cope-Marsh War." *Science* 131, no. 3408 (April 1960): 1171–76.
Wilgus, A. Curtis. "The Life of James Alexander Robertson." In *Hispanic American Essays: A Memorial to James Alexander Robertson*, ed. Alva Curtis Wilgus, 3–4. Chapel Hill: University of North Carolina Press, 1942.
———. "James Alexander Robertson." *Florida Historical Quarterly* 18, no.1 (July 1939): 3–10.
Williams, Carolyn. "The Female Antislavery Movement: Fighting against Racial Prejudice and Promoting Women's Rights in Antebellum America." In *The Abolitionist Sisterhood: Women's Political Culture in Antebellum America,* ed. Jean Fagan Yellin and John C. Van Horne, 158–78. Ithaca, N.Y.: Cornell University Press, 1994.
Williams, David R. "The Wilderness Rapture of Mary Moody Emerson: One Calvinist Link to Transcendentalism." *Studies in American Renaissance* (1986): 1–16.
Williams, Walter L. "United States Indian Policy and the Debate over Philippine Annexation: Implications for the Origins of American Imperialism." *Journal of American History* 66, no. 4 (March 1980): 810–31.
Williams, William Appleman. "Brooks Adams and American Expansionism." *New England Quarterly* 25 (1952): 217–32.
———. "The Frontier Thesis and American Foreign Policy." *Pacific Historical Review* 24, no. 4 (November 1955): 379–95.
Whyte, James H. "The District of Columbia Territorial Government, 1871–1874." *Records of the Columbia Historical Society* 51/52 (1951/1952): 87–102.
Wolgemuth, Kathleen L. "Woodrow Wilson and Federal Segregation." *Journal of Negro History* 44, no. 2 (April 1959): 158–73.
Woodburn, James A. "Reuben Gold Thwaites." *Indiana Magazine of History* 9, no.4 (December 1913): 298–301.
Woods, Randall B. "Integration, Exclusion, or Segregation? The 'Color Line' in Kansas, 1878–1900." *Western Historical Quarterly* 14, no. 2 (April 1983): 181–98.
Wright, Muriel H. "A Brief Review of the Life of Doctor Eliphalet Nott Wright." *Chronicles of Oklahoma* 10, no. 2 (June 1932): 267–86.
———. "Notes on the Life of Mrs. Hanna Worcester Hicks Hitchcock." *Chronicles of Oklahoma* 19, no. 4 (December 1941): 348–55.
———. "Rachel Caroline Eaton." *Chronicles of Oklahoma* 16, no. 4 (December 1938): 509–10.

Zorn, Roman J. "The New England Anti-Slavery Society: Pioneer Abolition Organization." *Journal of Negro History* 42, no. 3 (July 1957): 157–76.

Theses and Dissertations

Abel, Annie Heloise. "Indian Reservations in Kansas and the Extinguishment of their Title." Master's thesis, University of Kansas, 1900.

Amatniek, Joan Cindy. "The Women's Anthropological Society of America: A Dual Role–Scientific Society and Woman's Club." Master's thesis, Harvard University, 1979.

Anderson, James S. "Annie Heloise Abel (1873–1947), an Historian's History." Ph.D. diss., Flinders University of South Australia, 2006.

Akins, Damon B. "Lines on the Land: The San Louis Rey River Reservations and the Origins of the Mission Indian Federation, 1850–1934." Ph.D. diss., University of Oklahoma, 2009.

Bailey, Judith Bledsoe. "Nancy Towle, 'Faithful Child of God,' 1796–1876." Master's thesis, College of William and Mary, 2000.

Clark, Elizabeth Battelle. "The Politics of God and the Woman's Vote: Religion in the American Suffrage Movement, 1848–1895." Ph.D. diss., Princeton University, 1989.

Dale, Edward Everett. "A History of the Live Stock Industry in Oklahoma." Ph.D. diss., Harvard University, 1922.

Debo, Angie. "History of the Choctaw Nation from the End of the Civil War to the Close of the Tribal Period." Ph.D. diss., University of Oklahoma, 1933.

Eaton, Rachel Caroline. "John Ross." Master's thesis, University of Chicago, 1911.

English, Linda Christine. "Revealing Accounts: General Stores on the South Central Plains, 1870–1890." Ph.D. diss., University of Oklahoma, 2005.

Fulop, Timothy Earl. "Elias Smith and the Quest for Gospel Liberty: Popular Religion and Democratic Radicalism in Early Nineteenth-Century New England." Ph.D. diss., Princeton University, 1992.

Isenberg, Nancy Gale. "'Co-equality of the Sexes': The Feminist Discourse of the Antebellum Women's Right's Movement in America." Ph.D. diss., University of Wisconsin-Madison, 1990.

Jürisson, Cynthia A. "Federalist, Feminist, Revivalist: Harriet Livermore (1788–1868) and the Limits of Democratization in the Early Republic." Ph.D. diss., Princeton Theological Seminary, 1994.

Kellogg, Louise Phelps. "The Formation of the State of Virginia." Ph.D. diss., University of Wisconsin, 1897.

Kodumthara, Sunu Mary. "Anti-Suffragists and the Dilemma of the American West." Ph.D., diss., University of Oklahoma, 2011.

Lewis, Anna. "History of the Cattle Industry in Oklahoma, 1866–1893." Master's thesis, University of California, 1918.

Lewis, Anna L. "Early History of the Arkansas River Region, 1541–1800." Ph.D. diss., University of Oklahoma, 1930.

Moldow, Gloria Melnick. "The Gilded Age, Promise and Disillusionment: Women Doctors and the Emergence of the Professional Middle Class Washington, D.C., 1870–1900." Ph.D. diss., University of Maryland, 1980.

Pierce, Jason. "Making the White Man's West: Whiteness and the Creation of the American West." Ph.D. diss., University of Arkansas, 2008.

Rhea, John Mark. "Women and the Construction of American Indian Scholarship." Ph.D. diss., University of Oklahoma, 2012.

Romeyn, Sara N. "A Sentimental Empire: White Women's Responses to Native American Policy, 1824–1894." Ph.D. diss., Columbian College of Arts and Sciences of George Washington University, 2003.

Spear, Eloise. "Choctaw Indian Education with Special Reference to Choctaw County, Oklahoma." Ph.D. diss., University of Oklahoma, 1977.
Smith, Tash. "Grant's Peace Policy: Federal Indian Policy and the American Churches, 1869–1882." Master's thesis, North Dakota State University, 2004.
Wanken, Helen M. "'Woman's Sphere' and Indian Reform: The Women's National Indian Association, 1879–1901." Ph.D. diss., Marquette University, Milwaukee, Wisconsin, 1981.

Index

AAAS. *See* American Association for the Advancement of Science
AAW. *See* Association for the Advancement of Women
ABCFM. *See* American Board of Commissioners for Foreign Missions
Abel, Amelia, 139
Abel, Annie Heloise, 5, 10, 11–12, 114, 139, 142, 161, 172, 231n52; on benevolent imperialism, 140–41; dissertation of, 144–46; publications and career of, 147–50; review of *And Still the Waters Run*, 198–99; and slavery debate, 143–44
Abel, George, 139
ABHMS. *See* American Baptist Home Mission Society
abolitionism, 10, 19, 20, 22, 23, 200, 201; and ABCFM, 31–32; women and, 29–31
academic institutions, 11; professionalization of, 105, 237n50
acculturation, 26, 28, 54–55, 71, 91, 117
Act for the Sale of Part of the Reservation of the Omaha Tribe of Indians in the State of Nebraska and for Other Purposes, An, 97
Adams, Brooks, 116, 117, 123
Adams, George Burton, 188; and AHA, 146–47
Adams, Henry, 52, 57
Adams, Herbert Baxter, 110, 114, 142, 143

Adams, John Quincy, 31, 145, 211n42
Addresses to the Dispersed of Judah (Livermore), 25–26
African Americans, 10, 20, 23, 30, 32, 143, 200, 205, 217n1; suffrage, 31, 36–37
AHA. *See* American Historical Association
AHR. *See* American Historical Review
AIAA. *See* American Indian Aid Association
AIMA. *See* American Indian Mission Association
allotment, 43, 64, 72, 73, 81, 85, 104, 118, 191, 201, 221n2; Choctaw, 166–69, 179, 196, 235n9; coercive, 98, 99, 102, 103, 218n14; gradualist, 75; legislative, 96–97, 101, 103; Omaha, 65–66, 87, 88, 91–92, 93–94, 96–97; universal, 44, 58; voluntary, 71, 95, 102
Along the Arkansas (Lewis), 8, 163, 203; publication of, 175–76
Alvord, Clarence W., 143
AMA. *See* American Missionary Association
American Association for the Advancement of Science (AAAS), 49, 99, 101, 106, 109, 113
American Baptist Home Mission Society (ABHMS), 39, 40
American Board of Commissioners for Foreign Missions (ABCFM), 28–29, 31–32

American Darwinism, Darwinists, 11, 52, 54–55, 56, 58, 106, 110, 200, 201, 217n2
American eugenics movement, 106, 202
American Historical Association (AHA), 110, 111, 112, 188, 196, 231n56; Abel's membership in, 142, 143, 146; on professionalizing history, 113–14
American Historical Review (AHR), 142, 143
American Indian Aid Association (AIAA), 33, 41, 212n51, 213n63
American Indian as Participant in the Civil War, The (Abel), 149
American Indian as Slaveholder and Secessionist, The (Abel), 147–48
American Indian under Reconstruction, The (Abel), 149
American Indian Mission Association (AIMA), 32
American Missionary Association (AMA), 25, 32–33
American Nation: A History, The (Hart), 129
American Nonconformist, 60
American Social Science Association (ASSA), 95
American West: expansionism in, 123–24, 177; fossil discoveries in, 56–57; in Turner's Frontier Thesis, 115–16
American Woman Suffrage Association (AWSA), 36
Anaptomorphus cope, 56
Annual Report of the American Historical Association, 143
Anthony, Susan B., 33, 35–36
anthropologists: preprofessional, 7, 17, 25, 48–49, 52, 55, 57, 59, 60, 80–81, 98, 105; professional, 107–10, 113, 118–19, 179, 227n14
anthropology, 7, 9, 11, 49, 51–52, 147, 162, 202–203, 218n17, 227n27; Powell on, 56, 58, 105–108, 218n21; professionalization of, 108–109, 113, 119, 201
anti-removal campaigns, 28–29, 31–32, 212n47
antislavery campaign, 28, 29, 30–31, 36, 211n42
Apaches, in Arkansas River Valley, 176
Are the Indians Dying Out? Preliminary Observations Relating to Indian Civilization and Education (Clark), 101
Arkansas River Valley, 163, 203; Spanish and French colonialism in, 176–77; Lewis's research on, 171, 175
Arthur, Chester A., 73, 74, 97

ASSA. See American Social Science Association
assimilation, assimilationists, 4, 12, 19, 21, 28, 32, 33, 39, 51, 52, 56, 108, 141, 149, 164, 199, 202, 204, 217n3; Choctaw, 181, 191; coercive, 75, 98–99, 102, 218n14, 220n8, 224n55; Alice Fletcher on, 57, 59, 81, 89, 95–96, 119–20; gradual, gradualist, 47, 54–55, 71–73, 74–76, 96; ITKPA goal of, 43–44; Helen Hunt Jackson on, 76–77, 221n28; pan-Indian, 66–67; Philadelphia activism on, 40–42
Association for the Advancement of Women (AAW), 49, 82, 94
Atkins, John Dewitt Clinton, 99, 101
Atoka Agreement, 194
Austin, George Washington, 171
autonomy, 65, 195
AWSA. See American Woman Suffrage Association
Ayer, Edward E., 127

Babbit, Frances E., 109
Bacon, Nathaniel T., "Some Insular Questions," 144
Bancroft, George, 52
Bancroft, Hubert Howe, 52, 111, 213n64
Bannock War, 61
Banta Publishing Company, George, 150, 153, 157
Baptist General Convention for Foreign Missions (BGCFM), 32
Baptists, Plains Indian mission, 32–33
barbarism, 53
Barbour, James, 145
Barnard, Catherine Ann "Kate," 183, 196
BE. See Bureau of Ethnology
Beecher, Catherine, 27, 29
Beeson, John, 43, 213n63
Bergen, Fanny D., 109
BGCFM. See Baptist General Convention for Foreign Missions
BIA. See Bureau of Indian Affairs
Big Elk, 65
Bi-ku-de, Omaha Reservation, 85
Blair, Emma Helen, 4, 5, 10, 11, 12, 124, 137, 202, 229n21, 230n28; *The Indian Tribes of the Upper Mississippi Valley and Region of the Great Lakes*, 130–33; Philippines research of, 128, 129, 228n38; and Thwaites, 126–27; and Turner, 125–26, 130, 132

Bloom, Lansing Bartlett, 177; review of *Along the Arkansas*, 175–76
boarding schools, 62, 65, 104, 166
Board of Indian Commissioners (BIC), 32
Boas, Franz, 118, 132
Bolton, Herbert Eugene, 112, 115, 127, 137, 165, 169, 176
Bolton, Sara, 113
Bonney, Mary, 33, 40, 71, 201, 214n13, 216n25, 218n14; ITKPA, 39, 41–43
Boomers, 170
Borden, Lucy, 180
borderlands scholarship, 184; Lewis and, 171, 172, 175–76
Boudinot, Elias, 157
Boudinot, Elias C., 24
Bourne, Edward Gaylord, 127, 144, 146; research and publications of, 128–30
Bowers, Virginia K., 109
Brandt, Joseph A., 158, 159–60, 174; and Angie Debo, 196–97
Brewster, Benjamin H., 97
Briggs, Eugene, 189
British Regime in the Northwest, The (Kellogg), 137
Bronson, Ruth Muskrat, 204
buffalo kills, and Plains Indians, 88
Bulkley scholarships, 142, 231n52
Bureau of Ethnology (BE), 11, 57, 58, 108; American Darwinism in, 54–55, 106
Bureau of Indian Affairs (BIA), 18, 190, 225n59; Choctaw Nation archives in, 188–89
Burns, James Alexander, 153, 155
Burns, Rachel. *See* Eaton, Rachel Caroline
Burrows Brothers Company, 127–28

Cahuilla, 73, 78; *Ramona*, 76–77
Caldwell College, 167
Calhoun, John C., 145
California, Mission Indians in, 73–77, 201, 220n13
Callahan, Samuel Benton, 62, 63
Callahan, Sarah Elizabeth Thornberg, 62–63
Callahan, Sophia Alice, 62; *Wynema: A Child of the Forest*, 60, 63, 64–65
Carr, Lucien, 83
Catholic Church, and Mission Indians, 76
cattle drives, through Indian Territory, 169–70

cattle industry, 236n32; land cessions and, 170–71
Central Indian Committee (CIC), 43
Century Illustrated Magazine, and Helen Hunt Jackson, 73
A Century of Dishonor (Jackson), 7, 17, 34, 43, 48, 50, 72, 73, 78, 104, 131, 201, 208n7; reviews of, 70–71
Chardon's Journal at Fort Clark, 1834–1839 (Abel), 150
Cherokee Nation, Cherokees, 72, 149, 151, 152–53, 163, 170, 189, 197, 235n14; Eaton's scholarship on, 156–57, 158–61; nationalism of, 157–58
Cherokee National Female Seminary, 152–53
Cherokee Tobacco case, 87
Cheyenne tribe, Cheyennes, 72
Chicago World's Columbian Exposition, 118–19
Chickasaw Nation, Chickasaws, 175, 176, 189, 190, 197, 235n14
Child, Lydia Maria, 30
children, care for Indian, 18–19
Chisholm Trail, 170
Choctaw Advisory Committee, 180
Choctaw-Chickasaw Leased District, 189
Choctaw Leased District claim, 190
Choctaw Nation, Choctaws, 164, 168, 175, 176, 177, 192, 197, 235n14; assimilationist, 193–94, 195; land allotment, 166–67; Grady Lewis's research on, 188–89, 238n90; sovereignty, 190–91, 238n89
Choctaw Tribal Council House, 189
Christianization, as component of American Indian assimilation, 22, 25, 26, 32
Chronicles of Oklahoma, 171; Muriel Wright as editor of, 180–81, 194, 236n29
Church of Jesus Christ of Latter Day Saints, 24
CIC. *See* Central Indian Committee
citizenship, 43, 60, 71–72, 74, 95, 118, 119; Choctaw, 164; Omaha, 91, 92, 98
Civilization of the American Indian series (University of Oklahoma Press), 192, 207n5
civil rights movement, 10, 16, 23, 26, 200; African American, 32, 35–37, 39
Civil War, Indian participants in, 149
Clapp, Mrs. Almon M., Fletcher's letter to, 92–93
Claremore, Okla., 152, 153

INDEX

Claremore Mound, Okla., 152
Clark, Arthur Henry, 127–28, 129–30
Clark Company, Arthur H., 127, 128, 129–30, 133
Clark, Selden Noyes, *Are The Indians Dying Out?*, 101
Clark, William, 25
Cleveland, Grover, 102, 170
Coke, Robert, 102
Coke-Dawes bill, 100, 102
Colby, Clara Bewick, 15, 18
Collier, John, 198
colonialism: in borderlands, 176; British, 140, 144; settler, 4, 43, 61, 64, 67, 72–73, 77, 92, 116, 168–69, 173; Spanish, 76
colonization, 4, 25; Indian, 141, 145
Columbia Territory, suffrage in, 36–37
Columbia University, 108
Comanches, 175, 176
Communism, 198
"Compromises of the Constitution" (Farrand), 144
Conant, Claudius B., 48
Confederacy, and Five Tribes, 148, 149
Confederate Congress, Samuel Callahan in, 63
Congregationalists, 31
conservative ideology, women's, 26, 27–29, 31, 38, 43, 45, 211n42, 212n47, 212n50, 214n8
Cope, Edward Drinker, 56–57
Couch, W. L., 170
Council Fire and Arbitrator, 99
Crapo, Sarah Ann Davis, 94
Crapo, William Wallace, 94
Crook, George, 73
cultures, study of, 107
Cupeños, 73
Curtis Act, 64, 167

Dakotas, 72
Dale, Edward Everett, 112, 115, 165, 171, 236n32; and Angie Debo, 183, 186–87, 191–92, 193; scholarship of, 172–73
Dall, Caroline Healey, 19, 20
Davis, Pauline Wright, 20
Dawes, Anna Laurens, 95
Dawes, Electra Sanderson, 94
Dawes, Henry L., 44, 93, 94, 96, 97, 100, 101, 102, 224n55
Dawes Act/Dawes General Allotment Act, 64, 98, 102, 103, 107, 167, 207n5; blood quantum, 62, 63

Debo, Angie, 4, 5, 10, 12, 115, 150, 160, 162, 164, 172, 182; career of, 185–86; dissertation of, 192–93; ethno-politics of, 197–99, 203; and Grady Lewis, 190–91; master's thesis of, 184–85; *The Rise and Fall of the Choctaw Republic*, 193–94; *And Still the Waters Run*, 3, 161, 181, 195–96; at University of Oklahoma, 183–84, 186–89, 191–92; and Muriel Wright, 179, 194–95
Debo, Edward, 181
Debo, Lina, 181
Delaware tribe, Delawares, land rights, 72–73
Deloria, Ella Cara, 204
democratization, and Transcendentalist movement, 19
developmentalism, 54
Dewey, Lucy, 180
Diego, Juan, 76, 78
District of Columbia, 31; African American suffrage in, 36–37
Dixon, Joseph, 149
Dodd, William E., 12, 161; *Expansion and Conflict*, 157–58
Dorsey, Thomas, 90
Douglas, Henry, 61
Dow, Lorenzo, 20–21
Drury College, Missouri, Five Nations and, 151, 153
Dunning Prize, John H., Angie Debo and, 196
Dunning, William Archibald, 143
Dwight, Benjamin, 189–90

Early Narratives of the Northwest, 1634–1699 (Kellogg), 137
Early Western Travels (Thwaites), 137
Eastern Cherokees, 18
Eaton, Calvin, 152
Eaton, George Washington, 151, 152
Eaton, Joel Merritt, 155
Eaton, John, 98, 99, 101
Eaton, Nancy Elizabeth Ward Williams, 151, 152
Eaton, Rachel Caroline (Caroline B.), 5, 8, 10, 12, 150, 154, 162–63, 174, 184; education and career of, 152–53, 203; research and publications by, 155–61
economic independence, 166
education, 58, 62, 101, 213n1; Alice Fletcher on, 81, 89, 95
Edwards, Lettie, 63

egalitarianism, evangelical, 20–22
emancipation, compensated, 31
English language, racial evolution and, 58–59
Episcopal Church, 41
equality, gender, 21
ethnology, 49, 59, 193; Alice Fletcher's, 80, 86–87; Powell on, 58, 218n21
evangelicalism, women's ministry and, 20–26, 200, 209n20
evangelicals, assimilation movement, 33, 41
evangelization, 210n23; of Indians, 23, 25, 32, 39
Evarts, Jeremiah, 28–29
Everest, Kate Asaphine, 124
evolution, 11; American Darwinist concepts of, 54–55; language and, 58–59; racial, 55–56
Expansion and Conflict (Dodd), 157–58
expansionists, expansionism, 117, 118, 120, 177; Philippines and, 123–24, 228n38

Farley, Ed, 97, 103, 225n59
farmers, and ranchers, 170
Farrand, Max, "Compromises of the Constitution," 144
Father Junipero Serra and the Mission Indians of California (Jackson), 76
Fillmore, John, 119
Fiske, Deborah Vinal, 45–46
Fiske, John, 116, 117
Fiske, Nathan Welby, 45, 46
Five Tribes/Nations, 148, 149, 200, 234n14; and allotment, 64, 167; Angie Debo's work on, 12, 188, 193–98; intertribal conference, 189–90; Anna Lewis's scholarship on, 165–66
Fletcher, Alice Cunningham, 5–6, 10, 11, 18, 60, 78, 79, 106, 109, 110, 132; on allotment, 94–95, 224n55; as allotment agent, 103, 107, 118; on American Indian societies, 53–54; as anthropologist, 105, 227n27; on assimilation, 52, 59, 95–96, 108; career of, 48–49, 80–81, 226n1, 226n4; and Chicago World's Columbian Exposition, 118–20; *Indian Education and Civilization*, 7, 34, 50, 102–103, 104, 201; and ITKPA, 43, 45; at Lake Mohonk Conference, 99–100; Nebraska–South Dakota tour of, 82–86, 88, 92–93, 222n10; new nation idealism, 16, 17; and Omaha Allotment Act, 93–94, 96–97;

"Omaha Allotment Field Notebook," 86–87, 89–92, 221n6; and Peabody Museum, 97–98; on racial evolution, 55–56, 57; and WICCE, 100–101
Fletcher, Lucia Adeline, 48
Fletcher, Thomas G., 48
flexible ideology, women's, 38, 43, 45, 212n50
floods, Missouri River, 88
Foreman, Caroline, 191
Foreman, Grant, 191, 207n5
Forsyth, Thomas, 131
Fort Leavenworth, Kan., Osage at, 25
fossils, Cope and Marsh's discoveries of, 56–57
"Fox Indians during the French Regime, The" (Kellogg), 136
Freemont, Ezra (Wajapa), 82, 83, 84–85, 88, 89, 91, 103
Fremont, John C., 60
French colonialism, in Arkansas Valley, 176–77
French Regime in Wisconsin and the Northwest, The (Kellogg), 137
Frontier Advance on the Upper Ohio, 1778–1779 (Kellogg), 137
Frontier Retreat on the Upper Ohio, 1779–1781 (Kellogg), 137
Frontier Thesis, 11, 115, 128, 130; American Indians in, 116–17
Fuller, Margaret (Ossoli), 20; "The Great Lawsuit," 19

Ga-la-gi-noh, 24, 210n30
Gardner, Edward, 189
gender role reform, 21, 38, 205, 236n32
General Federation of Women's Clubs, 119
Georgia, removal debate, 29, 145
Giffen, Fannie Reed, *Oo-Ma-Ha Ta-Wa-Tha: Omaha City*, 60, 66
Gilder, Richard Watson, 73
Grant, Ulysses S., 36; Indian Peace Policy, 32, 33, 146
Great Britain, 144; benevolent imperialism of, 140–41; humanitarian legacy/principles, 145, 231n49
Great Depression, 179, 190
"Great Lawsuit, The" (Fuller), 19
Great Western Trail, 170
Greenville, Treaty of, 72
Grimké, Angelina, 27, 30
Grimké, Sarah, 29–30

Guide to the Indian Tribes of Oklahoma, A (Wright), 164, 180

Hako: A Pawnee Ceremony, The (Fletcher), 59
Hall, C. L., 96
Handbook of American Indians, 132
Harrell International Institute, 63
Harsha, William Justice, *Ploughed Under*, 60
Hart, Albert Bushnell, 110; *The American Nation: A History*, 129
Harvard University, anthropology program, 108
Hawley, Harriet Foote, 96
Hawley, Joseph R., 96, 107
Hayes, Rutherford B., 42
Henshaw, Henry W., 132
Hill, James, 160
historians, 204, 205, 227n14; professional women, 111–14, 133; slavery debate among, 143–44; women, 5–6, 7, 8, 11, 34, 70, 110, 150, 185
"Historical Background of the American Policy of Isolationism, The" (Debo), 184–85
Historical Sketch of the Omaha Tribe of Indians in Nebraska, 100
historical societies, 114–15
history, 52, 124, 193, 204, 227n27; academic professionalization and, 105–106, 108, 109, 237n50; American Indian, 7, 8, 9, 66–67, 126, 133, 135–36; American Indian political, 116–17, 136, 141; borderlands, 171, 172, 175–76, 184; Cherokee, 157–61; disputed, 143–44; professional, 110–11, 201
"History of the Arkansas River Region, 1541–1800, A" (Lewis), 173; University of Oklahoma Press reviews of, 174–75
"History of the Cattle Industry in Oklahoma, 1866–1893" (Lewis), 169–71
"History of the Cherokee Nation, A" (Eaton), submission and review of, 158–61
"History of the Choctaw Nation from the End of the Civil War to the Close of the Tribal Period" (Debo), 192
"History of Events Resulting in Indian Consolidation West of the Mississippi, The" (Abel), 142, 144–46
Hitchcock, Fanny, 109
Hodder, Frank Haywood, 139
homesteading, 167
Hopkins, Lewis H., 61

Hopkins, Sarah Winnemucca. *See* Winnemucca, Sarah
House of Kings (Muscogee Senate), 63
Howe, Julia Ward, 33
human rights, 20, 181, 183
Hunt, Edward Bissell, 46–47
Hunt, Murray, 46
Hunt, Warren, 46, 47

IHA. *See* Indian's Hope Association
IMA. *See* Indian Memorial Association
imperialism, 4, 123, 176; British, 140–41
Indian Civilization Fund Act, 28
Indian Diplomacy and the Opening of the Revolution in the West (James), 138
Indian Education and Civilization (Fletcher), 7, 34, 50, 101, 102–103, 104, 201
Indian Memorial Association (IMA), 189
Indian Peace Policy, 32, 33, 146
Indian reform movement, Bonney on, 41–42
Indian Reorganization Act, 197, 198
"Indian Reservations in Kansas and the Extinguishment of Their Title" (Abel), 141
Indian rights activism, 30, 229n28
Indian Rights Association (IRA), 94, 99, 103, 117–18
Indian Service, corruption in, 61
Indian's Hope Association (IHA), 41, 212n51
Indian Territory, 72, 168, 214n13, 235n14; cattle drives through, 169–70; missionary work in, 39, 40
Indian Territory Teachers Association, 153
Indian Treaty-Keeping and Protective Association (ITKPA), 33, 39, 40–41, 48, 58, 212n51, 215n24, 216n35, 218n14, 220n8; goals of, 43–45; petitions to Congress by, 42–43
Indian Tribes of the Upper Mississippi Valley and Region of the Great Lakes, The (Blair), 130; reviews of, 132–33; structure of, 131–32
Ingalls, George Washington, 39, 40
International Education Association, Fletcher's address at, 100–101
Intertribal sovereignty and claims conference 1930, 189–90
Ipais, 73
IRA. *See* Indian Rights Association
ITKPA. *See* Indian Treaty-Keeping and Protective Association
Ivey, Augustus E. ("Gus," Gustavus"), 157

Jackson, Andrew, 25, 29
Jackson, Helen Maria Fiske Hunt, 4, 5–6, 10, 11, 18, 45, 60, 68, 69, 201; on American Indian cultures, 53–54; on assimilation, 52, 71–72, 220n8, 224n55; *A Century of Dishonor*, 7, 17, 34, 43, 50, 104, 131, 208n7, 220n13; on fatigue and brain degeneration, 75–76; as historian, 70–71; marriage to Edward Hunt, 46–47; and Mission Indians, 73–75, 97; new nation idealism and, 16–17; on racial evolution, 55, 56; *Ramona*, 76–78, 221n26, 221n28; social consciousness of, 47–48
Jackson, William Sharpless, 47
James, James Alton, *Indian Diplomacy and the Opening of the Revolution in the West*, 1 38
Jameson, James Franklin, 111, 142, 143, 146
Jan-(th)ca'-te, Omaha Reservation, 85
Jefferson, Thomas, 144, 145
Jesuit Relations and Allied Documents, The, 126, 137
Jewish-Indian theory, 210n29; millennialism and, 24–25; Palestine and, 25–26
"John Ross" (Eaton), 153
John Ross and the Cherokee Indians (Eaton), 153; research and publishing history of, 155–61
Jumanos, 175, 176

Kansas, 139, 148; Delaware in, 72–73; women's suffrage, 35–36
Kansas State Historical Society (KSHS), 139
KCW. *See* Kentucky College for Women
Kellogg, Louise Phelps, 5, 10, 11, 12, 115, 202; American Indian history, 135–36; and Frederick Jackson Turner, 133–35; at Wisconsin State Historical Society, 136–38
Kentucky College for Women (KCW), 167
Kinney, Abbot, 74, 75
Kirkwood, Samuel J., 93
Klingberg, Frank, J., 142
KSHS. *See* Kansas State Historical Society
KU. *See* University of Kansas

Ladies' Association for Supplicating Justice and Mercy Toward Indians, 29, 212n49
Ladies' Circular, The, 29
La Flesche, Francis, 47, 58, 60, 65, 97; and Alice Fletcher, 98, 101, 221n8

La Flesche, Joseph (E-sta-mah-za), 60, 65, 82, 85, 90, 97, 103
La Flesche, Mary Gale, 65
La Flesche, Noah, 103
La Flesche, Rosalie, 97
La Flesche, Susette (Inshata Theumba), 47, 97, 102–103; Nebraska–South Dakota tour, 82, 83–84; *Oo-Ma-Ha Ta-Wa-Tha*, 60, 65, 66
Lake Mohonk Conference of Friends of the Indian, 58, 99–100, 101–102, 118
Lakotas, 72; Alice Fletcher and, 82
Lamar, Lucius, 102
Lamb, Martha, 113
land, 235n14; Choctaw Nation, 164, 166–67; "Free," 115, 116; loss of, 103–104
land rights, 29, 95; California Mission Indian, 74–75; Delaware, 72–73; Omaha, 87–88, 91–92, 93–94, 96–97
language, 58; and assimilation, 59
Lathrop, Henry B., 127
Lerner, Gerda, 204
Le Roy, Claude-Charles, 131
LeRoy, James Alfred, *Philippine Islands, 1493–1803* series, 129, 130
Leupp, Francis E., 108
Lewis, Anna Lazola, 5, 10, 12, 115, 150, 151, 161, 181, 189, 191, 234n5, 236n29, 238n89; *Along the Arkansas*, 8, 163, 175–76, 203; and Angie Debo, 185, 193–94; dissertation of, 173, 174–75; land allotments, 166–67; master's thesis of, 169–71; at Oklahoma College for Women, 164–65, 177; *Problems in Oklahoma History*, 173–74; scholarship of, 165–66; at University of California, Berkeley, 168–69; at University of Oklahoma, 177, 186
Lewis, Elizabeth Ann Moore, 164
Lewis, Eula Stroup, 166
Lewis, Grady, 12, 188–89; and Choctaw sovereignty, 190–91, 238n90
Lewis, William Ainsworth, 164
Lewis, Winnidell, 166, 168, 171, 173
liberal ideology, women's, 20–22, 26–30, 33, 36, 38, 43, 45–46, 210n23, 211n35, 211n42, 212n47, 212n50, 213n63
Life Among the Piutes: Their Wrongs and Claims (Winnemucca), 60, 62
Lincoln, Abraham, 31
Lincoln Independent, 60
linguistics, American Darwinism and, 58
Literary Society of Washington, 107

Livermore, Harriet, 21, 22, 210n30, 211n31; *Addresses to the Dispersed of Judah*, 25–26; and Jewish-Indian theory, 24–25, 210n29; public preaching of, 23–24
Lockwood, Belva Ann Bennett, 15, 18
"Long as Waters Run, As" manuscript (Debo), 160
Lottinville, Savoie, at University of Oklahoma Press, 158–59
Louisiana Purchase, federal administration of, 144
Louisiana Territory, 145, 177
Lovelock, Nev., Paiute school in, 62
Lubo, Ramona, 76, 78
Luiseño, 73

Malheur Indian Reservation, 61, 62
Mallery, Garrick, 83
Manifest Destiny, 110, 123, 140
Mann, Mary Tyler Peabody, 62
"Manuscript Sources of American History: The Conspicuous Collection Extant" (Winsor), 114
Mark, Joan, 86
Marquette University, 137
Marsh, Othniel Charles, 56
Marston, Morrill, 131
Mary Connor Junior College (MCJC), Anna Lewis at, 166, 234n5
Mathes, Valerie Sherer, 78
Ma-wa-da-ne, 103
McClurg, Alexander C., 127
McCosh, James, 58–59
McCoy, Isaac, 32
McGee, Anita Newcomb, 109
MCJC. *See* Mary Connor Junior College
McKinley, William, 117, 123
McNaughton, Clara W., 15
McNickle, D'Arcy, 197
Meacham, Alfred Benjamin, *Wi-ne-ma: The Woman Chief*, 63–64
Medicine, Beatrice, 204
Memorial of the Members of the Omaha Tribe of Indians for a Grant of Land in Severalty, 93
Merriam, Lewis, *The Problem of Indian Administration*, 187
Merrick, Joseph, land rights, 91–92
Methodists, and abolition, 31
"Mexican Projects of the Confederates" (Rippy), 184
middle class, evangelicalism and, 21–22

millennialism, Jewish-Indian theory and, 24–25, 26
Mitchell, Margaret J., 113–14
Mitchell, Maria, 49
missionaries, 23, 63; Quaker and ABCFM, 28–29
"Missionary Work Among Indians" (Ingalls), 39
Mission Indians, 55; Helen Hunt Jackson and, 18, 73–75, 97, 201
missions: California Spanish, 55, 76; Indian Territory, 39, 40; to Plains Indians, 32–33; southern, 31–32
Mississippi Valley Historical Association (MVHA), 137, 142, 143
Mississippi Valley Historical Review (MVHR), 143
Missouri River, floods, 88
MM. *See* Mother's Meeting
moderate ideology, women's, 38, 43, 45, 212n50, 214n8
Modoc War, 64
Monroe, James, 28, 145
Mooney, James, 132
Morgan, Henry Lewis, 55, 57
Morgan, John Tyler, 93, 94
Mother's Meeting (MM), 41
Mott, Lucretia, 33, 41, 213n63
Murphy, Jeannette Robinson, 109
Muscogee (Creek), 62, 63, 170, 189, 197, 235n14
Muscogee National Council, 63
Muscogee Supreme Court, 63
Muskogee Indian Journal, 63
Muzzey, David S., 180
MVHA. *See* Mississippi Valley Historical Association
MVHR. See Mississippi Valley Historical Review

Natchez, 175, 176
Nation, Carry (Carrie) A., 183
National Indian Association (NIA), 45
National Indian Defense Association (NIDA), 99
nationalism: Cherokee, 157–58; Oklahoma Indian, 189–90
Nebraska, and Omaha Reservation, 96
"Neglect and Destruction of Historical Materials in this Country, The" (Tyler), 114
New Discovery of a Large Country in America by Father Lewis Hennepin (Thwaites), 126–27

INDEX   289

"New Methods of Study in History"
   (Adams), 114
new nation idealism, 16–17
New Orleans, World's Industrial and Cotton
   Centennial Exposition, 100–101
New Woman movement, 16, 17, 51
Nez Perce tribe, 59, 60, 72; land allotment,
   103, 118
NIA. *See* National Indian Association
NIDA. *See* National Indian Defense
   Association
Nita-oshe, 164
Northern Paiutes, 60, 61, 62
Nuttall, Zelia, 49, 107, 109

OAA. *See* Omaha Allotment Act
OAFN. *See* "Omaha Allotment Field
   Notebook"
OCW. *See* Oklahoma College for Women
*The Official Correspondence of James S.
   Calhoun while Indian Agent at Santa Fé and
   Superintendent of Indian Affairs in New
   Mexico* (Abel), 148
OIA. *See* U.S. Office of Indian Affairs
Oklahoma, 150, 168, 183, 214n13, 235n14,
   236n32; land cessions and, 170–71
Oklahoma A&M College, 115
Oklahoma College for Women (OCW), 115;
   Anna Lewis at, 164–65, 171, 177
Oklahoma Hall of Fame, 155–56
Oklahoma Historical Society, *Chronicles of
   Oklahoma*, 180–81, 236n29
Oklahoma Indians, 39; nationalism, 189–90.
   See also Five Tribes/Nations; by tribe/nation
Oklahoma Territory, 40
Oklahombi, Joseph, 189
Omaha, Neb., Trans-Mississippi
   International Exposition, 66
Omaha Allotment Act (OAA), 75, 94, 96–97
"Omaha Allotment Field Notebook"
   (OAFN), 86–87, 94, 221n6; topics and
   themes in, 89–92
Omaha Citizen's (Citizen) Party, 84, 85, 89,
   90, 91
Omaha Daily Herald, 65
Omaha-Ponca tribes, Omahas-Poncas, 92
Omaha Reservation, Nebraska, 65, 83, 84,
   85–86, 96, 118; conditions on, 89, 91–92;
   land cessions on, 87–88
Omaha tribe, Omahas, 59, 60, 66, 92, 98;
   allotment, 65, 93–94, 96–97, 103, 225n59;

Alice Fletcher's study of, 82, 85–87, 89–91;
   land cessions, 87–88; World's Industrial
   and Cotton Centennial Exposition,
   100–101
Oo-Ma-Ha Ta-Wa-Tha: Omaha City (La
   Flesche and Giffen), 60, 65, 66
oral traditions, history and, 111
Organization of American Historians, 137
*Original Journals of the Lewis and Clark
   Expedition, 1804–1806* (Thwaites), 126, 127,
   137
Osage Indians, 25, 175, 176
Oskison, John Milton, manuscript
   submitted by, 160–61
"Our Indian Question" (Woodruff), 85
Owen, Robert L., 172, 236n32

Padoucas, 175, 176
Painter, Charles C., 103
Painter, Edward, 87
Paiute tribe, Paiutes, 60, 61, 62
Palestine, 25
Panhandle-Plains Museum, Angie Debo at,
   192, 193
Park Hill Publishing House, 152
Parkman, Francis, 52, 111, 208n7, 213n64
patriotism, maternal, 10, 38–39, 51, 94,
   117–18, 200
Pauma Ranch, Calif., 75
Pawnee, 59
Payne, David, 170
Peabody, Elizabeth Palmer, 20, 62
Peabody Museum, 109; Alice Fletcher and,
   97–98, 107
Pennsylvania, abolition organizations, 30
Pennsylvania Universal Peace Union (UPU),
   33, 41
Perrot, Nicolas, 131, 132, 136
PF. *See* Progressive Friends
Philadelphia, Indian reform in, 40–42
Philadelphia Protestant Tractarians, 40
Philadelphia Women's Anti-Slavery Society,
   30
Philippine Islands, 1493–1803, The, 129, 130
Philippines, American imperialism, 123–24,
   228n38; Blair on, 128, 228n38
Phillips Collection (University of
   Oklahoma), 188
philology, comparative, 58
Plains Indians, 10, 170; AMA missions to,
   32–33; land cessions and, 87–88

Ploughed Under (Harsha), 60
Plumb, Preston B., 44
Poito, 60
Political History of the Cherokee Nation, A (Wardell), 160
politics, 18, 52, 141; and ethnology, 86–87; racial, 116–17, 201; women's roles in, 27–28; Muriel Wright's, 179–80
Ponca Chiefs, The (Tibbles), 60, 68
Ponca tribe, Poncas, 47, 72, 222n10; and Omahas, 90, 91; removal of, 65, 68, 73, 82, 88, 92
Powell, John Wesley, 59, 60, 106; as American Darwinist, 54–55; on anthropology, 57–58, 107, 108, 218n21; and Alice Fletcher, 82, 83
Pratt, Richard Henry, 96
preachers, women, 20–26, 209n20, 210n22
Presbyterians, abolition, 31
Price, Hiram, 74, 75, 94, 225n59
Problem of Indian Administration, The (Merriam), 187
Problems in Oklahoma History: A Workbook for High School Students (Lewis and Taylor), 173–74
professionalization: academic, 105, 201; of anthropology, 108–109; of history, 110–11, 113–14, 237n50
Progressive Friends (PF), 33, 41, 212n51
Provost, William, 91
public realm (separate spheres ideology): women in, 22, 27, 212n47; women preachers, 20–26, 209n20
Putnam, Frederic Ward, 48, 49, 55, 83, 97, 108, 109, 118
Putnam, Mary, 49

Quakers, 28, 33
Quinton, Amelia Stone, 33, 39, 40, 82, 102, 201, 214n13, 218n14; on *A Century of Dishonor*, 70–71; ITKPA, 42–43, 44–45, 215n24; and WNIA, 95, 216n25
Quinton, R. L., 42

race, 128; in American Darwinism, 54, 55, 58
racial evolution theories, 11, 105, 108, 110; Fletcher and Jackson on, 55–56; McCosh on, 58–59
Rader, Jesse L., 174
Radin, Paul, 131
radium water, 152
Ramona (Jackson), 76–78, 221n26, 221n28

Ramsey, Arthur (To-oh-ka-hah), 91
ranching, and Indian land, 169–71
Reconstruction, 149
Records, Ralph H., 186
red-baiting, 198
removal, 28, 32, 72, 141, 149; Jefferson on, 144, 145; Poncas, 65, 68, 73, 82, 88, 92
Report on the Condition and Needs of the Mission Indians of California (Jackson), 74–75
Republican Party, and Choctaw Advisory Committee, 180
reservation system, 75, 96
Revolution on the Upper Ohio, 1775–1777 (Thwaites), 137
Rhoads, James E., 103
Richardson, R. N., 193
Riddle, Frank, 64
Riddle, Toby, 64
Riggs, Alfred L., 96
Rippy, James (J.) Fred, 12, 184, 185
Rise and Fall of the Choctaw Republic, The (Debo), 193–94, 196
Rise of the New West, The (Turner), 130
Rister, Carl Coke, 173
Robertson, Alice M., 96, 179
Robinson, Gertrude, 131
Robertson, James Alexander, 127, 128, 137, 229n9, 229n21; *The Philippine Islands, 1493–1803*, 130
Robinson, James Harvey, 110, 188
Rogers County Sequoyah Historical Society, Cherokee Nation, 156–57
Rolle, Andrew, 78
Roosevelt, Theodore, 52, 118, 120, 123, 208n7; on *A Century of Dishonor*, 71; on Frontier Thesis, 116, 117
Root, Elihu, 117
Rosebud Agency, 83
Ross, Daniel H., 95
Ross, John, 152, 153; Eaton's scholarship on, 156–61
Royce, Josiah, 52, 111

San Carlos Indians, 75
Santa Ysabel Ranch, Calif., 75
Santee Manual Training School, 89
Santee Sioux Mission, 83
Saunsoci, Louis, 90, 91
scholarship, 52, 105, 107; American Indian, 4–5, 7–8, 11, 34; anthropology, 57, 59;

INDEX

borderlands, 171, 172, 184; ethno-political, 9, 160, 197–99; frontier, 136–37; Philippine Islands history, 128–30
schools, 62, 166
Schurz, Carl, 48, 61, 68, 70
Second Great Awakening, 19, 20–21, 22
secularization, California missions, 76
Seelye, Julius Hawley, 72
segregation, 147–48, 179
Sells, Cato, 149
Seminole nation, Seminoles, 170, 189, 197, 235n14
Seneca Falls convention, 19
separate spheres ideology, 27
Sequoyah Historical Society, 156–57
Serranos, 73
Shaler, Nathaniel Southgate, 55
Shepherd, William R., 180
Sheppard, Edward Morris, 156
"Significance of the Frontier in American History, The" (Turner), 3
Sigourney, Lydia, 27, 29
Sin-da-ha-ha, 103
Sioux reservation, Alice Fletcher on, 53
slavery, 23, 30; historical debate on, 143–44; southern missions, 31–32
Smith, Erminnie, 49, 109
Smith, Jennie, 109
Smith, Joseph, 24
Smith, Lyndon A., 101
Smith and Company, H. J., 63
Smith College, Annie Abel at, 148–49
Smith College Studies in History, 185
Smithsonian, and Bureau of Ethnology, 57
Soboba, 73–74
social activism, 34
social reform, 8; public agendas of, 27, 28
social roles, women's, 27–28
"Some Insular Questions" (Bacon), 144
Sorosis club, 49
South, removal debate, 28, 29
Southeastern State Teacher's College (SSTC), intertribal conference at, 189–90
Southwest Press, 174, 175
sovereignty, 12, 62, 88, 141; Choctaw, 190–91, 238n89; Five Tribes, 188, 189; Indian, 146, 166, 181
Spain in America, 1450–1580 (Bourne), 129–30
Spanish-American War, 123, 128–29
Spanish colonialism: in Arkansas Valley, 176–77; in California, 76

Speer, John, 139
SSTC. *See* Southeastern State Teacher's College
Standing Bear, 47, 60, 65
Stanton, Elizabeth Cady, 35
Star Printery, 155, 158
Starr, Emmet, 153, 155, 156
Stevenson, Matilda Coxe, 49, 107, 119
Stevenson, Sara Y., 109
Still the Waters Run: The Betrayal of the Five Civilized Tribes, And (Debo), 3, 161, 181, 195–96, 197, 198–99
Studley, Cordelia A., 109
suffrage, 19; African American, 31, 36–37; women's, 35–36
Sunderland, Laura, 94
Supplemental Agreement, 194
"Survey of Indian Affairs" (Dale), 187

Tabeau's Narrative of Loisel's Expedition to the Upper Missouri (Abel), 50
Tae-on-ka-ha, 103
Taft, William Howard, 128–29
Talbot, Emily, 95
Talbot, Laura O., 109
Taylor, Howard, *Problems in Oklahoma History: A Workbook for High School Students*, 173–74
Teller, Henry M., 44, 74, 95, 96, 98; on allotment, 94, 224n55
Temple, Sam, 76
Ten Lost Tribes, 24
TFA. *See* Tuskahoma Female Academy
Thomas, Alfred B., 174–75
Thwaites, Reuben Gold, 115, 128, 132, 138, 202; and Emma Blair, 125–27; and Louise Kellogg, 135, 136, 137; Turner's friendship with, 126
Tibbles, Susette La Flesche. *See* La Flesche, Susette
Tibbles, Thomas Henry, 65, 66, 70, 82, 83, 90, 97, 102–103, 222n10; *The Ponca Chiefs*, 60, 68
Touacara, 175, 176
Towle, Nancy, 20–21, 22, 23
Transcendentalist movement, 200; and women's rights, 19–20, 21, 22
Trans-Mississippi International Exposition, 66
treaties, 47, 85, 164; abrogation of, 72, 222n10; histories of, 71, 72
Treaty of Dancing Rabbit Creek, 189
Treaty of Guadalupe Hidalgo, 184

Tru-ki-zo (Chief Truckee), 60
Tuboitonie, 60
Turner, Frederick Jackson, 127, 132, 142, 147, 202, 227n27, 228n38; Frontier Thesis, 3, 11, 115–16; and Louise Kellogg, 133–35; *The Rise of the New West*, 130; and women historians, 11, 112, 124, 201, 228n3, 229n21
Turner, P. L., 174
Tuskahoma Female Academy (TFA), 166, 238n89
Tyler, John, 31
Tyler, Moses Coit, 114, 141–42

U.S. Congress, 18; and District of Columbia, 36, 37; Fletcher's interactions, 93–94, 96; and Indian land, 87–88; and ITKPA petitions, 43–44; and Helen Hunt Jackson, 73, 220n13
U.S. Department of the Interior, 18, 99, 108, 163, 201
U.S. Office of Indian Affairs (OIA), 108; Annie Abel at, 147, 148
U.S. Supreme Court, 18
U.S. War Department, 89
Universal Peace Union (UPU), 41
universities, anthropology and history programs at, 108–109
University of California (UC), Berkeley, 108; Anna Lewis at, 168–69
University of Chicago, 108; Angie Debo at, 184–85; Rachel Eaton at, 153, 155
University of Kansas (KU), 148; Annie Abel at, 139, 143–45
University of Oklahoma, 115; Angie Debo at, 183–84, 186–89, 191–92; Anna Lewis at, 165, 171–72, 177
University of Oklahoma Press, 207n5; Angie Debo's manuscripts at, 192–93, 196–97; Anna Lewis's manuscript at, 173; Rachel Eaton's manuscript at, 155, 158–60; and Jesse L. Rader, 174; and Alfred B. Thomas, 174–75; and Morris Wardell, 160–61
University of Pennsylvania, anthropology program, 108
University of Texas, 115
University of Wisconsin, 137
UPU. *See* Universal Peace Union

Vandergrift, Roland, 173, 236n35
Vest, George Graham, 40
Vicissitudes (Towle), 23

WABHMS. *See* Women's American Baptist Home Mission Society
Wade, M. C., 96
Wajapa. *See* Freemont, Ezra
"Wa-ja-pa's letter" (La Flesche and Giffen), 66
Walker, Francis A., 116
Waller, J. L., 173
Wannmaker, Rodman, 149
Ward, Nancy, 151
Ward, William Hayes, 70
Wardell, Morris L., manuscript reviews by, 160–61, 197
Washington. *See* District of Columbia
Watie, Stand, 149
Wayland, Francis, 32
WBHMS. *See* Women's Baptist Home Mission Society
Wealaka Boarding School, 63
Weeks and Company, E. A., 63
Welsh, Herbert, 41; Indian Rights Association, 94, 117–18
Welsh, Mary Ross, 41
Welsh, William, 41
Western Confederacy, 72
West Texas State Teacher's College (WTSTC), Angie Debo at, 186, 192
Wheaton Seminary, Mass., 179
Whipple, Henry Benjamin, 41, 72
White, Richard, 177
Whittier, John Greenleaf, 25
WICCE. *See* World's Industrial and Cotton Centennial Exposition
Wilkinson, George W., 89, 96, 222n29
Williams, Nancy Elizabeth Ward. *See* Eaton, Nancy Elizabeth Ward Williams
Williams, Walter L., 123
Wilson, Woodrow, 117, 147
Win-dja'-ge, Omaha Reservation, 84, 85–86, 87, 88, 98, 103; demographics of, 90–91
Wi-ne-ma: The Woman Chief (Meacham), 63–64
Winnebago Reservation, 83, 88
Winnebago tribe, Winnebagos, 72, 87, 88, 103
Winnemucca, Sarah (Thocmentony): activism of, 61–62; as interpreter, 60–61
Winning of the West, The (Roosevelt), 71
Winsor, Justin, 52; "Manuscript Sources of American History: The Conspicuous Collection Extant," 114
Wisconsin State Historical Society (WSHS), 125–26, 133, 135; Kellogg and, 136–38

WNIA. *See* Women's National Indian Association
Wolff, Joseph, millennialism of, 24, 25
Women's American Baptist Home Mission Society (WABHMS), 40
Women's Baptist Home Mission Society (WBHMS), 39–40; ITKPA and, 42–43
women's ministry, evangelical movement and, 20–26, 209n20
Women's National Indian Association (WNIA), 40, 45, 70–71, 94, 95, 99, 103, 117, 216n25, 216n35, 224n55
women's rights movement, 10, 15–16, 17–18, 30, 39, 181, 201; evangelicalism and, 20–21, 23; and lateral diffusion, 35, 200, 214n9; and Territory of Columbia, 37–38; Transcendentalism and, 19–20; western expansion and, 35–36
Woodhull, Victoria, 38
Woodruff, Thomas M., "Our Indian Question," 85

World's Industrial and Cotton Centennial Exposition (WICCE), 100–101
Wright, Allen, 177, 194
Wright, Eliphalet Nott (E. N.), 177–79, 180
Wright, Ida Belle Richards, 177
Wright, Muriel Hazel, 5, 10, 12, 150, 161–62, 164, 191, 203; career of, 180–81; and Angie Debo, 185, 194–95, 197, 203; family of, 177–79; "playing Indian," 179–80
WSHS. *See* Wisconsin State Historical Society
WTSTC. *See* West Texas State Teacher's College
Wynema: A Child of the Forest (Callahan), 60, 63, 64–65

Yakima Reservation, 61, 62
Yale University, 142, 231n52

Zautoouy, 175, 176
Zionism, Indian-Jewish, 25, 26

www.ingramcontent.com/pod-product-compliance
Lightning Source LLC
Chambersburg PA
CBHW020831160426
43192CB00007B/600